Handbook for Evaluating Infrastructure Regulatory Systems

Handbook for Evaluating Infrastructure Regulatory Systems

**Ashley C. Brown, Jon Stern, and Bernard Tenenbaum
with Defne Gencer**

THE WORLD BANK
Washington, D.C.

ISBN-10: 0-8213-6579-7
ISBN-13: 978-0-8213-6579-3
eISBN: 0-8213-6580-0
DOI: 10.1596/978-0-8213-6579-3

Library of Congress Cataloging-in-Publication Data
Brown, Ashley C., 1946-
    Handbook for evaluating infrastructure regulatory systems / Ashley C. Brown, Jon
Stern, Bernard Tenenbaum; with Defne Gencer.
       p. cm.
    Includes bibliographical references and index.
    ISBN-13: 978-0-8213-6579-3
    ISBN-10: 0-8213-6579-7
      1. Electric utilities--Government policy--Developing countries. 2. Electric
utilities--Developing countries--Management. 3. Electric utilities--Finance--Developing
countries. 4. Infrastructure (Economics)--Government policy--Developing countries. I.
Stern, Jon. II. Tenenbaum, Bernard William. III. Title.

    HD9685.D442B76 2006
    333.793'2--dc22

                                                      2006045422

Cover design by: Serif Design Group, Inc.
Cover photo by: Dominic Sansoni/World Bank, Yosef Hadar/World Bank, Curt Carnemark/World Bank, Arne Hoel/World Bank.

Contents

Contents

Boxes

Figure

Tables

Foreword

Around the world, governments perform three main functions: they tax, they spend, and they regulate. And of those three functions, regulation is the least understood. It should not be surprising that regulation can produce harmful effects when it is poorly designed or executed. For example, an annual World Bank survey, *Doing Business*, has documented how too much general business regulation has hurt economic growth in many developing countries. Regulation is also a major concern in infrastructure industries where, for reasons of natural and sometimes unnatural monopoly, there are often extensive regulatory controls on maximum allowed prices, minimum quality standards, and access conditions to a common network. With the creation of more than 200 new infrastructure regulatory entities all over the world in the past 15 years, we have seen that the actions of the regulators can have major effects, both good and bad, on the performance of the sectors that are being regulated.

It is important to remember that the basic motivation for creating new infrastructure regulatory systems was to establish institutions that would encourage and support stable and sustainable long-term economic and legal commitments by both governments and investors. It was hoped that by promoting credible commitments on both sides, investors would then have adequate incentives to commit their capital to new investments to benefit existing and new customers. Despite these good intentions, there is now considerable evidence that the expectations of both investors and consumers—the two groups who were supposed to have benefited from these new regulatory systems—often have not been realized for both regulatory decisions and sector outcomes.

This can be seen in the fact that investors almost always cite poorly designed and non-credible regulation as one of their biggest disincentives for making new or additional investments. And there is evidence of similar dissatisfaction among consumers. One often hears of complaints from consumers that new regulatory systems have failed either to protect them against the monopoly practices of new private owners of infrastructure facilities or to provide promised improvements and expansion of service. So we are in the paradoxical situation where the two groups who were supposed to have benefited from the new regulatory systems often believe the opposite: the new regulatory systems have failed to provide either the commitment or the protection they had expected.

The fact that there is widespread dissatisfaction with the performance of these new regulatory systems does not mean that there is consensus as to what the problems are. Without such a consensus, it is hard to imagine how it will be possible to craft regulatory reforms that produce better outcomes, which are both economically desirable and politically feasible. Getting to such a consensus is further complicated by the fact that regulatory systems are dynamic, not static. Regulation exists within ever-changing social and economic conditions, and therefore, it must be both adaptable and predictable at the same time—a difficult challenge.

The best way to avoid getting stuck with poorly performing regulatory systems is to subject them to ongoing and periodic reviews to make sure they are fully functional and reflective of social and economic realities, and help to achieve the government's objectives for the sector. What is desperately needed are independent, objective, and fully informed analyses of existing regulatory systems. It is precisely this vacuum that this handbook is designed to fill. It provides a road map for evaluating the strengths and weaknesses of an existing system—a map that could lead to a shared understanding of existing problems and to realistic and effective recommendations for "second-generation" regulatory reforms. It does this by providing detailed guidance on how to perform systematic, objective, and publicly available evaluations of existing regulatory systems. It also presents practical advice on how to develop recommendations for improving these systems.

Four features of the handbook make it especially useful:

1. **Short, mid-level, and in-depth evaluations.** The handbook recognizes that evaluations take time and cost money and that not all countries or donors will be able to conduct intensive reviews. Therefore, the handbook presents options for three levels of evaluation

(short, mid-level, and in-depth) and provides detailed guidance and supporting materials (questionnaires, interview questions, and terms of reference) for each of them. Although the supporting materials are drawn mostly from the electricity sector, many of the recommended techniques would be equally relevant for other infrastructure sectors.

2. **Information on regulatory governance *and* regulatory substance.** Regulatory governance is the "how" of regulation, and regulatory substance is the "what." All too often, past evaluations of regulatory systems have been limited to describing the formal elements of regulatory governance—the laws, the processes, and the institutions. This handbook concludes that such a narrow approach easily can lead to mistaken conclusions. Therefore, it explains how to expand evaluations in two ways. First, it presents methods for analyzing whether the formal governance elements actually have been implemented. Second, it provides guidance on how to analyze regulatory substance—the real actions and decisions of regulators—because ultimately these actions and decisions most directly affect the performance of regulated enterprises and the overall sector. Building on this expanded analysis, the handbook provides guidance on how to evaluate the overall regulatory system as it affects the infrastructure sector and its consumers and investors.

3. **Discussion of the independent regulator model.** Over the past 15 years, the most commonly recommended model of regulation has been the independent regulator model. Often it has been proposed with only a vague understanding of what is required to implement it. The handbook presents a detailed checklist of actions to "operationalize" the independent regulator model. However, the handbook also recognizes that, from a practical point of view, this regulatory model may not be the appropriate starting point (that is, the best governance model) at all times and for all countries.

4. **Discussion of transitional regulatory systems.** In *The Brothers Karamazov,* Fyodor Dostoevsky, the famous Russian novelist, wrote "There you have it—reforms on unprepared ground, and copied from foreign institutions as well—nothing but harm." His insight applies equally well to regulatory systems. It is naïve to assume that one size fits all, especially for countries that are in the early stages of implementing a regulatory system and particularly if the new regulatory entity is surrounded by weak or corrupt institutions, or other government institutions that oppose change. The handbook accepts this reality, and it

provides practical guidance on designing and implementing transitional regulatory systems. The guidance is keyed to real-world problems that have been observed in World Bank client-countries that have created new infrastructure regulatory systems while still promoting the critical "meta-principles" of credibility, legitimacy, and transparency.

Finally, the authors of this handbook emphasize that regulation is a means to an end, not an end in itself. They are pragmatists rather than ideologues. If an evaluation shows that the regulatory system is preventing the sector from achieving good results (and the authors offer specific suggestions on how to measure these results), they offer concrete suggestions for how the system can be changed and strengthened. So their emphasis is not just evaluation for the sake of evaluation, but evaluation that can lead to practical reforms. I commend the authors (who have worked in a number of countries both as practicing regulators and as advisers to regulators) on producing a practical and insightful document. I am certain that the handbook will be of considerable value to government officials, regulators, managers of regulated enterprises, and consumer representatives in many developing and developed countries.

Jamal Saghir
Director, Energy and Water Department
Chairman, Energy and Mining Sector Board
The World Bank
June 2006

Acknowledgments

This handbook could not have been written without the assistance of many friends and colleagues inside and outside the World Bank. These people greatly contributed to our work. They gave us their time freely, and they shared with us their invaluable knowledge and insights on regulatory systems and issues facing the power sector and other infrastructure industries in developing and developed countries. We owe special thanks to Ian Alexander, Sanford Berg, Anton Eberhard, Raul Garcia, and Eric Groom, who provided extremely helpful comments on an earlier version of the handbook.

In addition, we would like to thank all the people with whom we have worked over the years on these issues in developing and transition countries—particularly regulators, their staffs, and those involved in the design and implementation of new regulatory systems. Economic regulation is not an academic exercise for these men and women. They have wrestled long and hard with the problems of regulatory governance and substance that are discussed in the handbook, and we have learned a huge amount from having worked with them.

Rebecca Kary provided thorough, insightful, and timely editorial support in the production of the handbook. She did a splendid job in completing the difficult task of dealing with four authors, and she made sure that we delivered our messages clearly and accurately.

We also would like to acknowledge the support for our work from our respective fathers: Allen Brown, David Stern, Meyer Tenenbaum, and Murat

Gencer. In their various ways they provided strong intellectual and practical guidance as well as powerful moral examples of how to apply professional skills to help improve people's lives.

Finally, we wish to acknowledge the financial assistance of the World Bank's Energy and Water Department in preparing this handbook. We owe a special debt of gratitude to the department's director, Jamal Saghir. He has given us consistent support and encouragement, and he has shared with us his vision and insights. Perhaps most important, he constantly reminded us that our goal was to produce a handbook that can be used by those who deal with the real-world issues of economic regulation.

About the Authors

Ashley C. Brown (abrown@harvard.edu) is executive director of the Harvard Electricity Policy Group at the John F. Kennedy School of Government, Harvard University. An attorney, he is also of counsel to the law firm LeBoeuf, Lamb, Greene, and MacRae. From 1983 to 1993 Brown served as commissioner of the Public Utilities Commission of Ohio. He has advised many governments around the world on infrastructure regulation. He is a frequent speaker and lecturer on both energy and regulatory matters at international conferences and universities, and he has published many articles and papers on the same subjects.

Jon Stern (jstern@london.edu) is an associate at the London Business School's Regulation Initiative, and a founding member of the Centre for Competition and Regulatory Policy at City University, London. He also works as an economic consultant with Cambridge Economic Policy Associates. He has worked on infrastructure reform and regulation with the World Bank and other agencies in more than 20 developing and transition countries, particularly in electricity. He has published a number of academic and other papers on regulatory governance in developing countries, including the criteria for good regulation and work on the impact of regulatory governance regimes on investment levels.

Bernard Tenenbaum (btenenbaum@worldbank.org) is a lead energy specialist in the Energy and Water Department at the World Bank. While at the

Bank, he has served as an adviser on power sector reform and regulation projects in Brazil, Cambodia, China, India, Mozambique, and Nigeria. Before joining the World Bank, he served as the associate director of the Office of Economic Policy at the U.S. Federal Energy Regulatory Commission. He is an author of *Regulation by Contract: A New Way to Privatize Electricity Distribution?* and *Governance and Regulation of Power Pools and System Operators: An International Comparison.*

Defne Gencer (dgencer@worldbank.org) is a power sector reform consultant in the Energy and Water Department at the World Bank. While at the Bank, her work has focused on power sector regulation, the investment needs of developing countries, hydropower development, demand-side management, wholesale market design, and off-grid electrification. Before joining the World Bank, she worked for the Energy Market Regulatory Authority of Turkey as a specialist on power sector regulation.

Abbreviations

ADR	alternative dispute resolution
AEI	American Enterprise Institute
AFUR	African Forum for Utility Regulation [*Forum Africain pour la Reglementation des Services Publics*]
ANEEL	National Electricity Regulatory Agency (Brazil) [*Agência Nacional de Energia Elétrica*]
ANRE	Energy Regulatory Authority (Romania)
BIT	bilateral investment treaty
CAB	Consumer Advocate Board
CCEE	Chamber of Electric Energy Commercialization (market administrator, Brazil) [*Câmara de Comercialização de Energia Elétrica*]
CDEC	Economic Load Dispatch Center (system operator, Chile) [*Centro de Despacho Económico de Carga*]
CEE	Central and Eastern Europe
CEER	Council of European Energy Regulators
CIS	Commonwealth of Independent States
CNE	National Energy Commission (Chile) [*Comisión Nacional de Energía*]
DRC	Democratic Republic of Congo
EBRD	European Bank for Reconstruction and Development
ERRA	Energy Regulators Regional Association
ERC	Electricity regulatory commission
EU	European Union
FIT	feed-in tariff

Abbreviations

GDP	gross domestic product
IFI	international financial institution
IPP	independent power producer
ITU	International Telecommunication Union
km	kilometer
kWh	kilowatt-hour
MIGA	Multilateral Investment Guarantee Agency
MW	megawatt
MWh	megawatt-hour
NER	National Electricity Regulator (South Africa)
NERA	National Economic Research Associates
NERC	National Electricity Regulatory Commission (Ukraine)
NGO	nongovernmental organization
O&M	operations and maintenance
OECD	Organisation for Economic Co-operation and Development
OUR	Office of Utility Regulation (Jamaica)
PLN	Perusahaan Listrik Negara [the state-owned national electric utility in Indonesia]
PPA	power purchase agreement
PPIAF	Public–Private Infrastructure Advisory Facility
PRG	partial risk guarantee
REDI	Recent Economic Developments in Infrastructure
RIA	regulatory impact assessment
SEC	Superintendency for Electricity and Fuels (Chile) [*Superintendencia de Electricidad y Combustibles*]
SERC	State Electricity Regulatory Commission (China)
SIC	Central Interconnected System (Chile) [*Sistema Interconectado Central*]
TOR	terms of reference
USAID	U.S. Agency for International Development

Executive Summary

It has been estimated that close to 200 new infrastructure regulators have been created around the world in the last 10 years. The basic rationale for creating these new regulators was to establish institutions that would encourage and support clear and sustainable long-term economic and legal commitments by both governments and investors. By promoting credible commitments on both sides, it was hoped that investors would then have adequate incentives to commit their capital in new investments to benefit existing and new customers. If there is any one lesson to be learned from the experience to date, it is that good intentions do not guarantee good outcomes. There is now considerable evidence that both consumers and investors—the two groups that were supposed to have benefited from these new regulatory systems—have often been disappointed with the performance of the regulators.

The mere fact that there is widespread dissatisfaction with the performance of these new regulatory systems does not mean that there is also a consensus as to what the problems are. A fundamental premise of this handbook is that once these new systems are in place, they tend to resist further reforms. Consequently, there's a real danger that they will fail to achieve what they were designed to accomplish, unless they face some outside pressure to improve. There is some evidence that independent, objective, and public evaluations of their performance can provide such pressure.

Such evaluations can be thought of as something akin to a periodic physical checkup. Just as one goes to a medical doctor for a regular health checkup, it is increasingly clear that economic infrastructure regulatory systems would also benefit from checkups in the form of periodic evaluations. At least six such in-depth evaluations have already been performed on electricity regulators, and similar evaluations have been conducted (or are in process) for water, sanitation, and telecommunications regulatory systems. Such evaluations provide a mechanism for ensuring accountability and for improving the design and performance of existing systems.

What the Handbook Does

Evaluation and criticism of regulatory systems began almost as soon as they were first established. The three most common forms of evaluation are cross-country statistical studies, cross-country descriptive analyses, and single-country structured case studies. The strengths and weaknesses of these different methods are analyzed. It is concluded that individuals who make decisions on whether to undertake changes in a country's existing regulatory system are typically not interested in multicountry studies that prove or disprove general propositions about the theory and practice of economic regulation. Instead, their principal concern is whether specific reforms should or should not be applied to their existing regulatory systems. Given the interests and needs of this audience, the handbook recommends that evaluations be performed through well-written, single-country case studies, supplemented by cross-country benchmarking, if possible. These structured case studies should be prepared by respected individuals who are familiar with the regulation of infrastructure industries and who understand the country's political, economic, and legal realities.

The handbook presents detailed, practical guidance on how to conduct *quick, mid-level,* and *in-depth* regulatory evaluations of existing national- and state- or province-level regulatory systems through structured case studies. The focus is on economic regulation of commercialized sector enterprises, whether publicly or privately owned.

The handbook discusses evaluation methods in detail and provides a set of evaluation tools. These tools include questionnaires, interview guidelines, a list of needed background documents, and a model terms of references for hiring the evaluators (appendixes B, C, D, E, and F). The handbook also gives detailed instructions on how to use each of these tools.

The questionnaires and interview guidelines have been designed specifically for power sector regulation. However, the basic techniques and many of the regulatory issues are also relevant for other infrastructure sectors. Consequently, the questionnaires can be used with little or no change when evaluating regulatory systems in other infrastructure industries. The handbook's focus is on the power sector because other ongoing World Bank research projects are examining how to improve the design and operation of regulatory systems in the telecommunications and water and sanitation sectors.

Quick Evaluation

The quick evaluation is designed to provide an initial overview of the basic characteristics of the power sector and its regulatory arrangements, including possible problem areas. It is a form of general reconnaissance conducted through a structured questionnaire (appendix C). Because time and resources are limited, the quick evaluation concentrates on describing formal, legal attributes of the regulatory system. However, if there is a significant gap between what is written in the law and what is actually practiced, focusing solely on the formal legal attributes could lead to mistaken conclusions on the overall performance of the regulatory system. To minimize this problem, a number of open-ended questions are provided to detect significant gaps between the formal and informal characteristics of the system.

The quick evaluation can be performed by individuals who have only general knowledge of the sector, including staff at multilateral and bilateral development agencies. A quick evaluation may take up to 5 person-days and could cost up to US$15,000. (This cost estimate and the comparable estimates for the mid-level and in-depth evaluations do not include travel costs.)

Mid-Level Evaluation

The mid-level evaluation provides a more substantial evaluation of a national-, state-, or province-level regulatory system. It reviews both the formal elements of the system and how these formal elements have actually been implemented (appendixes B, D, and E). It requires extensive interviews with the regulator and government officials, executives in sector enterprises, and consumers. Individuals with widely different perspectives need to be interviewed to ensure that the evaluation will not just reflect what government officials or regulators want it to say.

The mid-level evaluation should be performed by a small team consisting of a recognized specialist in infrastructure regulation from outside the country, a local consultant who is familiar with current sector conditions and the history of sector reforms, and a local lawyer who can make certain that any recommendations are consistent with existing laws or constitutional requirements. A mid-level evaluation could take up to 4 person-weeks and might cost up to US$65,000.

In-Depth Evaluation

The in-depth evaluation is similar to a mid-level evaluation, but it goes wider and deeper. It may involve the collection and analysis of a significant amount of quantitative data. Both the mid-level and the in-depth evaluations should examine the system's performance in implementing regulatory policies and actions to support the government's main reform initiatives. For the power sector, a series of interview questions is provided that will enable the evaluators to examine performance in implementing specific reforms that relate to electrification, grid-based renewable energy, distribution company regulation, the effect of regulation on the poor as consumers, open access and customer choice regimes, and competitive bulk power markets (appendix E). Most countries will pursue some, although not all, of these initiatives as part of their sector reforms. An in-depth evaluation could take up to 3–4 person-months and might cost up to US$125,000.

The general case study approach recommended in this handbook differs from other past regulatory evaluations in three ways. First, many earlier evaluations have tended to focus almost exclusively on the institutional and legal characteristics of regulatory systems with little or no attention paid to the actual decisions or actions of the regulator. Second, these previous evaluations have often not "drilled down" to see whether formal legal requirements have actually been implemented. Therefore, they tend to be overly positive because they fail to capture ground-level realities. And third, they generally do not attempt to assess how the regulator's actions or decisions have affected sector outcomes. Therefore, an important innovation of the handbook is its detailed consideration of these evaluation deficiencies and how they can be remedied.

What Should Be Evaluated?

It is important to be clear as to what is meant by *regulation.* At the most general level, regulation refers to government-imposed controls on business activity. The two universal tasks of economic regulation are the setting, monitoring, and enforcing of maximum tariffs and of minimum service standards. Most actual regulatory systems are broader than the formally designated regulatory entity. For example, it is not uncommon for regulatory decisions to be made by government entities other than the formally designated regulator. Therefore, a regulatory system should be defined as the combination of institutions, laws, and processes that, taken together, enable a government to exercise formal and informal control over the operating and investment decisions of enterprises that supply infrastructure services. Any evaluation of regulatory effectiveness must examine the entire regulatory system—not just the characteristics and actions of the formally designated regulatory entity.

Any evaluation must examine two basic dimensions of any regulatory system: *regulatory governance* and *regulatory substance.* Regulatory governance refers to the institutional and legal design of the regulatory system and the framework within which decisions are made. Regulatory governance is the "how" of regulation. It involves decisions about the independence and accountability of the regulator, the relationship between the regulator and policymakers; the process—formal and informal—by which decisions are made; the transparency of decisionmaking; the predictability of decisionmaking; and the organizational structure and resources of the regulator.

Regulatory substance is the content of regulation. It is the actual decisions, whether explicit or implicit, made by the specified regulatory entity or other entities within the government, along with the rationale for the decisions. Regulatory substance is the "what" of regulation. It typically involves decisions about tariff levels and structures, quality of service standards, automatic and nonautomatic cost pass-through mechanisms, investment or connection obligations and reviews, accounting systems, network access conditions for new and existing customers, and periodic reporting requirements.

ES

A complete evaluation of regulatory effectiveness must look at both regulatory governance *and* regulatory substance. Moreover, because regulation is a means to an end and the end is better sector performance, the evaluation must also try to assess how institutional and legal characteristics and actual decisions or actions have affected sector outcomes. This does *not* mean that the evaluator should spend a lot of time and effort trying to quantify the effect of regulatory governance and substance on overall sector performance. Instead, it will be more productive to look at specific elements of the regulatory system and assess whether they help or hinder in achieving goals that the government has established for the sector.

Because the goal of the evaluation is to provide recommendations that will improve the system, the most productive strategy is to focus on those elements of the regulatory system that, if changed, would clearly lead to better sector outcomes. In other words, the evaluation should take note of what is good, but focus on what is bad. To do this requires looking at weaknesses in governance and systematically examining bad decisions and their consequences arising from regulatory inaction (sins of omission), as well as bad decisions arising from regulatory actions (sins of commission). Specific examples of both types of decisions are given in the context of typical power sector reforms. The decisions may have been perfectly rational at the time they were made, but now turn out to be mistaken or ineffective with the benefit of the "20-20 hindsight" that comes from an ex post evaluation.

What Benchmarks?

Evaluations require benchmarks. Without benchmarks, the evaluation of a regulatory system would lack coherence, discipline, and meaning. The governance benchmarks used in the questionnaires are derived from the *independent regulator* model. This governance model has been chosen as the evaluation benchmark for three principal reasons. First, it has become the de facto governance model, at least on paper, in most of the 200 countries that have created new national or regional regulatory systems in the past 10 years. Second, there is some empirical evidence that shows that the independent regulator model, when adopted in both law and practice, leads to better sector outcomes. And third, the independent regulator model can accommodate a wide variety of sector structures and transactions.

The defining characteristic of the independent regulator model is independence in decisionmaking. To achieve this outcome on a sustainable basis requires implementation of a number of institutional and legal principles. The most commonly recommended principles are accountability, transparency and public participation, predictability, clarity of roles, completeness and clarity in rules, proportionality, requisite powers, appropriated institutional characteristics, and integrity. Although these are good, general principles, more detailed standards are needed if the principles are to be operationalized in day-to-day practices. Appendix A provides a detailed description and rationale for 15 standards that are designed to move the independent regulator model from theory to practice. The appendix is written to be used as a basic resource document in discussions with policymakers about regulatory design and implementation.

In addition, the handbook proposes three meta-principles for *all* infrastructure regulatory systems, including transitional regulatory systems:

1. *Credibility:* Investors must have confidence that the regulatory system will honor its commitments.
2. *Legitimacy:* Consumers must be convinced that the regulatory system will protect them from the exercise of monopoly power, whether through high prices or poor service, or both.
3. *Transparency:* The regulatory system must operate transparently, so that investors and consumers "know the terms of the deal."

Transitional Regulatory Systems

Although the independent regulator model is a widely accepted "best-practice" model of regulation, it is unrealistic to expect that the model can be adopted immediately in all countries and at all times. Transitional regulatory systems (with and without commitments for further reform) are likely to be needed for three reasons. First, a country may be unable to implement the independent regulator model because it lacks capacity or commitment, or both. Second, the full independent regulator model may simply be too risky a first step in creating a new regulatory system (that is, it is a "big jump"). Third, some aspects of the ideal model may be incompatible with established and accepted legal or cultural norms in a country. When one or more of these conditions exist, they are often manifested through the following:

- Unwillingness or inability to move toward commercialization with cost-reflective prices to small consumers.
- Unwillingness or inability to transfer regulatory decisionmaking powers.
- Weak and slowly operating law courts and regulatory appeals.
- Uncertainty about the nature and strength of regulatory commitments.
- Limited regulatory capability.
- Popular concerns that consumer interests are being ignored relative to investors' profitability.

In addition, all these weaknesses tend to worsen when there is a macroeconomic crisis.

Chapter 4 of the handbook discusses each of the main problem areas and a number of possible solutions to them (see table ES.1). It also assesses the strengths and weaknesses of these potential solutions.

These possible solutions constitute the building blocks for transitional regulatory systems. It is important that they be explicitly considered when

Table ES.1. Effective Regulatory Systems: Impediments and Possible Solutions

Impediments and problems	Possible solutions
Unwillingness or inability to commercialize the regulated enterprise	Explicit timetable supported by transitional subsidies with secure funding support
Unwillingness or inability to transfer regulatory powers	"Strong" rather than "weak" advisory regulator
Regulatory appeals to weak general law courts	• Arbitration • Specialized appeal tribunals advised by expert panels
Uncertainty about the strength of regulatory commitments	• Regulatory and infrastructure contracts • Regulatory partial risk guarantees and similar external risk mitigation measures
Limited regulatory resources and capacity	• Contracting out of regulatory staff functions on an advisory basis to consultants or other entities • Contracting out of regulatory decisions on a binding basis to other entities (for example, expert panels and regional regulatory bodies)
Consumer mistrust of reforms and regulation	• Openness and transparency • Emphasis on early quality-of-service improvements • Service expansion to unconnected customers • Protection of low-income customers • Open bidding for licenses or concessions
Macroeconomic crises	• Involvement of the regulator in post-crisis "workout" discussions

Source: All boxes and tables in the handbook are based on the authors' analyses, unless otherwise noted.

formulating recommendations for "next steps." Little is accomplished by just describing current deficiencies and then recommending a set of "best practices." A much more productive approach is to give concrete recommendations on workable transitional regulatory arrangements and to show how these arrangements can better achieve the goals that the government itself has set for the sector.

Specific elements of transitional regulatory systems will vary from country to country. No single transitional system will be applicable in all countries at all times. The handbook describes transitional regulatory systems for countries that have political will, but lack institutional experience (that is, the "weak but willing"); and countries that have considerable human and institutional resources, but are reluctant to move away from traditional forms of control over power sector enterprises (that is, the "strong but unwilling").

Finally, the handbook gives guidance on how these possible elements of transitional regulatory systems should be evaluated. The important point is that they need to be evaluated in terms of *both* how well they deal with current circumstances in the relevant country and sector *and* whether they provide a route and incentives for moving toward significant and sustainable improvements in regulatory practices and sector outcomes. The ultimate goal is a best-practice regulatory system—a regulatory system that transparently provides investors with credible commitments and consumers with genuine protections.

Note: Many documents cited in this handbook are described more fully in the selected annotated bibliography. To help users identify these documents, they are cited throughout the handbook in footnotes in author-date format and in boldface type. All other documents cited in footnotes are set in nonbold type; at first mention, the full bibliographic reference is given, after which the author-date format is used.

1

Evaluating the Effectiveness of Infrastructure Regulatory Systems: A Framework and Rationale

Not everything that is faced can be changed, but nothing can be changed until it is faced.
— James Baldwin, author

Why Evaluate Regulatory Effectiveness?

This handbook provides guidance on how to evaluate the effectiveness of infrastructure regulatory systems.[1] Regulatory evaluations can be thought of as something akin to a periodic physical examination. Just as one goes to a medical doctor for a health checkup, it is increasingly clear that new economic regulatory systems would also benefit from checkups in the form of periodic evaluations.

A Checkup

It is conceivable that such a regulatory checkup could be performed by the new regulator. This would be equivalent to a "self-examination." But just as

---

1. The term *regulatory system* is meant to be broadly encompassing. It includes all relevant laws, decrees, and regulations; all regulatory agency activities; all appellate processes; and relationships between regulatory agencies and all other organs of the state on policy and administrative matters relating to the sector that is being regulated.

one tends to ignore the early signs of illness for a variety of reasons (including the fact that one's own behavior may be causing the illness), a self-examination by a regulator runs the risk of denying symptoms that reflect underlying problems that may be obvious to everyone but the regulator. Therefore, a fundamental premise of this handbook is that serious regulatory evaluations should be performed by individuals, from both inside and outside the country, who are knowledgeable about regulation and the sector that is being regulated. It is equally important that the evaluations be performed by individuals whose judgments and recommendations will be widely perceived as fair and objective—that is, people who are not tied to the regulator or any constituencies affected by the regulator's decisions.

Throughout this handbook, the terms *evaluate, evaluation,* and *review* are used to cover all after-the-fact (ex post) examinations of existing infrastructure regulatory systems (or parts of them), as well as ex post examinations of specific regulatory decisions. In contrast, we use the terms *assess* or *assessment* and *appraise* or *appraisal* to cover all before-the-fact (or ex ante) examinations, typically, for specific proposed regulatory decisions or proposed changes in the regulatory system. The principal focus of the handbook will be on *how to conduct after-the-fact evaluations of existing infrastructure regulatory systems where a formally designated regulatory entity with decisionmaking or advisory authority is already in place, either inside or outside a ministry.*

Expectations and Performance

Separate economic regulatory systems for infrastructure sectors are a relatively new but important phenomenon in many developing and transition economies. It has been estimated that close to 200 new infrastructure regulators have been created around the world in the past 10 years. They were usually established as one component of a larger reform package that also included restructuring and privatization.

It is probably fair to say that most of the new regulatory entities were not created because governments suddenly saw the value in creating autonomous regulators. A more realistic assessment is that a large proportion of the new regulatory entities were established primarily because they were recommended by the World Bank and other multilateral lenders and bilateral aid agencies as a necessary component of a larger package of aid and reforms to encourage private sector participation in infrastructure sectors.[2]

2. In a recent review of African infrastructure reform, Nellis observed that "African govern-

The rationale was that a new regulatory system was needed to give commitments to investors and protection to consumers. In recent years, the "demand" for infrastructure regulatory entities may have become more "homegrown" as government officials, technocrats, and business people have seen—or had contact with—regulatory entities in other countries and have come to appreciate their potential benefits.

Despite these good intentions, evidence is now growing that those who were supposed to have benefited from the new regulatory systems—investors and consumers—often believe that the new regulatory systems have not met their expectations. For example, in a 2002 survey of private sector investors in power sectors, respondents stated that four of the top five factors that led to unsatisfactory investment experiences related to lack of fairness and commitment in the new regulatory systems.[3] Consumers also appear to be disenchanted. A 2001 survey of consumers in 17 Latin American countries found that only about 27 percent believed that privatization had benefited their countries.[4] This was a decline from more than 45 percent in 1998. Because Latin America's new economic regulatory systems typically were established to support privatizations, one could reasonably infer that consumers were probably also unhappy with the performance of the regulatory systems designed to protect them during and after these privatizations. *This seems to be borne out by the fact that 65 percent of Latin American consumers stated they would support privatization if it were accompanied by credible regulatory systems.* The implication is that a majority of Latin American consumers have concluded that the new regulatory systems have not protected them adequately.

In general, all parties (including the World Bank) probably had unrealistic expectations about what could be achieved—and particularly about how quickly regulatory agencies could establish their capabilities and reputation. Moreover, these expectations ignored the reality that even the best regulatory agency is likely to be ineffective in a country with high levels of corrup-

---

ments felt that they had little choice but to go along with policies requested and required by their financiers. They could marginally amend the content and slow the pace of the implementation of the policies, and they could employ passive noncompliance to dilute and delay their impact, but only in the rarest of cases could they and did they explicitly reject them." John Nellis, 2005, "The Evolution of Enterprise Reform in Africa: From State-Owned Enterprises to Private Participation in Infrastructure—and Back," Africa Private Sector Development Department, World Bank, Washington, DC, photocopy.

3. Ranjit Lamech and Kazim Saeed, 2003, "What International Investors Look for When Investing in Developing Countries," Energy and Mining Sector Board Discussion Paper 6, World Bank, Washington, DC, p. 10.

4. Latinobarómetro Survey (2002), http://www.latinobarometro.org/.

tion, a poorly functioning legal system, little or no history of or experience with independent regulation, and repeated macroeconomic crises.

Even if one ignored this frequently expressed disenchantment with new regulatory systems, there is also the unavoidable reality that investment in infrastructure industries has fallen dramatically over the past several years. When the World Bank announced its Infrastructure Action Plan in July 2003, a program to increase its infrastructure lending, the Bank highlighted the fact that private investment in infrastructure projects in developing countries had fallen substantially. On a worldwide basis, it fell from a high of US$128.4 billion in 1997 to US$41 billion in 2003. Because the creation of new regulatory systems was often justified as a way to promote more investment, it now seems reasonable to step back and assess whether the original design and the subsequent implementation of these new regulatory systems may have contributed to this observed decline in investment and, if so, what changes could be made to improve these systems.[5] In a sense, *this is a belated recognition of the fact that good intentions do not necessarily lead to good outcomes.*

Systematic evaluations of infrastructure regulatory entities, however, are recommended not only because of failures and disappointments. Rare is the new institution that performs exactly as it was intended. If a new regulatory system is encountering problems, corrections are more easily made sooner rather than later. Such corrections are more likely to be initiated if they result from prescheduled, periodic reviews. The value of regularly scheduled reviews has been recognized in developed countries. For example, in the European Union (EU), the EU Commission produces annual "benchmarking" reports on EU member-states' energy regulators, and individual countries conduct their own periodic reviews commissioned by government ministries, legislatures, or audit agencies. Similarly, U.S. regulatory agencies are subject to regular legislative oversight hearings to review their policies and practices, as well as the larger regulatory framework within which they operate. The fundamental presumption of this handbook is that developing countries

---

5. This handbook had its genesis in one component of the World Bank's Infrastructure Action Plan, which is referred to as Recent Economic Developments in Infrastructure (REDIs). The REDIs were designed to function as relatively standardized country-specific "diagnostics" of the investment, institutional, and policy frameworks of infrastructure sectors, such as water, power, transport, and telecommunications. This handbook was developed to provide guidance on how to perform a diagnostic of regulatory institutions and systems.

could benefit from conducting similar periodic evaluations of their new regulatory systems.

Recommended Approach

The overall purpose of this handbook is to provide systematic guidance on how to evaluate the performance of an existing infrastructure regulatory system. The handbook proposes that the evaluations be performed through structured case studies. To ensure that the case studies are comprehensive, the handbook provides a checklist of issues and topics that should be addressed. This checklist is incorporated in model questionnaires and interview guidelines. The handbook proposes different levels of review (short, mid-level, and in-depth), depending on the time and resources available to those who are making the evaluation. (See appendixes C, D, and E.)

The case studies are not intended for academic discussions. Instead, the primary purpose of the evaluations is to present information to a country's political leaders that will persuade them to make "second-generation" regulatory reforms. A president or infrastructure minister will often know very little about regulation and, equally important, may have had nothing to do with creating the regulatory system that is being reviewed. Therefore, if the case studies are going to have any impact on political decisions, they must combine objective evaluations with arguments for reform that will be persuasive to these individuals. The universal reality is that no reforms will be undertaken unless key policymakers and opinion leaders, such as the president, relevant ministers, and legislators, are convinced that the regulatory system, as currently operated, is failing to achieve outcomes they think are important (for example, more investment, reduction or elimination of subsidies from the treasury, reasonable prices, and expansion of access to unserved populations). Hence, the crafting of any recommendations must always be cognizant of these political realities.

What Should Be Evaluated?

The focus of the handbook is on how to evaluate infrastructure regulatory systems. If you are to avoid any confusion, it is important to be clear on what is meant by regulation.

1

The Meaning of Regulation

Regulation means government-imposed controls on particular aspects of business activity.[6] When government regulates an infrastructure sector, it imposes direct and indirect controls on the decisions or actions of enterprises within that sector. Government controls can cover many dimensions of business activities. In addition to economic regulation, a government may impose health, safety, and environmental requirements on infrastructure enterprises. Our focus will be on economic regulation of infrastructure entities for three reasons. First, economic regulation is the principal task that has been assigned to most new infrastructure regulators. Second, unless the economic regulatory system helps produce viable infrastructure enterprises, it is unlikely that health, safety, and environmental regulation will be very effective. Third, these other types of regulation raise a distinct set of issues that are best treated separately.[7]

Within economic regulation, the two core regulatory tasks are the setting, monitoring, and enforcing of maximum tariffs and of minimum service standards.[8] Of the two, control over the maximum prices that enterprises can charge is the more visible and controversial regulatory task. Although tariff levels usually receive the most public attention, they are by no means the only dimension of economic regulation. Economic regulation may also include controls over tariff structures, quality-of-service standards, the use of automatic pass-through and adjustment mechanisms, access conditions to networks, entry and exit conditions for participants, and investment obligations relative to existing and new customers. *A comprehensive evaluation of a regulatory system must look at all major regulatory actions—not just those relating to tariff levels.*

---

6. This does *not* mean that each and every business decision requires prior government approval. Instead, control will usually be exercised through a mix of prior approvals (for example, a request for a tariff increase) or after-the-fact reviews of performance (for example, connection of a specified number of new customers). Regulation is only one form of government control. Governments can also control enterprises through ownership and fiscal incentives.

7. Health, safety, and environmental regulation are discussed extensively in chapters 19–24 of W. Kip Viscusi, John Vernon, and Joseph Harrington, Jr., 2000, *Economics of Regulation and Antitrust*, 3rd ed. (Cambridge, MA: MIT Press).

8. Even though both tasks are core tasks, regulatory entities tend to spend more time on setting maximum tariffs because tariffs are more visible and are easier to observe and control. Monitoring of minimum quality-of-service standards is more difficult because it is multidimensional and requires investments and ongoing expenditures if the monitoring is to be effective.

Regulatory Systems

A regulatory system consists of more than just the formally designated regulatory entity. It is a broader concept. A regulatory system is defined by the combination of institutions, laws, and processes that give a government control over the operating and investment decisions of enterprises that supply infrastructure services. *Any evaluations of regulatory effectiveness must examine the entire regulatory system—not just the characteristics and actions of the formally designated regulatory entity.* The danger of limiting an evaluation just to the characteristics and decisions of the designated regulatory entity is that it can easily lead to flawed conclusions because the new agency may have only limited decisionmaking authority, both in law and in practice.[9] Therefore, this handbook recommends performing evaluations of the institutional characteristics and substantive decisions of the entire regulatory system, not just of those of the designated regulatory entity.

Regulatory Entities

Any evaluation must also recognize that designated regulatory entities can take many different institutional forms. Although there is a clear worldwide trend toward the creation of separate and specialized regulatory entities, these entities may exhibit "significant differences in their independence, powers and relationship with the executive branch of government."[10] Some may be new independent, nonministerial entities with final decisionmaking authority over tariffs and quality of service (an independent regulatory agency). Other designated regulatory entities may be autonomous entities with separate budgets, but which are located within an existing line ministry, with the minister retaining final legal authority over the regulatory entity's decisions (a separate advisory ministerial regulator). Still other designated regulatory entities may be located outside a ministry, but still may be granted nothing more than advisory powers (the advisory nonministerial regulator). Even though these latter entities may examine the same set of issues that would be reviewed by independent regulatory agencies, their rec-

---

9. **Ocaña** (2002, p. 18) reaches the same conclusion in his survey of new regulatory institutions in 23 Organisation for Economic Co-operation and Development (OECD) countries. He concludes that the norm is that "several organisations either deal with regulatory issues or influence regulatory outcomes."
10. **Ocaña** (2002), p. 13.

1

ommendations to the ministry, whether given publicly or privately, will be adopted at the sole discretion of the minister. Because they are advisory entities, they will not have any formal (that is, legally binding) decisionmaking authority. Any evaluation of a regulatory system must be able to accommodate these different types of regulatory entities.

Quasi-Regulatory Systems and Failed States

So far, our discussion has assumed that there is a designated regulatory entity for the power sector and other infrastructure industries. The creation of more than 200 new regulatory entities suggests a worldwide trend in this direction. However, in many countries, a separate, designated regulatory entity does not exist, either inside or outside a ministry. But even in the absence of a designated regulatory entity, if a functioning government is in place, some entity will still have to make decisions about the right to operate, the terms and conditions of operation, and frequently the allowed prices and acceptable investments. In other words, regulation—that is, government controls over commercial decisions—will often exist even if it is not explicitly called "economic regulation." The fallback is, of course, that these decisions are made by the relevant ministry, but in many Latin American and other countries, they may take place within the context of contractual arrangements that are monitored, interpreted, and enforced by an entity separate from the line ministry.

Such arrangements can be described as "quasi-regulatory" systems, for example, where infrastructure franchise contracts are monitored, enforced, and revised by a ministry or some other contract monitoring agency. Although the focus of the handbook is on countries with designated regulatory entities of one form or another, questions have also been developed to obtain information on the characteristics of these quasi-regulatory systems. To fully understand how these quasi-regulatory systems produce explicit or implicit decisions, more research will be needed that goes beyond the scope of what this handbook is intended to do.[11]

Finally, there is the special case of "failed states" where few, if any, government or legal institutions operate at all. In these countries, the supply of utility services can and does take place on a limited scale (for example, So-

---

11. A good discussion of the advantages and disadvantages of different types of regulatory systems can be found especially in chapter 2 of **Gómez-Ibáñez** (2003).

malia) using voluntary arrangements and private mechanisms (such as private militias) to enforce decisions, payment, and so forth. Government entities are not involved in these arrangements because government entities either do not exist or do not function. Because failed states represent a very different situation, we do not discuss these cases in the main text of the handbook. We do, however, make some observations on them in appendix I.

Old-Style Versus New-Style Regulation

Regulation is not new to infrastructure industries. Governments have always controlled infrastructure enterprises, especially when they were under total government ownership. The difference is that this "old-style regulation" was usually done by a line ministry and in a relatively opaque way. Old-style regulation (often described as coordination, review, or oversight) has been the prevailing mode in countries with substantial government ownership of infrastructure enterprises. Typically, it involved extensive and often ad hoc controls by one or more ministries over the operations of one or more government-owned infrastructure enterprises. With the growth of private participation in infrastructure since the early 1990s, a "new style of regulation" has emerged. This new style of regulation usually involves the creation of separate regulatory entities with some degree of independent decisionmaking authority, whether final or advisory, over the traditional regulatory tasks mentioned above.

Two Important Dimensions of Regulation: Governance and Substance

Any regulatory system has two important dimensions: *regulatory governance* and *regulatory substance*. Regulatory governance refers to the institutional and legal design of the regulatory system and is the framework within which decisions are made. Regulatory governance is defined by the laws, processes, and procedures that determine the enterprises, actions, and parameters that are regulated, the government entities that make the regulatory decisions, and the resources and information that are available to them. *Regulatory governance is the "how" of regulation.* It involves decisions about the following:

- Independence and accountability of the regulator.
- Relationship between the regulator and policymaker(s).

1

- Autonomy of the regulator.
- Processes—formal and informal—by which decisions are made.
- Transparency of decisionmaking by the regulator or other entities making regulatory decisions.
- Predictability of regulatory decisionmaking.
- Accessibility of regulatory decisionmaking.
- Organizational structure and resources available to the regulator.

Regulatory substance refers to the content of regulation.[12] It is the actual decisions, whether explicit or implicit, made by the specified regulatory entity or other entities within the government, along with the rationale for the decisions. *Regulatory substance is the "what" of regulation.* It typically involves decisions about the following:

- Tariff levels.
- Tariff structures.
- Automatic and nonautomatic cost pass-through mechanisms.
- Quality-of-service standards.
- Handling of consumer complaints.
- Investment or connection obligations and reviews.
- Network access conditions for new and existing customers.
- Accounting systems.
- Periodic reporting requirements.
- Social obligations.

Regulatory governance issues are similar for national or regional regulators regardless of whether the regulator is regulating electricity, natural gas transmission or distribution, telecommunications, transport, water, or sewerage. Therefore, the discussion of "best-practice" governance principles and standards in chapter 3 is generally relevant for all national and regional infrastructure regulators, regardless of sector. Similarities also exist across infrastructure sectors in regulatory substance. Although the specific issues may vary depending on differences in underlying economics and sector struc-

---

12. "Regulatory substance" is referred to as "regulatory content" by **Levy and Spiller** (1994). They argue for tightly defined regulatory governance arrangements for most developing countries so that a new regulatory entity will have little discretion over regulatory substance in its initial years of operation. The advantages and disadvantages of this approach (often implemented through detailed regulatory contracts or concessions) are discussed in chapter 4.

tures, all infrastructure regulators have to grapple with issues relating to tariff levels, tariff structures, and information requirements. *An important conclusion of the handbook is that any evaluation of a regulatory system will be seriously incomplete if the evaluation is limited to regulatory governance or regulatory substance alone.* Any serious evaluation of regulatory effectiveness needs to look at both dimensions.

Focus of This Handbook

As noted earlier, the focus of this handbook is on economic regulation rather than on health, safety, and environmental regulation.[13] Within economic regulation, the coverage of the handbook is limited in four other ways. *First, the emphasis is on evaluating effective regulation of enterprises with a commercial orientation.* Such enterprises are motivated by profits, which in turn implies that they are concerned about increasing revenues and reducing costs. Such enterprises are "more easily regulated than public operators because it is possible to design regulatory instruments that make it financially attractive for a company to act in the interests of consumers."[14]

Such enterprises will usually be privately owned or operated, although there are examples of state-owned enterprises with a strong commercial orientation in some countries. In these cases, a large proportion of investment is likely to be financed from private sources—for example, from equity investment, bond finance, or borrowing on commercial market terms. In addition, these state-owned enterprises usually operate in sectors that have a mix of public and private ownership. This mix of ownership facilitates benchmarking, which can put pressure on the performance of both private and state-owned enterprises. Unfortunately, however, the more common reality for many government-owned enterprises (especially in Sub-Saharan Africa

---

13. Economic regulation can have a major impact on the environment. For example, the success or failure of renewable energy and energy efficiency programs will depend critically on the pricing and power purchase policies established by the electricity regulator. The goals or targets for these initiatives are almost always established by the government in laws and decrees. However, once these goals or targets are established, any assessment of regulatory effectiveness should ask whether the regulatory system has helped or hindered the achievement of these goals.

14. Vivien Foster, 2005, "Ten Years of Water Service Reform in Latin America: Toward an Anglo-French Model," Water Supply and Sanitation Discussion Paper Series 3, World Bank, Washington, DC, p. 5; available at www.worldbank.org/watsan.

1

and many parts of Asia) is that they are unable to operate like a normal commercial enterprise because they are forced to satisfy multiple objectives, many of which are unrelated if not antithetical to commercial considerations. Often, a government enterprise will try to satisfy key political supporters, maintain high levels of budgets and employment, subsidize unrelated activities, and provide service on an uneconomic basis. The need to satisfy these multiple, non-economic objectives makes it impossible to operate as a commercially efficient enterprise.[15]

Moreover, it is unlikely that the government will put serious pressure on these state enterprises to improve their commercial performance if, as in some African countries, a portion of the salaries, cars, and housing of key ministerial officials comes from the state enterprise. *The presence of these additional (and often hidden) pressures and constraints implies that the regulatory systems discussed in this handbook, which presume that the regulated enterprise will respond to normal economic incentives, are not likely to be effective for most government enterprises.*[16] Other regulatory and governance systems are needed for public enterprises that face significant noncommercial pressures; these are discussed in other World Bank reports.[17] As a general rule, unless a government first makes serious governance reforms for the state-owned enterprise to ensure its commercial operation, economic regulation will be largely ineffective.

Second, the examples in the handbook are generally drawn from the power sector. This emphasis reflects the fact that the World Bank has supported, or

---

15. See the discussion in Mark Jamison, Sanford Berg, Farid Gasmi, and Jose Tavara, 2004, "Annotated Reading List for a Body of Knowledge on the Regulation of Infrastructure and Utility Services," World Bank, Washington, DC; photocopy; available at http://bear.cba.ufl.edu/centers/purc/Body_of_Knowledge.htm.

16. This has been a common complaint of the new state-level electricity regulators in India who have found themselves in the difficult position of trying to regulate state-owned power enterprises. The reality is that the state-owned power enterprises generally ignore the directive of their regulators because the regulators have little or no ability to impose rewards or penalties on them. As one Indian regulator observed, "My orders are just pretty poetry." Quoted in **Bakovic, Tenenbaum, and Woolf** (2003), p. 29.

17. Irwin and Yamamoto conclude that the biggest improvements in state-owned enterprises are more likely to come from changes in the corporate governance system than in the regulatory system. See Timothy Irwin and Chiaki Yamamoto, 2004, "Some Options for Improving the Governance of State-Owned Electricity Utilities," Energy and Mining Sector Board Discussion Paper 11, World Bank, Washington, DC; available at http://iris37.worldbank.org/domdoc/PRD/Other/PRDDContainer.nsf/All+Documents/85256D2400766CC785256FFC0074A7F4/$File/Energy_ImptheGov.pdf. See also World Bank, 1996, *Bureaucrats in Business* (Oxford, UK: Oxford University Press).

soon will be supporting, complementary initiatives that focus on evaluating and improving regulatory effectiveness in the telecommunications and water and sewerage sectors.[18] These parallel initiatives will provide a level of detail on sector-specific regulatory evaluations that would be impossible to replicate in this study. Therefore, we have opted to draw on examples mostly from the power sectors of developing countries. However, most of the general discussion, as well as the regulatory principles, standards, and outcome measures should be equally relevant to other infrastructure sectors that have regional or national regulators. Similarly, the questionnaires and other evaluation tools set out in the appendixes can provide a good starting point for designing evaluations of regulatory entities in other infrastructure industries.

Third, the focus of the handbook is on how to perform ex post evaluations of the design and operation of existing economic regulatory systems for infrastructure sectors.[19] This type of evaluation is not be confused with ex ante appraisals of specific proposed regulations, policies, or regulatory governance arrangements.[20] Before-the-fact assessments are often referred to as regulatory impact assessments (RIAs) and are discussed in great length in other studies and reports. (See section 3 of the selected annotated bibliography.) This does not mean that a connection is absent between the two types of reviews.

---

18. See NERA (National Economic Research Associates), 2004, *Framework for Evaluating the Effectiveness of Telecommunications Regulators in Sub-Saharan Africa,* a final report for the Global Information and Communication Technologies Department of the World Bank (London: NERA); available at http://wbln0018.worldbank.org/ict/resources.n sf/a693f575e01ba5f385256b500062af05/95c2062a88c0eb7c85256fe1006aedc8/$FILE/Te lecomFrameworkReport_AFR.pdf. A similar set of regulatory studies has been initiated for the water and sewerage sectors. See *Improving the Regulation of Water and Sanitation Services* at http://wbln0018.worldbank.org/ppiaf/activity.nsf/WebSectorWater (click on "[GLOBAL] Improving the Regulation of Water and Sanitation Services [WSS]").

19. Similar assessments are often made of proposed regulatory systems. The focus of this handbook, however, is on after-the-fact assessments that would be made after a new regulatory system has operated for several years.

20. Such ex ante assessments are often referred to as regulatory impact assessments (RIAS). RIAs usually involve a quantitative or qualitative assessment of a single *proposed* environmental, health, and safety regulation. RIAs are typically performed before the regulation is adopted by the government agency responsible for the specific regulatory action or another government body in charge of monitoring the regulator. In contrast, the regulatory evaluations discussed in this handbook are designed to determine whether an *existing regulatory system*, comprising its governance arrangements and actual substantive decisions, could be improved to obtain better sectoral performance. For more information on RIAs, see **U.K. Cabinet Office** (2003) and **Kirkpatrick, Parker, and Zhang** (2004).

Many of the benchmarks developed for the after-the-fact evaluations will be equally relevant for before-the-fact appraisals.

Fourth, where the private sector is involved, the focus of the handbook is on regulation of entities that have been fully privatized (that is, through an asset sale), and are operating under a long-term concession or other arrangement that transfers investment and operating responsibilities to the private operator or under a long-term lease that transfers operating—but not investment—responsibilities to the private operator. We focus on these more demanding forms of private sector involvement because private entities are more likely to be influenced by regulatory incentives if they are taking some significant demand and operating risks.

If the extent of private sector involvement is limited to a service or management contract (sometimes referred to as "entry-level" private participation), a regulator is likely to be marginal for at least two reasons. First is that the government has decided to turn over top management to a private entity, which means that the government essentially has chosen to relinquish its direct responsibilities for the management of the enterprise while still retaining control over the volume and financing of investments. Until there is a turnaround, it is unlikely that the enterprise will be operating with the "commercial orientation" that is a prerequisite for successful regulation. The second reason is that a regulator will not be effective if it is "micromanaging." Ideally, the regulator should focus on the overall performance of the regulated entity and not on the details of the regulated entity's contracts with outside contractors. Management contracts with outside contractors should be the responsibility of the owner (that is, government) and not of a sector-specific regulator.[21]

The Structure of the Handbook

This handbook is organized as follows:

- Chapter 2 describes three different approaches to evaluating economic regulatory systems:

---

21. A very perceptive analysis of the issues in designing and implementing management contracts for state-owned infrastructure entities can be found in David Erhardt, 2005, "Towards Sample Bidding Documents for Management Contracts," paper presented at an informal World Bank seminar, Washington, DC, May 10; available from the World Bank's Procurement Board.

- Type 1—cross-country statistical analyses
- Type 2—cross-country descriptive analyses
- Type 3—single-country structured case studies.

It concludes that the Type 3 approach is the best approach if the principal goal of the evaluation is to persuade political authorities to make changes in an existing regulatory system. Type 3 case studies, however, can be bolstered (that is, made more persuasive to political authorities) if they are accompanied by Type 2 studies that benchmark regulatory systems and performance within the same region or across comparable countries. The chapter describes how the recommended Type 3 case study approach differs from previous regulatory evaluations. It also analyzes how to evaluate the effect of the regulatory system on sector outcomes because sector outcomes must be the ultimate benchmark for judging the effectiveness of a regulatory system.

- Chapter 3 presents benchmarks for judging regulatory effectiveness. The benchmarks are contained in a hierarchy of meta-principles, principles, and standards for regulatory governance. From the three meta-principles, the chapter derives 10 principles that represent general ideal attributes of a well-functioning regulatory system. The principles, in turn, imply detailed and specific standards that are concrete legal and institutional arrangements through which the general principles can be "operationalized." Although the principles and standards are consistent with a good or best-practice "independent regulator" model—the most commonly recommended model of regulatory governance—they are also, for the most part, relevant and applicable to other forms of regulatory governance. This implies that it is also appropriate to use the principles and standards as a basis for the evaluations of other regulatory systems.

- Chapter 4 presents elements of "transitional" regulatory systems for countries that have in place a regulatory or quasi-regulatory system that is not the independent regulator model. A key consideration in evaluating transitional regulatory systems is whether they incorporate incentives and pressures that are likely to lead to improvements in regulatory practice and effectiveness over time. Among the transitional options considered are combinations of regulation with contractual arrangements, mechanisms that reduce the burden on regulatory resources, and the use of external regulatory guarantees. For any country, the choice of a transitional option—and its assessment— to

1

consider the country's starting conditions, both in the specific sector being regulated and in the country's overall governance capabilities. No single set of transitional regulatory arrangements will apply to all countries at all times. "Good fits" are harder to design than "best practices." The chapter concludes with a discussion of the implications of these issues for the evaluation of transitional and interim regulatory frameworks.

- Chapter 5 discusses how to recognize "good" and "bad" elements of a regulatory system, with respect to both regulatory governance and regulatory substance. It presents examples of "bad" regulation in the form of actions taken or not taken. The examples are tied to different types of reform initiatives commonly observed in developing and transition economies. In the power sector, such initiatives include promoting the expansion of grid and off-grid electrification, encouraging "open access" to allow customers to choose suppliers, subsidizing grid-connected renewable energy, and encouraging private sector participation in electricity distribution through long-term concessions or full privatization. This does not mean that a country can or should pursue all these reform initiatives. The threshold issue of "what should be reformed" will depend on a country's economic starting conditions and what the government wants to achieve from the reform. The chapter concludes with a list of measurable sector outcomes on which, if possible, data should be collected for use in regulatory evaluations of the power sector—including identifying the contribution of "good" or "bad" regulation.

- Chapter 6 describes the process for conducting short, mid-level, and in-depth regulatory evaluations. The level of evaluation will depend on the time and money that are available. Different levels of evaluation are illustrated with questionnaires and interview guides.

- Specific "tools" for evaluators and those who are managing evaluators are presented in nine appendixes:
  - Appendix A presents definitions and elaborations of the critical standards for effective infrastructure regulation that were presented in chapter 3. The material is written so that it can be used in discussions with government officials who have to make decisions on designing and implementing new regulatory systems.
  - Appendix B provides a checklist of background documents needed for mid-level and in-depth evaluations of regulatory systems.

- Appendix C contains questionnaires for short, basic evaluations of national, regional, and provincial power sector regulatory systems. It is intended for use by World Bank staff and a wider group of people who are not infrastructure or regulatory specialists.
- Appendix D describes how to conduct mid-level and in-depth evaluations. It contains a questionnaire, originally developed by the World Bank's Development Research Group, that can be used as a starting point for such evaluations in reforming power sectors.
- Appendix E discusses how to conduct structured interviews with sector participants. It presents specific interview questions keyed to regulatory issues associated with specific electricity reform initiatives. These include electrification; grid-based, renewable energy; distribution company regulation; effects on the poor as consumers; open access and customer choice regimes; and competitive bulk power markets.
- Appendix F contains a sample terms of reference for use by those evaluating an existing regulatory system. It discusses how to modify the terms of reference to match the particular situations of individual countries.
- Appendix G summarizes publicly available mid-level and in-depth evaluations that have been performed on the electricity regulatory systems in six countries—Brazil, Chile, India, the Russian Federation, South Africa, and Ukraine. It describes the context, principal findings, and recommendations for each evaluation.
- Appendix H presents an overview of the French and Anglo approaches to regulation, as well as a discussion of hybrid regulatory systems that have combined elements from these two regulatory traditions.
- Appendix I provides an introductory discussion of infrastructure provision and regulatory issues for countries with very limited institutional capacity, such as post-conflict countries and failed states.
- Finally, there is a selected annotated bibliography. Each cited entry describes what is in the document and how it relates to evaluations of infrastructure regulatory systems.

Chapter 2

Approaches to Evaluating Regulatory Effectiveness

I need solutions, not just observations.
— Government energy official in a South Asian country

Principal Methods of Evaluation

Because economic regulation is often controversial, it should not be surprising that the effectiveness of regulatory systems began to be examined and debated almost as soon as new regulatory systems came into existence. Such evaluations have taken different forms depending on what is being sought from the evaluation. In general, the evaluations are performed in one of three ways:

- Type 1—cross-country statistical analyses.
- Type 2—cross-country descriptive analyses (with and without benchmarking).
- Type 3—single-country structured case studies.

Type 1—Cross-Country Statistical Analyses

Type 1 studies use various statistical techniques (primarily econometric techniques based on variants of regression analysis) to examine whether various formal and informal characteristics of the regulatory system have produced positive or negative effects on the economic performance of the sector.[1] The data for these studies usually come from published information and questionnaires sent to the regulators in different countries. Typically, the studies try to determine whether certain regulatory characteristics or combinations of characteristics (such as institutional independence, existence of a regulatory statute, or type of tariff-setting system) have had positive or negative effects on different dimensions of sector performance (such as levels of investment and capacity utilization).

The studies attempt to use real-world data to test general propositions on the potential economic effects of regulation. *They are not designed to provide detailed recommendations on specific reforms.* This does not, however, imply that the studies are irrelevant to the real world of regulation. Presumably, policymakers will benefit from knowing whether different dimensions of regulatory governance (for example, an independent regulator) and substance (for example, cost of service versus price cap regulation) are associated with increases in infrastructure industry investment, productivity, and performance.

Quantitative answers to these fundamental questions can be found only from econometric studies of this type, whatever qualifications may be attached to specific studies. With the growing availability of "panel data" (comparable data for a good number of countries for a number of years), the quality of these studies has greatly improved. In general, the more recent studies increasingly confirm the view that good regulation (as defined by the governance principles and standards described in chapter 3) improves investment and productivity performance in developing countries both in telecoms and in electricity generation.[2]

Most government officials, however, do not have the time or background to delve deeply into these econometric studies. Nor are these cross-country statistical studies designed to provide an in-depth review of the performance of a single country's regulatory system (or some specific elements of the system). For this task, a country-specific evaluation based on specific data collection and interviews is required. Cross-country econometric studies and

---

1. For a discussion of these studies, see **Stern and Cubbin** (2005). Most of the early studies were done on telecommunications regulation. Some of the more recent studies have considered electricity regulation.
2. For a high-quality panel data study of regulatory outcomes in fixed-line telecoms, see **Gutierrez** (2003). **Cubbin and Stern** (2005) provide the first major panel data study of the effect of the quality of regulatory governance on developing countries' generation capacity.

single-country evaluations may complement each other, but the bottom line is that they are quite different in both objectives and methods.

Type 2—Cross-Country Descriptive Analyses

These are cross-country studies that are designed to compare the formal characteristics of regulatory systems in different countries.[3] Typically, they focus on legally specified elements of governance, such as appointment and removal procedures, funding sources, appeals of regulatory decisions, and the division of responsibilities between the regulator and other parts of the government. The end product is usually a published report with various tables designed to facilitate comparisons across countries. The general goal of such studies is to allow for benchmarking of regulatory systems rather than trying to prove or disprove the general propositions that are the focus of the Type 1 studies. These studies are usually conducted in the hope that a country's political authorities will be convinced that they need to improve their regulatory system if they see that it compares unfavorably with the regulatory systems in other comparable countries.

It is common for these cross-country descriptive studies to be commissioned by regional or international groups of regulators or organizations that want to promote "better" regulation. For example, the International Telecommunication Union (ITU) maintains a Web site that allows for comparisons among more than 100 national telecommunications regulators. Similarly, the U.S. Agency for International Development (USAID) has funded detailed surveys of the institutional and legal characteristics of energy regulators in Southeastern Europe. In this case, the motivation for the cross-country comparison was to determine whether the regulatory entity in a particular country met the requirements for membership in the European Union. It is almost always the case that these studies focus on characteristics associated with the independent regulator model (described more fully in chapter 3).

Regulators almost always end up liking these studies. Initially, most regulators are fearful that the studies will be used to evaluate their performance, but they soon realize that this is not the intent of such studies and that the studies can actually help them. For example, if regulators can show that their counterparts in neighboring countries have larger budgets, are able to

---

3. See **CEER** (2004); **Commission of the European Communities** (2005); **ITU** (2001); Ocaña (2002); and **Stern and Holder** (1999).

offer larger compensation packages, or possess more decisionmaking authority, they can use this information to argue for increasing their own budgets and autonomy. Because those studies usually focus on formally specified governance elements of regulatory systems, the studies provide little or no benefit to political authorities in making judgments on how the regulators have used their budgets or decisionmaking authority. In this sense, they tend to be one dimensional. The studies help the regulators argue for their institutional interests, or occasionally allow critics to argue that the regulators have inflated resources or powers. They are not, however, useful in reaching conclusions about whether the regulators made good use of the resources that were available or whether the regulators made decisions that helped or hindered sector performance.

Some of the studies even fail in their goal of trying to capture the attention of political authorities to improve on formal governance elements. This happens, in part, because of "how the message is delivered." Oftentimes researchers will present the results in table after table of cross-country comparisons of individual governance characteristics. Although such tables and the accompanying footnotes may be of considerable interest to other researchers on regulation, the reality is that most policymakers find it difficult to process all this raw information. Other studies do somewhat better by producing explicit rankings for different subdimensions (such as funding and transparency) rather than simply displaying the raw data in tables, but they still have a tendency to get lost in the trees rather than showing the forest.

If the goals are to capture the interest of policymakers and ultimately to influence their decisions on regulation, the better approach, in our view, is to present, at least initially, the "big picture" in a single overall governance ranking. A policymaker is much more likely to pay attention if he sees a single number that shows that his country's electricity regulatory commission ranks five out of six in his region rather than numerous tables filled with raw data that are hard to grasp, or six or seven separate subrankings where some numbers are high and other numbers are low. The advantage of first presenting a single number is that it captures the policymaker's attention (especially if the ranking is high or low) and is easier to remember. The same strategy is implicit in the golden rule of advertising: you first need to capture the consumer's attention before you start giving product details.[4]

---

4. A soon-to-be-completed study performed in Brazil adopts this recommended approach. Using the governance characteristics of the independent regulator governance model

Type 3—Single-Country Structured Case Studies

A third approach is single-country analyses of an existing regulatory system.[5] Typically, they take the form of structured case studies that focus on regulatory governance. Depending on the resources that are available, the evaluation may be limited to an examination of the formal legal and institutional aspects of the regulatory system, or it may go more deeply and review how the formal elements have actually been employed. The case studies are "structured" in the sense that the questionnaires and interview guidelines provide a checklist to ensure that case studies for different countries examine a similar core set of issues. Depending on the available resources, the case studies may involve quick, mid-level, or in-depth evaluations.

Quick Evaluations

A quick evaluation is a simple evaluation that uses a questionnaire, such as that set out in appendix C of the handbook, to get an initial overview of both the sector and its regulatory system. It may well be that no further evaluation is conducted, either because there are no pressing problems or because additional resources are not available. The quick evaluation will at least provide a brief overview of the state of regulation and the regulated sector, and it can provide a starting point for a useful public dialogue on regulatory issues. It also could serve as a useful diagnostic tool that points the way to further inquiry that needs to be done though the mid-level and in-depth evaluations presented in appendixes D and E. Thus, a quick evaluation can provide a form of reconnaissance without spending a lot of money. An additional advantage is that it can be performed by individuals who may have only general knowledge of the sector.

(see chapter 3), the evaluators produced overall governance rankings of 21 new federal- and state-level infrastructure regulators in Brazil. Although there are some methodological problems in comparing regulators at two levels of government, the overall approach should be effective in getting the attention of Brazilian policymakers at the federal and state levels. See **Correa, Pereira, Mueller, and Melo** (forthcoming).

5. For electricity, see **Brown and De Paula** (2002 and 2004) on Brazil, **Prayas Energy Group** (2003) on India, the **World Bank** (2004) on Russia, and **Moscote** (2004) on Ukraine. The principal findings and recommendations of these reports are summarized in appendix G. For telecoms, the 2001 ITU case studies of Botswana, Brazil, Morocco, Peru, and Singapore are also available on the ITU Web site: http://www.itu.int/ITU-D /treg/Case_Studies/Index.html.

2

Mid-Level and In-Depth Evaluations

These "deeper" studies often involve extensive interviews not only with the regulator but also with government officials, executives in sector enterprises, and consumers. The advantage of interviewing individuals with widely different perspectives is that it ensures that the study will not simply reflect what government officials or the regulator want the study to say.[6] The principal difference between a medium-level and an in-depth evaluation is that the latter goes wider and deeper on the issues and topics covered.

The better studies are performed by specialists in economic regulation who are not economically tied to organizations that can be helped or hurt by the evaluation. To ensure both the reality and the appearance of impartiality, it is usually best to pair an internationally known expert with one or more sector experts from the country that is being studied. This ensures that the outside experts will not waste a lot of time and money familiarizing themselves with the economic and political situation in the sector that is being studied. In addition, if the local experts are well known and have a good reputation, it will be easier to arrange interviews, and the interviews will be more productive. The local experts also will be able to suggest questions and, equally important, give an informed evaluation of the answers.

A useful supplement to the team approach, recently employed in Brazil, is the inclusion of a local lawyer as a third member of the team. If the president and legislature accept the substance of one or more of the recommendations, the lawyer can give specific advice on how the reform can be implemented. The lawyer can help frame issues in the context of local law and custom by addressing such questions as the following:

- Does the recommendation require a change in the constitution, in a law, or in a regulation?
- What specific legal language is required to implement the recommendation?

Having these legal questions addressed in the initial report avoids the delay of a second and separate legal analysis. It also avoids the criticism often directed at reports written by foreign experts, namely, that the recommenda-

---

6. It is not uncommon for trade associations or nongovernmental organizations (NGOs) to sponsor analyses of infrastructure regulatory systems. Such studies can be very helpful in

tions are irrelevant to or ignorant of local circumstances, are too academic or too theoretical, or constitute unnatural overlays on local jurisprudence.

Ideally, the study should be initiated by a country's legislature or government agency (or perhaps even by the regulators themselves). This is because they are the agencies either responsible for periodic reviews of regulatory agencies and similar bodies or likely to recognize flaws in the current system that need to be considered and corrected. However, as noted in chapter 1 and appendix A, it is not necessary to await the appearance of flaws in the system to evaluate the functioning of the system and examine what improvements might be made. It is prudent public policy for legislators and/or relevant executive agencies to conduct regular, periodic, transparent oversight hearings (for example, every four years) to review the institutional arrangements of and practices within the regulatory system. Such periodic reviews have become the norm in Europe and are quite common in the United States.

Although internally generated reviews do occur—usually triggered by a major sectoral or economywide crisis—it is more typical for such studies to be requested by an international aid agency or lender, such as the World Bank or one of the regional development banks. The external pressure for such a study may be presented as an explicit or implicit quid pro quo for a loan or grant. In either of these cases, the study is often initiated because of public controversies surrounding the regulated sector or over particular decisions that left some interest groups (often domestic consumers or international investors) seriously disaffected. Other evaluation studies may be commissioned by international or regional organizations such as the International Telecommunication Union or the Energy Regulators Regional Association with the objective of describing and disseminating regulatory best practices. In the future, international aid agencies and regional regulatory groups may request or promote more routine evaluations to encourage continued improvements and to disseminate best practices.

It should not be surprising that externally promoted, country-specific evaluations cause anxiety for a country's regulators and politicians. No one likes to be criticized. Even if a proposed evaluation is characterized as an evaluation of the "system," it is often viewed as a critique of the performance

---

identifying weaknesses or problems in both the design and the implementation of the system, but they also may be biased because they inevitably reflect the commercial or consuming interests of the organization that commissioned the assessment.

of particular individuals, especially if the report is publicized in national newspapers. Many regulators are fearful of such public evaluations.[7] Their fear is that the study may conclude that they performed poorly or that they did something that was illegal. Consequently, there is often strong pressure from both regulators and government officials to make the evaluation "confidential," so that it will not be seen by the general public.

Openness, however, yields considerable benefits, including making it easier to obtain consent and support for proposed changes. It also demonstrates that the government and regulator are not trying to cover up problems and are dealing seriously with difficult and often politically contentious issues. One country that has been very open and transparent in its handling of such evaluations is Brazil. In 2004, ANEEL, its National Electricity Regulatory Agency, and the Ministry of Mines and Energy agreed to the publication of an 85-page evaluation of the Brazilian electricity regulatory system that contained 29 recommendations for reform. Besides being made public, the report was extensively discussed by a cross-section of representatives from the entire Brazilian power sector before it was released.[8]

If this type of single-country evaluation is to be effective, it must be written in a style that is understandable to political authorities—presentation is as important as substance. But even if a study is well written and sensitive to current political sensibilities, this in itself does not guarantee that the recommendations will be adopted. Perhaps the hardest part of the evaluation exercise is to convince political decisionmakers that it is in their interests to adopt the recommendations. In fact, the reality is that it may not always be in their short-term political interests (that is, getting reelected) to adopt the recommendations. In other words, what is economically desirable in the long term may not be politically palatable in the short term.

---

7. Even though regulators may have such fears at the outset of the evaluation, they often find the exercise quite useful. Such was the case in Brazil where ANEEL, the electricity regulator, was concerned at the outset about whether the exercise would serve as a vehicle for criticizing them for their role in the country's electricity crisis. Over the course of the evaluation—a process in which they were very cooperative—the ANEEL commissioners came to view the evaluation as a very positive experience enabling them to demonstrate how the constraints under which they were compelled to operate were harmful. On its own initiative, ANEEL adopted almost all of the recommended improvements that were within the agency's power to adopt without legislative changes.

8. The full report is available at www.ppiaf.org.

The Approach of This Handbook and How It Differs from Earlier Approaches

This handbook proposes an evaluation methodology based on structured, single-country case studies.[9] This is the Type 3 approach, but with the modifications described below. The principal reason for proposing this approach is that the goal of the evaluation should be to produce a specific list of recommended reforms. The individuals who make decisions on whether to make changes in a country's existing regulatory system will not be interested in multicountry studies that prove or disprove general propositions about the theory and practice of economic regulation. Instead, their principal concern will be specific reforms that could be applied to their existing regulatory systems.

It is also important to remember that, even if the recommendations have considerable merit, they probably will not be adopted unless those who make the recommendations have demonstrated in-depth knowledge of what currently exists in the country. Credentials, reputation, and experience do matter because decisionmakers are more likely to pay attention to the recommendations of an internationally or nationally recognized expert. *In summary, the best way to establish credibility is through well-written, comprehensive case studies prepared by recognized and respected individuals who demonstrate a clear understanding of a country's political, economic, and legal realities.*

Although this handbook recommends the Type 3 approach, it does not mean that the case studies are irrelevant for Type 1 and Type 2 analyses. The proposed questionnaires (appendixes C and D), the interview guidelines (appendix E), and the general methodology of the case studies have been carefully designed to facilitate the collection of comparable information across countries. Therefore, an important side benefit of the case studies is that they will allow for better cross-country empirical analyses (Type 1 studies) or cross-country benchmarking (Type 2 studies).

This handbook also attempts to correct for three weaknesses in some of the earlier regulatory evaluation studies.

---

9. A similar, structured case study approach has been used in a Stanford University research project that examines the factors that contribute to the success or failure of independent power projects in five countries. For an explanation of the methodology used in the Stanford study, see David G. Victor, Thomas Heller, Joshua House, and Pei Yee Woo, 2004, "The Experience with Independent Power Projects (IPPs) in Developing Countries: Introduction and Case Study Methods," Program on Energy and Sustainable Development, Working Paper 23, Stanford University, Palo Alto, CA.

1. **Those studies have tended to focus almost exclusively on the institutional and legal characteristics of the regulatory systems, with little or no attention paid to the actual decisions made by the regulator.** Many earlier studies of regulatory institutions have emphasized cross-country comparisons of the institutional and legal characteristics of the new regulatory systems (that is, regulatory governance). The implicit assumption is that an infrastructure sector will achieve good outcomes if the regulatory law or decrees formally mandate independence, accountability, transparency, and other institutional and process characteristics of the U.S. and, more recently, European regulatory systems. The intentional or unintentional focus of these studies has been on regulatory governance (processes, funding, appointment procedures, and legal authorities) rather than on regulatory substance (tariff decisions and quality-of-service standards issued by the regulator or others). This is not an unreasonable approach. There is growing empirical evidence that regulatory systems with good governance characteristics, at least in middle- and high-income countries, are statistically associated with better sector performance.[10]

   Although poor governance is more likely to produce poor results, good governance is not an automatic guarantee of good outcomes. In other words, *good institutions can and sometimes do make bad decisions.* Moreover, what may be a workable regulatory institution in one country may not be workable in another country—that is, it may not be a good institutional fit. So if the goal is to assess the effectiveness of a regulatory system, one also must look at the actual decisions produced by the regulatory system in addition to its institutional and legal characteristics.

2. **The evaluations usually do not "drill down" to see whether the formal legal requirements actually have been implemented.** The reality in many countries is that a large gap often exists between the formally specified legal elements and how these legal requirements are actually implemented. For example, it was reported that the electricity regulators in two Eastern European countries were "encouraged" to resign because the prime ministers were displeased with their tariff decisions. The fact that regulators were legally protected because the law specified fixed terms for them apparently mattered very little after they is-

---

10. See **Stern and Cubbin** (2005).

sued decisions that the prime minister did not like. In another country, it was reported that individuals who wish to be named to a regulatory commission must provide the president with a signed but undated letter of resignation as a condition for being nominated.

These are not isolated incidents.[11] In Karnataka, India, the regulatory commission has the legal right to review and adjust tariffs on its own initiative, but on several occasions it was prevented from exercising this authority by the government. This is only one of many implementation problems that have been experienced by the new state electricity regulators in India. A study by Prayas, a leading Indian NGO, found that the new regulatory commissions suffered from inadequate funding, inadequate staff resources, problems with appointments and continuity, difficulties in enforcing compliance with their orders, lack of transparency and public participation, and a growing number of disputes with their state governments.[12] These are not isolated failures of the regulatory system. One often hears similar stories in other countries when regulators talk "off the record."

It should not be surprising that most evaluations of new regulatory systems have focused on formal governance characteristics. It is clearly easier (takes less time and effort) to obtain information on what is written in laws and decrees than to assess how the laws and decrees have actually been implemented. Moreover, most regulators and politicians will be understandably reluctant to talk about what happens behind the scenes, especially if it is of questionable legality. *The danger of limiting an evaluation to what is written in laws and decrees, however, is that it may give an inaccurate picture of how the regulatory system works in practice. Although such evaluations can be done quickly, they may also be very mistaken.*

3. **The studies usually do not attempt to assess how the regulator's actions or decisions have affected sector outcomes.** Regulation is not

---

11. A study by the European Bank for Reconstruction and Development (EBRD) finds that only 50 percent of infrastructure regulators in "transition" economies actually remain in office for their full assigned terms. This does not mean that all of the regulators were necessarily forced out by political authorities, but it tends to suggest that at least some of them left because of political pressures. The same EBRD study estimates that approximately 30 percent of the decisions made by regulators were overturned by governments. See **EBRD** (2004), pp. 37 and 43.

12. These implementation problems are well documented in **Prayas Energy Group** (2003).

an end in itself. Instead, it is a means to an end. *What ultimately matters is sector outcomes—not regulatory processes or institutional characteristics.* It is these sector outcomes (for example, capital investments, price levels, service quality, consumer satisfaction, profitability of regulated enterprises, productivity gains, expansion of basic service to new customers, subsidies that reach the genuinely poor, and the functioning of new and existing markets) that are the bottom line of any regulatory system. If the new regulatory system does not contribute to good outcomes, especially from the consumer perspective, the overall reform package and its regulatory component will be politically unsustainable. If the new regulatory system does not support commercially viable enterprises, it will be economically unsustainable.

For investors and consumers, it seems clear that *what matters most,* especially in the early years of sector reform, are earning profits on investments and experiencing discernible improvements in service at affordable prices, respectively, rather than a standard set of "best-practice" institutional characteristics for the regulator. For example, when a private Indian investor was asked for his opinion on the importance of independent regulatory commissions, his immediate response was that "regulatory independence is a fine concept, but it is of little comfort when I don't have enough money to pay my employees and creditors. I need money, not mantras."[13] Similarly, it is hard to imagine that a poor family in an African village without electricity will be very concerned about the transparency of a regulatory commission's processes and procedures if the regulated utility fails to meet its commitment to extend service to that family's village.

Sector Outcomes and Regulatory Evaluations

Measures of sector performance must be the bottom line for any reform package that includes a new regulatory system as one of its components. Conse-

---

13. Quoted in **Bakovic, Tenenbaum, and Woolf** (2003), p. 12. This is not an isolated comment. In the Lamech and Saeed (2002) worldwide survey of private investors in power sectors, "adequacy of cash flow" was mentioned as the single most important factor in deciding whether to invest. Ranjit Lamech and Kazim Saeed, 2003, "What International Investors Look for When Investing in Developing Countries," Energy and Mining Sector Board Discussion Paper 6, World Bank, Washington, DC, p. 10.

quently, sector performance needs to be measured on an ongoing and consistent basis. In chapter 5, we provide a recommended list of possible measures of sector outcomes or performance. Some of these measures, such as cost efficiency and quality of service, will be relevant for both industrial and developing countries. Other measures, however, will be of special interest just to developing and former socialist countries. For example, in many sub-Saharan African countries where less than 10 percent of the population has access to electricity, governments will want to know whether the overall reform package and its regulatory components have produced a significant number of new connections, whether grid or off-grid.[14] And in many developing and former socialist countries, the reduction of theft and nonpayment on distribution systems will be a major concern. For example, in India, where theft, nonbilling, and noncollections have been rampant, it has been estimated that in some states only 1 kilowatt-hour (kWh) actually is collected from paying customers for every 2 kWh produced by generators. The same is true in Nigeria.

Quantitative Versus Qualitative?

The importance of sector outcomes is indisputable, but this does **not** *imply that country-specific evaluations of infrastructure regulatory systems (Type 3 evaluations) should spend a lot of time and effort trying to quantify the effect of regulation on overall sector performance.* Such an exercise is likely to be unproductive for three reasons.

First, regulatory reform is almost always only one element of a larger reform package that usually includes sector restructuring, corporatization, commercialization, and some degree of private sector participation. It would be virtually impossible in a single-country case study to calculate the separate effect of the new regulatory system on overall sector performance or even particular components of sector performance. Such evaluations may be more amenable to cross-country statistical studies where there is observed variation in the regulatory systems across countries (Type 1 studies). Even in cross-country statistical stud-

---

14. Because more than 1.6 billion people do not have access to electricity, regulatory policies to achieve grid and off-grid electrification are of considerable interest to many countries in Asia, Latin America, and sub-Saharan Africa. This will be the subject of an Energy Sector Management Assistance Programme report, titled "Promoting Electrification Regulatory Principles and a Model Law," that will be published in 2006.

2

ies, it may be very difficult to distinguish between the separate effects of the various changes because many of the changes are occurring at the same time.

Second, sector outcomes also are strongly influenced by economic trends and events that are local, regional, and global. Regulated sectors of the economy are just as affected, for example, as any other segment of the economy when a country suffers a severe economic slump or when there is a collapse of macroeconomic policies. Recent events in Argentina bear witness to this reality. As a Latin American consultant observed, "The power sector pays for the sins of the macro economy."[15]

Third, even if it were possible to perform such calculations (that is, to quantify the effects of the regulatory system on overall sector performance), it is not obvious that these results would convince political decisionmakers to make specific "second-generation" reforms, the primary goal of any regulatory evaluation. The reality is that presidents and ministers do not think about changes in "consumer welfare" or "total factor productivity," the two most common measures used in empirical studies that attempt to assess the overall effect of infrastructure reform policies. Political authorities think in more concrete terms. They want to know what specific changes can be made in the current regulatory system to achieve politically beneficial outcomes.[16]

In other words, a president or minister is likely to pay attention to a regulatory evaluation only if it addresses immediate and politically visible issues, such as the following:

- How can we encourage more private investment in generation to reduce blackouts and brownouts?
- How can we get an existing distribution enterprise or some other entity to extend the main grid or to create stand-alone minigrids that will supply electricity to poor people who currently are not served?
- How can the regulator help the government meet renewable energy targets?
- Should some regulatory authority be transferred, at least temporarily, to the government ministry or board that is providing subsidies for electrification if the regulator is not helping achieve electrification?

---

15. Personal conversation with Bernard Tenenbaum, June 2002.
16. To be fair, an increase in connections will lead to an increase in consumer surplus, which is an economist's term for a measure of overall societal well-being. The issue, however, is obviously one of how to sell the reforms. A politician will have no problem in understanding that 25,000 households have been connected to the grid, but will likely have a totally blank look on his or her face if informed that consumer surplus has increased by 27 percent.

- Will the government need to offer a transitional subsidy to induce private investment? If so, how large must it be and for how long must it be given?
- Is there a risk that prices will go very high in a newly created bulk power market? If so, what should I do about it?

The Recommended Approach

Given the interests and needs of the likely audience—high-level government officials who have the power and the incentive to change the existing regulatory system—*the recommended approach is to look at specific elements of the regulatory system that relate to both regulatory governance and regulatory substance and to assess whether they help or hinder sector performance.* Stated differently, the evaluation should focus on actual characteristics and decisions of the regulatory system and assess whether these existing elements help move the sector toward better or worse outcomes.

This is a very different exercise from trying to assess the quantitative effect of a single element of the regulatory system or whether the overall regulatory system has a net positive or negative effect on overall sector performance. The proposed approach recognizes that the performance of the regulatory framework is only one of a number of factors that determine overall sector performance. It tries to determine whether particular actions or characteristics of the regulatory system are helpful or harmful in achieving desired sector outcomes. In other words, the recommended approach of the handbook, particularly for the mid-level and in-depth evaluations, is "forward looking" rather than "backward looking," "micro" rather than "macro," and "qualitative" rather than "quantitative."[17]

---

17. The approach recommended is in contrast with the full-blown cost-benefit analysis of an electricity or other infrastructure industry reform program. For an example of such a study, see David M. Newbery and Michael Pollitt, 1997, "The Restructuring and Privatisation of the CEGB—Was It Worth It?" *Journal of Industrial Economics* 45 (3): 269–303. This study and subsequent studies try to answer the question of whether an industry reform program *as a whole* has increased sector performance and economic welfare by providing quantitative estimates of the effects. To do so, they have to devise a plausible nonreform "counterfactual" (that is, how the entire sector would have performed without the reforms). Given the more limited objectives of identifying, in qualitative terms, positive and negative contributions, construction of an explicit general counterfactual is not proposed. However, the evaluators, in developing any recommendations for regulatory reform, implicitly will be assessing what might otherwise have happened if the regulator had taken a different view or made a different decision. This is a much less formal and more limited notion of a counterfactual than the one used in the academic studies to assess overall reform programs

Two Limitations of the Recommended Approach

The principal advantage of this "bottom-up" approach is that it focuses the attention of policymakers on specific reforms. However, this approach also has limitations that should not be ignored.

The Limits of Regulation

Any evaluation that focuses just on regulation will inevitably create the expectation that "better regulation" can solve most problems that exist in the sector.[18] This, however, ignores the fact that there are clear limits to what a regulator can and cannot do. *Regulation is not the answer to all problems.* For example, there is little that an electricity regulator can do if high bulk power prices are the result of a prior government policy decision to permit deregulated generation prices in a market that is too small or with too many transmission constraints to support effective competition. Similarly, a regulator will be equally powerless if he is trying to regulate the retail prices charged by a state-owned utility that was forced to buy high-priced power from an independent power producer (IPP) under the orders of an incompetent or corrupt minister.[19]

Another example would be regulatory actions to reduce technical and nontechnical losses. It is not uncommon for an electricity regulator to include explicit loss reduction targets in the allowed tariffs of distribution companies. The targets are designed to create incentives to reduce theft and improve collections. The regulatory action by itself, however, will accomplish very little if the government is unwilling or unable to provide effective police and judicial backup to support the distribution company in cutting off service to individuals who are stealing electricity. In other words, regulation cannot accomplish very much if basic "law and order" are absent.

In both of these cases, bad sector outcomes are not caused by flawed regulation. When a problem is beyond the scope of regulation because of a

---

18. This is true regardless of whether the evaluation is conducted through statistical techniques (Type 1), cross-country benchmarking (Type 2), or single-country structured case studies (Type 3).
19. In a survey of the role of African electricity regulators with respect to 25 independent power producer contracts in 13 countries, Anton Eberhard found that regulators were "frequently presented with a *fait accompli*." Presentation at World Bank Energy Week 2005. Available in the Learning Events section of www.worldbank.org/energy.

flawed sector structure or the actions of a government ministry, those who are performing the evaluation must state this in the public report. Specifically, the report must clearly highlight ministerial actions or sector characteristics that make it difficult or impossible for the regulatory system to achieve good outcomes. It is precisely at this moment that there is an advantage in having the evaluation performed by a respected outside evaluator. Clearly, if the regulator were to say the same thing, either publicly or privately, his or her statements would be heavily discounted as just a typical example of one government official trying to shift blame to another government official. In contrast, the outside expert has credibility that creates a unique opportunity to draw attention to fundamental problems that go beyond regulation. Stated differently, the outside expert has both an opportunity and an obligation to "speak truth to power."

The Good, the Bad, and the Uncertain

*It is unrealistic to expect that an outside evaluator **always** will be able to determine whether a specific element of the regulatory system—whether it relates to governance or substance—helps or hinders sector performance.* Some elements of regulatory systems are clearly good, some are clearly bad, and others are difficult to assess (see figure 2.1). A good element produces good sector outcomes, and there is no obvious change that will produce better sector outcomes. A bad element produces bad sector outcomes, and it can clearly be changed to

Figure 2.1. Regulatory Actions and Decisions

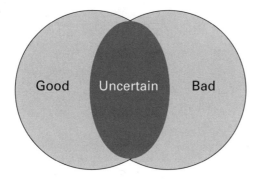

produce better sector outcomes. An uncertain element is an element whose effect on sector outcomes is difficult to assess.

Because the goal of the evaluation is to provide recommendations that will improve the system, the best strategy is to focus on those elements of the regulatory system that, if changed, would clearly lead to better outcomes for the sector while taking note of good features that are already in place. In other words, the evaluation should take note of what is good but focus on what is bad.[20] This is not so very different from the approach taken in most outside assessments of a company's performance. A management evaluation is worthwhile only if it leads to concrete recommendations on what needs to be improved. A competent company president or board of directors would not want to pay a lot of money to an outside consultant just to receive compliments. The same should be true of an outside regulatory evaluation.

Bad Regulation

Is it easy to recognize the bad elements of a regulatory system? The answer is "yes." Consider the following examples of regulatory characteristics and decisions drawn from World Bank client countries:

- Having no accounting system for calculating costs and tariffs.
- Imposing licensing and reporting requirements on small, community-based distribution entities that are the same as those for large, grid-connected distribution entities.
- Specifying a tariff-setting system for an initial five-year period and then providing little or no guidance as to the tariff-setting system that will be used in future tariff periods.
- Agreeing to the automatic pass-through of certain costs and then failing to honor this commitment.
- Imposing a ceiling on the price that distribution entities can pay for power purchased from generators that is lower than the generators' costs of production.
- Establishing a tariff structure that provides cross-subsidies to customers who are not poor.
- Failing to take account of congestion in setting transmission prices.

---

20. This is the approach generally taken in most of the single-country regulatory evaluations summarized in appendix G.

- Mandating "open access" for large industrial customers, but then failing to require separate, unbundled distribution and transmission tariffs that would allow them to purchase from alternative suppliers.
- Ignoring or suppressing seasonal and daily variations in electricity production costs in setting tariffs for customers who have the ability and incentive to respond to time-differentiated tariffs.
- Preventing the regulator from hiring staff on a permanent basis and from recruiting new staff at salaries other than entry level, or requiring that new mid- and senior-level hires must be approved by a sector minister.
- Failing to provide the regulator with a budget or diverting money that was specifically collected to support the regulator to other non-regulatory functions.
- Delaying or failing on the part of the regulator to make a decision.
- Creating long delays on appeals of the regulator's decisions in inexperienced courts.
- Forcing one or more regulators to offer "voluntary resignations" after a new government takes office.

The Strategy of the Recommendations

Characterizing these as "bad" elements of a regulatory system is saying, in effect, that there would have been a better outcome in the sector if the governance arrangements had been designed or implemented differently or if a different substantive decision had been made. This is a prediction based on a comparison between what actually happened and what might have happened if some other arrangement had been in place or some other decision had been made.[21] Therefore, any recommendation for a future change in the regulatory system inevitably will be based on a prediction of sector outcomes under the existing system versus a modified system. Because both states of the world require predictions about the future, it is impossible to be certain that either prediction will turn out to be true. However, there is enough worldwide experience with "good-practice" regulatory systems (see chapter 3) for us to have enough confidence that certain recommendations will lead to better outcomes in most countries.

---

21. This "what might have been" is usually referred to as "counterfactual" in the academic literature.

2

Although the recommendations may be easy to write, this does not imply that they will be easy to adopt. When presented with reform recommendations, it is not uncommon for a regulator to respond thus: "These are fine recommendations, but they will be impossible to implement in my country. You, as an outsider, simply do not understand the political and legal realities in my country."

Obviously, it is difficult for an outside evaluator to fully understand what is and what is not feasible in a particular country. Nor should it be surprising that individuals within a country will give conflicting assessments of the recommendations depending on whether they are defending the status quo or seeking changes to an existing system. For this reason, it is essential to involve experienced local experts in the evaluation team. The best advice for those who perform an evaluation is that they should give objective professional recommendations based on what they have observed in this and other countries. Unless an outside evaluator consciously tries "to push the envelope," it is very unlikely that anything will change.

Although the outside evaluator must try to understand the existing realities, he or she should always take the best practices and standards (chapter 3) as the basis of any evaluation. The evaluator also must be mindful that best-practice regulation does not necessarily require a single institutional framework. Historically, the independent regulatory agency model has been the model most associated with best-practice regulation. A number of industrial country variants of this model are available, however, and other governance models are certainly feasible. For electricity sectors in the early stages of commercialization or liberalization, other institutional arrangements may be as good—and in some cases possibly even better—provided that they can satisfy the principles and standards of good regulation and can deliver good outcomes in access growth, investment, and efficiency. These alternative arrangements are discussed in some detail in chapter 4.

In general, any "transitional" arrangements of the type discussed in chapter 4 should be evaluated according to whether they are likely to move the regulatory system toward a best-practice system even if that system is not immediately feasible. That, in turn, requires paying close attention to the context in which industry and regulatory reforms are taking place, including the industry and institutional developments of the previous 5–10 years.

Chapter 3

Benchmarks for Regulatory Governance: Key Principles and Critical Standards

3

Unless we can open up the black boxes labeled "rule of law," "regulatory independence," and the like, are we doing anything more than preaching "be good and avoid evil"?
— Outside reviewer of a World Bank publication

Why Benchmarks?

Evaluations require benchmarks. Without benchmarks, the evaluation of a regulatory system will lack coherence, discipline, and meaning. This chapter presents a set of key principles and critical standards that are represented in the best-performing versions of the *independent regulator* model, which exists in varying institutional forms in different countries. Taken together, these principles and standards represent the benchmarks for evaluation. The focus of the benchmarks, which are embedded in the questionnaires and interview guidelines, is on regulatory governance—the "how" of regulation.[1] The principles and standards are limited to regulatory governance because regu-

---

1. Governance, as noted in chapter 1, refers to the institutional and legal design of the regulatory system. It is the framework within and by which decisions are made. Governance is defined by the laws, processes, and procedures that determine the enterprises, actions,

latory substance—the "what" of regulation—tends to be more context-specific and, consequently, is less amenable to general principles and standards.[2] Issues that arise in evaluating regulatory substance are discussed in chapter 5 and the interview guidelines (appendix E).

What Is an Independent Regulator?

The key characteristic of the independent regulator model is decisionmaking independence. This means that the regulator's decisions are made without the prior approval of any other government entity, and no entity other than a court or a pre-established appellate panel can overrule the regulator's decisions. The institutional building blocks for decisionmaking independence are *organizational independence* (organizationally separate from existing ministries and departments), *financial independence* (an earmarked, secure, and adequate source of funding), and *management independence* (autonomy over internal administration and protection from dismissal without due cause).[3] The principal motivation for trying to create an independent regulatory entity is to "depoliticize" tariff-setting and other regulatory decisions by insulating the regulatory entity from day-to-day political considerations. It is an attempt to move away from a closed and often unpredictable, old-style ministerial regulation (see chapter 1).

The institutional and legal characteristics of the independent regulator model, along with the principles and standards to implement them, represent one model of regulatory "best practices." However, benchmarks need not always be based on best practices. As an alternative, *average* or even *worst* practices could have been used for the benchmarks, but that was not done for two reasons. First, it would have required detailed information on actual regulatory governance practices, information that is simply not available in

---

and parameters that are regulated, the agencies of the state that make regulatory decisions, and the resources and information available to them. It involves decisions about accountability, independence or autonomy, the roles of regulators and policymakers, transparency, predictability, organizational structure, and resources available to the regulator.

2. This is not entirely true. Certainly there is a generally accepted principle that overall tariffs must cover the long-term, efficient costs of supply.

3. See **EBRD** (2004), p. 58; Warrick Smith, 1997, "Utility Regulators—The Independence Debate," *Viewpoint* 127 (October); available at http://rru.worldbank.org/PublicPolicyJournal/Summary.aspx?id=127; and Bernard Tenenbaum, 1996, "Regulation: What the Prime Minister Needs to Know," *Electricity Journal* 9 (2): 28–36.

any systematic way. Second, it seemed reasonable to base the benchmarks on best practices because ultimately the purpose of any evaluation is to present recommendations on where the regulatory system should be, rather than on what is minimally acceptable or best avoided.

Why Use an Independent Regulator as a Benchmark?

Regulatory governance was chosen to be evaluated against benchmarks comprising the principles and standards of the independent regulator model for five reasons.[4]

First, the independent regulator model has become the de facto governance model, at least on paper, in most of the 200 countries that have created new national or regional regulatory systems in the past 10 years. For example, it is the recommended model in guidelines issued in 2003 by the African Forum for Utility Regulation (AFUR), the association of African infrastructure regulators.[5] It is the governance model that was used as a baseline in a recently completed benchmarking exercise of new energy regulators in Southeast Europe.[6] It is also the explicit or implicit governance model used in several recent single-country assessments of new regulatory systems. (See appendix G.) It is the recommended model of the ITU for telecommunications regulators.[7] Finally, it is the governance model most commonly recommended in the general literature on regulation.[8] Given the model's widespread formal acceptance and adoption, it would be difficult to justify a benchmark for evaluation based on a totally different model of regulatory governance.

Second, some preliminary empirical evidence shows that the independent regulator governance model, when adopted in both law and practice, leads to better sector outcomes. In particular, an increasing body of evidence from econometric studies is now showing that higher-quality regulatory governance incorpo-

---

4. However, the fact that we recommend the independent regulator model as an evaluation benchmark does not mean that it necessarily should be the first step in a regulatory reform process that seeks to create it as a long-range goal. See chapter 4.
5. See the position paper adopted by the AFUR General Assembly in **AFUR** (2003). The AFUR recommendation is a qualified recommendation. It states that the goal should be "independent or autonomous regulation where possible." However, it does not define what is meant by "where possible."
6. **CEER** (2004).
7. **ITU** (2001).
8. **Berg** (2000); **Office of Water Regulation** (1999); **Prayas Energy Group** (2003); **Rao** (2004); and **Stern and Holder** (1999).

rating elements of the independent regulator model results in higher investment levels, higher productivity levels, and higher privatization proceeds in the telecommunications sector. For the electricity sector, a recent study reports that good regulatory governance in the form of an independent regulator funded by license fees and operating under a primary law is associated with 25–35 percent higher per capita generation capacity in the long term. Even simply enacting a regulatory law with a ministry regulator is associated in one econometric study with approximately 15–20 percent higher long-term generation capacity.[9] Similarly, recent statistical evidence is showing that transparency, another key element of the independent regulator model, is associated with higher levels of private direct investment in a study of investment in 48 countries.[10]

This empirical evidence probably captures several advantages of the independent regulator model. When it is adopted in both law and practice, it tends to lead to decisions that are more focused on long-term policy goals than on short-term, political needs. In addition, errors in judgment are less likely to occur or to be repeated because of its emphasis on transparency. If mistakes are made, they probably will be corrected more quickly than in a closed regulatory system. Overall, these behavioral outcomes, which flow from the institutional and legal characteristics of the best-practice independent regulator model, seem to produce better sector outcomes.

Third, the independent regulator model can accommodate a wide variety of sector structures and transactions. In contrast, the pure public service concession model (in which no separate designated regulatory entity exists, and the regulatory framework is specified in a detailed concession or license) seems to work best in a limited set of circumstances. Typically, it can be used to regulate a single entity that has agreed to provide a well-specified service (for example, an IPP selling the output of one generating plant or a private operator providing stand-alone water and sanitation services to a municipality).[11]

---

9. **Cubbin and Stern** (2005); **Gutierrez** (2003); and Scott Wallsten, 2002, "Does Sequencing Matter? Regulation and Privatization in Telecommunications Reforms," Working Paper 2817, World Bank, Washington, DC; available at http://wdsbeta.worldbankorg/external/default/WDSContentServer/IW3P/IB/2002/05/03/000094946_02041804272576/additional/134534322_20041117184620.pdf.

10. Joel Kurtzman, Glenn Yago, and Triphon Phumiwasana, 2004, "The Global Costs of Opacity," *MIT Sloan Management Review* 46 (1): 38–44.

11. For an excellent survey of regulatory and other factors that have affected the success and

Since the pure public service concession model is based essentially on a bilateral contract between a lessor (usually some government entity) and a lessee (usually a private operator), its scope of regulatory coverage will be insufficient when there are many different types of entities in the sector (for example, generators, distributors, retail service providers, and transmitters or system operators) selling different services and continually interacting with each other, both physically and contractually, on a large interconnected grid. In other words, the regulatory coverage of the pure public service concession model will be too limited when there are many transactions between many entities, where the transactions and entities can take many different forms, and where the forms of the transactions are difficult to predict in advance.[12] Because these are the typical characteristics of many reformed power sectors, it is hard to imagine how these sectors could be regulated successfully just through a series of "stand-alone" concession documents.

However, this does *not* imply that the only available choices are limited to the pure public service concession model and the independent regulator model. In fact, the two can be combined. More complex sector structures can be regulated using a combination of detailed concession documents for distribution entities and more general, discretionary regulatory principles for other sector transactions and entities not covered by concession documents. Both forms of regulation can be administered by an independent regulator. In effect, the regulatory governance system can be bifurcated: very little regulatory discretion (at least initially) for new distribution entities combined with moderate to significant regulatory discretion over other sector entities and

---

failure of independent power producer projects in five countries (China, Mexico, the Philippines, Poland, and Turkey), see Erik J. Woodhouse, 2005, "The Experience with Independent Power Projects in Developing Countries: Interim Report," Program on Energy and Sustainable Development Working Paper 39, Stanford University, Palo Alto, CA; available at http://pesd.stanford.edu/publications/20819/.

12. In fact, France has now established an independent national electricity regulator to establish rules for access to the transmission and distribution grid and to adjudicate grid and market disputes between different industry participants. This regulator does not use concessions, but instead operates under general principles that are largely derived from France's obligations as a member of the European Union. This new French regulatory approach, which is similar to the regulatory approach taken in other countries that are trying to promote retail and wholesale competition, suggests that such regulatory functions (that is, approving terms and conditions of access to network facilities) are not amenable to effective regulation through concessions. However, as is discussed in appendix H, there is no obvious reason why the two forms of regulation cannot coexist within a larger regulatory system.

institutions (for example, transmission system operators and organized wholesale markets). Hybrid regulatory systems have become the de facto governance model in many developing and transition-economy countries. There is also empirical evidence that these hybrid systems tend to be more successful than either of the two regulatory governance models operating separately.[13] So, although there are often passionate debates between the proponents of the independent regulator model and the concession model, the real world of regulation in many developing countries has effectively moved beyond these debates simply by combining the two regulatory systems. (See the discussion of hybrid models in chapter 4 and appendix H.)

Fourth, the best-practice governance principles and standards adopted in this handbook can be used to evaluate the performance of almost any hybrid regulatory system, as long as there is an independent (or at least an institutionally separate) regulatory entity. This range of regulatory systems includes the independent regulator model as well as several of the more important hybrid models.

Fifth, it would be confusing to present multiple competing benchmarks. A single uniform standard of regulatory governance is favored to minimize the confusion that would arise with multiple governance benchmarks. It seems sensible to have a single benchmark that reflects the governance approach taken by most governments that have created new regulatory systems in the past 15 years or more.

Are There Meta-Principles for Regulatory Governance?

Although clear evidence exists that the independent regulator model can work well when implemented both in law and in practice (the sections that follow on principles and standards show how this can be done), it does not logically follow that such a model is the only model of regulatory governance that will work well (that is, achieve good sector outcomes) or that the model is feasible to implement at all times and in all places.[14] Some variants of the two models (described in appendix H) may be as effective as the independent regulator model. One obvious benefit of the case studies is that the

---

13. Using a sample of close to 900 Latin American and Caribbean infrastructure contracts, **Guasch** (2004) estimates that the existence of a regulatory body to monitor, enforce, and modify concession contracts reduces the expected renegotiation rate by 20–40 percent.

14. A similar observation was recently made by François Bourguignon, chief economist of the World Bank, in **Laffont** (2005, p. xi). Commenting on the lack of success in a num-

results from different evaluations should help shed light on the effectiveness of alternative regulatory models.

Without prejudging the institutional forms that these other regulatory governance systems may take, it is clear that a regulatory system can be effective only if that system satisfies three basic meta- or higher-order principles:

- *Meta-Principle 1: Credibility*—Investors must have confidence that the regulatory system will honor its commitments.
- *Meta-Principle 2: Legitimacy*—Consumers must be convinced that the regulatory system will protect them from the exercise of monopoly power, whether through high prices, poor service, or both.

Stepping back, it is clear that the common element in both of these principles is that investors and consumers believe the regulatory system operates fairly. Because investors and especially consumers are unlikely to perceive the system as fair if it is closed and opaque, this in turn implies a third principle:

- *Meta-Principle 3: Transparency*—The regulatory system must operate transparently so that investors and consumers "know the terms of the deal."[15]

This third principle is especially important for consumers. When regulators regulate in secret, consumers tend to assume the worst—that the regulator or government has been "bought out" by new private investors and that consumers will end up paying for this "secret deal." Such fears are not groundless. Sadly, there is a long history of bribery and corruption by government officials in many developing countries. In Latin America, the word for this widespread lack of confidence in government institutions is *desconfianza*. Even if regulators have done their best to protect consumer interests, it is naïve to expect that consumers will have confidence in the system if they do not understand what the regulator or government has agreed to. Without such knowledge, they will tend to assume the worst. Therefore, the long-

---

ber of reform and liberalization initiatives in developing countries, he notes that ". . . it was increasingly recognized that, in many instances, the problem was that reformers disregarded the functioning of regulatory institutions, assuming implicitly they would work as in developed countries."

15. Because our focus is on regulatory governance, meta-principles related to sector outcomes are not included. If the meta-principles were expanded to include both regulatory governance and substance, the fourth principle would be an "efficiency" principle: the regulatory system should promote pricing and production efficiency.

term sustainability of any regulatory system requires transparency because transparency is the first step to trust.[16]

The three meta-principles, if satisfied, will give overall legitimacy to a regulatory system. Without legitimacy, a regulatory system, even if technically competent, will not survive. Legitimacy requires that consumers and investors believe that the regulatory system is producing value for them. If consumers and investors do not see any value coming out of the regulatory system, it will not have any allies when there is a political crisis. It will be an institution "without any friends." This is another way of saying that there must be a demand for the regulatory system, and the demand must come from groups to whom politicians will pay attention.

This political reality also has implications for the assistance provided by donors. All too often, donors tend to think of regulation as a capacity-building exercise. This is too narrow a view. It is based on an assumption that a new regulatory system will be sustainable if new regulators can be trained, become technically competent, and have sufficient resources to perform their assigned tasks. The problem with this mindset is that it implicitly views regulation as just a supply-side exercise. It assumes that success in creating a new regulatory system is simply a matter of providing enough technical assistance (for example, number of training courses, number of study tours, or levels of staffing). What this ignores is that sustainable regulation has both a demand and a supply side. Although the supply side (that is, the technical capacity of regulation) is important, no regulatory institution will long survive, no matter how competent it may be, if there is no politically visible demand for its services. And the demand will not exist unless consumers and investors have concluded that the regulatory system is worthy of trust because it produces outcomes that are of value to them.[17]

Therefore, the three meta-principles should be viewed as necessary prerequisites for the sustainability of any regulatory system. The principles and

---

16. Francis Fukuyama argues that trust is central to economic development. His central thesis is that "[a] nation's well being, as well as its ability to compete, is conditioned by a single pervasive social characteristic: the level of trust inherent in society." See Francis Fukuyama, 1996, *Trust: The Social Virtues and the Creation of Prosperity* (New York: Free Press), p. 7.

17. Much the same conclusion was reached in a recent multicountry assessment of efforts to build the capacity of state institutions in Africa. The principal conclusion of the study was that future efforts at building government institutions need "to complement a narrowly technocratic focus on the supply side of public management and give more attention to the demand-side incentives for performance." See Brian Levy and Sahr Kpundeh,

standards for the independent regulator model of regulatory governance are derived from these meta-principles. However, most of the principles and standards are equally applicable to other models of regulatory governance. *Even though the independent regulator model has become the standard recommended model, it is not the one and only model of regulatory governance (that is, the only institutional and legal form) that can satisfy the meta-principles at all times and places.*

Although history demonstrates that the independent regulator model has clearly been successful when adopted in *both* law and practice, it is conceivable, as Dani Rodrik of Harvard University observed in another context, that "there are a multiplicity of institutional arrangements that are compatible with . . . higher order principles."[18] Moreover, for a variety of legal, political, cultural, and practical reasons discussed in chapter 4, it is unrealistic to expect that a fully functioning independent regulator governance model can be created from day 1 in many developing and transition-economy countries. Therefore, a benefit of the evaluations developed from the handbook is that they will provide specific knowledge of what, where, and why alternative regulatory systems work well.

Is the Independent Regulator Model Feasible in Countries with Limited Governance Capability?

The applicability and usefulness of the best-practice independent regulator model relies on a number of assumptions about the country in which it is being considered. For instance, it is much more likely to be viable if a country is, or is seriously trying to become, a constitutionally based government operating under rule of law and with a separation of powers—particularly between the legal and executive branches. This presumption about the nature of the overall legal system is implicit in the key attributes of the independent

---

2004, *Building State Capacity in Africa: New Approaches, Emerging Lessons* (Washington, DC: World Bank Institute), p. 11. A similar conclusion was presented in an award-winning study of how some U.S. government agencies have historically been able to achieve decisionmaking autonomy while other agencies have failed. See Daniel Carpenter, 2001, *The Forging of Bureaucratic Autonomy: Reputations, Networks, and Policy Innovation in Executive Agencies, 1862-1928* (Princeton, NJ: Princeton University Press).

18. See Dani Rodrik, 2004, *Growth Strategies* (Cambridge, MA: John F. Kennedy School of Government), p. 14.

regulator model: transparency, intellectual discipline and rigor, integrity and honesty, public accessibility, regard for the opinions of those affected by regulatory decisions, respect for property rights, relative isolation from short-term political considerations, and respect for law.[19] Given these required characteristics, it seems unrealistic to expect that the independent regulator model can operate within a highly centralized authoritarian state. Nor is it likely to be a workable fit in countries where there is a high level of corruption. *When other surrounding government institutions are closed, corrupt, or under tight, centralized control, it is hard to imagine that an independent regulator will be able to function as an island of openness, accountability, and independent decisionmaking.*

Similarly, it is unrealistic to expect that a full version of the model or anything similar can readily be created on day 1 in "weak" or "fragile" countries. These terms are used to refer to countries that have limited general governance capacity or a limited political will to implement an effective regulatory system, or both. In these countries, it will be counterproductive to insist on the immediate and complete implementation of a full-blown independent regulator model without taking a closer look at what is realistically feasible in the near term.[20] In such countries, more attention needs be directed to good-fit rather than best-practice regulatory systems. As one World Bank task manager asked, "Are we supposed to stop encouraging private investment until a fully functioning independent regulator comes into existence?"

Weak or fragile countries are at the extreme end of institutional capacity and effectiveness, but there are many other countries where regulatory capacity or commitment (or both) is limited. In these countries, there is considerable scope for developing "transitional" regulatory systems. These transitional frameworks should operate effectively and transparently. Although not incorporating all the elements of the best-practice independent regulator model, they should be designed to have good dynamic properties. Specif-

---

19. A recent report by the European Bank for Reconstruction and Development (EBRD) shows a high correlation between successful implementation of the independent regulator model of governance and generally accepted measures of constitutional liberalism. If these elements of constitutional liberalism do not exist in a country, the EBRD analysis shows that it is highly unlikely that the independent regulator model will "take." See **EBRD** (2004), p. 58.

20. One former aid official from a developed country criticized "lazy consultants" who provide the "standard regulatory recommendations report" with a "global search and replace" on the country name.

ically, they should contain elements that create incentives and pressures to move to better regulatory arrangements over time in whatever institutional form is most suitable for the country and the state of sector development.[21]

This implies that not all "hybrid" or transitional regulatory models are acceptable. Any hybrid or transitional regulatory model, if it is to be effective, must satisfy the three meta-principles described above. Hence, transitional regulatory systems need to be evaluated *both* on how far they are likely to evolve toward best practice in the future, *and* on how effectively they carry out their current tasks and how much of an improvement they have achieved relative to past regulatory arrangements. This applies both to their contribution to industry outcomes and to their regulatory processes and procedures.

Ten Key Principles for the Independent Regulator Model of Regulatory Governance

It is helpful to think of a hierarchy of principles and standards. The meta-principles are at the highest level. They must be satisfied by any infrastructure regulatory system for that system to be effective and sustainable. Beneath the meta-principles are principles that are specific to particular models of regulatory governance. This section presents 10 principles designed to implement the meta-principles in the specific context of the independent regulator governance model. In the next section of this chapter, 15 standards to implement the 10 principles are presented at a greater level of detail. Although the principles and standards were specifically designed to implement the independent regulator model (a best-practices rather than a transitional model), they also apply to some of the hybrid systems that are discussed in more detail in chapter 4 and appendix H.

1. Independence

Infrastructure regulators should, by law, be free to make decisions within their scope of authority without having to obtain prior approval from other officials or agencies of the government. They need to be adequately insulated from short-term political pressure.

---

21. Specific elements of possible transitional regulatory systems are discussed in chapter 4. See also Smith (1997).

2. Accountability

Regulators need to be held accountable for their actions. The mechanisms for ensuring accountability include the following:

- Appeal rights for parties believing their interests harmed by regulatory agency decisions that have been made against the requirements in the law, either on process or on substance.
- Substantive reporting and audit obligations on the regulatory agency.
- Oversight or performance reviews through evaluations and hearings.
- Ethical and procedural obligations.
- Extensive transparency obligations (for example, on regulatory decisions and their justification).

3. Transparency and Public Participation

The entire regulatory process must be fair and impartial and open to extensive and meaningful opportunity for public participation. The following are recommended with very limited exceptions:

- All documents and information used for decisionmaking should be available for public inspection.
- All procedures by which and criteria upon which decisions are made should be known in advance and made publicly available.

No major decision should be made by a regulatory agency without being set down in a publicly available written document. The document should include the following:

- A clear statement of the decision.
- A description and analysis of all evidence taken into consideration.
- A summary of the views offered by participants to the proceedings.
- A full discussion of the underlying rationale for the decision.

4. Predictability

The regulatory system should provide reasonable, although not absolute, certainty as to the principles and rules that will be followed within the overall regulatory framework. The following are recommendations for changes in that framework:

- Changes should occur only after extensive public notice and consultation so that stakeholders have a meaningful opportunity to provide feedback to decisionmakers before the change is implemented.
- To the extent possible, changes should be instituted gradually.
- Regulatory decisions and policy determinations, including laws and governing regulatory decisions, should apply prospectively and never retroactively.

5. Clarity of Roles

The role of the regulatory agency should be carefully defined in law. Similarly, the roles of other sector agencies (either government or nongovernment) should be carefully defined to avoid the following:

- Duplication of functions.
- Interagency conflicts.
- Mixed signals to stakeholders.
- Policy confusion.

6. Completeness and Clarity in Rules

The regulatory system, through laws and agency rules, should provide all stakeholders with clear and complete timely advance notice of the principles, guidelines, expectations, responsibilities, consequences of misbehavior, and objectives that will be pursued in carrying out regulatory activities.

7. Proportionality

Regulatory intervention in the sector should be proportionate to the challenges the regulators are addressing:

- Intervention should be the minimum necessary to remedy the problem being addressed and should be undertaken only if the likely benefits outweigh the expected economic and social costs.
- Regulators should have an array of powers and remedies at their disposal in order to ensure that they possess the ability to calibrate their actions to the circumstances faced.

3

8. Requisite Powers

Regulatory agencies should, under the law, possess all powers required to perform their mission. Those powers should, at a minimum, include the authority for the following:

- To set tariffs for regulated entities.
- To establish, modify, and monitor market and service quality rules.
- To address market power and market design problems adequately.
- To carry out normal administrative functions.
- To investigate, as well as adjudicate or mediate, consumer complaints.
- To provide dispute resolution facilities for the regulated entities.
- To compel the provision of needed information.
- To monitor and enforce its decisions, and to remedy problems.

9. Appropriate Institutional Characteristics

Regulatory agencies must be able to consistently perform professionally, competently, and thoroughly, which requires the following:

- Compensation and education or training opportunities for commissioners and staff that are competitive with what is available at regulated entities.
- A reliable, adequate, and independent source of revenue and adequate budgets.
- The ability to retain outside consultants when needed.
- Commissioners who are appropriately insulated from short-term political repercussions.
- Regulatory decisions that are, if possible, made by a board of three or five commissioners who come from diverse professional backgrounds.

All regulatory decisions should be subject to final appeal to a single, impartial or independent, legally designated court or tribunal with the following requirements. The specified appeal forum should possess regulatory expertise. The regulatory decision should, with very limited exception, remain in force while the appeal is pending. And the appeal body should affirm regulatory decisions unless the following is true:

- The regulators acted beyond their legal authority.

- The regulators failed to follow appropriate procedural requirements.
- The regulators acted arbitrarily or unreasonably.
- The regulators acted against the plain weight of the evidence before the court.

10. Integrity

Strict rules governing the behavior of decisionmakers should be in place so as to preclude improprieties or any conduct appearing to be improper. The rules governing behavior should be fully, fairly, and vigorously enforced so as to tolerate no breaches. Included among the subjects to be covered by ethical rules should be the following:

- Prohibition against bribes and gratuities of any kind.
- Prohibition of all forms of conflicts of interest.
- Prohibition against any form of preferential treatment.
- Reasonable disclosure of financial interests.
- Prohibition of use of inside information for personal gain.

Critical Standards for Effective Infrastructure Regulation

What is the difference between the principles in the previous section and the standards of this section? The principles present general governance goals and objectives for the independent regulator model. In addition, as noted above, they are very similar to regulatory principles recommended elsewhere.[22] In contrast, the 15 standards presented in this section go considerably beyond general goals and objectives. The standards are designed to show how the principles can be made operational. They constitute a checklist of specific institutional and legal actions necessary to implement the principles in a concrete way to produce a functioning independent regulator. Like the 10 principles from which they are derived, they represent best practices.

To the best of our knowledge, this discussion of these standards is the first time that a complete and detailed description of specific steps needed to implement the general governance principles of the independent regulator

---

22. See **Berg** (2000); **Office of Water Regulation** (1999); **Prayas Energy Group** (2003); **Rao** (2004); and **Stern and Holder** (1999).

model have been brought together in one place. The standards are designed to provide a checklist of specific measures that can be taken to achieve real-world implementation of the general principles. Appendix A provides a more detailed explanation and rationale for each of the standards.

1. Legal Framework

The regulatory agency should be created in a law (preferably in a statute or primary law) that fully articulates its jurisdictional authority, powers, duties, and responsibilities. Basic regulatory principles, practices, procedures, and policies to be followed should be articulated in law (preferably in a statute or primary law). All laws enacted on regulatory matters should be prospective in nature, and none should have retrospective application.

2. Legal Powers

The regulatory agency should have authority to make final decisions within its statutory domain without having to obtain approval of any other agency of government. It should also, at a minimum, possess the power to do the following:

- Set or approve tariffs at reasonable levels for the benefit of consumers and regulated entities.
- Set binding standards in such appropriate areas as technical and commercial service quality.
- Make rules and subsidiary policy for the sector as long as such policies and rules are within its legal authority, are reasonably necessary for carrying out its duties, and are not inconsistent with the policies and principles articulated in the applicable laws.
- Perform such routine functions as the agency may need to do in order to operate, such as making personnel decisions, spending money appropriately within its budgetary authorization, making relevant administrative decisions and taking relevant actions, and performing such other duties as government agencies ordinarily undertake to carry out their obligations.
- Fully enforce its decisions, standards, and rules, as well as relevant public policy. This requires the regulatory agency to have a range of remedies, including penalties, appropriate to the severity of violations that it is likely to meet.

- Compel the production and provision of the information as may be necessary to carry out the regulatory functions and serve the interests of transparency.
- Adopt and compel compliance with such appropriate accounting standards and practices as may reasonably be required for regulatory purposes.
- Adopt appropriate procedures for carrying out its duties.
- Adjudicate statutorily designated disputes between regulated entities and between regulated entities and consumers.
- Prevent the abuse of monopoly or market power.
- Promote competition where appropriate and feasible.
- Protect consumers from unfair or abusive business practices.
- Prevent undue discrimination in the provision and terms and conditions of services.
- Monitor the performance of regulated entities, the functioning of the market, and the maintenance of supply.
- Delegate or coordinate regulatory functions where another regulatory body could perform the function more efficiently, or where jurisdiction is concurrent or shared.

3. Property and Contract Rights

The property rights of all persons and entities should be protected, respected, and in no way treated arbitrarily, or unfairly abridged or violated by the regulatory system. Contracts between parties shall be afforded the full respect to which they are entitled under applicable law, and contract rights should not be unduly limited or abridged. No action that affects property or contract rights in any way shall be undertaken without first affording all affected parties proper notice of the action(s) being contemplated and affording such parties full, fair, and transparent opportunity to be heard on the matter before final decisions are made. No regulated entity should be held to account for any activity unless standards or expectations with which they are expected to comply are formally in place and publicly available.

4. Clarity of Roles in Regulation and Policy

The law should also provide for clear and comprehensive provisions concerning the allocation and demarcation of responsibilities, powers, and duties between the regulatory agency, governmental bodies, and all other agencies (for example, market administrators) that have authority over the sector. Basic policy for the regulated sector should be formally set out in law by legislative or executive branch action, or both, and be made prospectively binding on the regulatory agency.

The regulatory agency should implement and enforce all public policy as embodied in law and relevant government pronouncements consistent with other legal obligations. To do so, it should be able to make subsidiary determinations on policy issues to fulfill its obligations. Regulatory agencies cannot be required to adhere to government policies that are not publicly articulated in advance of decisions. Ministers and government agencies seeking to influence regulatory decisions should be able to do so, but only in a fully transparent and open manner.

5. Clarity and Comprehensiveness of Regulatory Decisions

The key principles and methodologies on which major regulatory decisions will be made (for example, tariff reviews, compliance with service quality requirements, market surveillance, and approvals for investment) should be set out clearly in advance in appropriate legal documents (for example, statutes, decrees, guidelines). The rules should, to the extent possible, be thorough, complete, and clear as to the rights, responsibilities, expectations, and consequences that all stakeholders enjoy or face.

6. Predictability and Flexibility

Regulatory decisions should, to the extent reasonable and feasible, be consistent with previous decisions or determinations on similar matters in the past. When deviation from previous practice is necessary, it should be undertaken by regulators only after first providing public notice of such a possibility and providing all interested parties with a meaningful opportunity to be heard on the matter. Any fundamental change in regulatory practice or policy should, to the extent feasible, be undertaken on a gradual basis and applied prospectively.

7. Consumer Rights and Obligations

The central purpose of regulation is to protect consumers, including future consumers, and look after consumer interests in the short and long terms. To help achieve this, regulatory agencies should adopt a consumer statement of rights. This should, at a minimum, include the following:

- Quality-of-service standards the consumers are entitled to expect.
- Remedies to which the customer is entitled in case of breach.
- Access to the regulatory agency to seek redress of grievances.

8. Proportionality

Regulation should always be kept to the minimum necessary to ensure efficiency and fairness. Regulatory intervention should be made only in the following instances:

- Where there is demonstrable market failure that cannot be removed by other means.
- Where the economic and social benefits of intervention can reasonably be expected to exceed the likely economic and social costs.
- Where a natural monopoly is an important element of the industry.
- Where significant market power exists (for example, because of market design problems or abusive behavior).
- Where fundamental consumer protection requires it.
- Where clearly specified, government-mandated social policy requires action, and where regulation is likely to be the most efficient method of providing this.

Where regulatory actions are necessary, they should be well targeted, proportionate to the problem being addressed, and measured against the alternatives. A regulatory agency should possess the legal latitude to vary its regulatory methods and practices so that it can accomplish the objective at minimum cost to itself and regulated entities. The following are guidelines to accomplish its objectives:

- Act with proportionality (for example, not revoke a license for a small offense or limit mandated refunds for an offense to affected customers).
- Act in ways that are relevant to the nature of the regulated entity (for example, state- or privately owned, small or large).
- Delegate regulatory responsibilities to other agencies or entities (for example, from national to regional or local regulators), although the regulatory agency should remain responsible for the performance of these delegated bodies.

- Coordinate regulatory responsibilities with other agencies that share legal jurisdiction or responsibility over specific matters (for example, competition regulators).

Regulatory agencies should periodically and regularly review their activities and methods to determine their relevance and need in changed circumstances. These periodic reviews should include public consultation, as appropriate.

Political authorities—on a regular, periodic, and fully transparent basis (for example, every four years)—should conduct reviews of the regulatory framework and performance of regulatory agencies in order to evaluate whether the laws or other governing instruments require changes. These reviews should include the formal publication of conclusions and recommendations.

9. Regulatory Independence

Regulatory agencies should be created by law (or constitution), rather than by decree or other subsidiary legislation. Under the law, regulatory agencies should have the following powers and characteristics:

- Regulatory decisions should, if possible, be made by a board of three or five commissioners. Regulatory agencies headed by a single person are, in general, not recommended except for either (a) an initial period during which the agency is being established or (b) use in countries with major resource constraints—or both.
- They should have a stable and reliable source of revenue for their operations.
- They should offer staff competitive compensation packages and viable career opportunities, as well as appropriate training and education.
- They should establish the table of organization within the agency and have the authority and ability to make all relevant personnel decisions, including the hiring of personnel on a full- or part-time basis, or on a permanent or temporary basis, and the engagement of consultant services as needed.
- They should set such rules and policies as may be necessary to carry out their responsibilities.
- They should promulgate a code of ethics applicable to agency personnel and to those who conduct business with them so as to ensure both the reality and the appearance of honest, fair, and impartial decisionmaking.

- They should retain the services of such independent experts as may be required to carry out their obligations and, where justified by the circumstances, order affected regulated entities to pay the consulting fees.
- They should be encouraged to join or participate in relevant professional, research, and educational groups, as well as in regional or international cooperative regulatory organizations.

Regulatory agency commissioners or directors should satisfy the following terms:

- They should be appointed to fixed terms of office.
- The terms of the directors or commissioners should not be coincident with the terms of governments and legislatures.
- Commissioners or directors should be appointed only if they are not legally precluded from serving their full terms (for example, because of mandatory retirement conditions in the law).
- Appointments of single-person agency directors and commission chairs and other commissioners or board members should be made by the head of government or head of state, with possible legislative approval.
- In the case of collegial bodies, the terms of the directors or commissioners should be staggered to ensure continuity.
- Directors or commissioners should be removed only for good cause as defined in the law (that is, proven, nontrivial legal and ethical misbehavior or nonperformance of their duties) as found by an independent complaint investigation.
- The terms and conditions of employment of any regulatory commissioner or director should not be altered during the course of a term (except where predetermined automatic adjustments are not subject to administrative discretion).
- Directors or commissioners should come from diverse professional backgrounds and training (for example, economics, law, engineering, or accounting).

10. Financing of Regulatory Agencies

By law, the level of funding of the agency should be adequate to enable it to meet all its responsibilities competently, professionally, and in a timely manner. A minimum level of funding, expressed in terms of a percentage of regulated revenues, should be set out in law.

The agency funding should be obtained from a levy assessed on regulated entities—and not from the general treasury, except (a) where the government requires the agency to undertake a specific project that is beyond the scope of normal regulatory functions or possibly (b) for an initial period after the agency's creation.

Regulated entities should be able to pass through funds collected for the levy to their customers in their tariffs. The levy should be assessed as a percentage of the revenues of a regulated entity, not tied in any way to the profits of regulated entities. Funds collected from the levy should be held in a special account and earmarked for the exclusive use of the regulatory agency, and any other use should be expressly prohibited. The following recommendations apply to changes in the amount of funds available:

- If there is a significant surplus of funds, the surplus should be returned to the customers of the regulated entities or to a public benefits fund for sector improvement (for example, to assist low-income customers). The surplus should not be available to the government to divert for other purposes.
- *Any reduction in the spending authority of the regulatory agency in the middle of a normal budget cycle should occur only as part of an overall reduction in government spending, and not as a mandated reduction applicable only to the regulatory agency.*

The ordinary fiscal controls, auditing policies and practices, and budgetary controls of the government should apply to the regulatory agency. The overall spending authority of the agency should be subject to government approval. If government approval is not obtained in timely fashion, the agency should be allowed a budget authorization (in real terms) equal to its budget in the previous fiscal period.

The regulatory agency should, where circumstances warrant, and without regard to agency spending authorization, be able to retain the services of a consultant to perform specified tasks and to require payment for the specific costs of that engagement from the regulated entities affected.

11. Regulatory Accountability

Legislative committees or the relevant ministries and executive task forces, or both, should periodically conduct hearings reviewing the performance of regulatory agencies. Among the issues that should be covered are the following:

- The functions of the agency and continued appropriateness of the division of authority between it and other relevant agencies.
- The transparency, effectiveness, and timeliness of regulatory procedures.
- The clarity, coherence, consistency, and timeliness of agency decisions.
- The proportionality and effectiveness of targeting in agency decisions.
- The quality of agency decisions and their sustainability on appeals and in practice.
- The efficiency of the agency's use of its resources.
- The degree of independence, integrity, and credibility in agency processes and actions.

The government or legislative authorities should periodically engage the services of a panel of financially disinterested outside experts (for example, international experts and regulatory staff from neighboring or similar countries) to prepare a report on the overall performance of the agency, or on specific areas of interest.

Regulatory agencies should be subject to periodic management audits and to other types of effectiveness review (for example, policy audits). Regulatory agencies should be required, at least on an annual basis, to submit a report on their activities to legislative or executive authorities, or both. The report should be a public document.

12. Regulatory Processes and Transparency

Except for defined emergency circumstances, no decision should be made by a regulatory agency until the following have occurred:

- Proper legal notice has been given notifying all parties that a matter is under formal consideration.
- The public notice should identify the matter being considered, the initiator of the action being contemplated, and a full schedule for the consideration of the matters.[23]
- All parties who wish to do so have been afforded a meaningful opportunity to provide input to the agency.

---

23. The initiator in some regulatory models might be a specific party. In other models, the initiator might not be a party, but rather the fulfillment of a legal or contractual requirement by the regulatory agency.

In cases of emergencies, actions may be taken, but interested parties should be afforded a fair opportunity to participate ex post in any review of the matter. The criteria for defining an emergency should be stated in law. No decision should be made by a regulatory agency without being set down in a publicly available document. The document should include the following:

- A clear statement of the decision.
- A description and analysis of all evidence taken into consideration.
- A summary of the views offered by participants to the proceeding.
- A full discussion of the underlying rationale for the decision.

All regulatory agencies should have clearly defined, published procedures under which they make, announce, and publish regulatory decisions and their justification. Multimember regulatory agencies normally make their decisions *either* (a) by majority voting *or* (b) by consensual, nonvoting methods. If a multimember regulatory agency decides to use a formal voting process for making decisions, the result of the vote should be made publicly available at or soon after the date of the decision. When a formal voting process is used, these procedures should be followed:

- All decisions should be made at a meeting at which or following which the votes of all members should be made public.
- Board members voting "no" should have the option to file formal opinions expressing the rationale for their vote.
- Board members who concur in the result, but do so for reasons that differ from those set forth in the decision, should have the option to file concurring opinions expressing the rationale for their decision.

If the regulatory agency decides to use a consensus approach for decision-making, these procedures should be followed:

- A record of the discussion should be made, reflecting the range of opinions expressed, both supporting and dissenting.
- A summary of the discussion should be made publicly available, along with or soon after the publication of the regulatory decision and its justification.
- Board members should have the right to state their views concerning the decision publicly and on an attributable basis.

All documents in the possession of a regulatory agency, particularly those being relied upon in making decisions, should be presumed to be available for public inspection, unless the regulator rules otherwise (for example, on the grounds of commercial confidentiality).[24] Further guidelines concerning transparency are as follows:

- No document should be treated as confidential unless the regulator finds that the document (or some part of it) falls specifically into a category that the law or binding articulated policy deems legitimately confidential (for example, personnel matters, verifiable trade secrets, draft decisions not yet finalized, or documents related to pending litigation). Confidentiality issues, it must be noted, only involve the question of how the regulator treats the document. Claims of confidentiality do not constitute grounds for a party to withhold a document from the regulator.
- The primary law—or failing that, the regulatory agency—should publish its criteria in advance for judging whether documents (or some parts) will be treated by them as confidential and establish systems for handling and storing confidential material.

The procedure the agency will follow in making decisions should be set out in clearly defined rules and made publicly available.

13. Public Participation

There must be ample opportunity for all affected parties who wish to participate meaningfully—that is, in a time and form that will reach the regulators in such fashion that they could take it into account before rendering a decision—in regulatory proceedings to do so. Regulatory agencies should take all reasonable steps to facilitate and encourage public participation.

14. Appellate Review of Regulatory Decisions

All appeals from a regulatory agency decision should be directed to a single, independent appellate forum, the decision of which would, in the absence of a constitutional issue, be final. The appellate forum should be either a specif-

---

24. The requirement for public availability of documents need not, and perhaps should not, apply to internal documents drafted by regulatory agency personnel for purposes of making specific decisions. Thus, for example, early drafts of decisions being circulated internally within the agency for review need not be made publicly available.

ically designated court or a specialized appellate tribunal with the authority to review the decisions of one or more infrastructure regulatory agencies. In either case, the forum should possess relevant expertise in regulatory matters.

The regulatory agency must provide parties with an opportunity to seek rehearing or de novo review by the agency itself or, if called for by law, by some other duly designated body (for example, a competition agency). The deadlines for filing an appeal should be suspended during the rehearing application or process.

Any parties who believe they were adversely affected by an agency decision should have the right to make an appeal of that decision within a reasonable period after that decision has been made (for example, 30 days). That right, however, should belong only to a party who formally participated in the agency proceedings on the matter in question and who raised that issue in the regulatory proceeding, including any rehearing process. No interested party should be able to put forward new issues or new evidence on appeal that was not first raised in the proceedings at the regulatory agency (including any rehearing).

Regulatory agency decisions should be affirmed on appeal, unless the agency acted unlawfully or exceeded its lawful authority, failed to follow the required procedures in making its decision, or made decisions that were clearly flawed in the light of evidence presented at the appeal. The decision of the regulatory agency should remain in effect for the duration of the appeal, unless the agency or the appeals tribunal decides otherwise. Such a delay should not be granted without a demonstration of irreparable harm to the appellant and a likelihood that the appeal will succeed.

If the appellate forum reverses or changes the decision of the regulatory agency, the preferable course is for the matter to be sent back to the regulatory agency to conclude a remedy consistent with the decision of the appellate forum.

15. Ethics

To the extent not already covered by applicable law, regulatory agencies should promulgate a binding code of ethics applicable to all agency personnel, including directors or commissioners. Such a code should, at a minimum, include the following:

- Prohibitions on gratuities, favors, or other gifts from parties having any business involving the agency.
- Limitations on subsequent employment by staff or commissioners on matters they worked on while employed at the agency or with parties doing business with the agency.
- Limitations on subsequent employment with parties who have had matters decided by the agency.
- Prohibitions on actual or apparent financial or other conflicts of interest involving agency personnel or their immediate family.
- Prohibitions on conduct giving rise to an appearance of favoritism or ethical compromise.
- Appropriate financial disclosure.
- Prohibitions of employment or other work by agency personnel (or their close family members) in companies or areas of work covered by the agency for a reasonable period after leaving the agency.

3

These principles and standards are designed to accomplish internal and external objectives. Internally they are aimed at ensuring fairness, balance, deliberativeness, and substantive discipline in the decisionmaking process. Externally they are designed to protect the integrity, legitimacy, independence, and accountability of regulation. Although adherence to these principles and standards, in and of itself, does not guarantee the accomplishment of the objectives, failure to adhere to them will almost certainly imperil the possibility of achieving them.

4

Transitional Regulatory Systems and Criteria for Evaluating Them

There you have it—reforms on unprepared ground, and copied from foreign institutions as well—nothing but harm!
— Fyodor Dostoevsky, *The Brothers Karamazov,*
book 11, chapter 9

. . . the sequence of reforms is crucial.
— Joseph Stiglitz, *Newsweek*

If you don't know where you are going, any road will get you there.
— Unknown

In this chapter, we present various options for transitional regulatory systems and criteria for evaluating the effectiveness of such systems. *Transitional* means different things to different people. Some people use the term to denote a *temporary resting place on a path from one position (or point) to another* (for example, while in transit). Other people use the word to imply something less restrictive. An alternative definition would be *intermediate positions within a range of options from which change is likely, but not inevitable.* This latter definition would include what might be called "intermediate" regulatory options.

The key difference between these two definitions is whether the transitional regulatory system is expected to move to some best-practice variant within, say, 5–10 years, or whether the system is anticipated to stay as it is unless or until the underlying industry or market structure changes. In other words, the distinction is between the following:

- A transitional regulatory system with clear commitments for further reform.
- A transitional regulatory system without commitments for further reform.

In this handbook, we use the term *transitional* to refer to both types of systems.

Although the three meta-principles of credibility, legitimacy, and transparency are critical for the design and evaluation of all regulatory systems—whether transitional or best-practice—the meta-principles can accommodate a variety of institutional arrangements. To be more specific, our discussion of transitional regulatory arrangements does not imply that there is an inevitable or required path for the regulatory system of any developing country to evolve to some ideal regulatory system, such as the Australian, French, British, or American regulatory models. All countries differ. They can and should develop their own institutional solutions on how to achieve good-practice regulation. At the same time, however—as discussed below—this does not imply that "anything goes."

Overview of Transitional Regulatory Systems

Why Transitional Systems?

Transitional regulatory systems may be needed for three reasons. First, a country may be unable to implement the independent regulator model because it lacks capacity, commitment, or both. It is unrealistic to expect that the requisite capacity and commitment will appear overnight when a country has little or no prior experience with autonomous regulation and when political authorities may be suspicious of a government entity over which they do not have full control.

Second, the full independent regulator model may simply be too risky as a first step in creating a regulatory system. There is always a risk of trying to do too much too soon. If a country tries to jump to the independent regulator framework in a single big step and the new regulatory system fails or is widely perceived to have failed, this failure or perception of failure may stop or significantly delay the overall sector reform. Therefore, a better strategy may be to work toward an independent regulator or another agreed-on best-practice model rather than trying to do it all at once.

Third, some aspects of an ideal model may be incompatible with established and accepted legal or cultural norms in a country. For example, a country's constitution may prohibit a minister from delegating final decisionmaking authority to a nonministerial body. In such a situation, the minister may, however, be able to create a body that provides advisory opinions in a public document on tariff levels and structures even if all final decisions are legally required to remain with the minister.

Good Fits Versus Best Practice

The existence of these real-world constraints suggests that more attention needs to be paid to obtaining good fits instead of just insisting on best practices. However, this is easier said than done. Almost any consultant with hands-on working experience in designing regulatory arrangements in developing and transition countries will admit that designing a best-practice regulatory system is relatively easy because it is the equivalent of a canned and off-the-shelf approach. In contrast, it is much more difficult to develop concrete recommendations on what should be done over the next one to two years to move a country that has no background in independent regulation to a best-practice system while avoiding major failures during the transition. In other words, specifying an ideal is easy. It is much more difficult, however, to define workable next steps that will lead to that ideal. Any regulatory evaluation will be of little or no use unless it develops realistic recommendations for good stepping-stones that can move a country from a starting point of no formal regulatory system to a best-practice regulatory system, while satisfying the three meta-principles of credibility, legitimacy, and transparency.[1]

Types of Transitional Regulatory Systems

As noted earlier, there are two general types of transitional regulatory systems:

- Regulatory systems for which a government has made no formal commitment to go beyond the specified transitional arrangements.

---

1. These principles are set out and discussed more fully in chapter 3.

- Regulatory systems for which a government has made a clear commitment to move beyond the transitional arrangements to a best-practice system.

The current electricity regulatory system in China and the 1990s Jamaican telecommunications system are examples of the first type of transitional system. In both instances, there was or is no legislative or clear, time-bound policy commitment to deepening the regulatory or other reforms. (See box 4.1.)

This first type of system can be described as a *transitional regulatory system without commitments* for further reforms. Such a system may create a basic, initial regulatory structure—which will probably be better designed and more

4

Box 4.1. Transitional Regulatory Systems—Type 1

1. Jamaican Telecommunications

The Jamaican telecommunications example shows how incentives on "intermediate" transitional policies can operate to promote good-practice regulation. Initially, the Jamaican Office of Utility Regulation (OUR) was given the limited role of advising the relevant minister on the enforcement of the concession contract with Cable and Wireless, the monopoly supplier. The minister, not the OUR, was the decisionmaker. Within 10 years, however, the OUR had become an independent, decisionmaking regulatory agency operating with all the powers, duties, and procedures of an independent regulatory regime overseeing a competitive telecom industry.

The change in the status and powers of OUR arose partly because it performed well in its original, limited role and partly because of a 1997–98 policy change by the Jamaican government to move to a competitive telecom industry. (See box 4.8 for further discussion of the Jamaican telecom example.)

2. Chinese Electricity

China established the State Electricity Regulatory Commission (SERC) as an electricity regulatory agency in 2002. SERC was established primarily to oversee the development of wholesale generation markets and transmission access in China's regions, together with oversight of technical quality standards, codes, and so forth. In its initial form, it has a number of features that, at least in general, one would not identify as good regulatory governance practice. For instance, it was established by a State Council Decree rather than by a law; it shares its functions in unclear ways with other agencies; and, at least by the standards of other countries, it has no noticeably open or transparent procedures.

The current arrangements appear to be just a first step, however, and there are strong pressures within China to increase SERC's scope, establish its powers by primary legislation, and enhance its openness. Further, China is currently seeing large increases in generation capacity (35 gigawatts in 2003 and 51 gigawatts in 2004), which are helping reduce current high levels of excess demand. Hence, the deficiencies of the current regulatory system do not seem to be impeding high levels of investment, at least in recent years. Moreover, as private investment and ownership increase and as SERC builds up its experience and reputation, the incentive to enhance, widen, and codify SERC's powers and duties is likely to grow—and to provide good opportunities for developing a more autonomous and transparent regulatory framework.

---

transparent than what went before—on which future changes can be built. Even though the current government may be unable or unwilling to commit to future enhancements, some future government might make further changes provided that the transitional arrangements lead to obvious improvement and the regulatory system gains a reputation for fairness and efficiency.

The second type of transitional arrangement exists in countries that have taken some initial regulatory steps and combined these actions with a clear legislative or policy commitment to deepening the regulatory reforms within a certain and relatively short period, typically within 5–10 years. This type of system can be described as *a transitional regulatory system with commitments for further reform*. The commitment may be specified in legislation or given as a public policy statement by the government, or both. The new electricity and telecommunications regulatory systems in the Central and Eastern European (CEE) countries that have joined the EU (or that expect to do so in the near future) and that have accepted EU regulatory requirements are an example of this second type of transitional regulatory system. In these cases, the need to comply with current and future EU directives is a powerful force for ensuring that the current regulatory system will not get stuck in a transition that never ends.

The Danger of Transitional Regulatory Systems That Never Evolve

Even if there is a formal government commitment to move beyond a transitional regulatory arrangement, there is no guarantee that this actually will happen. This suggests that, apart from any formal government commitments, the transitional system should be designed so that there are strong built-in incentives and pressures to move beyond any initial regulatory arrangements. These incentives and pressures are needed because not all transitional regulatory systems develop as planned.

Although there are some examples where transitional regulatory arrangements do evolve toward best practices, there are also many cases where the transition gets stuck and the reform either unravels and is reversed or continues in ways that leave the full promise of reform unrealized. There are examples, such as in Ukraine, where transitional concession contract arrangements were used as a way of avoiding some critical political choices (for example, on prices and ownership) and where the reform unraveled or achieved less-than-expected results because of the inability or unwillingness of governments to confront and address the underlying issues.

Regulatory reform also may fail because the infrastructure industry reform programs are overtaken by adverse economic or political shocks (as was the case with the macroeconomic collapse in Argentina in 2002) or because a new government may disavow a regulatory commitment on the grounds that the regulatory system was created by the previous government. In addition, powerful new vested commercial interests that benefit from the initial reform (frequently incumbent utilities) are likely to resist deeper electricity industry and regulatory reforms.[2] This is particularly so if, as is usually the case, they have invested time and effort in learning to maneuver and manipulate the new industry and regulatory system to their advantage. Such resistance can be very powerful, as has been shown by experience in Russia and some other Commonwealth of Independent States (CIS) countries, in India and some other Asian countries, and in several Latin American countries.

To minimize the likelihood that a transitional regulatory system will get stuck in a bad equilibrium, mechanisms should be in place to create incentives or pressures to continue moving toward a best-practice regulatory system. One such mechanism would be *prescheduled, public evaluations of the transitional regulatory system* (such as those proposed in this handbook). This would be strengthened if the evaluation were combined with legislative oversight hearings (as discussed in more detail in chapter 3 and appendix A).

A second mechanism that creates pressures for improvements is transparency. A transparent regulatory system—one that facilitates ongoing and open discussion—will usually generate new pressures for improvements in regulatory practice. It is particularly powerful if it is combined with moves toward the following:

- Service provision by companies with a strong commercial orientation.
- Expectations of improved services to consumers.

The combination of these factors generates incentives and pressures for accountability of service providers, regulatory entities, and governments, which can, as in the Jamaican telecom example, create strong pressures for improvements in an existing regulatory system.

---

2. This risk may be exacerbated in countries where the staff of the new regulatory agency are seconded from the incumbent company or enterprise. This risk is most obvious where the people involved are expected to *return* to their previous company.

The Importance of Starting Conditions

The particular transitional regulatory arrangements that may be feasible for a country will depend on the country's starting conditions. Two important starting conditions that need to be considered are the following:

- Governance conditions in the country.
- Commercialization of the utilities.

In analyzing starting conditions, an evaluator must consider the historical and current socioeconomic context in which the regulatory agency was designed and in which it operates. For instance, it is important to consider whether any utility reform or regulatory entity operates in a good/improving or bad/deteriorating country governance framework, and whether commercialization and any necessary price rebalancing and price increases had been started or at least clearly signaled before the new regulatory entity started work. Problems with the country governance regime and an inability or unwillingness to stay the course on commercialization are the two most common causes for the breakdown of infrastructure industry and regulatory reforms in developing and transition countries.

We now turn to a discussion of these two key starting conditions.

Governance

In what follows, we consider transitional regulatory options for countries grouped into two broad categories of overall country-level governance: countries with some effective and well-functioning institutions, and countries with few well-functioning government institutions. Following Kaufmann and his colleagues, we define country-level governance as "the traditions and institutions by which authority in a country is exercised."[3] (See box 4.2.)

Economic regulation of utility industries is one specific form of governance. Therefore, it seems reasonable to expect that the higher a country's general level of overall governance, the greater is the likelihood that it will be able to develop effective regulatory arrangements and move toward sustainable autonomous regulatory agencies along the lines of the best-practice independent regulator model.[4] This, then, raises the issue of how to measure a

---

3. See **Kaufmann, Kraay, and Mastruzzi** (2003), p. 2.
4. The **EBRD Transition Report** (2004, p. 58) finds a relatively clear correlation between

---

Box 4.2. Country Governance Measures

During the past 10 years, Daniel Kaufmann, Aart Kraay, and Massimo Mastruzzi have produced an important series of World Bank publications on country governance and its measurement.[1] Using this methodology based on a variety of subjective measures, Kaufmann and his colleagues have created a major data set that now measures overall governance in more than 200 countries.

Definition of Country Governance

The Kaufmann definition of country governance is "the [set of] traditions and institutions by which authority in a country is exercised." This general definition includes the three governance "clusters":

1. The process by which governments are selected, monitored, and replaced.
2. The capacity of the government effectively to formulate and implement sound policies.
3. The respect of citizens and the state for institutions that govern economic and social interactions between them.

(See **Kaufmann, Kraay, and Mastruzzi** 2004, p. 2.)

Different Indicators of Country Governance

To measure these three governance clusters, Kaufmann and his colleagues focus on six specific indicators:

1. Voice and accountability.
2. Political stability and the absence of violence.
3. Government effectiveness.

4. Regulatory quality (primarily regarding regulation of trade, business development and start-ups, financial systems, and the like).
5. Rule of law.
6. Control of corruption.

Empirical Measures of Country Governance

Kaufmann, Kraay, and Mastruzzi have developed an extensive data set on governance. The 2004 version provides estimates of governance levels for almost all countries in the world for 1996, 1998, 2000, and 2002. For 2002, the data set includes measures of the six governance indicators and 250 specific governance elements within the six. These measures were calculated for 199 countries using 25 different data sources produced by 18 organizations. Kaufmann, Kraay, and Mastruzzi (2005) have updated the indicators to include 2004 and to cover 209 countries.

The indicators and the estimates are an extremely useful policy and research tool but, as Kaufmann, Kraay, and Mastruzzi recognize, they must be interpreted with caution because of the inevitably subjective nature of much of the original source data.

1. Most of the references are to **Kaufmann, Kraay, and Mastruzzi** (2004). The World Bank now has a Web site devoted to this work, which includes the 2004 updates and much supporting material. See http://www.worldbank.org/wbi/governance/govdata/ for the latest data set. The data and methodology used to construct the indicators are described in Daniel Kaufmann, Aart Kraay, and Massimo Mastruzzi, 2005, Governance Matters IV: Governance Indicators for 1996–2004 (Washington, DC: World Bank); available at the same Web site.

---

country's overall level of governance. The most comprehensive work in this area has been undertaken by Daniel Kaufmann and his colleagues (Kaufmann), and this is now the standard reference. (See box 4.2.)

---

measures of regulatory quality (measured by formal measures of independence, transparency and accountability—three of the key regulatory governance principles) described in chapter 3—and constitutional liberalism (measured by respect for the rule of law, control of bureaucratic corruption, protection of property rights, and freedom for the media).

Although all six of the Kaufmann governance issues are important for effective utility regulation, *the rule of law is probably the single most important governance indicator for economic regulation.* Within the rule of law, the two most important elements are the following:

- Sound law courts.
- The ability to enforce commercial contracts.

These two elements are critical for ensuring that regulatory commitments will be honored.

A tariff-setting system may look fine on paper, but private investors are not likely to invest if they have good reason to believe that whatever regulatory commitments have been established will not be honored. Success in implementing regulatory commitments requires more than good intentions. A government or its regulator may have the best of intentions to honor the terms and conditions of a tariff-setting system, but they probably will be unsuccessful if they lack the capacity to operate the new regulatory institutions.

Commitment and Capacity

This suggests that the overall effectiveness of a new regulatory system will depend on both the government's commitment to establishing such a system and its capacity for doing so. Both elements are included in the Kaufmann rule of law country governance indicator. In other words, *an effective regulatory system requires both "commitment" (will) and "capacity" (ability to develop, implement, and honor policies, programs, and regulations) on the part of the government.* When designing and evaluating a regulatory system, it is helpful to think of countries as falling into one of four categories that are defined by combinations of commitment and capacity (see table 4.1).[5]

Category 1 countries have strong capacity and strong commitment. They are countries that have a high probability of creating well-functioning and

Table 4.1. Commitment and Capacity Combinations

Category 1 Countries	Category 2 Countries
Strong commitment Strong capacity	Weak commitment Strong capacity
Category 3 Countries	Category 4 Countries
Strong commitment Weak capacity	Weak commitment Weak capacity

---

5. This typology can be found in Magüi M. Torres and Michael Anderson (2004), "Fragile States: Defining Difficult Environments for Poverty Reduction by DFID." This can be downloaded from http://siteresources.worldbank.org/INTLICUS/6413734110945714517 60/20357055/P RDE_W P_1%20Defining%20Fragile%20States.pdf.

effective utility regulatory institutions without long delays. Most Organisation for Economic Co-operation and Development (OECD) countries would fall into this category. Even if they have not had any history of separate regulatory entities, their overall governance endowment (particularly their respect for the rule of law) should enable them to establish well-designed regulatory systems that could incorporate most of the best-practice principles and standards presented in chapter 3.

For most developing and transition-economy countries, this situation is not likely to exist. As a general proposition, they are likely to be Category 2 (competent, but with uncertain or limited commitment) and Category 3 (weak but willing) countries. Commitment is inherently a political phenomenon, therefore, there is little that can be done if a country lacks the political will to create a viable regulatory system for its commercialized (or commercializing) utility industries.

The two governance categories that we focus on in the remainder of this chapter are:

- Countries with some effective and well-functioning government institutions (Category 3 and Category 2).
- Countries with few well-functioning government institutions (Category 4).

Countries with Some Effective and Well-Functioning
Government Institutions—Category 3 and Category 2 Countries

Category 3 and Category 2 countries have sufficient regulatory resources and an overall quality of governance that would enable them to move toward a regulatory system that reflects the best-practices model. In table 4.1, they would normally be Category 3 countries with a strong commitment to developing effective utility regulation, but with weaknesses in capacity and experience. However, some may be Category 2 countries where the potential capacity for effective regulation might be reasonably strong (for example, in terms of staffing and funding), but the political willingness and commitment of the government might be weak or variable. Typically, the countries that fall into these two categories are middle-income or larger countries but, particularly among Category 3 countries, they include a number of low-income and small countries. On the Kaufmann rule of law governance indicator, it is likely that they will have scores that place them some way above the bottom 25 percent of countries.

Category 3 countries have the political will, but lack the institutional experience and capacity to develop effective regulatory or other institutions (that is, the willing but weak). For these countries, the question is typically how best to enhance and develop what is already in place. Formal and informal transitional regulatory mechanisms need to be created that produce initial and observable successes from both an investor and a consumer perspective. It is hoped that these early wins will create a demand for the more sophisticated forms of regulation. In electricity, examples of such countries might include Brazil, South Africa, Turkey, and Uganda.

Category 2 countries may have considerable human and other regulatory resources. For historical, political, or other reasons, however, they may be reluctant to move away from state control and let go of regulatory control of electricity (and other infrastructure industry) investment and prices. One can think of these Category 2 countries as unwilling but strong. They are unwilling in the sense that they have a limited or very low (if any) commitment to an independent regulatory entity but, if they did have this commitment, they would certainly have the technical and administrative capability to operate such an entity. This will be true of many former socialist countries with a long tradition of state planning and control. Because of this history, they may be reluctant or opposed to the notion of a minister ceding economic controls to some governmental entity that is not under a minister's direct control. This phenomenon has been observed in Russia.[6] China and India are also examples of Category 2 countries where successive governments have made some moves toward commercialization of their electricity and other infrastructure industries, but the new emerging regulatory agencies face opposition, usually from powerful forces that prefer continued and extensive state influence. The experience of the new Chinese and Indian regulatory entities shows both what can be achieved and the difficulties that can arise in Category 2 countries.

Countries with Few Well-Functioning Government Institutions—Category 4

These are countries where regulatory resources are very limited or where the overall quality of governance is low—typically very-low-income countries,

---

6. The Federal Tariff Service, the national electricity regulator, initially operated outside of a ministry, but then was moved under the prime minister's direct control in 2004. See **World Bank** (2004).

4

small countries, and countries emerging from widespread civil conflict. In terms of table 4.1, they would fall into Category 4 countries with a weak commitment to developing effective utility regulation, as well as major weaknesses in capacity and experience. However, some may be Category 3 countries where the potential capacity for effective regulation is weak (for example, in terms of specialist staff), but the political willingness and commitment of the country leadership might be relatively strong.

At the limit, these are countries where both the capability and the willingness of government to establish a regulatory system are weak to nonexistent. Although the capacity may be very limited, there may be some willingness on the part of supply companies and others to begin developing regulatory arrangements—for example, for telecom interconnection or for the recommencement of electricity network expansion investment. For these countries, the question is how best to initiate—in some cases to kickstart—some utility regulatory activity that will promote investment and stimulate increases in the volume and quality of output supplied. The Category 4 countries are likely to fall into the bottom 25 percent (or 10 percent) on the Kaufmann overall rule of law governance indicator.

Examining experience and utility regulatory steps taken in the first group of countries (Categories 3 and 2) can help identify where and how reasonable progress in developing utility regulation can take place. We will make suggestions about practical measures that may be useful as intermediate steps and for moving toward best-practice regulation. This analysis also will help identify the necessary minimum conditions needed for making any further progress. It will set the framework for the evaluation of regulatory arrangements that is the focus of chapters 5 and 6.

Commercialization

Good-practice utility regulation is feasible for *all* countries, rich or poor, where sector enterprises are operating on a commercialized basis *or are clearly moving toward it.*

Commercialized enterprises are motivated by profits. This, in turn, implies that they are primarily concerned with providing services that increase revenues and with reducing the costs of these services. Often, such enterprises will have substantial involvement of private investment, or will be privately owned or operated. Private ownership is not a requirement for commercialization, particularly for monopoly network elements.[7] There are examples of government-owned enterprises doing business on a strong commercial basis (such as Eskom in South Africa). However, it is more common for publicly owned enterprises in developing countries to be used for political or policy ends that cannot be commercially justified.

We define a fully commercialized electricity enterprise as one that satisfies the following two general conditions:

1. It is operated on the expectation that its sales revenues will be sufficient to enable it to cover its operating expenses and earn a reasonable return on its assets, so that it can finance new investments without *general* taxpayer subsidies or guarantees. Alternatively, the combination of its sales revenues and transparent and explicit subsidies (for example, for rural electrification, renewable generation, or mandated below-cost lifeline rates) will be sufficient to cover operating expenses and a reasonable return on assets.[8]
2. Its principal incentive is to maximize profits by increasing revenues and reducing costs. Alternatively, in the case of fully commercial state-owned enterprises, its principal incentive is to meet its service obligations by the most cost-effective, productive means, including a positive, real rate of return to its public sector asset providers.

Starting points matter a lot in new regulatory systems. If there is a big gap between revenues and costs, it is unrealistic to expect that the gap will be closed by a new independent regulator acting through technical economic solutions, even if the regulated enterprise has been corporatized and notionally commercialized. In such a situation, the fundamental problem is political, not regulatory. Little will be accomplished unless the government is willing to commit to a credible transition strategy for raising tariffs and unless the government supports the regulator in implementing this strategy.

The expectation that a regulatory agency acting on its own initiative will be able to close a big revenue–cost gap when a country's political authorities have been avoiding the same problem for years is unrealistic. When the gap

---

7. For potentially competitive services, it is harder to reconcile state ownership with effective competition. That was one of the major problems with the Asian IPP developments of the 1990s.
8. Note that commercialization by implicit subsidy or cross-subsidy, as in India and Russia, does not satisfy this criterion.

is large, the path to commercialization must depend on some form of transitional, time-limited subsidies for the shortfall in revenues. The subsidies will need to be provided either openly and directly by explicit subsidies or indirectly through publicly mandated cross-subsidies and subsidized inputs. The former is preferable where possible, but if not feasible, limited cross-subsidies or implicit subsidies may have a role as intermediate or transitional steps—provided that they are transparent and published.

Governments also can make a major contribution to commercialization by ensuring that all customers pay their bills. That means ministries, military installations, and all other governmental agencies, as well as private customers. Further, governments need to resist claims from previously favored industries either to continue not paying their bills or to continue receiving very-low-cost electricity, or both. The police power of the state will be needed to enforce laws against theft of service. These issues have been important in establishing the credibility of commercializing electricity reforms—and newly installed regulatory regimes—in India, Russia, and many other countries.

A commercialized electricity industry is likely to be one with significant amounts of private involvement (or at least private financing of investment) in some or all elements. In theory, commercialized electricity entities could be either publicly or privately owned. Australia and Norway provide good examples of a commercialized and largely publicly owned electricity industry. However, this is not the case for most electricity enterprises in developing or transitional economies. In most such economies, the power enterprises are politicized and inefficient, so that the willingness of governments to encourage private investment on a significant scale (and preferably to privatize or lease the assets of government-owned power enterprises) is very important. It provides a concrete sign that the government has recognized that the industry cannot be commercialized without substantive changes in management objectives, control, and ownership.

Box 4.3 provides a more detailed checklist of important requirements for commercialization and corporatization. The criteria assume that the company or enterprise operates as a *corporatized,* privately owned, municipalized, or state-owned enterprise—that is, *not* as an unincorporated state-owned enterprise operating under the control of a line ministry. State-owned corporatized utilities operate under varying degrees of commercialization.[9]

---

9. A good discussion of commercialization and corporatization of state-owned enterprises can be found in Timothy Irwin and Chiaki Yamamoto (2004), "Some Options for Improving the

---

Box 4.3. Commercialization Criteria for Utility Service Industries and Enterprises

The relevant company or enterprise should:

- Have corporatized status and not operate as a government department
- Be governed by a board with a significant number of non-executive board members who should not be government officials
- Be in full compliance with internationally accepted accounting standards (including its own balance sheet)
- Pay taxes at the same rate as other companies or enterprises
- Borrow at interest rates that are market based

- Earn a commercial rate of return on capital or equity
- Have the autonomy to borrow within limits set by the board and regulator
- Have the autonomy to procure equipment, consultancy, and other services
- Have the autonomy to hire and fire staff
- Adopt commercial salaries and employment conditions (including total level of employees)
- Raise financing from capital market sources rather than from low-cost government fiscal sources.

4

For electricity, noncommercialized operation was the rule before 1990 in the former Soviet bloc and is still the case in many middle-income and developing countries, including many CIS countries.[10] In the water and sewerage industry, as well as the railway and postal industries, the noncommercial industry model still operates in most middle-income and developing countries (and, to a considerable extent, in many rich OECD countries). In these cases, not only is the "ideal" or best-practices regulatory model largely irrelevant but any major steps toward it realistically can be made only once some major initial steps have been made toward genuine commercialization (for example, as has been achieved since 1990 for electricity in most of the CEE countries).[11] Nevertheless, as we shall illustrate below, some initial regulatory or quasi-regulatory arrangements may, in the right circumstances, help promote commercializing reform.

Governance of State-Owned Electricity Utilities," Energy and Mining Sector Board Discussion Paper 11, World Bank, Washington, DC; available at http://iris37.worldban k.org/domdoc/PRD/Other/PRDDContainer.nsf/All+Documents/85256D2400766CC7852 56FFC0074A7F4/$File/Energy_ImptheGov.pdf). See also World Bank, 1996, *Bureaucrats in Business* (Oxford, UK: Oxford University Press).

10. David Kennedy argues that significant progress toward cost recovery has been made in some parts of the former Soviet Union, particularly the Baltic States that have now joined the European Union. Using a baseline of US$0.075 to US$0.08 for full cost recovery, Kennedy calculates that the average retail power sector tariff is US$0.061 in the Baltics contrasted with US$0.025 in the CIS. See David Kennedy (forthcoming), "Lifelines in Europe and Central Asia: Refocusing the Infrastructure Transition Agenda," Europe and Central Asia Region, World Bank, Washington, DC.

11. This is described more fully in **EBRD** (2004) and in Kennedy (forthcoming).

Evaluation Criteria for Transitional Regulatory Systems

Any mid-level or in-depth evaluation of a regulatory system should do the following:

- Establish the current situation.
- Establish whether and how far the observed regulatory system has moved to improve its regulatory practices relative to previous arrangements (using the meta-principles plus the principles and standards of chapter 3 and appendix A as the evaluation benchmarks).
- Establish industry outcomes, and assess the contribution of the regulatory arrangements and decisions to the quality of outcomes achieved.
- Assess the regulatory arrangements and industry outcomes with those in comparable countries.
- Identify the internal incentives and pressures that are
  - likely to improve regulatory processes and industry outcomes
  - likely to impede or retard progress, or threaten the viability of current regulatory arrangements, or both.

These criteria are important for evaluations of infrastructure regulatory arrangements in all countries, *but they are especially important for the transitional regulatory arrangements discussed in this chapter.* This is particularly true for the second through fifth criteria.

Regulatory Options for Countries with Some Effective and Well-Functioning Government Institutions

In this and the following sections, we describe transitional regulatory options for countries with functioning governmental, legislative, and judicial institutions that have the potential to develop autonomous infrastructure regulatory agencies, but for various reasons have not yet done so.

Some Prerequisites

The countries concerned need the following:

- Legislative bodies that can enact adequate primary and secondary laws.
- A functioning court system (or an equivalent dispute-resolution or appellate process).

- Policymaking institutions (usually ministries) with the administrative capability to make policy decisions and implement them.
- Commercialized utility service industries or, at the least, a clear policy objective of moving to commercialization in the short to medium term.
- Governmental bodies that can prepare and bid out franchise or concession contracts in an honest and transparent way.
- A reasonable overall quality of country governance (for example, a country score above the bottom quarter of the Kaufmann index).

Countries that satisfy these prerequisites can go beyond simply awarding contracts with dispute resolution mechanisms and begin tackling the fundamental issue of utility regulation: *how to provide for the review and modification of utility franchise or concession contracts and rules that will protect consumers without unduly or unreasonably jeopardizing the interests and confidence of investors.*

Utility Franchise and Concession Contracts, Private Investment, and the Development of Utility Regulation

Concession contracts often play an important role in introducing private capital into infrastructure industries, particularly in the earlier stages. This is especially evident in water and railways, but also is evident in electricity and natural gas distribution. Box 4.4 provides a stylized outline of how utility regulation and regulatory functions often evolve.

Of course, not all attempts to introduce private concessions into infrastructure industries are successful. In the 1990s, there was a boom in the use of concession contracts for infrastructure in Latin America and the Caribbean. However, many of them, particularly the Latin American water and toll road concessions, have had major renegotiations early, and some have failed completely. The record is not as bad in energy, but, by end-2003, 11 percent (by value of all electricity and gas projects with private participation started since 1990) had either been cancelled or were in serious financial distress, many of them with concession-type regimes.[12] This is a lot better than in water (40 percent), but not nearly as good as in telecommunications (4 percent). However, as is discussed later in this chapter in the section on combinations of regulatory agencies with infrastructure contracts, the per-

---

12. See Ada K. Izaguirre (2004), "Private Infrastructure," Public Policy for the Private Sector Note 274, World Bank, Washington, DC, pp. 3–4.

Box 4.4. The Stages of Regulatory Development

The development of regulatory arrangements for infrastructure sectors often goes through three separate stages:

- **Stage 1—Contract Enforcement.** The first stage is an institutional arrangement by which long-term commercial (and franchise) contracts can be written, approved, and enforced. This can be achieved through formal oversight by impartial courts of law that are enforcing an effective commercial law system.[1] Alternatively, the contracts might be administered by the executive or legislative branches of government, or both.
- **Stage 2—Monitoring and Enforcement of Contracts by Separate Entities.** The second stage is some institutional arrangement under which utility service licenses or concession contracts can be monitored and enforced on an ongoing basis by a third party, such as an informal arbitration entity or a formal regulatory or quasi-regulatory body.
- **Stage 3—Separate Regulatory Entity with Tariff-Setting Authority.** The final stage is the emergence or creation of a separate regulatory entity that can act of its own volition and that has the authority, in consultation with regulated companies and their consumers, to modify existing regulatory obligations (for example, maximum tariffs and minimum quality-of-service standards) and to establish new rights and obligations. In other words, it is a regulatory entity that has all the powers needed to act as a full regulator, including a degree of bounded and accountable discretion.

This pattern of regulatory evolution has been observed in the development of regulation in the U.K. railways, electricity, and telecom industries, as well as in the French water industry.[2] It also has been common in the more recent development of regulatory institutions in some industries in some countries in Latin America and the Caribbean.[3]

1. This includes the development of the French water concessions—initially "tight" concessions that subsequently, under the legal supervision of the Conseil d'Etat, evolved into *regies* (in which investment and operation are realized by a public body, the municipality) and *affermages* (in which investment costs are borne by the municipality, with operation being taken over by a private entrepreneur, the operator). See **Pezon** (2003).

2. See **Gómez-Ibáñez** (2003), **Pezon** (2003), and **Stern** (2003).

3. The Jamaican telecom experience since 1980 is a classic example. See box 4.1. For a full discussion of the role of regulatory and quasi-regulatory agencies in Latin American infrastructure concession contract experience, see **Guasch** (2004).

---

formance of concession contracts is much better *if there is a regulatory or quasi-regulatory agency external to the contract to monitor and enforce the contract*—in other words, if the country is, in the typology suggested in box 4.4, at least at Stage 2 rather than Stage 1.

Considering where the country is located in its regulatory development is very important when assessing problems and proposing remedies. It is on these issues that we focus in our discussion of specific intermediate and transitional options by identifying and suggesting solutions for the most common problems in creating effective regulatory systems. In particular, we consider in some detail how to build the incentives to move to Stage 3 in the suggested typology.

Constraints on the Development of
Effective Regulatory Institutions

Even if the country-level governance prerequisites discussed above are satisfied, that in itself does not guarantee that a country will be successful in creating an effective regulatory system. Most countries that are trying to create new regulatory systems also will have to deal with one or more constraints or impediments that will hinder the development of a fully functioning, independent regulatory agency. The most commonly observed constraints include the following:

1. An unwillingness or inability to move toward commercialization with cost-reflective prices to small consumers.
2. An inability or unwillingness to hand over decisionmaking powers to a nonministry or nonpolitical agency even if it is formally required by law.
3. Weakly functioning or slowly operating law courts that create considerable uncertainty when there is an appeal of a regulatory decision.
4. Uncertainty about the nature and strength of regulatory commitments.
5. Limited regulatory resources (particularly the lack of money and specialized, experienced staff, such as economists, lawyers, and accountants).
6. Popular opposition, especially from consumers, because they believe that their interests are being ignored to provide large profits to private investors (particularly when private foreign investors are significantly involved).
7. Macroeconomic crises (or fears of rapid inflation, currency devaluation, and the like) and their aftermath.

Some of these problems may also affect countries with well-established, nontransitional regulatory systems, but they tend to be much more manageable where institutions are stronger and better established. In those circumstances, these problems (particularly numbers 5–7 above) typically will not threaten the viability of the regulatory framework. In contrast, the problems tend to be markedly more acute in countries that have transitional regulatory regimes. In the rest of this chapter, we discuss each of these constraints and some possible solutions.

4

Unwillingness or Inability to Move toward Commercialization

Sustainable private investment is virtually impossible if unwillingness or the inability to move toward commercialization is an absolute and binding political constraint. However, given the alternative of continued sector stagnation, many countries are deciding to move toward cost-reflective tariffs—*but over a relatively extended period* (for example, over five years).

The best approach, particularly in electricity and water distribution, is to establish an explicit timetable for the transition that is written into the law or in a concession or privatization contract that is externally monitored and enforced.[13] If low prices have been supported in the past by subsidies or cross-subsidies, explicit and clear measures must be in place either to phase out the subsidies or to convert them into direct, explicit subsidies that the government can reasonably be expected to pay. This also applies to implicit subsidies, such as subsidized power purchase costs for newly privatized electricity distribution entities, or even more commonly in the absence of a requirement, the utility earning a commercial rate of return on its assets.[14] In many regions, the most common implicit subsidy is requiring that a state-owned power company cover only its current costs and that it not be required to earn a positive rate of return on its assets or pay a dividend to the government.

If the government fails to make its promised subsidy payments, the regulator faces a major problem. Although the regulator could, in theory, raise overall tariffs to cover the subsidy shortfall, the popular backlash could be enormous. Therefore, the World Bank and other international financing organizations have been discussing the possibility of loans and grants for tran-

---

13. This has been done very clearly and explicitly in the Peruvian water sector. The Peruvian water law requires a three-stage process for "tariff convergence." In the *etapa preparatoria* (preparatory stage), tariffs must cover operating expense while water companies work on defining their investment plans. The second stage is called the *etapa de mejoramiento* (improvement stage). During this stage, tariffs are supposed to raise the level of long-term marginal cost. The final stage is called the *etapa definitiva* (definitive stage). A similar arrangement exists in the Colombian water sector. See Vivien Foster, 2005, "Ten Years of Water Service Reform in Latin America: Toward an Anglo-French Model," Water Supply and Sanitation Discussion Paper Series 3, World Bank, Washington, DC; available at www.worldbank.org/watsan.

14. Input subsidies in electricity are usually provided through subsidized power purchase costs. For example, electricity privatizations or concessions are often accompanied by subsidized "vesting" contracts for the sale of power to distribution companies at below-market prices (Argentina and Panama) or by a commitment to sell power from state-owned generators at subsidized prices (Delhi).

sitional subsidy funds, as well as partial risk guarantees (PRGs) to increase the likelihood that promised subsidies actually will be paid. We discuss these in more detail in the section that follows on external regulatory risk mitigation and World Bank PRGs for new regulatory systems.

A process involving combinations of regulation with contractual underpinnings has been used in a number of countries to jump-start privatizations or long-term leases and/or concessions. It is especially common in electricity distribution, where it is usually implemented through a prespecified, performance-based, multiyear tariff system that involves benchmarks or targets for controllable costs, pass-throughs for noncontrollable costs, and a subsidy mechanism.

Examples of this approach include most of the Latin American electricity distribution privatizations and concessions from the 1990s, as well as ongoing (mid-2005) distribution privatizations in Bulgaria and Romania, the long-term leases implemented or planned for Lesotho and Uganda, and the electricity distribution privatization in Moldova. Typically, the prespecified regulatory agreement will be negotiated by a privatization entity within the government.[15]

This combination of a commitment to an initial prefixed regulatory arrangement accompanied by a subsidy-delivery mechanism seems to work reasonably well in privatizations and concessions of *distribution and retail sales* entities for electricity (and natural gas). It has been much less successful in electricity generation—as well as in water and railways—and has been virtually nonexistent in electricity transmission.

This is for various reasons—perhaps the most obvious of which is that subsidy problems relating to prices to final consumers are much more easily addressed where they occur, that is, at the distribution level. The Asian financial crisis in 1997 and the Argentina peso crisis left power distribution companies (and consumers) unable and unwilling to pay for the generation prices of the private generating companies at the new exchange rate. Because there was no subsidy mechanism at the distribution level, the generation contracts collapsed because the distribution companies were unable to

---

15. A critical issue with such privatizations is the goal of the government and the Ministry of Finance. Some privatizations are primarily designed to fund investment in the privatized entity, whereas others are designed to maximize short-term treasury receipts. The appropriate side conditions for incorporation in accompanying contracts are likely to be very different between these objectives. The failure to adequately balance these conflicting government objectives can lead to severe consequences for the viability of the regulatory arrangements.

buy—or were prohibited from buying—power from the independent power producers at the substantially higher local currency price.[16]

For evaluation purposes, the critical issues are whether the mechanisms that are established

- have clear and transparent procedures
- foster cost-reflective tariffs
- help support an increase in maintenance and investment expenditures
- provide a platform and incentives for further movement toward best-practice regulation.

Unwillingness or Inability to Transfer Regulatory Decisionmaking Powers

The concept of an independent regulatory entity with final decisionmaking authority is not familiar to political authorities in most developing and transition-economy countries. It was reported that the president of one Latin American nation, when informed that the electricity regulatory commission had raised retail electricity tariffs by more than 10 percent without consulting him, said, "Who is this guy and how can I fire him?" Obviously, political authorities will always be concerned about the political effects of raising highly visible electricity tariffs, especially if there have been no obvious improvements in quality of service. This phenomenon is universal; it is not limited just to developing and transition economies.[17] Occasionally, political figures will view the existence of independent regulatory agencies as a

16. The delivery price of power in the relevant power purchase agreements (PPAs) typically was denominated in U.S. dollar terms (apart from Thailand) and relied on dollar debt finance. For Argentina, the underpinning was the fixed dollar-peso link. Given that prices to domestic consumers were denominated in local currency, the contracts became financially nonviable, unless the IPPs were able to raise the price of delivered wholesale power by the amount of the currency depreciation. Even if this happened, power retailers continuing to purchase from the IPPs would make unsustainable losses, unless these wholesale price increase were passed through into retail prices. In fact, both in Asia in 1997–98 and in Argentina in 2002, retail distribution companies suspended purchases and, almost always, as in Argentina, governments fixed wholesale delivery prices at the old local currency price. In all cases, governments fixed the allowed retail price at the predevaluation level for a considerable period after the depreciation, resulting in the financial nonviability of the PPAs because of the inability to meet the debt-financing commitments. The PPAs, therefore, collapsed and either were sold or were substantially renegotiated, with major losses to the investors and, in many cases, to the debt providers.

17. Mark Jamison, director of the Public Utility Research Center at the University of Florida,

positive development because it frees them from having to make politically difficult decisions. If regulators make the decisions, politicians are free to criticize the unpopular ones and support the popular ones without having to accept any direct responsibility.[18]

Some ministers may want control over tariffs for more personal reasons. Implicit or explicit control over the approval of tariffs, such as long-term power purchase agreements (PPAs), provides opportunities for bribes that might disappear or become more difficult to obtain if the PPAs have to be reviewed and approved by an independent regulatory entity. All of this suggests that it is unrealistic in some countries to expect that a truly independent regulatory entity with final decisionmaking authority can be created on day 1 of the reform process.

Faced with this reality, what can be done? The most commonly observed alternative to a fully functional and independent regulator with final decisionmaking authority is an advisory regulator.[19] This is a regulator who provides advice on regulatory decisions to a minister or prime minister. The final decisions—whether tariffs should go up by 6 percent or 14 percent—formally remain with the minister or prime minister and not the regulator.

Although this is a politically convenient compromise, it also clearly has the potential for being a dead end rather than a short-term transitional arrangement. As always, the devil is in the details. Whether the "advisory"

---

writes that "[w]hen the Governor of Iowa appointed Dennis Nagel to be chairperson of the Iowa Utilities Board several years ago, the only thing that the Governor requested is that Dennis *not* do anything that would cost the Governor the next election. The Governor didn't mention protecting consumers, protecting shareholders, or obeying the law. The Governor asked only that Dennis not cost him the next election." Mark Jamison, 2004, "Survival Guide for the Independent Regulator," Working Paper, Public Utility Research Center, University of Florida, Gainesville, Fla., p. 1; available at http://bear.cba.ufl.edu/centers/purc/.

18. An excellent example of a politician finding it to his advantage to have independent regulators was implicit in the story of a newly elected governor of a U.S. state who once asked a veteran governor of a neighboring state for advice on the types of persons best suited for regulatory appointments. The advice was that a governor should only appoint two types of people, a very close friend or irreconcilable enemies. The reason for such appointees, the veteran governor noted, was that sooner or later, after the regulator made an unpopular decision, a governor would have to go on television and proclaim that he was betrayed, and his friend would understand and his enemy would not care.

19. In a recent survey, Kennedy (forthcoming) finds that 3 of 6 new electricity regulator entities in Central and Eastern Europe and the Baltic states are advisory (that is, they do not have full tariff-setting authority), 5 of 10 are advisory in Southeastern Europe, and 4 of 12 are advisory in the CIS.

regulator eventually evolves to an independent and fully functioned regulator will depend very much on the specific features of the arrangement.

To be more concrete, it is useful to distinguish between a weak advisory regulator and a strong advisory regulator. The important characteristics of these two types of advisory regulators are listed below:

1. **Weak advisory regulator** (inside or outside a ministry).
   a. There is no separate earmarked budget (depends solely on ministry budget).
   b. The regulator's advice to the minister is not given publicly and is often kept confidential.
   c. The minister's policy and other directives or other communications to the regulator are not made public.
   d. There is little or no public consultation by the regulator with affected parties.
   e. The ministry is under no obligation to respond to the regulator's advice within a specified period.
   f. If the minister rejects or modifies the regulator's recommendations, the minister is under no obligation to give any public explanations for rejecting or modifying the regulator's recommendations.
   g. There are no conflict-of-interest rules for the decisionmakers and key staff members of the regulatory entity.

2. **Strong advisory regulator** (inside or outside a ministry).
   a. Separate and earmarked funding is outside the ministry's budget.
   b. The regulator's advice must be given in a publicly available document that provides a clear statement of the decision, a description and analysis of all evidence taken into consideration, a summary of views offered by the different parties, and a full discussion of the rationale for the recommendations.[20]
   c. The minister's policy directives and other communications to the regulator must be given in a public document.[21]
   d. The regulator has public consultations with affected parties (U.S.-style rate cases, Australian-style consultations, or Latin American *audiencias públicas*).

---

20. This approach recently was taken by the advisory electricity regulator in Peru when he transmitted his distribution tariff recommendations to the minister.

21. This is required in Pakistan for the electricity regulator. See http://www.nepra.org.pk for examples of government policy directives to the electricity regulator.

e. The minister can reject or request reconsideration of the recommendations and must do so within a specified number of days. If the minister fails to act before the deadline, the regulator's recommendations are deemed to have been adopted.[22]

f. If the minister rejects or modifies the regulator's recommendations, the minister must give a written, public explanation for this action.

g. Conflict-of-interest rules are in place for decisionmakers and key staff of the regulator.

h. The effectiveness of this governance arrangement is periodically reviewed in prescheduled evaluations by independent sector and regulatory experts (preferably including one or more individuals from outside the country) in a public document.

It is probably safe to say that the weak advisory regulator rarely leads to anything useful. Essentially, it is a repackaged version of the previously existing regulatory system but with a different name and, typically, with weak legal protection. Indeed, it is sometimes used to hide the reality that little or nothing has changed—a substitute for the introduction of autonomous regulation while maintaining ministry or government control rather than a genuine reform step.

If, however, the advisory regulator is established by law with clear functions and duties and fully transparent processes, even relatively weak advisory regulators can begin to act with a degree of independent authority, provided that there are sound, functioning law courts. This is also true of ministry regulators where their powers and duties are set out in primary law.[23]

In contrast, the strong advisory regulator, while satisfying short-term political needs, has considerable potential for evolving to a more effective regulatory system over time. Although the regulator will not have the critical element of final decisionmaking authority, this arrangement does introduce strong elements of transparency and accountability that did not exist before. It is these elements that will create pressures in most political systems for improving regulatory practice.

---

22. For example, the recommendations of the advisory Pakistani gas regulator to the government are "notified" (that is, they go into effect) if the government does not take any action within 45 days. In contrast, the government does not have to take any action on the recommendations of the electricity regulator within any specified period.

23. See **Cubbin and Stern** (2005) for empirical evidence on the role of all regulators (including ministry regulators) having their powers established under primary law.

Unfortunately, most experience with advisory regulatory agencies in developing countries has been that countries that have adopted the weak advisory regulator option have not moved forward to developing effective decisionmaking regulators. This is most obvious in East Asia (for example, Thailand). In the CEE in the 1990s, the advice of advisory regulators was frequently overruled (particularly on tariff cases), so that they rapidly lost credibility with investors (for example, the 1990s Hungarian electricity regulator). However, in the CEE cases, the advisory regulators have evolved into genuinely autonomous regulators—because such a change was required as a condition of joining the EU. There is as yet little sign of the electricity or other infrastructure regulators moving toward exercising substantive influence in the CEE or CIS countries apart from those that have joined or are likely to join the EU.

There are other examples of advisory regulators becoming autonomous, final decisionmaking agencies. As discussed earlier, the Jamaican Office of Utility Regulation (OUR) was set up initially as an agency to advise the minister on monitoring and enforcing the concession contract with Cable and Wireless. It was successful in establishing a good reputation and has now become a full-blown final decisionmaking regulator for electricity and water, as well as for telecommunications. This, however, represents a relatively rare success and it is interesting that, when in advisory mode, the Jamaican OUR had a number of the key features of the strong advisory regulator—at least for its telecom regulation.

It may be that the advisory regulator model, as based on the strong advisory regulator, can work better in the future than the typically adopted weak model has in the past. It remains to be seen whether the above-cited examples of recent moves to the adoption of a strong advisory regulator, as in Pakistan, will be more successful or whether they also become marginalized over time.

For regulatory evaluation purposes, the critical issues are whether the advisory regulator variant in the relevant country

- has clear and transparent procedures, particularly for publication, recommendations, and ministerial responses
- fosters commercially based operation of electricity companies
- helps support an increase in maintenance and investment expenditures
- develops a body of experienced regulatory staff
- provides incentives and a framework for further movement toward best-practice regulation.

Weak or Slowly Operating Law Courts and Regulatory Appeals

Weak or dysfunctional judicial systems frequently are encountered in developing countries. The problem with such systems is that they can be slow, bureaucratic, ineffective, and weak in enforcing judgments. Dysfunctional court systems also may be biased or uninformed in adjudicating matters. They may make unwarranted intrusions in areas best left to regulators and may operate in a politicized manner. Finally, they also may be corrupt (that is, judicial decisions can be bought).

A strong, functional judiciary is a prerequisite for an effective regulatory regime. Without one, commercial contracts, labor contracts, and other critical business practices will be almost impossible to carry out and enforce on any reliable, consistent basis. A credible and fair judicial system is also needed for appealing decisions from regulatory agencies. Regulators must be held accountable to ensure that they are operating consistent with and fully within the bounds of the law.

In the long term, no economic reform, whether in infrastructure or other sectors, can work without a fully functional legal and judicial system. That being said, however, it must be acknowledged that judicial and legal reform is beyond the scope of this handbook. For purposes of this chapter, the question is how one puts in place legal arrangements that will support a transitional regulatory system if the judicial and legal system has not yet undergone reform and if it is still weak or dysfunctional.[24] For regulation, the main relevance of the judicial system is whether it is a suitable forum for hearing appeals from regulatory decisions.

Two Possible Solutions

Two basic mechanisms may be used for dealing with weak or dysfunctional courts:

1. Contractual mechanisms such as arbitration.

---

24. Even in countries with reasonably competent judicial systems, dealing with regulatory matters can be very difficult. The concept of independent regulatory agencies is new, and the subject matter is often arcane and outside the normal experience of judges. This is particularly the case where courts have historically played a limited role in regard to administrative matters. Moreover, judicial systems may not be structured in such a way as to handle regulatory matters expeditiously. Bureaucratization and multiple layers of appeals

2. Alternative adjudicatory institutions, such as specialized tribunals or formal advisory panels.

The latter is preferable for the reasons discussed below.

The Alternative Dispute Resolution Option

In commercial situations, where parties to a contract are aware of the shortcomings of the judicial system and wish to avoid the system for dealing with contract disputes, they often will agree to alternative dispute resolution (ADR) mechanisms (such as arbitration,) by which the parties select "private judges" to adjudicate and provide resolution to any dispute.[25] They may even agree to dispute resolution according to the laws of a foreign jurisdiction rather than the laws of the country within which the transaction occurs.

ADR can work well where the only interests to be considered are those of the specific parties to the dispute and

- where public policy determinations are not at stake
- where the power of the state in making critical decisions is not at issue
- where the validity of the underlying contract that gave life to the arbitration is not in question[26]
- where there are no constitutional, legal, or political barriers.

Unfortunately for those seeking a "quick fix" to weak, dysfunctional, or even inexperienced courts in regulatory matters, particularly for regulatory appeals, most of these conditions usually are not present.

---

can be quite disruptive to effective regulation, even in those circumstances where the courts are fully functional. Thus, transitional arrangements are always something that might be contemplated in regard to the role of the courts.

25. One must be careful, however, in defining what is meant by ADR. The term has come to mean many things to many people. For purposes of this handbook, the definition is limited to circumstances in which a contractual entity (presumably, although not necessarily, private) is called on or empowered to resolve a dispute or hear an appeal from a regulatory agency. ADR, as defined here, does not include judicial bypass by means of referral to special tribunals or other mechanisms created by law, such as the Competition Commission in the United Kingdom or the regulatory appellate tribunals created in Bolivia, India, and Tanzania. In short, for purposes of this handbook, ADR does not refer to de jure (that is, created by law) tribunals, but only to contractually created ones.

26. In Indonesia, power supply contracts between IPPs and the Perusahaan Listrik Negara (PLN), the state-owned national electric utility, contained provisions calling for arbitration in the case of disputes or alleged default. Some IPPs did allege default by PLN and began arbitration

It is important to note that, in no small measure, regulatory agencies themselves are often created to avoid mechanistic reliance on judicial oversight of contracts and contractual mechanisms. Certainly, over the years, advocates of regulation by contract have been moving toward having contractual disputes concerning the arrangements resolved in the courts. The more prevalent view, however, has been that regulatory or quasi-regulatory agencies be created to enforce regulatory arrangements, whether by contract or by statute, and that they be the initial forum for resolving such disputes over such matters.[27] Where these agencies are created, of course, the question of the forum for hearing appeals from regulatory decisions must still be addressed.

Regulatory disputes, whether they are formal appeals or disputes over tariffs, license conditions or service quality, almost always involve the interests of "nonparties" (for example, third-party beneficiaries, such as consumers). In addition, more often than not, they involve public policy issues well beyond the scope of matters typically addressed in commercial disputes, and inherently address the power of the state (including, but not necessarily limited to, regulatory agencies) to make policy decisions. In consequence, the use of ADR mechanisms, as defined here, to resolve regulatory disputes, particularly ones that are taken to an appeals stage from regulatory decisions, are not likely to be workable.

Apart from such theoretical constraints on bypassing judicial or legally created appellate tribunals, there are practical, realpolitik reasons not to favor such options. They include the difficulty of enforcing ADR decisions in the face of governmental opposition, as well as public resentment that "outsiders" are deciding critical infrastructure matters in a country other than their own (particularly where international arbitration or arbitrators are used, or foreign law is applied, to resolve disputes).

---

proceedings. The legality and enforceability of the arbitration clauses, however, were thrown into considerable legal doubt by Indonesian courts, which found that the validity of the contracts themselves was open to doubt, because of corruption in their formation. Whether the facts supported the finding can be debated, but the legal point is almost universally acceptable: if arbitration is created in contract, then its validity and enforceability is largely dependent on the validity of the underlying contract. A similar court decision in Brazil led to precisely the same result, although the court's reasons for rejecting the arbitration process were not identical.

27. These include concession contract monitoring and enforcement agencies, set up under primary law to handle infrastructure contracts once they are in operation, as well as utility regulatory agencies.

4

In addition, there are basic legal and constitutional questions about using private means to enforce or overrule the otherwise lawful decisions of duly constituted agencies of the state. We note the practical difficulties that have arisen in many countries over trying to enforce regulatory appeals referred to international arbitration and other agencies, including the Hub Valley Project in Pakistan and other power projects in places such as Brazil, Indonesia, and Vietnam.

Legal, constitutional, and other constraints found in many countries also preclude the use of ADR as a mechanism for appealing regulatory decisions. Examples of this include constitutional provisions guaranteeing rights of judicial review, the inability to enforce contracts including arbitration results, refusal to recognize private restrictions on the powers of the state and its agencies, and nonrecognition of various forms of arbitration. (See box 4.5 for a fuller discussion.)

Specialized Tribunals and Expert Advisory Panels

There are two other principal options for developing appeals processes in transitional regulatory systems. Both are consistent with the underlying principles and standards we recommend in chapter 3. Both of these options also provide incentives and pressures to move toward legal arrangements that would support better-practice regulation.

The first option is to statutorily create an independent, specialized tribunal to hear regulatory appeals. The tribunal would be composed of specially trained personnel who would adjudicate regulatory disputes, including appeals from regulatory agencies. The advantage of such a body is that regulatory matters would be channeled to experts, thereby increasing the probability that decisions would be made in a consistent manner with a coherent and discernible pattern. It would be difficult to get such predictability if regulatory appeals were simply turned over to courts of general jurisdiction. The mechanism of a tribunal is also appealing because it can very easily become the permanent forum for adjudicating regulatory disputes. Thus, the transition would be simple in that no major institutional adjustments would be required. Such specialized courts have been created in Australia, Bolivia, India, Tanzania, and the United Kingdom and have been proposed in Brazil and Chile.

The second option would be to allow appeals to be heard in the courts, but to require (or encourage) the courts to use independent advisory panels to assist them in making decisions. These panels would be ad hoc committees or

---

Box 4.5. Regulatory Appeals and Alternative Dispute Resolution—Underlying Legal Problems

Two basic problems are associated with using ADR for appeals of regulatory decisions. The problems arise from the basis of authority of an ADR body. Such authority can be derived from only two sources, statute or contract. From such a statutory perspective, many, if not most, countries will not give private parties (for example, a private arbitration panel) veto powers over a decision of an agency of the state (for example, a regulatory agency). From both legal theory and political perspectives, this is certainly an understandable doctrine. Such considerations, however, generally do not exist for the statutory (or constitutional) creation of a de jure special tribunal to hear such matters. In fact, a regulatory agency itself could be described as such an entity, so an appellate tribunal created in the same way could easily meet these requirements.

Two issues are associated with ADR created through contracts. The first is whether formal, infrastructure regulatory decisionmaking (including hearing appeals of regulatory decisions) is a power that can be delegated at all. The second is whether the legal basis for arbitration (almost always a contract of some form) is lawfully binding. The answer to the first question in most countries is no. Given the public interest and the general impact on society, regulatory matters most often are not delegable by the state to a private party. The answer on the second issue, where the appeal mechanism is contractual, is more complicated. It tends to be very fact specific.

The answer depends on whether the state has the power to contractually bind individual consumers, whether the contract itself is legally binding and enforceable, and, of course, whether the specific details of the contracts are both lawful and enforceable. In short, considerable legal uncertainty shrouds the availability of ADR, as defined in the handbook, to deal with regulatory matters, particularly appeals of regulatory decisions. Moreover, depending on how it is designed, ADR will contribute little or nothing to building the local capacity to handle such matters in the long term.

If ADR is not an option, another approach would be to bypass the judiciary entirely and allow appeals or disputes concerning concession contracts to go to the government. Although this option is workable from a purely functional point of view, it is contrary to the fundamental principles of independent regulation and will almost inevitably politicize the regulatory process and reduce transparency in decisionmaking. It also seems very likely to expand the scope of legal appeals well beyond the scope recommended in chapter 3. Moreover, appeals to the government offer little in the way of facilitating better practice according to the standards set out in chapter 3. Indeed, in many ways, appeals to the government may well sustain undesirable elements of the prereform infrastructure arrangements.

4

individuals who have relevant expertise and no conflicts of interest. They could be either international or local experts, or some combination thereof. Their role, however, would be purely advisory. The final decisionmaking authority would remain with a judge or a panel of judges. Thus, the process would obtain the benefit of independent expertise without any delegation of the power of the state.[28] The arrangement also facilitates the transition be-

---

28. Expert panels also have been proposed to advise or replace decisionmaking by a regulatory entity (that is, first-level regulatory decisions). The pros and cons of such an arrangement are discussed later in the section on regulatory commissions with limited resources.

cause it could easily become permanent or, if not, the judges would gain experience in and knowledge of regulatory matters by working closely with experts.

Whatever option is pursued, evaluators also ought to look at the training that court personnel are receiving in regulatory matters and appeals. Obviously, capacity building is central to the success of regulatory and legal reform. (See appendix A for further discussion of appeal issues and methods that may be useful for transitional and intermediate regulatory frameworks.)

We recommend that whatever appeals mechanisms are put in place be evaluated against the following criteria:

- How well they operate in their own terms (for example, in providing effective, transparent, reasonable, and prompt legal appeals processes).
- The quality and consistency of the decisions made and the criteria on which they are based.
- The degree to which they support efficient economic outcomes (for example, in service quantity and quality, investment, productivity growth, costs, and prices).
- How far the appeal processes established have developed or can be expected to develop into good-practice, long-term, effective, and sustainable legal institutions.

Uncertainty about the Nature and Strength of Regulatory Commitments

Private investors usually have two principal concerns about new regulatory systems: obtaining a clear regulatory commitment from government, and receiving some assurance that the commitment actually will be honored.[29] Even if there is an explicit regulatory agreement, investors often are fearful that governments and regulators will succumb to political or other pressures that will cause them to renege on the commitments contained in the agreements.

Investors' concerns about commitments are greatest when infrastructure industries are only partly or semicommercialized. The problems are most acute when

- overall tariffs do not cover the full costs of supply

---

29. Ranjit Lamech and Kazim Saeed, 2003, "What International Investors Look for When Investing in Developing Countries," Energy and Mining Sector Board Discussion Paper 6, World Bank, Washington, DC, p. 10.

- some consumers (for example, households and small farmers) pay very low prices for their supplies
- the cost of this support is met by cross-subsidies from large customers or, as is most often the case, by implicit subsidies arising from a zero or low allowed rate of return on invested capital.[30]

This is often the case in electricity, but these circumstances are even more common in the water industry and with passenger railway services. In these situations, investors will understandably be very concerned about the commitment of current and, even more so, of *future* governments to commercialization and the likelihood that these regulatory commitments will be honored—particularly in countries where there is a history of failed or stalled previous attempts at commercialization.

There is no easy or obvious answer to ensuring that regulatory commitments will be honored. However, some techniques can increase a government's ability and resolve to make credible commitments and then to comply with these commitments. The common feature of these techniques is that they are designed to raise costs to current or future governments of reneging on regulatory and contractual commitments to investors.

Combinations of Regulatory Agencies with Infrastructure Contracts

The techniques usually involve some *combination of the use of regulatory agencies established under primary law and infrastructure contracts,* sometimes bolstered by external arbitration or guarantees, or both. Infrastructure regulation and contracts can be—and historically have been—combined in various ways. The three main variants usually coincide with the three main stages of regulatory developments described in box 4.4. Variant 1 corresponds to Stage 1, whereas Variants 2 and 3 are alternative design possibilities for Stage 2.

- **Variant 1: Informal Monitoring and Enforcement Procedures**—Infrastructure contracts that include within the contract some regulatory

---

30. The pattern of cross-subsidies and implicit subsidies identified here is prevalent in South Asia, the CIS countries (and to a lesser extent CEE countries), and in many African countries. However, in some Latin American nations, including Brazil, prices are unbalanced because small consumers cross-subsidize large ones.

obligations or review procedures, but do not have a formally designated regulatory agency or some other monitoring and enforcement entity.

- **Variant 2: Semiformal Monitoring and Enforcement Procedures**—Infrastructure contracts that include prespecified tariffs and other regulatory elements fixed for an initial period (such as three to five years); and that are monitored, enforced, reviewed and, for elements other than the prespecified ones, subject to agreed review and modification by an external regulatory or quasi-regulatory agency.

- **Variant 3: Formal Monitoring and Enforcement Procedures and Detailed Prespecification of the Tariff Methodology for an Initial Period**—Infrastructure contracts that are monitored, enforced, reviewed, and sometimes modified by an external regulatory or quasi-regulatory agency; and that include prespecified tariffs and other regulatory elements fixed for an initial period (for example, three to five years).

The infrastructure contracts, which typically are awarded by a government entity, transfer ownership and operational responsibility for providing infrastructure services to some private entity. The contractual vehicle can be a franchise license, a concession agreement, or a combination of the two. The regulatory elements, which may be embedded in this contract or in a separate document, usually establish rules or standards for setting maximum prices and minimum quality-of-service requirements. Particularly in Variant 3, the contract is likely to lay down detailed cost and tariff methodologies, which are fixed for at least the initial period.

A critical issue with all hybrid regulatory and contract arrangements is that what is in the contract must correspond entirely with what is in the legal framework (both primary and derived legislation), regulatory licenses, and so forth. This correspondence includes an alignment of regulatory and legal *processes,* as well as the *substantive content* of the contract and the legislation. There have been cases (such as in Belize and Mali) where serious problems have emerged because of inconsistencies between the contracts and the regulatory legislation.

Infrastructure and regulatory contracts can vary considerably in several key dimensions, including

- Duration of the contracts
- Degree of ownership and control that is transferred
- Degree of specificity for price and quality-of-service regulation

- Processes for modifying the terms of the contracts at the end of a specified period or if certain prespecified events occur
- Extent to which the contracts are legally supported by higher level documents (laws and decrees)
- Extent to which the contracts are supported by an explicit risk mitigation mechanism (for example, a regulatory PRG)
- Whether there is a separate regulatory entity or some other government entity that has the authority to monitor, enforce, and modify the contracts
- Whether this is the same entity that negotiated the original terms and conditions of the contracts
- Provisions for handling disputes.

When there is a high degree of specificity in the regulatory elements of the contracts, the contracts are sometimes referred to as "regulation by contract." The problem with using this term, however, is that it has no generally accepted definition. For example, one definition is "regulation without a regulator." This has recently been proposed in the water industry context by Shugart and Ballance who define it as "a formal agreement between the two parties (rather than being imposed unilaterally by law or by a discretionary regulator) and that the organizations with responsibility for applying or adjudicating the regulatory rules are those typically used for commercial contracts—i.e., courts or arbitrators and do not include a statutory regulator."[31] An alternative definition is "a detailed tariff-setting agreement administered by a separate regulatory entity."[32] Because there is no general agreement on the meaning of the term, we think that it is more productive to describe different combinations of regulation by agency and infrastructure contracts that can be used to strengthen regulatory commitments. The common element in all these arrangements is that the government or regulator has made some regulatory commitments of varying degrees of specificity in a document that has some degree of legal enforceability either in a domestic court or through international arbitration.[33] It is this element of legal enforceability that distinguishes a "contract" from a "promise."

---

31. **Shugart and Ballance** (2005, p. 6).
32. This is the definition by **Bakovic, Tenenbaum, and Woolf** (2003, p. 16) in their analysis of regulatory approaches used in the privatization of electricity distribution.
33. If the regulatory commitments are highly precise and specific, they are sometimes referred to as "low discretion rules" because they have been designed to limit the discretion of the regulator or any other entity that administers the rules.

This does not mean, however, that a regulatory contract is the same as a normal commercial contract. In fact, regulatory contracts differ from commercial contracts in two important respects. First, one of the parties to the contract—the government—will usually be performing two roles. It may be the seller or lessor of existing assets while acting as the initial enforcer of the contract. Second, there are asymmetric rights in the contract. In a normal commercial contract, there is a balance of rights between the two parties, and these rights are specified in the contract. In contrast, a government usually reserves some extra-contractual rights for itself in a regulatory contract. For example, it may reserve the right to early termination, the right to make unilateral amendments to the contract, and the right to prohibit early terminations to the contract by the private party. These are traditional rights that a government reserves for itself when it authorizes a private company to perform a public service. However, if the contract is to be credible to investors, a government must somehow convince potential investors that it will impose restrictions on the ability of future governments to exercise these extra-contractual rights or compensate the private operator for higher costs or lost revenues if the government exercises these reserved rights. Three combinations of institutional and legal options for doing this are discussed below. They correspond to the three stages of regulatory development in the typology discussed in box 4.4.

Variant 1: Informal Monitoring and Enforcement Procedures

In the United States and the United Kingdom, 19th- and early 20th-century railway and other infrastructure industry franchises were awarded for long periods (for example, 21 years) or for indefinite periods. The framework for U.K. railways was initially established through a Private Act of Parliament. In effect, it was a regulatory contract granted by Parliament and enforced through the law courts. These Acts operated like private contracts because they were enforced by regular courts.

Although these arrangements were successful in inducing significant amounts of private investment, they had a number of major disadvantages both in the 19th century and even more strongly in the inflationary periods of 1914–18 and after 1939. The key problems were the following:

- The absence of any periodic regulatory review to realign prices with costs when costs fell because of technical progress or economies of scale (leading to *very* substantial profits by railway companies in the 19th century).

- The inability to impose any general conditions on companies (for example, for consumer services and protection and technical standards) beyond those specified in the original Act.
- The inability to obtain or publish comparable information on costs, prices, investment, financial accounts for different railroads, and so forth.
- The inability to prevent widespread anticompetitive behavior, including massive price discrimination between industrial customers.

Because of these problems, in 1873 the United Kingdom established the Railways and Canal Commission, one of the world's earliest specialist utility regulatory agencies.[34] Similar concerns led to the establishment of canal and railroad regulatory bodies in the United States in the 19th century. In both the United Kingdom and the United States, the national regulatory agencies for railways were established to provide monitoring and enforcement of franchise contracts designed to prevent monopoly abuse and enforce common rules, standards, and practices.[35] The fact that these separate regulatory entities were created in both countries shows that the British Parliament and the U.S. Congress reached the common conclusion that these regulatory activities could be performed more effectively by a separate, specialist regulatory agency than by the legislative body.

In the United Kingdom and the United States, the move away from putting regulatory provisions in "closed" railway franchise contracts *without* a specialist regulator and toward establishing a regulatory agency to monitor, enforce, and review them (some years or even decades later) was followed by similar regulatory arrangements for electricity, natural gas, and urban transport. The common problem that motivated the shift was that it proved extremely difficult, without a separate and ongoing regulatory entity, to find a stable and orderly way of revising these long-term franchise contracts. This

---

34. Some U.S. public utilities commissions were established earlier, such as in Ohio in 1867. Before the Interstate Commerce Commission was established as a national railroad regulator in the United States, some states had public utilities commissions that had tariff-setting authority.
35. See **Stern** (2003) for a discussion of U.K. historical experience, and **Gómez-Ibáñez** (2003) for U.S. experience. Both relate historical experience to recent and current utility industry issues in developing countries.

Box 4.6. Contract Incompleteness

All contracts are inevitably incomplete. It is difficult to specify in advance how to deal with unforeseen and unforeseeable events. No contract can be fully specified even for the present let alone for the next 15–25 years. Economic conditions will change, and unanticipated events will occur. The implication is that there must be provisions for dealing with these unanticipated events either (a) through dispute resolution procedures written into the contract, or (b) through modifications of the contract, or both.

This is a problem that affects all industries where long-term contracts are important. For infrastructure industries, the standard solution to the contract in-

completeness problem is to specify an external regulatory or quasi-regulatory entity (for example, a court, a contract monitoring and enforcement agency, or an international arbitrator) to handle these issues following agreed procedures. This resolves the incompleteness problem and has the major benefit of allowing the writing of much simpler and clearer franchise, concession, or privatization contracts.

Note: Contract incompleteness and its consequences is discussed in detail in Oliver Hart, 1995, *Firms, Contracts and Financial Structures* (Oxford, UK: Oxford University Press). For its implications for infrastructure industries and their regulation, see **Gómez-Ibáñez** (2003) and **Stern** (2003).

---

is because long-term concession contracts are particularly likely to suffer from problems of *contract incompleteness.* In other words, no contract is ever "complete." (See box 4.6.)

The history of the French water industry follows the same general path from fixed contracts treated like any other contract to ones in which, as is now generally the case, the regulatory entity has powers to review and modify the contracts according to clear predetermined criteria. The difference is that it was the Conseil d'Etat, the highest administrative court in France, that has remained in charge of water regulation. In the past, the Conseil d'Etat has functioned as a quasi-regulator or super-regulator.[36] In particular, it has always performed at least one regulatory function: it has resolved disputes between customers (the municipalities) and the suppliers (the private operators). It also is arguable that the Conseil has effectively expanded its regulatory scope because other legal decisions have now indirectly established tariff-setting methods. For example, until the early 1900s, the Conseil's decisions favored fixed price caps that could not be changed during the life of the contracts. However, in the early 1900s, it began to favor the introduction of one or more explicit tariff adjustment mechanisms to reflect major cost changes.[37]

Similar combinations of contracts with regulatory or quasi-regulatory contract oversight and review have been created in Latin America and the

---

36. **Frilet** (2004).
37. **Pezon** (2003).

Caribbean. Within this region, more than 1,000 infrastructure concessions were awarded between 1985 and 2000. Of these contracts, excluding telecoms, more than 40 percent had renegotiations.[38] For water and toll roads in particular, the average time before renegotiation was three years or less. Across all the infrastructure industries considered, however, if there was a pre-existing regulatory entity in place to monitor and enforce the contract (Variant 2), the probability of a company-induced renegotiation was significantly reduced.[39] (See box 4.7.)

The brittleness of long-duration infrastructure contracts without external regulatory support also is shown in the high failure rate of the Asian independent power producer contracts. This was the case even where external guarantees were in place, as in the Indonesian IPP projects supported by the Overseas Private Investment Corporation and the Multilateral Investment Guarantee Agency, and the Hub Valley Project in Pakistan. This suggests that a regulatory guarantee will not be effective if the underlying economics are not viable or if there are strong allegations of corruption.

For these reasons, contracts without external regulatory support are recommended only for countries where the institutional environment or available human and other resources prevent the establishment and operation of some regulatory or quasi-regulatory institution to oversee the regulatory contracts.[40] This may well be the only option realistically available for fragile conflict and post-conflict countries with few functioning institutions (see appendix I). Infrastructure contracts without external regulatory (or quasi-regulatory) support, however, are emphatically not recommended for countries that can sustain some moderate level of institutional regulatory support.

Variant 2: Semiformal Monitoring and Enforcement Procedures

As discussed above, many regulatory agencies in developed countries evolved from concession contract enforcement agencies. Hence, it should not be surprising that this route also has been followed in many developing countries in

38. There were large differences between renegotiations across sectors. For electricity concessions, the incidence of renegotiation was 9.7 percent. For the transportation and water industries, the respective percentages were 54.7 and 74.4 percent.
39. For further details and discussion, see **Guasch** (2004); and J. Luis Guasch, Jean-Jacques Laffont, and Stéphane Straub, 2005, "Concessions of Infrastructure in Latin America: Government-Led Renegotiation," Working Paper, University of Edinburgh, Scotland, p. 28; available at http://www.econ.ed.ac.uk/papers/gov_led_reneg_april05.pdf.
40. This was the situation in Tajikistan. The Tajikistan government's Pamir project involved the awarding of a 25-year concession to a private company to operate a vertically integrated

4

Box 4.7. Renegotiation Rates for Infrastructure Concession Contracts and Regulatory Arrangements

A recent study by **Guasch** (2004) of early company-initiated renegotiation rates for 895 infrastructure transport (mainly toll-roads) and water concession contracts implemented in the 1990s in Latin America and the Caribbean showed that the probability of an early renegotiation was much lower if there was an external regulatory entity and if the regulatory framework existed in a legal document (for example, a law or decree) other than in the concession contract.

Guasch's key findings were the following:

Incidence of renegotiation	%
Regulatory body in existence	17
Regulatory body not in existence	61
Regulatory framework embedded in law	17
Regulatory framework embedded in decree	28
Regulatory framework embedded in concession contract	40

Source: **Guasch** 2004, table 6.15, p. 90.

Using his sample of recent Latin American and Caribbean concession contracts, Guasch estimates that the existence of a regulatory body to monitor, enforce, and modify the concession contracts reduces the expected renegotiation rate by 20–40 percent.

Guasch and his colleagues suggest the benefits of an external regulator are that it

- leads to better-designed contracts (for example, clauses adapted to the type and circumstances

of the specific concession) by encouraging simpler, more transparent contracts with fewer objectives and trade-offs between objectives
- improves the quality of enforcement by enhancing "learning by doing" in contract design, monitoring, enforcement, and operation.[1]

Guasch, Laffont, and Straub (2005) find that, for government-initiated renegotiations, the existence of a regulatory body to monitor, enforce, and modify the concession contracts reduces the expected renegotiation rate by about half the amount estimated for company-initiated renegotiations. They also find evidence that a nonministry regulator had a much larger impact than a ministry regulator, and that a regulatory agency had a larger effect the greater the level of country corruption. Hence, they concluded that "the impact of a regulatory agency is especially important in weak governance environments."[2]

1. J. Luis Guasch, Jean-Jacques Laffont, and Stéphane Straub, 2003, "Renegotiation of Concession Contracts in Latin America," volume 1, Policy Research Working Paper 3011, World Bank, Washington, DC, pp. 21–26; available at http://econ.worldbank.org/files/25200_wps3011.pdf.

2. J. Luis Guasch, Jean-Jacques Laffont, and Stéphane Straub, 2005, "Concessions of Infrastructure in Latin America: Government-Led Renegotiation," Working Paper, University of Edinburgh, Scotland, p. 28; available at http://www.econ.ed.ac.uk/papers/gov_led_reneg_april05.pdf.

power system in one of Tajikistan's poorest regions. The concession, which was awarded by the parliament, was one element of a larger reform package. Because Tajikistan has no separate electricity regulatory commission, it was decided that the concession would be monitored and enforced by the Ministry of Energy. To date, the concession has survived problems involving the mechanism for social protection, billing in the absence of reliable meters, and tariff levels for commercial customers. See Anil Markandya and Raghuveer Sharma, 2003, "Tajikistan: Pamir Private Power Project," Paper presented at the World Bank Shanghai Poverty Conference, December 11, 2003; available at http://www.worldbank.org/wbi/reducing poverty/Cases-SearchThematic.h tml#infr.

recent years. The creation of a separate regulatory or quasi-regulatory entity to monitor and enforce regulatory contracts seems to produce two benefits. First, it appears to lead to a significantly lower incidence of concession contract renegotiation. (See box 4.8.) Second, it facilitates a natural transition to a fully independent regulatory agency possessing regulatory authority (bounded by whatever limits are established in the regulatory contract or other legal documents). (See box 4.8.)

The establishment of a regulatory agency to monitor franchises has been a successful transitional tool in establishing a best-practice regulator in a number of countries. For example, it has been used in a number of successful electricity distribution privatizations in Latin America performed through either asset sales or long-term leases (Chile and Peru). It also has been adopted in Uganda and is now under active consideration in Lesotho. Both of these African examples involve long-term concessions. In both instances, the regulatory commitment will be bolstered by PRGs as a form of "insurance" to back up the specifics of the agreed tariff-setting system. (See the section on external regulatory risk mitigation and World Bank partial risk guarantees for new regulatory systems in this chapter.)

Variant 3: Formal Monitoring and Enforcement Procedures Combined with Detailed Prespecification of Tariff-Setting Formulas for an Initial Period

Under this type of arrangement there is a prespecification, in one or more formal or explicit agreements between investors and the government or regulator, of the formulas that determine the prices that a power enterprise (usually a distribution entity) can charge for the electricity it sells. This formula typically applies for an initial period, for example, three to five years. In electricity, implementation of the formula is almost always performed by a separate regulator.[41] The tariff-setting formula usually is more detailed than in Variants 1 and 2. The specifics of the regulatory agreement may be set out in a concession, a license, a privatization agreement, or other documents. Similar regulatory arrangements have been adopted in the water and

---

41. However, both Ehrhardt (in **Castalia Strategic Advisors** [forthcoming]) and **Shugart and Ballance** (2005) contend that this model of regulation might work best in the water and sanitation sectors without a formal and separate regulatory entity. They are, in effect, arguing for "regulation without a regulator."

4

Box 4.8. The Use of a Regulator to Monitor and Enforce Concession Contracts—The Case of Jamaican Telecoms

The Jamaican telecom industry was run by Cable and Wireless under general regulation until the 1970s when serious regulatory imprudence led Cable and Wireless to hand back its franchise. After failed attempts by the Jamaican government to run the company as a nationalized industry or to bring in alternative operators, Cable and Wireless was given a new license in 1987 to run the company with a guaranteed rate of return of 18 percent on equity in U.S. dollar terms and a guaranteed 25-year monopoly on national fixed-line services and the right of first refusal for other telecom services. (See the classic account by Levy and Spiller [1994]).

Although the license had been negotiated and awarded by the Government of Jamaica, it was monitored and enforced beginning in 1998 by the Jamaican OUR, a multisectoral regulatory authority that also had authority over electricity, water, and some transport industries. Under the leadership of two strong heads, the OUR quickly developed a reputation for effective enforcement of the license and for protecting the rights of Jamaican consumers. It also was able to build up its regulatory expertise through the exercise of its monitoring and enforcement roles. In consequence—and because of other changes, such as the Jamaican adoption of the 1998 World Trade Organization telecom provisions—the Jamaican Telecommunications Act of 2000 was passed, which established the OUR as a fully fledged telecom regulator similar to the U.K. Office of Telecommunications (Oftel) model. New legislation gave it decisionmaking powers—for example, for imposing tariffs and interconnection charges, and for issuing, monitoring, and enforcing licenses—as well as the authority to carry out and implement regulatory reviews with full regulatory autonomy as specified in primary law.

This increase in the OUR's regulatory powers was accepted by all parties, including Cable and Wireless and new entrant companies, as part of an overall reform package that included phased liberalization and the introduction of competition much earlier than written into the 1987 concession contract. Although this expansion of the OUR's authority from a monitoring and enforcement entity to a regulatory entity with full and final decisionmaking authority may not have been planned in advance, it does illustrate that governments and other parties can become more comfortable with transferring full regulatory authority to an independent regulatory body after they have seen it operate effectively in a lesser mode. It appears that the OUR's early years provided a helpful and comfortable transition for all parties. In particular, it seems clear that the Government of Jamaica felt much less exposed than if the OUR had been set up initially as a fully independent regulator. This suggests that, for some countries, the path for moving from an "advisory regulator" with strong publication duties on regulator and government to an independent regulator with full and final decisionmaking authority can be a successful process.

For an account of the post-1997 changes, see Martin Lodge and Lindsay Stirton, 2002, "Regulatory Reform in Small Developing States: Globalisation, Regulatory Autonomy and Jamaican Telecommunications," *New Political Economy* 7 (3): 415–33.

---

sanitation sectors. As with any regulatory agreement, it will not survive, no matter how sophisticated or detailed it might be, if the underlying economics do not compute (that is, if tariff revenues and external subsidies do not cover costs). Because the use of Variant 3 has become widespread in many developing countries, it would be useful to take a closer look at how the variant has been designed and implemented.

What Is Prespecified?

In developing countries, the use of such arrangements does *not* mean that the actual electricity distribution (or water distribution) prices are prespecified during the initial period. Instead, what is prespecified is the tariff-setting method (usually some combination of indexing, automatic pass-through, or benchmarking) for individual cost elements that together determine the overall tariff level. Typically, the tariff-setting method will be specified on a multiyear basis for a given number of years and will include benchmarks or targets for controllable costs and automatic pass-through for noncontrollable costs.

In addition, the formal or explicit agreement may specify minimum quality-of-service standards and targets for connection of new customers, as well as any commitments to provide general subsidies for a transition period or targeted subsidies for the performance of specific tasks. In effect, the explicit agreement represents an attempt to prespecify and precommit the government and regulator to the key elements of the tariff-setting, quality-of-service, and subsidy systems, at least for an initial period.

Role of the Regulator

These arrangements seem to work better where a regulatory agency or similar entity is in place that can monitor the arrangements and recommend or take remedial action if that becomes necessary. Ideally, the regulator also should be heavily involved in drawing up the specifics of the regulatory contract because the regulator is likely to be more sensitive to implementation problems.[42]

A key characteristic of Variant 3 is that the regulator's discretion on the crucially sensitive issue of price setting is constrained for an initial period by an explicit agreement involving the government and the regulated companies.[43] Therefore, the regulator is more of an implementer than a designer of the tariff-setting system. The hope is that the regulatory agency will use the transition period to build up its regulatory resources and experience so that there can be a successful transition to another regulatory system in which it has more decisionmaking discretion. Ideally, this transitional arrangement

---

42. However, this obviously will not work if the regulator is opposed to private sector participation or did not exist when the private sector participations were being drawn up.

43. Under this arrangement, the regulator's role in the first period is limited "to making certain that the tariff formula . . . is correctly applied and the true-ups and pre-scheduled tariff adjustments are processed in a timely way." **Bakovic, Tenenbaum, and Woolf** (2003, p. 72).

should help speed up the inflow of local and foreign private funds for maintenance and investment.

The End of the Transition Period

The most difficult issues seem to be how and when to move from a contractually fixed basis for service supply to a more flexible regulated regime, and whether there can be a prespecified transition arrangement rather than some ad hoc, regime-shift break. These are particularly difficult issues for privatization contracts, such as the 2003 Delhi electricity privatization in which the contract terms for tariff setting were laid down for an initial period of five years or so, but were largely silent about what happens at the end of that time. Because of this deficiency, after the initial five-year period some observers noted that there was a risk of falling off a "regulatory cliff."[44]

A similar situation existed in Brazil. Most of the concession agreements for new privately operated distribution companies contained a general reference to "repositioning" tariffs at the end of the first tariff period. The guidance on what repositioning meant typically was limited to a single vague sentence stating that the regulator

> ... shall process the revision of the amounts of rates for commercialization of power, altering them upwards or downwards, taking into account the cost of and market structures of the Concessionnaire, the levels of rates charged by similar companies in the nationwide and international context, [and the] stimuli for efficiency and for reasonableness of rates.[45]

The vagueness of the guidance for subsequent tariff-setting periods led to major controversies at the end of the first tariff-setting periods in Brazil. In contrast, other Latin American countries, which had prespecified key elements of the tariff-setting methodology for subsequent tariff periods in their primary or secondary legislation, have had much easier transitions at the end of their initial tariff-setting periods. Although there have been disagreements in these other countries between the private companies and regulators in subsequent tariff-setting periods, the disagreements have been over the specific values rather than over the methodology itself.

---

44. **Agarwal, Alexander, and Tenenbaum** (2003).
45. As quoted in **Bakovic, Tenenbaum, and Woolf** (2003, p. 25).

Prerequisites for Success

Fixed regulatory commitments in the form of concession or license agreements (with or without an external monitoring or enforcement agency) have been widely used throughout the world, particularly for privatization or long-term leasing of electricity distribution systems.[46] However, the mere fact that a tariff-setting system is written down in considerable detail in some document issued by a government ministry or regulator is, by itself, no guarantee that the terms and conditions will be implemented as written.

The regulatory framework is most likely to be successful if accompanied by the following:

- An economically coherent and viable plan within which the tariff-setting system is set up.
- A subsidy mechanism in cases where tariffs need to be raised to commercial levels (or where there is substantial undercollection of bills).[47]
- A politically palatable arrangement established with full, explicit agreement with the relevant governmental institutions, preferably after widespread consultation.
- An effective dispute resolution process (which may be contracted out).
- Possibly a regulatory PRG.

Evaluating Regulatory Systems That Combine
Regulatory and Contractual Arrangements

As noted above, the specific elements for these three regulatory systems can differ widely. Therefore, in any mid-level or in-depth regulatory evaluation, it is not enough to say that there is a "regulatory contract" because the term can mean many different things. The evaluator must clearly describe the specifics of the regulatory contract in the evaluation. In particular, the evaluator must determine the following:

- Who established the agreement within the government (for example, a ministry, the parliament, or the regulator)?

---

46. A detailed discussion of the specifics of such regulatory contracts for electricity privatizations can be found in **Bakovic, Tenenbaum, and Woolf** (2003).

47. For example, this is a key element of the actual or planned concession agreements in Lesotho, Tajikistan, and Uganda. It also was proposed recently by the Government of India in a proposal to create a "viability gap fund" that would be a backstop to a multibillion-dollar program to encourage private investment in rural infrastructure. See "World Bank to Support Rural Infrastructure in India," World Bank Press Release, August 20, 2005.

- What is its duration?
- What is its level of specificity on key tariff elements (for example, regulatory asset base, pass-through of power purchase costs, extent of benchmarking) in the initial and later tariff-setting periods?
- Is the agreement tied to the provision of subsidies by the government or some other entity? If subsidies are not provided as promised, is the operator relieved of any regulatory obligation?
- If there is a regulator or contract monitoring and enforcement entity, how much discretion does this entity have in implementing key tariff elements in the initial and later tariff-setting periods?
- How are key risks shared among the operator, the government, and the customers?
- What is the level of the government's formal legal commitment?
- Is the agreement legally enforceable? If so, where and how? Is the government or regulator liable for any penalties if either one fails to honor the agreement?
- How much discretion, if any, does the regulator have to change the terms of the agreement? If the regulator has such discretion, what constraints are there on exercising it?

Each of the above combinations of discretion and contracts has advantages and disadvantages both in theory and in practice. Different methods (and variants) will be more appropriate in some countries than others, given the legal, political, human resource, financial, and other constraints. For the evaluator, the important questions to ask about the overall regulatory arrangements are as follows:

- Is the chosen method well suited to the country in question and its electricity (or other infrastructure industry) sector?
- Has it worked smoothly in terms of sustainability and readily resolved conflicts?
- Has it produced real economic benefits in service quantity and quality, investment, productivity growth, costs, and prices?
- Has it helped foster a commercially viable industry?
- Has it enabled and encouraged progress toward best-practice regulation and industry reform?
- What type of sector outcomes have occurred? Are they consistent with outcomes that the government is seeking (for example, increased access rates, investment, and reduction in budget subsidies)?

External Regulatory Risk Mitigation and World Bank Partial Risk Guarantees for New Regulatory Systems

None of the combinations of regulation and contracts described in the previous section will be of much value unless the investors have good reason to believe that the contracts will be honored. Increasingly, private investors in infrastructure have been asking for an extra-contractual mechanism that will bolster the commitments of governments to honor the contracts that they have signed. As a consequence, more attention is now being paid to develop what is broadly described as risk mitigation mechanisms. They are typically one or more mechanisms involving either insurance or international arbitration and dispute resolution. (See box 4.9.)

oped, PRGs for regulatory systems have received considerable attention. Regulatory PRGs are a relatively new phenomenon. The essence of a regulatory PRG is to provide private investors with explicit financial compensation

4

Box 4.9. External Regulatory Risk Mitigation Methods and Partial Risk Guarantees

Most market or international financial institution external regulatory risk mitigation techniques, including World Bank PRGs, provide lenders and/or investing companies with insurance or other protection against prespecified events. One exception that, at least in principle, can provide more comprehensive protection is the use of bilateral investment treaties (BITs).

A BIT is a treaty between two countries intended to provide for investors in the two countries with protection against unreasonable behavior by governments and other public agencies against investments made by investors of the other country. Because BITs are voluntary agreements, decisions by infrastructure regulators are frequently excluded from their remit. However, regulatory decisions are sometimes covered. Hence, in 2005 the risk insurers who provided political risk insurance for the Dahbol project in India were able to obtain compensation under the India-Mauritius BIT for the regulatory abuses of the Maharashtra State authorities. They were able to do this because the project company was registered in

Mauritius. However, BITs vary as to whether they provide protection against the actions of third-party regulatory and quasi-regulatory agencies. The Dahbol case seems to be the first in which investors were able successfully to use a BIT for compensation against infrastructure regulatory risk. Other attempts to use BITs for protection against regulatory risk have been unsuccessful in providing effective legal redress (for example, in a Bolivian water case that was discussed in the *Financial Times*; July 26, 2005).

Other external risk mitigation methods include the following:

- Comprehensive credit insurance—only applicable to lenders, not to equity holders or investors.
- Denial of justice cover—which like BITs can have serious enforcement issues when used in international courts.
- On-demand guarantees.
- Self-insurance—by big companies with many projects.
- The use of local currency financing.

---

if a government fails to live up to a specified regulatory commitment that has been guaranteed.

PRGs issued by the World Bank (and other international financial institutions [IFIs]) have an extra force that other risk mitigation methods do not have. Reneging on a PRG agreement with an IFI is likely to have much more far-reaching consequences for the country than reneging on a private concession contract with private political risk insurance or refusing to implement an international arbitration decision. It is the requirement that the country government provide a counterguarantee to the World Bank or other provider that gives the PRG its force.

At the time of writing (September 2005), World Bank PRGs have been agreed and concluded in two countries: Romania and Uganda (see box 4.10). The PRGs provide private investors with explicit financial compensation if a government fails to live up to a specified regulatory commitment that has been guaranteed. Equally important, it serves as a mechanism to make governments and regulators think twice about reneging on regulatory commitments.

What Are They?

PRGs for regulatory systems are a form of insurance against defined regulatory risks. Specifically, they are designed to pay an investor some quantity of money if the investor can demonstrate that the regulator or its government failed to comply with the pre-established regulatory framework, especially with respect to tariff setting. If the investor can show noncompliance, the World Bank (or some other financial institution) will make a payment to the investor. However, the PRG is structured so that the government must then reimburse the World Bank for any payouts that it makes to the investor. This counterguarantee is intended to provide an incentive for the regulator and government to live up to the terms of the regulatory framework.

The PRG concept is designed to be flexible. It can provide insurance regardless of whether the specifics of the regulatory system are embedded in a concession, a license, a government support agreement, or in some combination of these instruments.[48] It can provide support both for debt financed on specific projects or for the initial years of a privatization or long lease.

---

48. Moreover, PRGs need not be limited to guaranteeing the performance of regulatory systems. For example, they also have been used to guarantee that governments pay their electricity bills. In the future, it is conceivable that PRGs could be used to guarantee delivery of promised subsidy payments.

A particular strength of World Bank PRGs is that the investor receives a prompt payout if there is a demonstrable infringement by the country government or infrastructure regulator. The payment is not delayed to the end

---

Box 4.10. The First Two PRGs

Uganda

The first application of a World Bank PRG for a utility regulatory system was approved for a new 20-year electricity distribution concession in Uganda in 2004. The lessor is the Uganda Electricity Distribution Company, a government-owned company, and the lessee or investor is Umeme, a joint venture between Globeleq and Eskom of South Africa. The transaction was completed on March 1, 2005. The PRG was designed to protect the investors against the regulator's making decisions that do not comply with the tariff-setting provisions in the concession agreement.

The PRG is for a relatively modest amount (US$5 million) and is limited in time to the first regulatory review period of seven years. It insures for potential loss of regulated revenues resulting from a "guaranteed event" according to a predefined loss-of-revenue formula. The PRG specifically covers noncompliance by the regulator with the previously agreed tariff framework, full pass-through of the bulk electricity tariff supply from the Uganda Electricity Transmission Company (the state-owned transmission and bulk supplier company), and timely adjustments of tariffs (that is, within 45 days of submission).[1] The PRG also provides for provisional payments pending resolution of a dispute.

Romania

The PRG was used to facilitate the privatization of Electrica Banat and Electrica Dobrogea, the first two of eight planned electricity distribution privatizations. Enel, the Italian energy company, purchased 51 percent of the equity shares of the two companies. The PRG, which was approved by the World Bank in December 2004, provides a five-year guarantee to Enel for the recovery of revenues in case of a loss of regulated revenue caused by the failure of the Romanian Energy Regulatory Authority (ANRE) to implement the

agreed regulatory framework *or* revocation or modification of the framework by ANRE or the government.

If the guarantee is triggered, the World Bank has agreed to pay up to 60 million euros, or about 15 percent of the expected total annual revenues of 416 million euros. The World Bank, in turn, has required a counterguarantee from the Romanian government so the Bank will be reimbursed for any payments it makes. By agreeing to the counterguarantee, the Government of Romania has, in effect, purchased insurance that covers its own future behavior, as well as the actions of the regulator.

The regulatory framework initially was presented in a white paper issued by ANRE that described in detail how it would regulate tariffs, investments, and quality of service for the two distribution companies. The white paper was later formalized in an order that ANRE issued prior to the privatization. Even though ANRE negotiated the details of the regulatory framework with Enel, ANRE is not a legal party to the PRG. Moreover, ANRE's commitment to the specified regulatory framework is unilateral because ANRE's commitment exists in one of its orders and not in some separate "contract" with Enel or the Government of Romania. Even though ANRE has unilaterally committed to implementing all elements of the regulatory framework in its order, ANRE, like most regulatory commissions, does not have the legal ability to force future commissions to honor this commitment. So there is always a risk that a future ANRE could change its mind about the reasonableness of one or more elements of the regulatory framework.

1. The PRG also provides insurance for other nonregulatory events, such as nonpayment of electricity bills by agencies of the Government of Uganda and termination payments for undepreciated investments triggered by an early termination of the concession by the investor because of a breach of the concession agreement by the government.

4

of potentially long legal or arbitration processes. This liquidity support is greatly valued by investors.

Who Benefits?

The principal motivation for regulatory PRGs is to give comfort to investors that whatever regulatory commitments the government or regulator may have made will actually be honored. Or, in the words of one investor, "We need some assurance that the regulatory commitments are worth more than the paper that they are printed on." While regulatory PRGs are of obvious direct immediate benefit to investors, they also can benefit consumers in two ways:

1. *Regulatory PRGs may help consummate transactions that otherwise would not have occurred.* This will benefit consumers if the transaction leads to better service or to the establishment of service where no service is currently provided.
2. *They will lower investors' perceptions of country and regulatory risk.* This, in turn, should lower investors' required cost of capital, which leads to lower cost of supply, and ultimately to lower tariffs for consumers.

With respect to the second benefit, a high-level Romanian government official estimated that his country's use of PRGs for its first two disco privatizations (described above) will produce tariff savings over time of approximately US$200 million for customers of these two discos and customers of other discos that are expected to be privatized in subsequent rounds.[49] The savings result from investors' willingness to accept a lower return on their investments because of lower perceived country risks.

General Observations on PRGs

Because the first PRGs have been issued only recently, it is too early to judge their long-term effectiveness. Nevertheless, some general observations can be made even at this early stage in their development. First, PRGs will not work unless the underlying economics of the transaction make sense. This is another way of saying that the numbers have to add up. A PRG is not worth

---

49. See Dorin Mucea (2005), "Persuading the Investors That the Romanian Energy Sector Is Reliable, Stable, Predictable, and Transparent," Presentation at World Bank Energy Week 2005. Available at www.worldbank.org/energy/energyweek).

pursuing unless the combination of tariff revenues and subsidies can be expected to cover investors' and lenders' costs, including a normal rate of return. Neither a PRG nor any other regulatory risk mitigation method can turn loss-making projects into profitable ones. However, where a PRG reduces the required loan rates, it may make low-return or marginal projects commercially viable.

Second, a PRG can work with different forms of private sector participation. The Romanian privatization is based on a full asset sale (that is, a full transfer of ownership). In contrast, the Ugandan transaction is a long-term lease with the government still retaining ownership of the distribution entities' assets that existed at the time of the transfer.

Third, a PRG will be feasible only if it is accompanied by a fairly detailed tariff-setting system. No insurer, whether it is the World Bank or some other financial institution, will be willing to provide insurance unless the nature of the insurable event is reasonably clear. Not all tariff-setting systems can satisfy this standard. For example, it is unlikely that the World Bank or any other potential insurer would be willing to insure a tariff-setting system like the U.S. system where the only legal requirement is typically a general statement that tariffs must be "just and reasonable and not unduly discriminatory." Although there is a regulatory commitment to a principle in the United States (and the principle has been made more specific by various court decisions), the principle is still very general and not likely to be insurable.[50]

This does not mean that everything must be prespecifed and that all regulatory discretion must be eliminated. For example, even after the Romanian Energy Regulatory Authority (ANRE) tariff order was issued, there have been ongoing disputes between ANRE and Enel, an Italian energy company, over implementation of certain elements of the tariff formula. There is always fuzziness around the edges of words, and not all issues or events can be anticipated.[51] The success of the regulatory system ultimately will depend on the willingness of the parties to negotiate their disagreements, and if they fail to reach agreement, on the existence of a dispute resolution mechanism that can render a quick decision. Without an efficient dispute resolution system, the PRG is not likely to be effective.

---

50. See **Shugart and Ballance** (2005) for a good discussion of "precise rules" versus "general principles" in regulatory contracts.

51. In the economics literature, this is referred to as "bounded rationality." See box 4.6 for a description of incomplete contracts.

PRGs, like all external insurance and comprehensive risk mitigation techniques, must be carefully drafted and administered in order to offset the moral hazard implicit in them. Insured companies may find loosely drafted or administered PRGs convenient mechanisms for avoiding the risks justifiably associated with their own violation of relevant rules and regulations. PRGs should be carefully constructed to protect investors against arbitrary, unjustifiable, or unlawful regulatory actions, but never to insure investors against their own foibles or transgressions.

Fourth, the PRG need not cover all revenues for all time. For example, the World Bank–provided PRG in Romania will cover about 15 percent of total revenues for the first five years. The Ugandan PRG covers an even smaller percentage of revenues. Although the financial coverage is limited, the PRG creates incentives to comply because noncompliance has reputational consequences.[52]

Fifth, PRGs are more likely to work if the insurer is an IFI like the World Bank. Although the PRG is a specific and self-contained form of insurance, it is important to remember that the insurer, the World Bank, will usually have a multifaceted relationship with any country using the PRG. For example, the Bank probably will be providing loans and grants in other sectors of the country. Obviously, a country will not want to take actions that would jeopardize its relationship with the World Bank. This gives a World Bank PRG much more force than insurance against regulatory event risks arranged from, say, private markets.

Overall, PRGs can provide strong incentives for countries to maintain their regulatory commitments. They represent a new and promising method for providing regulatory risk mitigation. It is likely that we will see the development of various other event-based and more comprehensive methods of risk mitigation, perhaps including more coverage of regulation in bilateral investment treaties. Such mechanisms should not be viewed as magic bullets. They raise the costs of reneging but, as has been experienced with similar schemes before, they can only reduce rather than eliminate the likelihood of breakdown (for example, Moldova electricity distribution and the Pakistan Hub Valley IPP). Finally, they will not be workable unless the regulatory system being insured offers the potential for commercial viability. If

---

52. Arguably, this would be an important consideration for Romania, which would not want to take any action that would jeopardize its chances of becoming a member of the EU.

the basic numbers do not work, neither a PRG nor any other risk mitigation tool can provide a solution.[53]

In evaluating PRGs and other risk mitigation methods, the evaluator should consider the following:

- The coherence and clarity of the arrangements.
- How successfully they have operated (for example, in terms of sustainability, readily resolved conflicts, and continued operation and investment by private investors).
- The impact on decisions and economic outcomes (including service quantity and quality, productivity growth, costs, and prices, as well as maintenance and investment levels).
- The extent to which they have helped foster a commercially viable industry.
- The extent to which they have enabled and encouraged progress toward the establishment of best-practice regulation and the development of a reputation for effective regulation.

Limited Regulatory Capability

The problem of limited regulatory capabilities in newly established regulators is frequently mentioned in the discussion of the difficulties that arise with new regulatory regimes, particularly in low-income countries with small numbers of experienced professionals. In this section, we discuss two potential solutions that have received much attention: first, the contracting out of regulatory work and, second, the use of expert panels.

Contracting Out

In the process of commercializing their electricity and other infrastructure sectors, many countries have created small regulatory agencies with very limited resources, little or no experience in performing regulatory functions, and difficulty in attracting and retaining competent staff. Many of these new

---

53. Mechanisms to mitigate regulatory risk in private infrastructure investment are the subject of an ongoing Public-Private Infrastructure Advisory Facility study being conducted by the World Bank's Infrastructure Economics and Finance group. Reports should be available in 2006.

regulatory entities have realized quickly that they will not be able to operate as fully functioning regulatory entities, especially in their early years. Given their inability to perform many basic regulatory functions, some of these new entities have chosen to contract out some or all of the work that would otherwise be done by the agency staff. *Contracting out* has been defined as

> [T]he use by a regulator or an external contractor, instead of its own employees to perform certain function(s). Such external contractors can be consultants, individuals, other government entities (in country or outside, including at a regional level) or NGOs.[54] Contributions by external contractors can either be solely advisory in nature or binding on the ultimate regulatory decision. The overall exercise of functions, however, usually continues to be the ultimate responsibility of the regulator, who is accountable to taxpayers for the role conferred to it by the relevant statute(s).[55]

Contracting out has a number of potential advantages for new regulatory agencies. The four most important potential benefits relate to competency, independence, legitimacy, and cost reductions. Contracting out can help increase competency by helping agencies respond to variable workloads and changing market structures, by drawing on specialized skills only when needed, and by getting access to international experience in specialized areas. Contracting out can improve independence by enabling the regulatory agency to benefit from the reputation of an external consultant and by providing more control over the quality of the work especially in countries where civil service rules establish major constraints on hiring. Contracting out also may improve the legitimacy of a fledgling regulatory agency because the work of an outside consultant often will be perceived as more credible, especially if the work is performed in an open and transparent manner. Fi-

---

54. The possibility of contracting out some regulatory functions, either on an advisory or binding basis, was suggested as a transitional regulatory arrangement at a recent all-Africa conference on private participation in infrastructure. The French aid agency, Agence Française de Développement, commissioned a feasibility study to examine how to create a regional regulatory body for electricity in West Africa that could provide an expert panel service. See "Towards Growth and Poverty Reduction: Lessons from Private Participation in Infrastructure (PPI) in Sub-Saharan Africa," Cape Town, South Africa, June 6–7, 2005.

55. **Trémolet, Shukla, and Venton** (2004, p. i). Our discussion draws heavily on their work

nally, contracting out may be able to accomplish a regulatory task at lower cost and higher quality than if it were performed internally. These are *potential* benefits. There is no guarantee that they actually will be achieved.

The single most comprehensive study of developing countries' new infrastructure regulatory agencies' actual experience with contracting out was performed by Sophie Trémolet and colleagues in 2003 and published in 2004. Using a questionnaire, they found that contracting out is a relatively common phenomenon for new regulatory agencies. More than 75 percent of the agencies that answered the questionnaire engaged in some form of it.[56] In the majority of cases, the contracting out involved international consultants. More than 60 percent of the respondents rated their experience as "good." About a third of the respondents devoted more than 20 percent of their budgets to contracting out for external expertise. Contracting out was used for tasks relating to tariff reviews, monitoring compliance, legal opinions, and dispute resolution.

Observations on Contracting Out

Although contracting out has been used widely by new and existing regulatory agencies, it does raise a number of concerns.[57] Among the most important concerns are the following:

- *Difficulty in implementation.* New regulatory agencies reported a number of problems in trying to implement contracting out. The most commonly mentioned problems were budget constraints, lack of appropriate consultants (that is, the supply of qualified consultants was not extensive), and difficulty in specifying the elements of the contract and then in monitoring performance.

  The first problem—budget constraints—is also an issue for regulatory agencies in developed countries. In the United States, state regulators sometimes are able to avoid budgetary constraints by contracting out certain regulatory activities that the regulated companies

---

56. Trémolet and her colleagues received responses from 51 regulatory agencies for a response rate of 38 percent.
57. For example, in the United States, the Federal Energy Regulatory Commission contracts out market monitoring, and in the United Kingdom, Ofgem and Ofwat (the electricity and water regulators) always contract out a significant amount of work during the price reviews that occur every five years.

want done. They do this by having the companies pay for consultants selected and supervised by the regulatory agency. This is clearly not something one would recommend in general. Regulatory agencies, like regulated companies and governments. should have clearly defined and binding budgets, if at all possible. In some circumstances, however, arrangements of this type can be a useful safety valve for special projects or determinations that clearly benefit only one particular enterprise.

The second problem—specifying the task to the contracted experts—reflects the reality that new regulatory agencies, with limited or no experience with regulation, may have considerable difficulty even in specifying the tasks that need to be performed on their behalf. Therefore, it is not uncommon for the terms of reference (TOR) for the contracting out to be written by specialists at donor agencies or by consultants who are hired to write the TOR. It is clearly not the best solution, but it is one that moves an agency forward at least during a transition.

- *Delays in the creation of in-house capabilities.* The concern here is that the agency will never become a fully functioning regulatory entity if it makes extensive use of outside consultants. However, the importance of this concern depends very much on the set of functions that the agency believes it eventually must perform in-house.

    Significant differences are observed across countries. In the United States, most state regulatory agencies have staff members who conduct detailed cost-of-service studies that are used in setting the retail tariffs for end-use customers. In contrast, Peru and several other Latin American countries have consciously avoided developing this internal capability. When a new tariff study is needed (typically at five-year intervals), the role of the regulatory commission staff within these countries is limited to preparing a TOR that specifies methodology and important assumptions for the studies that will be performed by consultants to the commission and regulated companies. In other words, there is no expectation or plan for tariff studies to be performed by the commission itself. At most, the commission staff's role is limited to preparing the TOR and then advising the commission in deciding on the merits of the competing tariff proposals presented in different studies.

- *Controversy if the contracting out produces binding regulatory decisions.* Although most contracting out is advisory in nature, Trémolet and her colleagues found that about 14 percent of contracting out is binding (that is, legally enforceable) in nature. This included binding decisions on payments to a regulated water company in Gaza based on its success or failure to meet quality-of-service standards and binding decisions of an arbitration panel in Chile on water tariff disputes.

Expert Panels

Recently, two groups of well-known regulatory consultants recommended a more radical form of contracting out.[58] Their recommendation was to create independent, nongovernmental expert panels to make binding tariff decisions in the water and sanitation sectors of many developing countries.[59] The decisions of such panels either would be binding on the regulatory commission or, in the extreme, might eliminate the need for any separate regulatory entity at all (that is, the panel would become the de facto regulator).

Shugart and Ballance (2005) argue that expert panels are needed because it is unrealistic to expect that fully functioned, "conventional utility regulators" could become immediately operational in many developing countries. In addition, they conclude that the need for "periodic comprehensive price reviews" makes it infeasible to rely just on "simple regulation by contract." Their solution is to combine an expert panel and a detailed, prespecified tariff-setting agreement that is part of the license or concession. Essentially, the panels would be used to replace the regulator at the time of periodic tariff review. The rationale is to create a regulatory system of "constrained discretion." Shugart and Ballance recommend this because infrastructure sectors in general and the water sector in particular have enormous investment needs. Hence, "enhancing regulatory certainty is more important than introducing a high degree of discretion."[60] Shugart and Ballance also suggest that this might be a permanent arrangement rather than just a transition mechanism.

---

58. See **Castalia Strategic Advisors** (2004) and **Shugart and Ballance** (2005).
59. Expert panels have been used in more limited ways. For example, expert panels are used in Chile as an appeals body to adjudicate disputes over regulatory decisions. In Romania, an expert panel has provided advisory decisions on tariff adjustments and binding decisions on quality-of-service obligations and performance. See **Shugart and Ballance** (2005). Throughout the world, panels have been used frequently for dispute resolution, arbitration, and appeals.
60. **Shugart and Ballance** (2005, p. 28).

Because the Shugart and Ballance proposal represents a more radical form of contracting out, it is useful to describe their proposal in more detail. Its key elements are as follows:

- *A multidisciplinary three-person panel.* The panel would consist of experts in the fields of economic regulation, technical operation of the entity that is being regulated, financial modeling, and regulatory accounting systems. An independent appointing authority would prepare a short list from which the parties would select the three members of the panel (chair, technical member, and financial member).

- *A standing or ad hoc panel.* The expert panel could operate as either a standing or an ad hoc (that is, called into existence on an as-needed basis) panel. The advantage of a standing panel is that it could be convened more quickly, would be more familiar with the regulated entity, and would bring greater consistency to its decisions. The disadvantage is cost. Shugart and Ballance estimate that a panel of three experts who are on retainer for two days per month would have an annual cost of US$172,800.[61] The cost per decision could be reduced if the overall cost of the panel is shared across a number of regulated enterprises. This would increase the overall cost of the expert panel, but would probably reduce the per-unit cost of individual decisions.

- *Narrower responsibilities than a conventional regulatory entity.* The principal task of the expert panel is to produce estimates of reasonable future costs of the regulated company upon which tariffs will be based. This inevitably requires discretion, but the discretion is more of a technical than a policy nature. The policy decisions (for example, on service-quality levels, how to share efficiency gains between consumers and the regulated enterprise, and what kinds of embedded costs should be accepted because they are locked in by previous government or regulatory decisions) still would be made by the government or the regulator.

- *Binding decisions with limited review by a national or international adjudicator.* The expert panel's decisions would not be reviewed de novo if appealed. Instead, any review of a panel decision by a national or international arbitration panel would be limited to whether there was a serious error of law, whether no reasonable person having the requisite expertise could have reached the panel's decision given the infor-

---

61. This assumes that each panel member is paid the daily rate for consultants hired by the International Centre for the Settlement of Investment Disputes: US$2,400.

mation that was available to it, or whether there had been gross non-compliance with procedural rules.

The Shugart and Ballance proposal raises a number of concerns. Some major concerns and possible solutions are as follows:[62]

- *Expert panels would hinder the development of regulatory entities.* One major concern is that the regulator will never "grow up" if tariff-setting and other key regulatory tasks continue to be performed by an outside expert panel. The underlying argument is that the regulatory entity needs hands-on experience in performing these functions. It will never acquire this experience if an expert panel is always performing these functions as a shadow or substitute regulator.

    The underlying presumption is that the regulator is not really a regulator unless it is capable of performing the detailed work of calculating costs and then setting tariffs. The experience of some new Latin American regulators, however, suggests a different possible end point. As discussed earlier, many of these Latin American regulators have no stated plans to develop in-house capability to calculate efficient costs and the tariffs based on these costs. Instead, their steady-state goal is limited to creating sufficient internal staff capability to give guidelines on the general tariff-setting approach and to specify certain important assumptions to be used in cost and tariff calculations rather than trying to perform the calculations themselves. Because these Latin American regulators envision (or have been assigned) a more limited role, outside consultants, whether constituted as an expert panel or in some other form, will be an ongoing necessity rather than simply a transitional mechanism.

- *Most governments and regulators would be deeply reluctant to cede binding decisions over tariffs to a nongovernmental expert panel.* Shugart and Ballance emphasize the importance of giving binding authority over tariff-setting to the expert panel. Many would argue that this is impossible in most countries because binding tariff setting is too politically sensitive to be handed over to a group of experts outside the government. The political sensitivity will be even greater if one or more members of the panel are noncitizens.

---

62. The Shugart and Ballance proposal was the subject of a one-month online discussion on the World Bank's Rapid Response Web site. To read this discussion, see http://rru.world bank.org/Discussions/Topics/Top ic66.aspx.

These political concerns are understandable and cannot be ignored. However, they probably can be addressed with hybrid arrangements that are between the two extreme options of full binding authority and nonpublic advice. For example, one option between the two extremes would be to specify that final decisionmaking authority over tariffs remains with the government or regulator, but to require that the expert panel's recommendations be given publicly and, if the government or regulator rejects some or all of the panel's recommendations, that it give a public explanation of why it disagrees.[63]

Another option would be to offer the advisory expert panel as a service of a regional regulatory body or some other regional economic entity if a regional regulatory body does not exist. This has been discussed in Africa. It has been observed that the political acceptability of such an arrangement would be greater, especially if one or two members of the panel are ex-African regulators or utility operators. Such an arrangement would have the additional advantage of providing a natural vehicle for spreading the fixed costs among several countries. Some countries (for example, Belize and Honduras) have used international expert review as an appeal method against regulatory decisions. For Belize, however, the international expert provides nonbinding advice to the regulator.

- *Expert panels are more suitable for water than for electricity.* Infrastructure sectors are not the same. Water and sanitation services are often provided by small, self-contained enterprises that will have few, if any, physical and contractual connections to other entities in the industry. In addition, competition is relatively limited, and the technologies for providing the services are fairly stable. All these conditions make it more feasible to create a fairly detailed tariff-setting system that could be administered by an expert panel.

  The electricity sector is quite different. Electricity enterprises often are vertically integrated so that they may be in several different businesses functioning at the same time—generation, transmission, distribution, and retail supply. Even when there is vertical separation, the separate enterprises are almost physically connected to each other over a national or regional grid. The fact of a physical connection

---

63. Note that this is very similar to our earlier recommendation for strong rather than weak advisory regulators.

leads to many transactions and contracts between the separate entities. In other words, most electricity enterprises do not operate as isolated and self-contained business entities. In addition, electricity sector structures are continuing to evolve in many countries with the spread of competition and technological changes. Given this more complicated sector structure and the continuing structural changes that are likely to occur, it would probably be more difficult to create an expert panel to administer a well-defined tariff-setting system for many of the sector's activities.

Difficult, however, does not mean impossible. In fact, numerous Latin American countries have adopted one element of the Shugart and Ballance proposal—the detailed, prespecified tariff-setting agreement for many distribution enterprises.[64] But the difference is that, to varying degrees, these agreements are administered by separate regulatory entities rather than by nongovernmental expert panels. And in those instances where the regulator has been assigned a smaller role in administering the tariff system (for example, developing the tariff-setting TOR, but not making decisions on the results of the studies), this lack of experience seems to have hurt when crises arose. For example, a number of commentators have asserted that Chile was slow in dealing with obvious imperfections in its bulk power market system because the regulator had limited authority and experience.

One final point: It is important that any independent expert input into regulatory decisionmaking or appeals provides the expert(s) with clearly defined instructions and responsibilities. The recently established three-person standing expert panels for the Chilean electricity and water sectors do this. But their functions are more limited—arbitrating dispute over regulatory decisions. They do not make the initial regulatory decisions.

Evaluation of Contracting-Out Arrangements

The evaluation of contracting-out arrangements (whether advisory or binding) should cover the following:

- The degree to which they are well suited to the country and industry in question.

---

64. See **Bacovic, Tenenbaum, and Woolf** (2003) for how this has been done in Latin America and other regions.

- How well they have functioned in speed and quality of decisionmaking, analysis of dispute, and so forth.
- Economic outcomes (for example, on service quantity and quality, investment, productivity, costs, and prices).
- The degree to which they have enabled and encouraged progress toward best-practice regulation and industry reform.

Popular Concerns That Consumer Interests Are Being Ignored Relative to Investors' Profitability

In many countries where utility service industries have been privatized, there have been widespread complaints (and, in some cases, more extreme protests—including riots) that the reforms and the regulatory arrangements have led to large and growing profits to companies and investors at the expense of consumers. Perhaps inevitably, this opposition has been particularly evident where privatization has transferred significant ownership shares to *foreign* investors.

In some cases, the opposition is to the process of commercializing the operations of the industry—of which privatization is usually the last step. In other cases, it arises because existing consumers either do not see themselves as benefiting significantly relative to investors or rapidly discount the benefits from improved coverage and quality of service. This appears to have happened in Argentina around—and certainly after—the peso crisis in 2002.[65]

If such opposition is sufficiently strong, there is little that any regulator can do. In many cases, however, the regulator can bolster support for the reform by taking actions that protect the interests of consumers, ensuring that all price increases can be justified and that efficiency gains are shared with consumers. This is very important for increasing the *legitimacy* of such reforms.

What Can a Regulator Do?

A first action for allaying the suspicions of consumers is for regulatory agencies to operate under a policy of openness and transparency. This includes ensuring that the operating culture and style should be one where

- Decisions are based on sound arguments.
- All relevant parties (particularly consumers) can make their case before decisions are made.

---

65. See **Estache** (2004b).

- Decisions are published with justifications.
- The general public has access to important documents, such as PPAs, licenses, and concessions that are the basis for regulatory decisions.
- Reconsideration and appeal opportunities are presented against regulatory breach of procedures and apparently perverse decisions.

Other aspects of openness and transparency are set out in detail in chapter 3. Of particular importance are opportunities for public participation, creation of a permanent consumer advocacy function, and access to information being used for making decisions. In the context of the discussion of intermediate, transitional, and quasi-regulatory agencies, we would point to the importance of public communication by the regulatory agencies, including maintaining a good Web site and publishing annual reports. In general, the importance of the agency's willingness to debate and answer questions openly and publicly cannot be overstated. These issues are particularly important for new regulators acting in support of utility reforms that have attracted populist opposition.

A second action is to try to ensure significant and early improvements in the quality of service. Particularly where prices to consumers are having to be raised, it is important that consumers perceive improvements in the quality of service. For electricity, these improvements will include the following:

- Quicker connections and reconnections.
- Better bill collection.
- Fewer and shorter outages.
- Better frequency control.
- Faster peri-urban and rural electrification.

If the regulator is proactive in generating early service improvements and linking service improvements to perceived price rises, this will increase the perceived legitimacy of the reforms. Nevertheless, it is important to remember that the benefits of past changes are rapidly taken for granted so that continuous progress is necessary.

The third action is service provision and protection for low-income consumers. This is a very difficult issue for regulatory and quasi-regulatory agencies. Any decisions on subsidies and cross-subsidies are essentially policy decisions and hence the responsibility of government. However, regulators can be active in protecting and promoting the interests of low-income consumers (for example, by providing prepayment meters and encouraging lifeline tariffs).

4

The fourth action is the enactment of a clear regulatory law. This is an important step in developing a regulatory system. Even with a ministry regulator, a good regulatory law can have significant effects by providing incentives to all parties to take seriously the regulatory powers and obligations.[66] Particular issues here are (a) specifying clearly the objectives of regulation and (b) providing a clear delineation of the responsibilities of the regulator relative to the policy responsibilities of government. If the government decides to maintain some control of certain regulatory issues for a certain period (for example, a power of veto over household price increases), that should be clearly stated as well.

A fifth action is open bidding for concessions, franchises, or privatizations and for new investment projects. Recent experience, including analysis of Latin American concession contracts, shows how crucial sound, fair, and transparent bidding processes can be for private sector participation in electricity and other infrastructure industries. This should include the use of a concessions law. New and small regulatory and quasi-regulatory agencies can have an important role in devising and supervising criteria and procedures in this area. For instance, regulatory enforcement of sound bidding arrangements can greatly reduce the risk of corruption in contract awards— as well as provide effective investigations of corruption accusations. This, in turn, helps discourage unfounded accusations. In addition, regulatory action to ensure proper bidding also is important in ensuring that bid winners are properly qualified to take on their tasks and that they are unlikely to default or opt out.[67] All these regulatory actions are important in ensuring the legitimacy of controversial decisions where opportunistic behavior by bidders and others should be expected.

In many countries, electricity and other infrastructure industry reforms that have been beneficial in overall economic efficiency terms have suffered a popular backlash because lower-income customers came to believe that they lost out at the expense of higher-income or corporate customers. This can greatly damage the legitimacy or at least the perception of legitimacy of the reforms—particularly when utility companies also are increasing their

---

66. See **Cubbin and Stern** (2005) who find that, in developing countries, enacting a regulatory law is associated on average with 15–20 percent higher per capita investment in generation capacity over the long term.

67. See **Guasch** (2004) for a discussion of good and bad practice in bidding arrangements for infrastructure concessions, including the appropriate role of regulatory entities.

profitability. Regulatory agency recognition of the interests of low-income consumers and support for measures to help therefore can be important—provided that this does not go so far as to become a screen behind which existing consumers revert to being overprotected, and serves as an excuse to prevent the utilities from earning a reasonable rate of return.[68]

All of the aspects discussed above should be evaluated in terms of the following:

- The quality and success of the arrangements per se.
- Their effect on decisions and economic outcomes (including maintenance and investment levels).
- The degree to which they incorporate features that lead to better regulation and regulatory governance.

4

Macroeconomic Crises and Their Aftermath

A macroeconomic crisis may require the temporary emergency suspension of autonomous regulatory agencies for a certain period. (Such suspension of authority is explicitly provided for in the United Kingdom and in most other electricity regulatory laws.) It does not, however, require a long-term or permanent downgrading or suspension of the functions of the regulator. In some countries (for example, Bulgaria), the recovery period following a major macroeconomic shock has provided the opportunity for a step-change improvement in the quality of utility regulation arrangements.

Indeed, a good test of whether regulatory agencies are well rooted in a country is whether they are used in post-crisis discussions over contract, price adjustment, and other workout issues. They were not used in this way in Thailand and other South Asian countries after 1997, nor have they been used in Argentina since 2003. In consequence, the electricity, telecom, and other regulatory agencies in these countries appear to have permanently lost many of their powers to one or more ministries.

Any evaluation of regulatory arrangements should include the quality of the macroeconomic environment—beneficial or adverse on their performance and development. In the specific case of a country that has suffered a major macroeconomic or exchange rate shock, the evaluator should address the following issues:

---

68. See **Estache** ([2004a]; World Bank paper and chapter in von Hirschhausen, Thorsten Beckers, and Kay Mitusch book [2004]) for a fuller discussion of these issues.

- The powers and duties of the regulatory agency or similar entity pre- and post-crisis; for example, whether their powers and duties have (a) been reduced or enhanced and (b) whether the change is likely to be temporary or permanent.
- The role of the agency, if any, in renegotiating concession and other contract arrangements post-crisis.
- The role of the agency, if any, in adjusting prices and working out an appropriate post-crisis transition path.
- The role of the regulatory agency in all other post-crisis adjustments (for example, redefinition of license conditions).

Implications for the Evaluation of Regulatory Agencies

The overall goal of any evaluation of an existing regulatory system should be to recommend specific improvements that will lead to better outcomes. A problem with some past evaluations is that they often have been limited to describing deficiencies and recommending regulatory best practices—and not much more. This is not a productive approach. Little is accomplished by giving lectures to government officials, either in writing or in meetings, on ideal regulatory systems. If an evaluation is going to be useful, it also must give concrete recommendations on realistic short-term actions that will move the existing system to these end points.

Many of these earlier evaluations have tended to ignore two basic realities. The first reality is that infrastructure regulatory systems are new and unfamiliar institutions for most developing and transition economies. Moreover, they often were created in response to pressures from the World Bank or other aid institutions rather than self-initiated by the reforming country. The second reality is that there are numerous real-world impediments, constraints, and problems that make it difficult, if not possible, to transplant best-practice regulatory systems from developed countries to developing and transition-economy countries.

If the evaluation of the regulatory system is going to be of any practical use, it needs to closely examine these impediments and then recommend "first steps" that create political and economic incentives that will create pressures to move to a better system over time. In other words, it is not enough to repeat the mantra of regulatory best practices as if that is all that is necessary to persuade government officials that improvements are needed.

Table 4.2. Effective Regulatory Systems—Impediments and Possible Solutions

Impediments and problems	Possible solutions
Unwillingness or inability to commercialize the regulated enterprise	• Explicit timetable supported by transitional subsidies with secure funding support
Unwillingness or inability to transfer regulatory powers	• Strong rather than weak advisory regulator
Regulatory appeals to weak general law courts	• Arbitration • Specialized appeal tribunals advised by expert panels
Uncertainty about the strength of regulatory commitments	• Regulatory and infrastructure contracts • Regulatory PRGs and similar external risk mitigation measures
Limited regulatory resources and capacity	• Contracting out of regulatory staff functions on an advisory basis to consultants or other entities • Contracting out of regulatory decisions on a binding basis to other entities (for example, expert panels and regional regulatory bodies)
Consumer mistrust of reforms or regulation	• Openness and transparency • Emphasis on early quality-of-service improvements • Service expansion to unconnected customers • Protection of low-income customers • Open bidding for licenses or concessions
Macroeconomic crises	• Involvement of the regulator in post-crisis workout discussions

According to a famous Chinese proverb, if the goal is to go from one side of the river to the other, what matters most are the small but critical decisions as to what should be the next stones to step on as one moves across the river.

Table 4.2 lists some of the most commonly observed impediments to effective regulation and some possible solutions. Taken together, these potential solutions constitute the building blocks of various transitional regulatory systems. One thing should be clear from the discussion in this chapter: *there is no single "best" transitional regulatory system that applies to all countries at all times.* The transitional regulatory system needed for a particular country will depend on the specific problems that exist in that country. This, in turn, implies that the first task of an effective evaluator is to be something akin to a detective. The evaluator must determine the problems or deficiencies in the existing regulatory system that prevent the infrastructure sector from achieving better performance. Realistically, this requires talking to many people in the sector, and then stepping back and recommending one or more first steps that could remedy these real-world impediments. It is these steps, when taken together, that constitute the elements of a transitional regulatory system.

Chapter 5

How to Recognize Good and Bad Regulation: Regulatory Decisions and Sector Outcomes

. . . [G]rant me the serenity to accept the things that I cannot change, the courage to change the things I can, and the wisdom to know the difference.

— Reinhold Niebuhr

The purpose of the handbook is to provide guidance on the relevant criteria for evaluating infrastructure regulation. Two dimensions of regulation need to be evaluated: regulatory governance—the institutional and legal framework within which decisions are made—and regulatory substance—the actual decisions, whether explicit or implicit, made by the designated regulatory body or other entities within the government. It makes little sense to limit the evaluation to the decisions of a formally designated regulatory body if important regulatory decisions actually are made by other government entities, such as ministries and agencies.

The handbook provides evaluation tools in the form of questionnaires and interview guidelines. These tools can be used by individuals working in regulatory agencies, governments, international agencies, and donor agencies—as well as World Bank staff—so that they can evaluate specific infrastructure regulatory systems and the performance of designated regulatory bodies within this system.

The relevant criteria for regulatory governance—that is, the "how" of regulation—were discussed in chapter 3 where a set of best-practice principles and standards was presented. They provide benchmarks that can be used in evaluating the design and operation of regulatory institutions and processes. This chapter now shifts to the relevant criteria for judging, first, regulatory substance—that is, the actual decisions that are the "what" of regulation—and, second, the effect of regulatory decisions on sector outcomes. Thus the chapter marks the transition from discussion of the quality of regulatory decisionmaking processes and regulatory institutions to the quality of the decisions themselves, the factors that caused them, and the sector outcomes affected by these decisions.

Regulatory Decisions and Sector Outcomes

Regulatory decisions are the means by which regulatory agencies interpret their powers and duties to try to achieve the purposes of the law—they are the outputs of the agency. Regulatory decisions affect sector outcomes. Economic regulation is justified only if it produces better sector outcomes—for example, in terms of prices, productivity, investment, access, financial viability, service quality, and social objectives—than some other system of control. In other words, regulation is a means to an end, and the end is better sector performance. Even though sector outcomes must be the ultimate benchmark for judging regulatory performance, this does not imply that country-specific evaluations of infrastructure regulatory systems (the Type 3 evaluations used in this handbook) should spend a lot of time and effort to *quantify* the effect of specific regulatory decisions on overall sector performance.

Such an exercise would be unproductive for three reasons. First, regulatory reform is almost always only one element of a larger reform package that usually also includes sector restructuring, corporatization, commercialization, and often some type of private sector participation. As a consequence, it is virtually impossible in a single-country case study to calculate the separate effect of a new regulatory system on overall sector performance or even on particular components of sector performance because many other reforms will have been made at the same time. Second, sector outcomes also are affected by local, national, and global trends and events (see the next section) over which the regulator has little or no influence. Third, even if it were possible to perform such calculations (that is, quantify the effects of the regulatory system on overall sector performance), it is not obvious that these calculations, however sophisticated or precise they might be, would convince political decisionmakers to make specific "second-generation" reforms the primary goal of any regulatory evaluation. Such calculations may be of considerable interest to researchers, but they will not address the immediate concerns of most government decisionmakers.

High-level government officials and legislators who have the power to change the existing regulatory system are the most important audience for the evaluation. *Given their interests and needs, the recommended approach is to look at specific elements of the regulatory system, relating to both regulatory governance and substance, and to evaluate whether these elements help or hinder sector performance.* Stated differently, the evaluation should focus on actual characteristics and decisions of the regulatory system and on whether they move the sector toward better or worse outcomes. This is a very different exercise from trying to quantify the separate effects of one or more characteristics or decisions of the regulatory system on sector performance.

What Other Factors Affect Sector Outcomes?

5

This narrower focus recognizes the reality that many different variables affect sector outcomes. Although these variables certainly include regulation, they also include many other factors, such as macroeconomic conditions (local, regional, and global), currency fluctuations, interest rates, management skills and capabilities, political and social conditions, and global conditions of the regulated market. These external influences are clearly beyond the control of the regulator. This implies that, in many cases, sector outcomes are heavily driven and, in some cases, directly determined by external forces and events that regulators simply cannot control. For these external forces and events, the regulator is a bystander, not an actor. Some examples of external factors not controlled by regulators include

- Inability to enforce contracts and commercial or regulatory decisions.
- Cumbersome or inadequate process for appellate review of regulatory decisions (for example, judicial delays, judicial corruption, lack of judicial expertise, and inappropriate standards and processes for review).
- Government interference, seizing of authority that is illegal under existing laws, or other politicization that adversely affects the ability of the agency to carry out its legal mandate.
- Inadequate powers or discretion granted to regulators, or disputes over authority between regulators and other agencies of the state (for example, ministries).

- Government or company tolerance of failures to pay bills and an unwillingness or inability to enforce payment (for example, through litigation or cutting off of service to nonpaying customers)
- Constitutional or other legal system constraints that prevent effective operation of the regulatory agency.
- Government establishment of an inappropriate market structure (for example, insufficient competition to sustain a well-functioning and viable generation or telecom market).
- Adverse macroeconomic circumstances, currency problems, and fiscal or monetary policies that are beyond the ability of the regulators to control.
- Lack of adequate resources—human, technological, or financial—to meet assigned regulatory responsibilities.
- Perception of overall country risk by investors.
- Natural or human-caused disasters or shortages of essential resources (for example, lack of water for hydroelectric generating plants).

Given the existence of these many external influences on sector performance, assessing the quantitative effect of substantive regulatory decisions on performance would not be an easy task. Although it is certainly possible to measure the performance of the regulated sector, it would be almost impossible to quantify the effect of sector decisions on sector outcomes. *Although bad regulation will lead to adverse consequences, the converse—that bad outcomes in the regulated sector are the result of poor regulation—is not necessarily the case.*

Should the Evaluation Ignore External Factors beyond the Regulator's Control?

The fact that these external nonregulatory factors are beyond the control of the regulator does *not* imply that they should be ignored in the regulatory evaluation. Although some external factors are beyond the control of the national government, other external factors can be clearly influenced by a country's government. This is especially true for government policy failures and sector structure failures. In other words, although these failures may be beyond the control of the regulator, they are still within the control of the national government.

It would be a mistake for the evaluator to ignore government policies or sector structures that make it difficult or impossible for the regulatory system to achieve good sector outcomes. The outside evaluator has the advantage of credibility that the regulator may not have. If a regulator talks publicly or privately about government policy failures, his or her statements will often be viewed as just a typical example of one government official trying to shift blame to another government official. In addition, if the regulator "goes public," there is a risk that he or she will be forced to leave the regulatory entity, despite legal guarantees that are supposed to prevent that from happening.

In contrast, an outside expert has more degrees of freedom and, therefore should take advantage of the opportunity provided by the evaluation to draw attention to important nonregulatory influences on sector performance. If the evaluator does not take advantage of this opportunity ("I only do regulation"), he or she will create an unrealistic expectation that changes to the regulatory system can solve sector problems that actually have little or nothing to do with regulation. If the evaluator stays silent, he or she may end up hurting rather than helping regulatory reform.

5

Judging the Quality of Utility Regulatory Frameworks and Decisions: Asking the Right Questions

The objectives of a good regulatory system are

- To produce a flow of good regulatory decisions.
- To minimize the number of poor or mistaken decisions.
- To correct errors speedily.
- To avoid repeating mistakes or poor decisions.

Failing to meet these objectives or any significant subset of them—to the extent that the failures are attributable to regulation—is significant evidence of flaws in the design and operation of the regulatory system.

The questionnaires (appendixes C and D) and interview guidelines (appendix E) have been designed to produce information on which to base a determination of whether these objectives are being met. The discussion below is intended, first, to provide a context for understanding what is included in the questionnaires and why; and second, to assist in determining how the questionnaires should be interpreted and used. The discussion also provides a basis for measuring a regulatory regime's success or lack of it.

In a medium-level and in-depth evaluation, the evaluator is looking for patterns of behavior. Therefore, information is needed to answer the following questions:[1]

- Have regulatory decisions (including appellate decisions) been consistent or inconsistent?
- Have the regulatory decisions (including appellate review of them) helped the sector improve its performance, or have they been damaging to sector performance?
- Has the regulatory agency or ministry regulator (where no independent regulator is in place) actively helped resolve problems, or has it tended to create difficulties?
- Has the government supported or hindered the regulatory agency in carrying out its legally mandated functions?
- Is the regulatory agency used to help resolve key issues, or is it bypassed?

In addressing each of these questions, the evaluator should be looking for specific examples and patterns of behavior. When there are obvious problems in observed behavior or conduct, it usually means that the underlying structure of the regulatory system is flawed.

The principal value of answering these questions is to provide the following:

- Critical analysis of the country's regulatory system and recommendations for improving the system.
- A basis for learning *from the experience* of the countries evaluated.
- Examples of useful things to do and avoid based on experience in other countries and sectors.
- Lessons for the World Bank and other lenders and donors for infrastructure projects in developing countries.

In the section that follows, the specific examples are drawn primarily from the electricity industry, but the same or similar problems are often observed in the telecommunications, water, and transport sectors. In consequence, it should be a relatively straightforward process to modify the evaluation questionnaires for other infrastructure industries.

---

1. The evaluator, of course, will need to exercise judgment as to which questions should be posed to which interviewee. Although some of the people interviewed may provide insights to all the queries, it seems likely that each person interviewed will add particular value in those specific areas where his or her experience has been greatest.

Good and Bad Regulatory Decisions

Regulatory decisions are the concrete outputs of a regulatory system. They can have an immediate and direct effect on sector outcomes. This section discusses what is meant by a regulatory decision and how to distinguish good decisions from bad decisions.

What Is a Regulatory "Decision"?

It is important to be clear about the meaning of a *regulatory decision*. Throughout the handbook, this term is used very broadly. It refers to any action or inaction of the designated regulatory body or other government entity that affects the economic interests of participants in the sector. In other words, an action is "regulatory" if it affects the costs and revenues of sector enterprises that, in turn, affect the prices paid and services received by current or future consumers.[2]

A regulatory decision can take different forms. It can be a formal decision that is publicly announced in an official document. Two examples of a formal decision would be a tariff order that applies to a specific enterprise or a general rule that applies to a class of enterprises (for example, new generators). Alternatively, it might be a phone call from an energy minister to the regulator informing him or her that the government does not want average residential tariffs to increase by more than 5 percent in 2005.[3]

It may be an action taken or an action not taken. The failure to act is effectively a decision because it will have real-world consequences in the sector. For example, suppose that the government has decided that new large industrial customers should have the right to choose alternative electricity suppliers. If the regulator fails to issue or approve an unbundled "wires" tariff, this inaction represents a regulatory action. The important point then is that a regulatory decision cannot and should not be limited just to decisions formally and publicly announced by the designated regulatory entity if the purpose of the evaluation is to assess the actual operation of the regulatory system.

---

2. However, this is limited to sector-specific actions and decisions. It is not meant to include governmentwide policy actions. For example, a government may decide to raise rates on the general corporate income tax. Although this would certainly affect the costs of power enterprises that are corporations, this would not be considered a regulatory action.
3. This does *not* mean that the evaluator would ever know about the phone call, but the evaluator would see the outcome in whatever tariff order the regulator issues in response to the minister's call.

The Meaning of "Good" and "Bad"

Usually when one talks of something as being *good* or *bad,* it implies an ethical determination. However, this is *not* how the two terms are used in this handbook. Rather, they refer to determinations by the evaluator as to whether specific regulatory decisions have helped or hindered the sector in achieving sector outcomes that have been adopted as government goals (see the next section). Good regulatory decisions move the sector closer to a goal; bad regulatory decisions move the sector farther away or only slowly toward a goal.

Another set of designations could have been chosen. For example, it could have been the evaluator's job to determine whether certain regulatory decisions are *functional* or *dysfunctional* in light of the government's goals for the sector. The designations of good and bad were chosen because they are the terms that are most commonly used when individuals in the sector make their own informal judgments about a regulator's performance.[4] Equally important, if the evaluator uses these designations, he or she is more likely to capture the attention of those who have the authority to make improvements.

What Are the Goals?

The government's goals for the sector are usually written down in legislation and government policy documents. A typical electricity law will specify goals in very general terms, such as "a more efficient sector" or "greater access of the population to electricity service." In contrast, the goals in policy statements (for example, white papers or sector strategies), which are almost always derived from the law, tend to be more specific. A government policy statement may state that technical and commercial losses should be reduced by 12 percent over four years; 200,000 new customers should be connected to the grid in five years; and the government should no longer provide subsidies to the sector after seven years. In almost every instance, whether the goals are general or specific, they will be stated in terms of one or more of the sector outcomes described below (see regulation and sector outcomes section). This then is consistent with the handbook's fundamental presumption that sector outcomes must be the one and only standard for judging regulatory performance.

---

4. Although the terms *good* and *bad,* as used in this chapter, relate solely to substantive effects and not to ethical matters, it is the unequivocal view of the authors that decisions derived either in part or wholly from unethical practices or influences are always unacceptable, regardless of their substantive effects.

What If the Evaluator Disagrees with the Government's Sectoral Goals?

The evaluator should begin by taking the government's goals as a given when performing an evaluation. In other words, the initial job of the evaluator is to assess whether observed regulatory decisions are moving the sector closer to or farther away from the goals that the government itself has established for the sector. The evaluator should be saying, "Here is what you said you want to accomplish for the sector, but the regulatory system you have established is not doing a good job of moving toward those goals because. . . . "

This does not preclude the evaluator from having opinions about the appropriateness of government goals for the sector. For example, if the government has established the goal of creating a competitive spot market, but the country is too small to support such competition, the evaluator should not be precluded from stating that this sectoral goal is inappropriate for the country's size. Similarly, the evaluator should point out that the goal of a commercially sustainable power sector is an impossible goal if the regulator is prohibited, either directly or indirectly, from raising tariffs to cost-recovering levels. In other words, the evaluator should not feel constrained from offering opinions about the appropriateness or realism of government goals. However, as a general strategy and especially in an initial evaluation, the better approach, is to evaluate the regulatory system against overall sector goals that the government itself has formally and publicly espoused. If the evaluator shows that he or she can be objective and helpful in performing this initial task, government decisionmakers are more likely to be receptive to comments that the government's goals may be unrealistic or inappropriate for the country's economic and social circumstances.

How Can Good Decisions Be Distinguished from Bad Decisions?

This is a judgment call. It is not based on the application of some mathematical formula. The evaluator's judgment largely depends on answering a single question: Has the decision or action helped or hindered the sector from achieving outcomes that the government has specified for the sector? Answering the question depends on common sense and logic. When all is said and done, the evaluator must be able to write a sentence that reads, "This [specific regulatory action or decision] has hindered the sector from achieving [for example, greater access, less costly generation, reduction in technical

5

and nontechnical losses, or efficient subsidies for poor people] because. . . . " What comes after "because" must be both logical and convincing.

As discussed in chapter 2, it may not always be possible to make this determination. Clearly, there are some regulatory decisions where it is simply unclear whether the decision is good or bad for the government's goals. For example, it probably would not be productive for an evaluator to offer an opinion on whether an average tariff increase should have been 8 percent rather than the 6 percent that actually was granted. It makes little sense for the evaluator to waste much time trying to evaluate "gray areas." The better approach is to focus on decisions and actions that are generally accepted as bad by those who have no direct commercial influence.

Real-World Examples of Bad Regulatory Decisions

To illustrate these concepts, some bad decisions that have been observed in World Bank client countries are listed in tables 5.1 and 5.2. The decisions are grouped into two categories: bad decisions arising from regulatory inac-

Table 5.1. Bad Decisions Arising from Regulatory Inaction—Sins of Omission

- Failure to institute a uniform system of regulatory accounts.

- Failure to systematically collect and effectively analyze all information required for regulatory decisions.

- Failure to articulate fully which risks are internalized into rates and which are externally adjusted (for example, currency risks, fuel risks, or purchased power risks).

- Failure to audit regulated enterprises adequately.

- Failure to define regulatory methodologies sufficiently (for example, pricing, market power criteria, and assessment of penalties for poor performance).

- Failure to comprehend fully the implications of incentives inherent in methodologies used for pricing and other regulatory activities.

- Failure to articulate fully the social and other noneconomic obligations being imposed on regulated enterprises.

- Failure to institute adequate quality-of-service standards or to monitor these standards effectively.

- Failure to adopt adequate methods for handling consumer inquiries and complaints, or failure to look for patterns in complaints being received, or both.

(continued)

Table 5.1, *continued*

- Failure to monitor competitive behavior or market abuse effectively in electricity generation or telecom markets that are intended to operate competitively.

- Failure to investigate or understand the cost structures of the regulated industries.

- Failure to impose access charges and adopt rules for industries where there is competition over networks (primarily telecoms, electricity, and natural gas, but also, to a lesser extent, water and railways).

- Failure to understand or consider demand elasticity or other socioeconomic results of decisions.

- Failure to provide the general public with access to important documents such as power purchase agreements, licenses, and concessions that are the basis for regulatory decisions.

- Failure to adequately consider public feedback and critiques of regulatory decisions.

- Failure to provide effective competitive bidding procedures for new capacity.

- Failure to monitor and mitigate market power in competitive markets.

- Failure to set tariffs at fully compensatory levels.

- Failure to eliminate unjustifiable cross-subsidies and to efficiently target and make transparent justifiable cross-subsidies.

- Failure to adopt clear standards for tariff setting for future tariff periods (for example, clear standards for power purchase costs or distribution costs, or definition of the regulatory asset base).

- Failure to institute a mechanism for relating payment—or nonpayment—of contributions in aid of construction or government subsidies to tariffs.

- Absence of any attempt to progress on eliminating cross-subsidies between customer classes, even when the law supports it.

- Failure to prevent a regulated company from purchasing services or products from an affiliated company at above-market prices.

5

tion (sins of omission) and bad decisions arising from regulatory actions (sins of commission).[5]

It must be emphasized again that the point of carrying out an informed, unbiased, and credible evaluation is to provide the basis for learning—and that means learning from mistakes, which in turn requires being able to identify and analyze the causes of mistakes and bad decisions. All utility regulatory systems in all countries make mistakes; parties other than the regula-

---

5. The severity of the consequences of each of the bad decisions noted may vary depending on a number of factors, including the particulars of the regulatory regime being examined.

tory agency are usually involved (for example, governments or regulated companies). The point is not to assign blame for mistakes, but to learn from them—not least so that they are not repeated. In the words of the old adage, "Those who do not learn from history are doomed to repeat it." This definitely applies to economic policymaking institutions, such as infrastructure industry regulatory agencies.

The Effect of Regulation on Sector Outcomes

In evaluating the role regulation plays in sector outcomes, the first issue is to define the current state of the infrastructure industry whose regulatory framework is being studied and define appropriate evaluation criteria for each identified outcome.[6] This is done below. The information is identified for collection in one or other of the questionnaires in the appendixes.

Much of this factual material should be available from regulated enterprises (for example, from accounts and annual reports), regulatory agencies, ministries, and so forth. A key point is that, wherever possible, information should be collected *for a number of years,* not merely for the last available year or for a single year. This is particularly important when a major restructuring and regulatory reform have taken place and it is *very* important that the comparable outcome data are collected for a few years before as well as after the reform. It is also important so as to normalize data by avoiding any anomalous circumstances encountered in a particular year.

A critical issue is how the outcome data can and should be used in an evaluation of regulatory outcomes. Chapter 6 will say more about this, although *the key point is that regulatory aspects are only one determinant of industry outcomes—and by no means necessarily the most important.* General economic conditions, industry and market structures, and the reliability of legal institutions are the most important. A good regulatory framework that is

---

6. Several ongoing World Bank studies are examining the issues involved in measuring "core electricity sector performance indicators." The focus of these regional studies is on developing measures of sector outcomes that can be used in cross-country comparisons. The studies will emphasize physical and economic outcomes that would be of particular relevance to the electricity sectors of developing and transition-economy countries. They will also use statistical techniques to determine whether certain regional regulatory and institutional characteristics affect such performance. When the studies have been completed, the results will be available on the Bank's energy Web site (www.worldbank.org/energy).

charged with regulating an incoherent or contradictory industry or market structure is likely to achieve little in improved sector performance and investment. This has been observed in many countries and regions with generally sound regulatory frameworks that were burdened with severely flawed market designs or privatization arrangements (for example, California electricity, U.K. railways). Similarly, major macroeconomic and exchange rate crises can swamp the best regulatory framework, at least temporarily.

Collecting data on outcomes and attributing them to regulatory or other causation is extraordinarily complex. Trying to do so, however, may provide

Table 5.2. Bad Decisions Made in Regulation—Sins of Commission

- Setting inappropriate benchmarks for efficiency or operational improvements.
- Unnecessarily or unreasonably reopening investment decisions or privatization agreements ex post.
- Setting prices on the expectation that governments will deliver promised subsidies, even when it is highly unlikely that governments can or will do so.
- Permitting price changes that allow for a growing divergence between prices and costs—either from failure to allow a pass-through of unavoidable cost increases or because of overly generous regulatory reviews or automatic adjustments.
- Having severe penalties assessed for minor offenses or, alternatively, light penalties assessed for serious deficiencies (for example, revoking a license for minor billing errors or minimal financial penalties for excessive profits earned through above-market self-dealing with unregulated affiliate companies).
- Inappropriate differentiation between different classes and types of customers (for example, rural and urban, industrial, commercial, or residential).
- Establishing low caps on power purchase prices that eliminate incentives to build new generation stations.
- Using inaccurate data or misapplying accurate data.
- Applying inappropriate benchmarks or standards.
- Using costly and time-consuming tariff-setting methodologies (such as requiring that regulatory asset base be calculated on an asset-by-asset basis).
- Sending poor price signals (for example, encouraging wasteful or inefficient use of energy) by under- or overpricing or failing to require meters.
- Providing perverse incentives (for example, encouraging overinvestment or discouraging service quality).
- Creating a regulatory entity whose decisionmakers are chosen to represent different constituencies or regions (that is, regulators as politicians) rather than to be independent decisionmakers.

5

good pointers to the role of regulation relative to other factors, but the question is highly subjective. Although extensive econometric modeling might yield more empirically supported conclusions, evaluators of regulatory regimes need not go that far in conducting their evaluations because they are looking at the substantive role regulation played in sector outcomes, and that role was carried out in a social, institutional, economic, and political context.[7] For the evaluation to be effective, it need not yield empirical results attributing x percent of the outcome to the regulatory action. Instead, it is limited to determining whether the regulatory system helped or hindered in achieving outcomes sought for the sector.

To illustrate the point, assume that an important outcome is whether sufficient investment was attracted to the regulated sector. If the answer is no, then, for purposes of evaluating the regulatory regime, the central question is not precisely why was that the case, but rather, given all other circumstances being encountered, what role did regulation play in causing inadequate investment? There are many potential answers to that question. Perhaps, in the case of an economic meltdown, the answer is virtually none. At the other end of the spectrum, in the case of an otherwise booming economy, a bad market design (perhaps enshrined in law or in regulation) or gross misunderstanding of the cost structure of the regulated industry by the regulators caused significant underinvestment. The question is not literally an empirical one, but rather a matter of what, if any, deficiencies in regulation contributed in whatever measure to the result of inadequate investment? An evaluator need not determine that regulation played a dominant role in the outcome of underinvestment to find that the regulation was flawed in specific ways, and that to the extent that those flaws are remedied—whatever role regulation plays in attracting future investment—its effect will be more positive.

The point that is critical for evaluators scrutinizing the regulatory regime is that although other factors may play a critical role in defining outcomes, regulation needs to be sufficiently flexible to adjust to an ever-changing backdrop. Although it may not be the primary determinant of all sector outcomes, it al-

---

7. Recent econometric studies with better data on the components of regulation are suggesting markedly stronger and better-determined effects of regulation on outcomes than those based on weaker, self-administered questionnaires. See, for instance, the studies by **Cubbin and Stern** (2005) for electricity and the study by **Gutierrez** (2003) for Latin American and Caribbean telecoms.

ways has an influence and a role to play. How it plays that role is what is critical for evaluators to analyze. It also is important in this context to remember, as noted earlier, that there is an asymmetrical element in the role of regulation in sector outcomes. *Good regulation does not necessarily produce good outcomes for the regulated sector, but bad regulation will almost always contribute to bad outcomes.*

Measures of Relevant Outcomes and Criteria for Infrastructure Industries

The questionnaires are designed to assist and guide the evaluators in their inquiry and to ensure that they possess at least the minimal information required to perform their mission. They are not meant to be straitjackets. If one hoped to conduct meaningful surveys across a number of countries, the data collected would have to be systematically obtained and uniformly analyzed to maintain the type of discipline and rigor required to make the survey meaningful. The purpose of the questionnaires in the context of regulatory assessment is somewhat different. Although the rigor and discipline of the evaluation remains critical, the uniformity of data collection is less so. Each country inevitably will have unique circumstances that affect both the nature of regulation and the results obtained. The regulated sectors are almost certain to be in different circumstances and the institutional, political, and legal contexts of regulatory regimes are likely to vary from country to country. Certainly, the same is true of the social and economic contexts. As a result, the same issue will not have the same importance for one country as it may for another. The criteria used for measurement might vary, including, of course, the possibility of adding criteria other than those listed below. The obstacles to effective regulation are likely to vary as well. Although, as was pointed out in chapter 1, there are lessons to be learned that transcend political boundaries—hence the need for an international expert as part of the evaluation team—the priorities in an evaluation are likely to vary significantly from one country to another. Based on the initial feedback they receive, evaluators should focus on characteristics and outcomes that are generally recognized as problematic.

For each of the criteria below, the relevant question is whether, in the country, region, or province, the relevant outcome for the industry (for example, electricity supply industry) or sector (for example, electricity distribution and supply) has improved or worsened over time or relative to other similar countries, regions, or provinces. The main relevant outcomes are set

5

forth below. The general headings would apply to a range of network-based utility service industries (for example, water and sewerage, telecommunications, railways, airports, or natural gas), but the specific measures identified all refer to the electricity industry.

Note that for some indicators (such as investment and prices), the criteria and specific measures may differ between countries, in particular between richer OECD countries and middle- or low-income countries. However, the majority—and the most important measures of final outcomes—are common to all countries (for example, those covering efficiency, access, adequate supply, costs, quality, and financial viability). In what follows, specific outcome measures are grouped under appropriate general headings. *Again, it is worth repeating that the role of the regulatory regime and a regulatory agency in achieving successful outcomes on these indicators is only one factor and will, in many cases, be a subsidiary factor.* This should be borne in mind when considering and using the questionnaires for evaluation purposes.

5

Indicators for Output and Consumption

The following are indicators for output and consumption:

1. The percentage of households and businesses with access to the utility service, and growth in access levels (electricity access rates, rural electrification rates, and grid and off-grid connections).
2. The level and rate of growth of consumption per head and per unit of gross domestic product (GDP) by main customer group (for example, electricity consumption in kilowatt-hours and its sectoral composition).
3. Measures of unsatisfied demand (for example, the length and duration of connection queues, degree of uneconomic self-generation, and peak demand cuts).

Indicators for Efficiency

The following are indicators for efficiency:

1. Level and rate of growth of productivity—preferably total factor productivity, but also labor productivity (for example, kilowatt-hours generated per employee, customers served per employee, and electricity sales per employee—kilowatt-hour and value).

2. Level of costs and changes in cost levels—total (average) costs, operating costs, and capital costs (for example, average costs of supply, generation costs, and fuel costs).
3. Capital availability and utilization (for example, generation reserve margins and availability).
4. Wasted output (for example, technical losses and commercial losses on transmission and distribution systems, or lack of effective demand-side management).

Indicators for Quality of Supply

The following are indicators for the quality of supply:

1. Continuity of supply (for example, outages as measured by minutes of supply interruption per year or numbers of major blackouts).
2. Quality of supply (for example, frequency and voltage control and the incidence of damaging variations, and the time taken to restore power and make repairs).
3. Quality of customer service (for example, numbers of customer complaints and the average response times to resolve supply interruptions and complaints).

Indicators for Financial Performance

The following are indicators for financial performance:

1. Financial surpluses and losses for individual companies and electricity industry segments, as well as for the industry as a whole.
2. Achieved rates of return on capital—preferably at replacement cost, as well as historic cost and allowed rates of return on equity for privately owned companies.[8]
3. Capital structure issues (for example, debt-to-equity balance and term structures of debt).
4. Measures of indebtedness and interest burden.

---

8. Low attainment of allowed rates of return do not necessarily indicate regulatory shortcomings, because they also are likely to reflect management quality and general economic circumstances.

5. Sources of finance (for example, domestic versus foreign, state versus private, and share of local banks and local state-owned banks).

6. Amounts and average duration of payables and receivables (that is, lead and lag).

7. Nontechnical losses (for example, from electricity that has not been paid for, including through theft and fraud).

Indicators for Capacity, Investment, and Maintenance

Note that for some richer developed OECD countries and some transition economies, there may be excess electricity capacity—particularly in generation. This is highly unlikely to be the case for middle-income and low-income countries or in countries where access to the infrastructure service is significantly less than 100 percent. This is much less likely to be an issue for telecoms and some other infrastructure industries.

In what follows, it is assumed that there is unsatisfied demand and a sufficient margin of unserved households and businesses so that higher rates of (efficient) investment are desirable.

The indicators for capacity, investment, and maintenance are these:

1. Levels of maintenance expenditure (in physical and financial units).

2. Levels of capacity (for example, installed generation capacity in megawatts, transmission and distribution route length, and usable as well as rated book capacity).

3. Levels of investment (in each of generation, transmission, distribution, and supply and sales, and in both financial and appropriate physical units).

4. Amount of investment from private and foreign investors.

5. Terms of investment (for example, borrowing rates and bond coupon rates).

Indicators for Prices

The following are indicators for prices:

1. Relationship between prices and full economic cost or long-term marginal cost, including a reasonable rate of return on assets. This should be calculated for all major customer classes and on average across all customer classes. When possible, it should be calculated for genera-

tion prices, final retail prices, and for other major wholesale prices such as bulk supply tariffs.

2. Relationship between prices and full economic cost or long-term marginal cost, on average and for the major customer groups. If there is a positive or negative gap between prices and cost measures, there should be an analysis to determine if the gap is increasing or if it is decreasing.

3. Efficient tariffs that provide effective signals for production and consumption (for example, in terms of capacity charges, marginal energy use signals, and environmental externalities).

4. Economically efficient congestion management procedures and prices, as well as transmission and distribution access terms and prices (where appropriate).

5. Explicitness and transparency of subsidies and cross-subsidies.

6. Efficiency of subsidies and cross-subsidies (for example, well targeted at intended beneficiaries, such as the poor and those seeking connection).

7. Financial self-sufficiency of the sector (for example, no need for state subsidies or sovereign guarantees).

Indicators for Competition

The following are indicators for competition:

1. Measures of competition in competitive segments of the industry (for example, share of the largest and the three largest companies in relevant generation markets, Herfindahl-Hirschman indexes in relevant generation markets, and proportion of customers served by other than incumbent companies).

2. Performance of competitive markets (for example, evidence of anticompetitive behavior in generation and supply markets, price spikes, and duration of prices).

3. Numbers and quality of bidders in bids (for example, for transmission projects, new generation, franchises, and privatizations).

4. Prices achieved in competitive bids (for example, for competitively bid IPP contracts).

5. Well-functioning spot or other short-term energy markets (where appropriate).

6. Variety of products and services being offered.

7. Merger and acquisition (convergence) standards.
8. Evidence of physical and institutional bottlenecks that create subnational markets.

Social Indicators

The following are social indicators:

1. Market penetration (for example, percentage of households connected and the nature of the unserved market).
2. Subsidies and cross-subsidies (design, implementation, sustainability, and efficiency).
3. Effects on economic development.
4. Affordability of service (for example, the number of disconnections for nonpayment or the scope of nontechnical losses).

Conclusion

Collecting good data on these indicators should enable an evaluator to make a judgment on the role of the regulatory framework in achieving improved sector outcomes along the lines discussed above. These criteria, if accurately measured and evaluated correctly, should help the evaluator make some critical judgments on how regulation affects sector outcomes.

The Process of Conducting a Regulatory Evaluation: Discussion and Evaluation Tools

Change is inevitable; progress is not.

— Winston Churchill

This chapter discusses the process for evaluating infrastructure regulatory systems in developing countries. As noted previously, our emphasis is on the evaluation of *economic regulation* in the electricity sector. Consequently, the detailed examples in the proposed questionnaires (appendixes C and D) and interview guidelines (appendix E) are focused on the power sector. However, the general approach taken in these evaluation instruments also would apply to any infrastructure sectors (such as natural gas, water and sewerage, and telecommunications) with national or regional economic regulators. Therefore, the questionnaires and interview guidelines can be used as models for developing similar instruments in other infrastructure sectors.[1]

Any regulatory evaluation must be performed against some implicit or explicit principles and standards. In this handbook, our benchmark for evaluation is the set of principles and standards presented in chapter 3. This does not imply, as was discussed in chapter 4, that all countries immediately can or necessarily should develop institutions that incorporate these best-

---

1. A similar set of instruments was developed in a World Bank–financed evaluation of telecommunications regulators in several African countries. See http://wbln0018.world bank.org/ict/resources.nsf/InfoResources/.

practice principles or standards. However, the benchmarks implicit in these principles and standards can be used for evaluation purposes, at least in countries with reasonably well-functioning governmental, legal, and other institutions. This is the case whether the country in question has developed regulatory practices that are close to best practice, or whether they have a transitional regulatory regime, as described in chapter 4. (For developing countries, particularly lower-income or less institutionally developed countries, a transitional regulatory regime is likely to be the norm rather than the exception.) In consequence, the chapter 3 benchmarks, combined with the questionnaires and interview guidelines, can be used for the evaluation of utility industry regulatory arrangements to establish the following:

- How effective they are on their own terms, given the circumstances of the country in question.
- How effective they are in providing incentives to move toward best-practice standards, including a clear pathway.

Although they are clear on the benchmark standards, the questionnaires and interview guidelines take a deliberately neutral view on the choice of institutional framework for utility regulation. This follows the logical framework for the choice of evaluation criteria relevant for transitional regulatory systems as set out in chapter 4. In evaluating any regulatory system, the overarching concern is whether the system is doing some or all of the following:

- Developing and implementing clear legal frameworks.
- Providing an effective basis for writing, issuing, enforcing, updating, and revising its regulatory rules.
- Granting licenses and concessions in an efficient and fair manner.
- Operating in an open and transparent manner.
- Developing institutional experience and independence—both from government and/or from regulated companies/entities and/or other specific interests.
- Building a reputation for sound, justified, and consistent decisions.

The Three Levels of Evaluation

Three possible levels of evaluation are discussed below:

1. A short basic overview evaluation.

2. A substantive, mid-level evaluation.
3. A fundamental, in-depth evaluation.

The discussion that follows examines how each of these evaluations should be conducted and what can be expected from them. The choice between the three levels of evaluation depends on the purpose of the evaluation and on the resources and time that are available. Table 6.1 summarizes how the short, mid-level, and in-depth evaluations differ in scope, data collection methods, duration, and cost.

A Short Basic Evaluation

This level of evaluation is designed to provide a description of the *basic characteristics* of the sector and its regulatory arrangements, including possible problem areas. Carrying out the evaluation through the use of a structured questionnaire primarily with precoded responses is strongly recommended (appendix C). The questionnaire that is proposed also includes a small number of open-ended questions on regulatory and industry outcomes, successes, and setbacks.

This type of evaluation provides a form of general reconnaissance. Because time and resources are limited, the evaluation will be largely limited to

6

Table 6.1. Summary of Recommended Evaluations

Type of evaluation	Scope	Data collection methods	Duration	Likely cost and resource need[a]
Short basic evaluation	Provide a summary overview of regulatory framework and sector	Structured questionnaire; primarily precoded questions	Up to 5 days	Up to US$15,000; specialist staff not required
Substantive, mid-level evaluation	Provide a substantive analysis of regulatory arrangements and sector performance with recommendations for change	Structured questionnaire combined with open-ended interviews based on topic headings	Up to 4 weeks	Up to US$65,000; specialist staff required, e.g., World Bank or similar professionals; and consultants in regulatory and utility reform
Fundamental, in-depth evaluation	Provide a fundamental analysis with recommendations for development of a regulatory system and sector reforms	Wide range of open-ended interviews; possible augmentation by use of structured questionnaires, and statistical analysis of other data	3–4 months	From around US$125,000; specialist research teams required, e.g., from a specialist academic or policy research institute

a. Includes labor costs, but excludes travel and related costs.

the formal (for example, legal) attributes of the regulatory system. If there is a significant gap between what is written in the law and what actually is practiced, there is a danger that the evaluation may lead to a faulty understanding of the performance of the regulatory system in practice, but the inclusion of the additional open-ended questions is intended to provide some check on this. However, this questionnaire will provide little information on *how* the regulatory system actually operates and the degree to which its day-to-day performance has supported or hindered sector performance. The latter requires a more detailed mid-level or in-depth evaluation.

The questionnaire for this limited evaluation could be completed by World Bank staff, their counterparts in other agencies, and by researchers in the area of infrastructure industry regulatory and sector policy in developing countries. Because the evaluation is relatively basic, it can be performed by nonspecialists in infrastructure industries or regulatory systems. This basic evaluation should take no more than 5 staff-days, including the time needed to prepare a short write-up of the results.

A Mid-Level Evaluation

This level of evaluation is more extensive. It is designed to provide a substantive analysis and understanding of the sector and its regulatory arrangements, including both formal (legislative) and informal (in practice) elements of the regulatory system. The mid-level evaluation will involve an in-depth analysis of two to three areas of regulatory governance and two to three areas of regulatory substance. In-depth analyses are undertaken to evaluate whether these specific characteristics or decisions have helped or hindered in achieving sectoral outcomes that the government has specified as goals in either legislation or policy statements. Therefore, the purpose of the mid-level evaluation is to understand what aspects of the regulatory system work well, what aspects work less well or badly, and what changes usefully could be made.

The evaluation is carried out using both a structured questionnaire (as in appendixes D and possibly C)[2] and more open-ended interview questions (ap-

---

2. The recommended questionnaire in appendix D is the Electricity Regulatory Survey prepared by the American Enterprise Institute and the Brookings Institution for the World Bank's Development Research Group. We are grateful to them for the permission to use it in the context of this handbook. The basic-level questionnaire in appendix C also may be useful in the preparatory phase (for example, in providing some basic information and diagnostics).

pendix E) keyed to the principal areas of sector reform and the regulatory policies that are intended to support these reforms. The nature of the reforms will vary from country to country. To date, major areas of reform in the power sectors of developing and transition economies have included expansion of access to unserved customers; creation of open access regimes; establishment of organized bulk power markets; promotion of renewable energy and energy efficiency; reduction of technical and commercial losses; and rationalization of pricing, subsidies, and cross-subsidies. Appendix E contains questions designed to evaluate the effectiveness of regulatory policies to support reforms in all these areas.

A mid-level evaluation should be carried out by utility sector or regulatory specialists, or both. A large proportion of these evaluations are likely to be performed by consultants to the World Bank, regional development banks, or other donor agencies. Although this is the current norm, it would be a major advance if more of these evaluations were initiated by national or regional legislative or audit groups. The mid-level evaluation should produce a substantive report and would probably take up to 4 staff-weeks.

An In-Depth Evaluation

An in-depth evaluation is designed to provide *a wide-ranging, in-depth, and fundamental analysis* of the state of reform and regulation in the sector, including an understanding of how the major constituencies view the reforms, and recommendations on how the sector structure and its regulatory system can be improved. It is designed to go wider and deeper than a mid-level evaluation.

The evaluation would be carried out through an initial review of relevant written materials (appendix B), followed by extensive interviews with all parties or interests significantly involved in and affected by the sector and its regulation. The interviews would be open-ended, although the interviewers should prepare a list of the issues they seek to explore to establish the basic agenda for the interviews. Although the list is important, it should not serve as a limitation on the flexibility of the interviewers to pursue added areas of inquiry as they arise. The client for the evaluations (for example, a ministry, regulatory agency, legislative committee, or an international donor organization) should have input into the preparation of the list.[3]

6

---

3. The identity of the client and nature of the interface between client and consultant are discussed further in appendix F.

To initiate the review process, the evaluators should use the structured questionnaires in appendixes C and D developed for the basic and mid-level evaluations (if such evaluations have been made). This will allow them to collect a good initial data set on the industry and its regulatory framework.

For an in-depth evaluation, it also may be appropriate to supplement the interview material with other data collection and to carry out more formal analysis (for example, economic, econometric, legal, policy, financial, or technical) to complement the case study results. An in-depth evaluation always should result in a major report that is published.

In-depth evaluations are likely to be carried out only by specialist evaluation teams. Expert-led teams, possibly based in academic or policy research institutes, can provide a pool of individuals to perform these evaluations. The team members should be from both inside and outside the country. (See appendix F for more discussion of the composition of the team.) An in-depth evaluation normally should take 3–4 staff-months to complete.

Each level of evaluation will go *wider and deeper* than the previous level. In addition, each higher level is likely to require a greater amount of input from senior regulatory, management, business, professional, political, and academic experts involved in the sector and its regulation. Evaluations that lead to changes in the regulatory system or operations almost always will require a mid-level or an in-depth evaluation.

Six examples of mid-level and in-depth evaluations are summarized in appendix G to provide a better sense of the effort required to perform such evaluations. These evaluations were performed on the power sectors of Brazil, Chile, India, Russia, South Africa, and Ukraine. Each summary contains the main findings and recommendations.

The Questionnaires and Interviews

The purpose of the questionnaires and interviews is to understand fully the current situation "on the ground." The questionnaires and interview framework are meant to be broadly applicable across the whole range of developing and transitional countries—and, if desired, in high-income OECD countries. The standards and principles implicit in these documents are intended to serve as guides for evaluators to make judgments about the efficacy of existing arrangements and to develop recommendations for improvements.

The appendixes provide a questionnaire for the short basic evaluation (appendix C) and a questionnaire plus topic headings that can be used as

6

the starting point for mid-level evaluations (appendix D). Each one can be used directly for evaluating electricity regulatory frameworks—and with some modifications for other infrastructure industries. They are intended to be tools for country officials, World Bank and other IFI staff, consultants, academic investigators, and others. The questionnaires deliberately have been designed to incorporate and build on previous questionnaires so as to allow as much comparison as possible.

We do not provide a questionnaire for the in-depth evaluation. Instead, we have developed an interview guide that will use the responses to the medium-level questionnaire as a starting point for the evaluation process (see appendix E). By providing a checklist of issues and concerns, this interview guide can be used for structured discussions with individuals from the government, the regulatory entity, and industry, and from consumers. Appendix F provides guidance on writing the terms of reference for defining, initiating, and conducting an in-depth evaluation.

The questionnaires cover both regulatory governance and regulatory substance. The issues relating to regulatory governance—independence, transparency, and accountability—are likely to be common to all countries. The issues relating to regulatory substance, however, will depend on the nature of the sector and its structure, as well as the goals that are most important to the government. For example, in Central and Eastern Europe the overriding regulatory issues are usually driven by the need to satisfy the requirements of the EU's Electricity Directives to gain membership in the EU. This, in turn, implies considerable focus on issues relating to transmission pricing and wholesale market design. In contrast, the overriding issues for most sub-Saharan African countries are how to improve service, commercialize the sector, make the sector financially viable, and expand access to electricity to those who currently do not have it. Each of these government policy goals requires regulatory actions, and the interview guides are designed to determine whether regulatory actions have supported the country's sector reform goals.

The Alternative of Self-Completed Questionnaires

In the course of preparing this handbook, we became aware of a significant number of questionnaires that have been or are being developed to explore various aspects of utility service industry regulation in developing countries. Most of these questionnaires are *self-completed or self-administered* questionnaires—that is, they are mailed, faxed, or e-mailed to regulatory agencies. Self-

6

completed questionnaires provide a very effective way of collecting relatively small amounts of factual information on regulatory frameworks. They are often used for statistical analyses and benchmarking exercises, but with the following limitations:

- They are inherently unsuited for evaluation where *external* interpretations and judgments of laws, procedures, and outcomes are crucial.
- There are serious limitations on the amount and type of data that can be collected reliably. For instance, self-reported responses are not likely to produce candid assessments that would be detrimental to the reputation of the government or the regulator of the country concerned. In addition, it is unrealistic to expect people to spend several hours or more in completing a questionnaire.
- They usually exhibit response rates of 50 percent or less.[4] In addition to the low response rate, the sampling of agencies responding is likely to be concentrated among the better agencies. Hence, the results will probably be biased for estimating statistics for the underlying population. In particular, they are likely to provide an overly optimistic picture of the state of regulatory development. Unfortunately, it is often difficult to test explicitly for such biases.

There is no question that self-completed questionnaires can provide important information (for example, on the characteristics of utility regulatory agencies or the number of staff they have) about the *formal* structure of the regulatory system. Even for this level of information, however, they need to be used carefully with extensive checks on the quality of the data and their comparability across countries. They are of little or no value for evaluating the *actual operation* of the system and how it can be improved. The significant disadvantages of self-completed questionnaires, even for collecting standard data, are the reason why the basic-level evaluation questionnaire in appendix C has been designed to be used by an outside observer rather than set up as another self-completed questionnaire.

For these reasons, the regulatory evaluations proposed in this handbook—and the questionnaires used to support them—should be administered on site. In addition, they should be carried out by people outside the

---

4. The **Trémolet, Shukla, and Venton** (2004) survey of the contracting out of regulatory functions had a response rate of 38 percent—51 of the 136 agencies approached. This is a typical—and perfectly respectable—response rate for a mail-out, self-completion survey.

regulatory agency and its processes. The people doing the evaluations could be consultants or staff members from the World Bank and other IFIs or donor agencies. They also may be individuals from within the country—for example, people or teams appointed by legislative committees, policy audit commissions, or similar bodies.

An important point to remember is that—like justice—a regulatory evaluation must be seen to be impartial if it is to be accepted as legitimate. In-country evaluators will not be perceived as credible unless they are free of commercial and political interests that could benefit from the report's recommendations. Because it may be almost impossible to find such individuals—especially in smaller countries—a local consultant's role may have to be limited to that of an informant and facilitator rather than that of an evaluator. One possible way to deal with this problem is to employ electricity sector officials or regulators from other countries within the region, but even so there are still risks of potential conflicts of interest.

Conducting the Evaluations

6

The discussion below provides some guidance on how to carry out each of the three proposed levels of evaluation discussed above. The discussion covers the purpose and objectives of each of them, as well as the most important issues concerning how to carry them out successfully—including the question of how they should be presented to give the best chance of their recommendations' being implemented.

Conducting Short Basic Evaluations

The short basic evaluation is intended to serve as a basic stock-taking exercise. It is the equivalent of a health checkup for the regulatory system, which is largely limited to taking "vital signs." It relies on a relatively simple and straightforward questionnaire that is intended to be usable by people with limited previous experience and expertise in utility regulation.

One of the purposes of the questionnaire is to enable appraisals to be made on the core information concerning the regulatory framework (for example, laws, codes, governance, market and industry structures, access levels, prices, and investments), as well as on key events—including both successes and setbacks in the practical application of the regulatory framework. The other purpose of the questionnaire is to collect such data systematically and on a comparable basis across countries and utility service industries. This will allow for the creation of a database that would do the following:

- Help the people carrying out such evaluations in new countries or regulated industries.
- Over time, support the standardized-format assembly of the information that is required for more formal statistical and econometric analysis of the impact of regulation on country and industry outcomes.

The kind of information that is covered in the questionnaire also is needed regularly, for example, by World Bank and similar staff in considering loan and grant applications and preparing for missions or for infrastructure project appraisal reviews. In addition, it can be useful for officials involved in benchmarking regional performance (for example, the Energy Regulators Regional Association [ERRA] for Central and Eastern Europe) and for individuals in policy review and audit groups in individual countries.

The specific questionnaire for the short evaluation in appendix C is designed for use in the electricity industry. However, the first part of the questionnaire would require little change for use in other infrastructure sectors with national and regional regulators. In contrast, the second part, which focuses on substantive reform policies, would need to be modified significantly for use in other infrastructure industries.

The following are the primary elements of the questionnaire for the short basic evaluation:

- The characteristics of the legal framework under which the regulatory entity operates (including the degree of independence, funding, appointment and dismissal criteria, and appeals procedures).
- The number and types of entities regulated.
- The composition of the regulatory entity (both decisionmakers and staff).
- The regulatory entity's decisionmaking powers over the regulated industry.
- A short open-ended exploration of major recent changes in regulatory responsibilities and disputes.
- Basic data on the electricity industry, including industry characteristics and structure, ownership structure, trading arrangements, and so forth.
- The role and scope of price regulation and the nature of price regulation methods used.

6

- The role of government policy in electricity supply and the regulation of the industry.

The questionnaire is primarily designed for use in countries with specific and legally established electricity or other infrastructure regulatory agencies, whether organizationally separate or ministry-based. However, the questionnaire also includes a few questions that cover intermediate and transitional regulatory or quasi-regulatory entities, including infrastructure concession contract monitoring and enforcement agencies. More work on designing evaluation tools for these agencies is clearly needed.

Because this survey is intended to provide answers to a common set of questions across a number of countries, it is strongly recommended that those who use the questionnaire do so without modifying the questions. Although adding questions will not cause problems, deleting or redrafting questions would greatly reduce the value of the questionnaire in providing comparative information across a range of countries.

Conducting Mid-Level Regulatory Evaluations

6

The nature of a mid-level review can be best understood through answers to certain fundamental questions.

1. What Is a Mid-Level Regulatory Evaluation?

A mid-level regulatory evaluation involves a substantial evaluation of a country's or subregion's (such as a state's or province's) utility service industries' regulatory system. Its coverage can be narrow or broad. For example, the evaluation may be sector specific (for example, electricity or telecommunications), or it could be on a specific subject, such as pricing or service quality or decisionmaking processes. Alternatively, it could cover all infrastructure industry regulation in the country or region.

Once the scope of the evaluation is defined, the evaluation should be designed to develop an understanding of the current system and to provide recommendations for improvements.

2. When Should a Mid-Level Evaluation Be Carried Out?

Two primary sets of circumstances can be useful for a medium-term evaluation:

1. When specific problems are being encountered and the service of an objective, experienced, outside observer can be of value.
2. On a periodic basis, for instance, as part of an overall effort to evaluate the effectiveness of the regulatory system, including but not necessarily limited to the performance of the regulators themselves.

3. Who Should Sponsor a Mid-Level Regulatory Evaluation?

Ideally, the evaluation should be sponsored by an agency of the government. The potential sponsors of an evaluation could include

- The regulatory agency itself.
- A ministry or another agency of the government with overall management responsibilities for the government.
- A congressional or parliamentary committee, or people responsible for conducting review and oversight hearings or policy audits of utility regulation and regulatory agencies.

In many cases, the World Bank or another international financial agency or international body may have requested the evaluation. Even if the evaluation was initiated by an external authority, the prime responsibility for conducting the evaluation should be with the relevant governmental body of the country involved.

4. Who Should Carry Out the Mid-Level Evaluation?

The evaluation is best carried out by a small team of consultants with the following requirements:

- At least one of the consultants should be experienced in regulatory matters in a variety of countries. Familiarity with international standards and practice is essential for a successful evaluation.
- The international consultant needs to be carefully balanced with a local consultant who is familiar with current conditions in the sector and the history of the reforms.
- It is also essential that the team include a practicing local lawyer who can make certain that the recommendations contained in the final evaluation are consistent with existing laws or constitutional requirements.

- All consultants should be independent actors exercising their own professional judgments with no financial or other conflict of interest and with no preconceived agenda or conclusions.

If it is not possible to find a local consultant who satisfies these requirements, the role of the local consultant should be limited to that of an informant and facilitator. This is important because the evaluation will have little or no influence unless it is perceived as independent and objective.

5. How Is a Mid-Level Evaluation Best Carried Out?

The consultants should begin by surveying the materials they will need to familiarize themselves with the relevant issues for the evaluation. Those materials include relevant laws, decrees, rules, and constitutional provisions. They also should examine articles in scholarly journals, official reports, trade and general press articles, speeches about the sector, and, of course, relevant regulatory agency reports and decisions. (See appendix B for a listing of background documents.)

If the World Bank or another comparable institution (for example, the Asian Development Bank, the African Development Bank, or the Inter-American Development Bank) has had a formal questionnaire completed about the sector and its regulation, this also would be essential reading. The medium-term questionnaire in appendix D provides an example of this type of questionnaire for the power sector. It should become the standard evaluation tool for mid-level evaluations of power sectors. Although adding new questions might well be useful, it is not advisable to omit questions or redraft them, unless there is very good reason to do so. Again this is to try to maximize comparability across evaluations, countries, and industry sectors.

After gaining some familiarity with the subject, the consultants need to negotiate a well-defined, flexible scope of work with the sponsor. The scope of work should include the following:

- A description of the subjects to be covered.
- A statement of the scope of the expected work product.
- A schedule for project milestones.

The description of the subjects should be specific enough to be meaningful, but not so specific as to preclude the consultants from pursuing a line of inquiry that might be of value, but that was unanticipated in the planning

6

stages of the work. Appendix F contains a sample terms of reference that could be used to hire consultants.

The consultants should prepare a list of queries designed to cover the assigned subjects. Those queries should be the basis of a submission in writing to key actors. More importantly, however, the queries should be used as a major element in the interviews with critical figures in the sector. The interviewees should be broadly representative of the sector. In electricity, for example, interviewees should include people from the following groups:

- Commissioners and staff from the regulatory agency.
- Senior people involved in generation companies or entities, transmission operators, distribution companies or entities, system operators, and market administrators.
- Representatives of consumers, large and small.
- Environmental experts and lobbyists, judges, local officials, and specialist journalists.

The consultants should make inquiries as to whom they should interview and then endeavor to interview all those people. The interviews should be somewhat uniform in the sense of beginning with the same queries, but the consultants should not be constrained from following important leads that develop during the course of discussions.

The ground rules of the interviews are critical, of course, if people are to speak candidly and openly. Accordingly, it is best that the consultants indicate at the outset that the interviews are on a "not-for-attribution" basis.[5] It is important that the consultants gain the trust of the interviewees so that they are comfortable enough to speak candidly and openly.

At the conclusion of the interviews and other information collection, the consultants should prepare a draft report to be delivered to the sponsors of the evaluation. After giving the sponsors time to review the draft report, the consultants should meet with them to get their feedback. The consultants should then make whatever revisions, if any, are necessary in the consultants' independent judgment. The revised draft should then be circulated in draft form to all the interviewees, and to other interested parties, in order to get wider feedback—and, it is hoped, to generate discussion and debate. It is also

---

5. *Not for attribution* means that what interviewees say may well be used—or even quoted—but the source of the thoughts or comments will not be identified other than in the most general of ways (for example, "an electric generator executive informed us that . . .").

useful to conduct a workshop or seminar with all interviewees and other interested parties in order to obtain more detailed and nuanced feedback.

Once the process of getting feedback is complete, the consultants should finalize the report and submit it to the sponsors. It is desirable to release the report to the media as well to get more coverage of the recommendations and analysis. If the sponsors are agreeable, it might well be worth presenting the report to legislative and executive branch leaders as well. The final report should then be published.

It may well be appropriate to arrange some kind of seminar or workshop involving interested parties and outside experts to discuss the report and accompanying conclusions. It may also be worth considering the establishment of a Web-based discussion facility to involve a wider range of people within the country and from outside. (See the Web site of the World Bank's Rapid Response Unit for examples of structured Web-based discussions: http://rru.worldbank.org/Discussions/.)

For further discussion of mid-level evaluations, see appendixes D, E, and F.

Conducting In-Depth Evaluations

The guidance provided for conducting mid-level evaluations applies equally well to in-depth evaluations. The principal difference between the two is that the in-depth evaluation should go wider and deeper. Specifically, this means that more issues would be covered and more individuals would be interviewed. For both the mid-level and the in-depth evaluations, the evaluators always should be mindful that the goal of the exercise is to be of genuine assistance to the government in thinking through some needed changes to its existing regulatory system. This is a different mindset from the more typical mindset of writing a report with the expectation of just moving on to write another report in another country.

Ensuring That the Evaluation Is Taken Seriously

If a country's decisionmakers are to take the evaluation seriously, they must be convinced of two things: its credibility and its usefulness. Credibility requires both the appearance and the reality of independence and professionalism. An evaluation will be ignored if decisionmakers believe that the evaluators are simply representing the interests of one or two sectoral constituencies. Therefore, the evaluators always must be conscious of how they interact with everyone with whom they come into contact. Even the manner in which they ask questions can influence whether the report is taken seriously or is ignored.[6] Finally, the credibility of the evaluators is enhanced by how they present their analysis and recommendations. Both "what is said" and "how it is said" are of equal importance. In the authors' experience, the recommendations of a report dealing with sensitive and controversial issues are more likely to be accepted if the tone of the report is "here is how we have thought about this problem and possible options for solving it," rather than "here are international best practices, and we recommend that you adopt these practices."[7]

Particularly for in-depth evaluations, the recommendations are likely to carry more weight if the analysis in the evaluation includes some systematic, quantitative analysis of data on sectoral performance, for example, examination of trends over time, their determinants, and, if possible, the contribution of regulatory agencies to the changes. The appropriate form of quantitative analysis may well vary between evaluations and countries. In some cases, relatively informal quantitative economic analyses may be sufficient. In other cases, more ambitious economic evaluation methods and formal modeling may be justified. However, it is clear that the presentation and analysis based on quantitative data—both from within the country and from reasonably comparable countries—always will help carry out the qualitative, interview elements of the evaluation. It also is likely to add significantly to the credibility of the final report and to convince policymakers and their advisers to implement the report's recommendations for change.

It is important for evaluators to think about how to gain the trust and attention of busy ministers. Typically, the terms of reference for mid-level and in-depth evaluations will state that the objective is to "evaluate the overall effectiveness of the electricity regulatory system." This should be the primary goal—but even if a minister has agreed to this goal, it is the authors' experience that most, although not all, ministers are usually more concerned with immediate problems than with long-range strategies. In most bureaucracies, the day-to-day reality is that the "immediate" almost always takes precedence over the "important." Given this reality, a good strategy is to reserve some

---

6. See the discussion on how to conduct interviews at the beginning of appendix E.
7. See, for example, the style of presentation for recommendations 18, 21, and 25 in the recent evaluation of the Brazilian regulatory system. Brown and de Paula (2004).

time in the contract for advising the minister on short-term issues that may arise during the contract but can rarely be predicted in advance. If the evaluator can demonstrate usefulness to the minister on the *crise du jour,* the minister is much more likely to be receptive to any longer-term recommendations for reform from that same person. To put it in another way, there is nothing that builds up trust as much as "a shared experience in the policy trenches."

Conclusions and Implications for Regulatory Evaluation

The purpose of this chapter has been to provide guidance on how to conduct short basic, mid-level, and in-depth evaluations of electricity and other infrastructure regulatory systems. It also provides tools—questionnaires and interview guidelines—to perform these evaluations and explains how they can be used for evaluating the performance of an entire regulatory system, not just that of the designated regulatory entity.

It may be useful to step back and remind ourselves why such evaluations need to be performed. Almost all the new infrastructure regulatory systems were created as one element of a larger package of infrastructure reforms. These reforms were intended to benefit consumers and attract private investors. After a decade or more of experience, the widespread perception is that many infrastructure reform programs have been only partially successful in achieving these outcomes, at least for electricity and particularly in low-income countries. Because regulation has been one important component of the reforms, this inevitably has raised the questions, first, of whether the new regulatory systems have contributed positively or negatively to the reform outcomes, and second, of how one can make this determination objectively. More importantly, whatever the degree of success of the reformed regulatory arrangements, we would strongly argue that periodic evaluations of new institutional systems are necessary to facilitate proper oversight and review of the new regulatory frameworks and to help facilitate "mid-course" corrections that would otherwise be difficult to make.

Therefore, this handbook has presented a methodology that allows for the systematic evaluation of the design and operation of new regulatory systems and their strengths and weaknesses. By strengths and weaknesses, we mean aspects of the rules, organization, processes, and decisions of a regulatory system that make it easier or harder to achieve government goals for the sector.

6

To carry out such an investigation, we have recommended a methodology based on structured case studies that differs from earlier efforts in several key respects. The principal difference is that the handbook has presented a methodology designed to enable an evaluation team to do the following:

- Go beyond what is written in laws to evaluate what is done in practice.
- Examine regulatory substance, as well as regulatory governance.
- Analyze how the regulatory system helps or hinders the achievement of sector outcomes that are important to government.
- Present recommendations for changing the regulatory system in a form that is likely to be persuasive to government decisionmakers.

Although the handbook has used the independent regulator model as a benchmark for evaluating existing regulatory systems, we also have suggested elements of possible transitional or alternative regulatory systems. We believe that this will make the handbook more relevant for developing and transition-economy countries. However, it makes the evaluator's job more difficult. The independent regulator has a fairly well-defined set of characteristics. (See chapter 3 and appendix A.) This is not true for transitional regulatory systems. Such systems can take many different forms, depending on the characteristics of the sector and a country's governance endowment.[8] Therefore, if the evaluator is evaluating or recommending a transitional system, it will inevitably require more effort than if he or she were simply evaluating or recommending the independent regulator model.

It would be presumptuous to imply that this handbook represents the last word on regulatory evaluations. The evaluation of such a system is clearly more of an art than a science. There are significant gaps in our knowledge. In particular, more research should be conducted in the following areas:

- Developing transitional or alternative regulatory systems that satisfy the basic meta-principles in chapter 3.
- Designing dynamic elements that allow transitional and alternative regulatory systems to evolve as the infrastructure sector changes.

---

8. Although the precise nature of the institutional model may vary, the criteria advanced both in chapter 3 and in appendix A are relevant to all institutional models, with the possible exception of those specifically linked to regulatory independence. It would be inconceivable, for example, to find a model acceptable in any way if it were devoid of ethical standards, meaningful opportunities for public participation, intellectual discipline, or transparency.

- Establishing regulatory systems that can accommodate different forms of private sector participation (such as full privatization, concessions, leases, and management contracts).
- Assessing what, if any, regulatory systems may be appropriate for state-owned enterprises that exhibit different degrees of corporatization and commercialization.
- Understanding how regulatory systems help or hinder the achievement of government goals for the sector being regulated.

To date, too many of the regulatory evaluations have been done in isolation. For example, it took considerable effort just to track down the six evaluations of power sector regulatory systems that are summarized in appendix G. As a consequence, synergies probably were lost that could have improved these evaluations. Therefore, we would recommend that the World Bank, another international organization, or a group of universities create a central database of publicly available evaluations. One possible location would be the World Bank's Rapid Response Web site (http://rru.worldbank.org/), which already includes a collection of important articles and reports from regulatory literature. Another possible location would be the multi-university "regulatory body of knowledge" Web site (http://bear.cba.ufl.edu/centers/purc/Body_of _Knowledge.htm) maintained by the University of Florida. In addition to providing a depository of regulatory evaluations, such a Web site could provide a location for an electronic message board for regulators and evaluators. Such a system could make a major contribution to improving the quality of future regulatory evaluations.

Finally, we would be delighted if practitioners were to find our evaluation tools useful in judging and improving the performance of infrastructure industry regulatory systems. We would be even more delighted if, in 5–10 years, the methodology proposed in this handbook had been field-tested, built upon, and significantly improved. We have identified some specific areas where we think more work is necessary. However, we also are aware of—and look forward to—future developments in evaluation methods and practice that will help improve the performance of regulatory systems in providing improved access to infrastructure services that are of better quality and that are produced more efficiently by commercially sustainable enterprises. A regulatory system that helps achieve these goals can make a genuine and lasting contribution to the alleviation of poverty in developing countries.

6

Critical Standards for Effective Regulation of Infrastructure: A Detailed Exposition

This appendix defines the "best-practice" regulatory governance standards presented in chapter 3 and elaborates on them. The focus of these 15 standards is on the institutional and legal framework of the regulatory system, as well as its processes and procedures, rather than on substantive decisions, which are discussed in chapter 5. The purpose of the standards is to create a checklist of specific actions that would be needed to implement the 3 meta-principles and 10 general principles of chapter 3 in a concrete way to produce a functioning independent regulator. In other words, the standards provide the bridge to go from the "general" to the "specific" and from the "theoretical" to the "practical."

It is sometimes difficult to explain to policymakers why standards such as those set forth in this chapter are necessary. The difficulty can arise for a variety of reasons ranging from a reluctance or unwillingness to put into place a truly transparent process to a simple lack of knowledge of what is required to implement effective regulatory reform. The purpose of this appendix is to provide a common-sense, experienced-based explanation of what is required to implement each standard, along with the benefits, both political and practical, that would be derived from adopting the standard. The appendix is intended to be a document that open-minded policymakers can digest easily and consider carefully. It is designed to ensure that all participants in the regulatory process, whether they agree or disagree with the outcome of a regulatory proceeding, at least will be assured that the decision was honestly derived, that their interests and views were adequately considered, and that they were treated fairly in the process. For reform-minded policymakers, the possibility of attaining such a result should be very persuasive.

1. Legal Framework

1.1. Create a law

The regulatory agency should be created in a law, preferably in a statute or primary law, that fully articulates its jurisdictional authority, powers, duties, and responsibilities.

The basic rules governing the full authority, powers, duties, and responsibilities should be set out in primary law.[1] The reason for the preference is that primary law is both more representative of political will and consensus to create and sustain an independent regulatory agency and inherently more permanent and stable than the alternative of an executive decree of some sort. Primary law can be changed, of course, but only through the full legislative process.

The alternative method of creating a regulatory agency, through presidential or ministerial decree, has been used in some countries. Mere executive action is problematic because, in contrast to primary law, it is relatively easy to change, or even to use as a threat for the government to wield in ways that could compromise the independence of regulatory agencies. It is also highly susceptible to reassessment every time the government changes. Moreover, whereas legislative processes are often insufficiently transparent, they are likely to be more transparent than the process of issuing ministerial or even presidential or cabinet decrees. Thus, changes in the basic laws governing regulation will be difficult to make without public debate and awareness of what is being contemplated.

The necessity of such a process to alter the regulatory regime is precisely what should occur and, although it does not fully insulate the regulator from pressure, it exposes those pressures to greater public scrutiny than do the alternatives.

1.1.1. Articulate the principles and practices in the law

Basic regulatory principles, practices, procedures, and policies to be followed should be articulated in law, preferably in a statute or primary law.

The law itself should be reasonably thorough in defining the scope of the agency's jurisdiction, the public policies and methodologies it is obliged to follow and apply, the specific duties and responsibilities it is assigned, and the powers it possesses to carry out its work.

The substance of the various elements, which should be addressed in law, is laid out fully over the course of this handbook. The principle is precisely the same as that articulated with regard to creating and empowering the regulatory agency, namely that there be a degree of *stability and permanence* in the substance, methodologies, and processes of the entire regulatory system. Such stability and predictability is not perfect, but it does allow for more rational and efficient decisionmaking by investors and

---

1. For purposes of this handbook, *primary law* is defined as a formal statute enacted by the legislative authority of the country and, if required, approved by the executive authority. It can be altered only by an act of the legislature. Although it is rarely done, creation and empowerment of a regulatory agency by constitutional provision also meets the definition of primary legislation. *Secondary legislation* is defined, for purposes of this handbook, as a decree or rule promulgated under lawful authority by executive officials (for example, the president or minister). That same authority also possesses the power to alter the decree or rule.

consumers alike than a regime whose substantive basis is easily and readily alterable—whether or not that basis is actually altered.

1.1.2. Create laws that are forward-looking

All laws enacted on regulatory matters should be prospective in nature, and none should have retrospective application.

The laws should set the boundaries of, and guidelines for, regulatory action. They are not an alternative to, or recourse from, regulatory decisions. To serve their boundary-setting and guidance objectives, the laws can only be prospective and future looking. Regulators, for example, can hardly be expected to follow principles that appear only after action has been taken. Similarly, retrospective reversal of otherwise lawful regulatory decisions by legislation, either primary or secondary, seriously compromises both regulatory independence and transparency for the reasons discussed below.

2. Legal Powers

2.1. Grant final decisionmaking authority

The regulatory agency should have the authority to make final decisions within its statutory domain without having to obtain approval from any other agency of government.

The ability of a regulatory agency to make a final decision[2] without having to obtain approval from any other agency of the government is, in theory and practice, the most fundamental element of meaningful independence[3] of the regulatory agency.

In some countries, the regulatory agency has the power only to advise the ministry or government on regulatory matters, such as tariffs. The dynamics of that advisory function vary from country to country. In some places, the agency's decision is often determinative, whereas in others it is largely a symbolic effort. As a long-term arrangement, this is emphatically not a best practice or ideal standard.

If used at all, advisory regulation should be adopted only as an introductory transitional step toward fully independent decisionmaking for regulation. Any advice should be given publicly and openly. It is also important that any use of such an arrangement should be subject to an explicit date for going to full, independent regulation (for example, through a

A

---

2. By matter of definition, *final decision* in this handbook means the last administrative decision. The decision, of course, is subject to the appellate process. The existence of an appellate process, as discussed below, should certainly *not* be understood to mean any compromise of regulatory independence.

3. In some legal systems (for example, in Brazil and some other Latin American countries), the terms *autonomy* and *independence* for such institutions as regulatory agencies have *different* meanings. Where the distinction is made, *independence* denotes a greater level of freedom from possible government interference or influence than does *autonomy*. For the purposes of this handbook, however, the terms are used interchangeably.

"sunset" clause). A number of developing countries have failed to take this second step in spite of policy statements that they intended to do so.

Subject to the possible transition issues above, anything less than the ability to make final binding decisions is a serious compromise of the agency's independence and perhaps of the transparency of the entire regulatory process.

2.2. Establish minimum jurisdiction

The regulatory agency should, at a minimum, possess the power to do the following:

2.2.1. Set tariffs

Set or approve tariffs at reasonable levels for both consumers and regulated entities.

The power to set tariffs for monopoly providers of basic infrastructure services is at the heart of what a regulatory agency is created to do. The tariff-setting process is central to protecting consumers against the abuse of monopoly power. Conversely, in the absence of competition, tariffs are the most critical aspect of providing incentives for regulated companies to invest and perform in efficient and desired ways. Although the law—and licenses or concession or franchise contracts[4]—should state clearly what methodologies should be employed, the actual calculations and application of the principles embodied in tariff methodology fall to the regulator.

In addition to the broad purposes of the tariffs, of course, the regulators must have the power to deal with a host of subsidiary tariff questions, such as in the following areas:

- Cost and risk allocations.
- Determination of asset base.
- Cost of capital assumptions.

Indeed, just as important as it is to lay out the approved methodologies in law, it is equally advisable that the law be stated in broad principles rather than in explicit detail. However, a government may find it necessary to specify a detailed tariff-setting formula for a first tariff-setting period to gain the confidence of investors. This is especially true if no regulatory entity exists at the time that a particular transaction is being negotiated. In general, it is far better that a regulator be created prior to negotiating a transaction, so that it can advise the government on the workability and feasibility of the proposed regulatory system. The regulator can, and should, also act as a control mechanism on government's inherent "moral hazard" in privatization, name-

---

4. In this handbook, we use the terms *license*, *concession*, and *franchise* interchangeably.

ly the conflict between "sweetening" the initial arrangement in order to gain the short-term advantage of maximizing the purchase price paid by the investor for a state-owned asset, and looking out for the long term best interest of the consumer and of the sector itself. The failure to guard against such perverse incentives in privatization has proven to be a problem in a number of countries, notably in Brazil.

A host of issues exist in every pricing methodology that need to be carefully considered and dealt with in an expert, balanced, and technically competent manner. Regulators need to have sufficient discretion to act in such a manner. These issues are almost always implicit in the general power to set tariffs, although the law or concession documents may well contain specific directions.

The omission of details on these matters in law or concession documents can sometimes prove to be a problem. Such was the case in Brazil, where the method for valuing assets in the recalculation of distribution tariffs was left entirely to the discretion of the regulators. Distributors claimed they had been promised that the asset base would be the purchase price at the time of privatization, whereas others suggested that there was no such commitment and that both the law and the concessions were silent on the question. The issue, from the broad perspective of regulatory standards, is not who was correct, but rather that such critical elements of tariff calculation should be addressed in either the law or the concession documents in order to provide both some degree of predictability to investors and consumers and some guidance to the regulators.

Another issue inherent in tariff-setting is the question of cross-subsidies. Part of the cross-subsidy question, of course, is inherent in how one analyzes costs and risks, and allocates them across customers or customer classes. Allocating costs and risks is a highly subjective series of judgments that regulators are compelled to make. What may seem a legitimate allocation to one person may be seen as a cross-subsidy by another. This is an inherent aspect of tariff-setting. The important legal point is that the regulator needs to be left with some degree of discretion in making cost-allocation and related judgments.

In addition to that, however, is a question of deliberate cross-subsidies being built into rates. They may sometimes take on the characteristic of a transfer from large customers to small ones or, as is sometimes the case, the other way around. There may also be explicit cross-subsidies designed to achieve desired social results. Examples of this include subsidies to low-income customers to promote economic development and support for rural electrification.

It can be argued that such cross-subsidies in tariffs are inherently inefficient and undesirable, but political and social reality often makes them unavoidable. Indeed, some contend that regulatory administration of cross-subsidies is more likely to make

A

them better targeted and more efficient than politically administered cross-subsidies. As interesting as that debate may be, for purposes of this handbook, the questions from the standpoint of the regulator's powers are as follows:

- What cross-subsidies, if any, are mandated by law?
- What is the degree to which the regulator is required to ensure that they are efficiently targeted to achieve the desired result and to make them as transparent as possible?

If there are to be cross-subsidies, they should be explicitly stated in law, concession, or other policy in language either binding upon or empowering of regulators. If some discretion on those matters is left to the regulator, the scope of that discretion should also be clearly specified.

The critical point on the legal powers of regulators concerning tariffs is that there should be clear empowerment of regulators to establish tariffs and undertake all activities required to do so. Additionally, there should be sufficient guidance and clarity in law, concession documents, or binding policy pronouncements concerning both the methods to be employed and the cross-subsidies to be put in place in order to provide all stakeholders with a reasonable expectation of how tariffs will be formulated.

Although clarity and guidance are in order, it should also be noted that leaving some discretion to the regulator to deal with ever changing circumstances is both desirable and necessary.

2.2.2. Set standards

Set binding standards in such appropriate areas as technical and commercial service quality.

After tariff-setting, perhaps the next most important task of the regulators is to set the minimum service standards that regulated entities are expected to meet. If regulated companies operate under licenses, the service standards may be specified in the license.

These standards could include service quality, interface with consumers, safety, social obligations (for example, expansion of service availability), and a variety of other matters that are not inherently or exclusively economic in nature and that are, therefore, not internalized in the tariffs.

The regulator must be given the authority to articulate in some detail the precise standards with which all regulated entities will be required to comply. As in the question of tariff methodology, both investors and consumers have a right to know what is expected. Because standards are often of a technical and complex nature, it is perhaps best that the delegation of powers to the regulators be of a general, not overly detailed, nature that allows for the exercise of broad discretion. The law should make clear those subjects on which regulators are required to publish standards, but leave to the regulators the discretion to articulate them in other areas as well. Regulators should also have the discretion to change the standards, with sufficient notice, over time. In most developing countries, the technical and commercial quality-of-service standards will need to be phased in over time.

2.2.3. Make rules

Make rules and subsidiary policy for the sector, as long as such policies and rules are within its legal authority, that are reasonably necessary for carrying out its duties and not inconsistent with the policies and principles articulated in the applicable law.

It is sometimes suggested that the job of the regulator is simply to implement law and policy. This is an oversimplification of the regulatory role. The law or other binding policy documents will set forth policies that the regulator is obliged to follow. They can be labeled "primary policy." Inevitably, however, the primary policy will prove to be lacking in detail and will have to be flushed out in greater detail in order for the regulator to make actual decisions.

Stated simply, in order to make necessary regulatory decisions, the regulator will need the authority to interpret the primary law in the face of actual events and in consideration of the details of individual cases. This requires them to develop a regulatory approach within the primary law and government-declared policy. In this handbook, this process is described as the making of "secondary policy."

Although one could contend that making secondary policy is an inherent part of the exercise of regulatory authority, there has been considerable controversy in many countries over the regulators' ability to "make policy." It is important that the laws empowering regulators not be overly restrictive in preventing the regulator from exercising this function.

2.2.4. Carry out responsibilities

Perform such routine functions as the agency may need to do in order to operate, such as making personnel decisions, spending money appropriately within its budgetary authorization, taking relevant administrative decisions and actions, and performing such other duties as government agencies ordinarily undertake in carrying out their obligations.

Although it seems self-evident that an agency created by the government would have the power to administer itself, there are special considerations to keep in mind for an independent regulatory agency. Unlike other agencies of the government that might be subject to general administrative rules, regulatory bodies have particular

A

special requirements for salary conditions, ethical rules, the need for freedom from retaliation for unpopular decisions, and budgetary considerations, among others. All these matters will be discussed below.

What is important in the law is that the agency be duly authorized to conduct its own affairs, and that it not be subject to any provisions that impede its ability to pay competitive salaries, hire and retain senior and skilled personnel, and employ permanent or temporary staff as the agency requires. The agency also needs to be able to maintain stable funding and to subscribe to the very highest ethical standards.

Regardless of their special needs, however, regulatory agencies should be subject to fiscal oversight (for example, audits) by the government.

2.2.5. Enforce rules

Fully enforce its decisions, standards, and rules, as well as relevant public policy. This requires the regulatory agency to have a range of remedies, including penalties, appropriate to the severity of violations it is likely to meet.

Regulators cannot fulfill their obligations if they lack the ability to enforce their decisions. The law needs to provide them with the means to do so. Two specific issues must be considered in that regard. The first is the *nature of the enforcement,* and the second is the question of the *remedies available* if it is determined that a regulated entity is in violation of a rule or other regulatory requirement.

a. **Nature of enforcement**

Regulators can enforce their decisions in two general ways. In some countries, it is by issuing their own order. The order would be enforced by the government in the exercise of its general police powers. The second would be through the courts where the agency issues its decision. If a regulated company does not obey the order, however, the agency would go to court to give the order legal effect so as to be able to enforce it.

The first method is more direct and more efficient, although the second provides for greater procedural protections against abuse. The latter course has the added risk that the court could try to substitute its judgment for that of the regulator—something that is best avoided. Nonetheless, either approach can be effective.

The critical point is that in the law, there should be an explicit means for the regulators to enforce their decisions.

b. **Remedies available to regulators**

The second issue is the remedies available to regulators under the law. In some countries, the only remedy available is the suspension or termination of a license. Such remedies are to regulation what nuclear weapons are to war-

A

fare. They are the remedies of last resort when all other means of obtaining compliance have been exhausted and the harm being caused or threatened is overwhelming.

Thus, if license suspension or termination is the only method legally available, the regulator, when faced with a small violation, is left with no effective remedy at all. *It is, therefore, necessary that the law provide the regulator with very broad discretion to penalize violators in proportion to their violation.* Such remedies as refunds, fines, injunctions, and rebates should be available to the regulator under law, along with suspension and termination of the license.

2.2.6. Obtain information

Compel the production and provision of the information as may be necessary to carry out the regulatory functions and serve the interests of transparency.

Regulators cannot perform their job without access to accurate, documented, and complete information. It is not reasonable to believe that parties will voluntarily produce all the information needed by the regulator. Certainly individuals and companies have powerful incentives to conceal information that is adverse to themselves from regulators. *It is essential that the law provide the regulator with the means to compel the production of needed information from all necessary parties.*

Although a party can—and should—be afforded the right to be free from unreasonable or irrelevant information requests—or to request confidential treatment for legitimately confidential information, as discussed further below—that assertion or claim needs to demonstrated. The regulator (or reviewing court) needs to be persuaded of the reasons why the requested information should not be supplied to the regulator.

It is also important that the law clearly states the power to compel the production of needed information and documents. This includes the authority to compel regulated companies to issue periodic reports (for example, annually or quarterly) that set forth such information as the regulator can show is necessary and appropriate.

2.2.7. Require adoption and use of accounting standards

Adopt and compel compliance with such appropriate accounting standards and practices as may reasonably be required for regulatory purposes.

Most countries have a uniform system of accounts with which businesses are required to comply for financial reporting and tax purposes. For many, if not most, regulatory matters, such accounting rules are adequate.

If no such generally applicable rules exist, regulators will need the power to impose them. There are also circumstances where special financial accounting is required for regulatory purposes, such as the following:

A

- Where companies combine regulated and unregulated businesses—which may well require separate accounts, separate management, or more.
- Where certain expenses, which might be perfectly legitimate business expenditures, cannot be recovered from consumers in cost-of-service regulation.

Some separate regulatory accounting treatment is necessary in these cases. Regulators need to have the authority to mandate such accounting when circumstances demand it.

2.2.8. Adopt procedures

Adopt appropriate procedures for carrying out its duties.

For the regulatory process to be transparent, the procedures to be followed in decisionmaking must be known to everyone affected. *Well-defined and transparent procedures are not only fundamental for fairness, they also provide the ultimate protection for consumers, regulated companies, and investors alike.* (The details of the optimal model of a transparent process will be discussed in greater detail below.)

For the purposes of basic regulatory law, however, two things are important to note:

- The regulatory agency should be required to set out in writing precisely what the procedures will be for deciding the various matters that come before it.
- Any elements of general procedural fairness or transparency required by a country's laws or culture should be laid down by law.

2.2.9. Resolve disputes

Adjudicate statutorily designated disputes between regulated entities and between regulated entities and consumers.

For the rules concerning the interface between consumers and regulated entities to be interpreted consistently and predictably, it is best that the law require, if possible, that all unresolved disputes between them be mediated or adjudicated by the regulator, or both.

Concerning disputes between regulated entities, the law should specify which types of disputes should be resolved by the regulator and which should be left to the courts to resolve as ordinary commercial controversies would. The law should be clear on this delineation in order to avoid jurisdictional disputes between the courts and the regulator.

2.2.10. Prevent exercise of monopoly power

Prevent the abuse of monopoly or market power.

The regulatory agency requires the ability to prevent the abuse of monopoly power in two contexts. The first is where the regulated entity is a monopoly provider, such as an electric distribution company or a water supply company. The regulatory agency needs

A

the power to protect consumers from such an entity's abuse of its powers, including authority over business practices and undue discrimination (subsections 2.2.12 and 2.2.13 below), and the tariff standard setting detailed above.

The second refers to the need for the regulator to prevent the abuse of monopoly power in areas where the market is open to competition, such as it might be in electricity generation or retail supply, as well as in telecom services. To remedy or to prevent any market participant (or set of participants) from abusing their market power, the regulator needs to have the authority to do a number of things, such as the following:

- Instituting a code for competitive behavior.
- Separating functions where vertical market power is exercised.
- Ordering separation of accounts.
- Requiring divestiture of particular businesses.
- Ordering refunds or rebates, or disgorgement of ill-gained profits.

There is also an institutional issue concerning the matter of controlling abuse of market power. Some developing and transition countries have a competition (antitrust) regulator, who might also have responsibilities in these areas.

Although the infrastructure sector regulator clearly should have explicit legal responsibility for controlling any abuse by a monopoly provider, in the context of a competitive market, the law should specify whether the competition or sector regulator has primary responsibility for dealing with abuse of market power. In the alternative, the law should require the two agencies to coordinate on these matters. Conflict in authority between the sector and competition regulator should be avoided, and the terms of the law should provide the best way to do so.

2.2.11. Promote competition

Promote competition where appropriate and feasible.

Some aspects of the electricity market are natural monopolies, and some are not. The same is true for other infrastructure industries, such as railways, natural gas, and telecoms. While the electric wire businesses of transmission and distribution, for example, are likely to remain natural monopolies, competition in generation and perhaps retail supply have the potential to be—and in many places already are—competitive businesses.

The regulator needs sufficient legal authority to promote, shape the transition to, and maintain competition where it is decided that it is both viable and desirable to rely on competition rather than regulation for the electricity sector, the necessary powers include issues for electricity, such as the following:

- The formulation and enforcement of market rules.

195

- Market governance arrangements.
- Oversight of dispatch.
- Formation and oversight of independent system operators (where they exist),
- Interconnection rules.
- Network policies and pricing.[5]

2.2.12. Protect consumers

Adequately protect consumers from unfair or abusive business practices.

The regulator has a fundamental obligation to protect consumers against fraudulent, abusive, or other unfair treatment by a regulated entity. Much of this authority is exercised through the adoption of quality-of-service standards or a consumer bill of rights, and vigorous enforcement of their provisions. However, circumstances may also exist where the code provisions might not be fully applicable, for example, to a competitive retail supplier.

The law should clearly provide the regulatory agency with the power to redress abuse or other unfair treatment of consumers by all regulated entities.

2.2.13. Prevent undue discrimination

Prevent undue discrimination in the provision, terms, and conditions of services.

Monopoly providers should be barred from unduly discriminating against any customer in the provision of services. Undue discrimination means to discriminate among similarly situated customers without good cause (for example, cost basis, competitive market circumstance, or legitimate, authorized social objective).

This is a basic principle to guard against favoritism, arbitrariness, corruption, and other undesirable results. The regulator must have the clear authority to protect against it.

This issue is particularly important for infrastructure companies that combine network and service elements. It is an issue that has been central to effective regulation since the development of the railways in the 19th century and that regularly recurs in telecoms, natural gas, and railways, as well as in electricity supply. Because behavioral or conduct regulation in this area can be very difficult to sustain effectively,

---

5. Just as in the case of preventing abuse of monopoly power, there may be other agencies with regulatory or policy-making power in this area (for example, the competition regulator or energy ministry). The respective authorities of each of those entities need to be specified. Jurisdictional disputes among competing agencies of the state, as noted elsewhere in the handbook, are disruptive and make unpredictability and policy incoherence the likely outcomes. Confused jurisdiction complicates dispute resolution as well. In that regard, however, it is vital that the sector regulator, at a minimum, have considerable input into the formulation and enforcement of competition in the regulated sector.

structural separation is often advocated as superior.[6] However, structural separation can also create problems even for electricity, particularly in small countries.

2.2.14. Monitor performance

Monitor the performance of regulated entities, the functioning of the market, and the maintenance of supply.

Regulators must be able to track developments closely in the market over which they have legal authority. The law needs to provide all the requisite legal tools to enable the regulators to do so. The information-gathering power, mentioned above, is part of the equation.

In addition, the law should actually require the regulator to conduct market monitoring and issue periodic reports on the state of the market, and should focus on the following:

- Competition issues.
- Supply adequacy.
- The operations of market institutions.
- Similar topics.

3. Property and Contract Rights

3.1. Respect for property rights

The property rights of all persons and entities should be protected, respected, and in no way treated arbitrarily, or unfairly abridged or violated by the regulatory system.
Regulation is not a regime for either confiscating or arbitrarily diminishing the value of private property. Rather, it is an environment in which the risks and rewards associated with investment in the regulated sector are assessed and treated in a rational, symmetrical, and, to the extent possible, predictable and consistent way. Property rights—and incentives for their efficient and productive use—is an essential element of a successful regulatory regime. Those rights should be honored and protected, and property itself should be treated with respect.

In practical terms, respect for property means that owners should not be deprived of their ownership rights and that economic decisions concerning the use of property should respect the value of the assets in question. That is, the regulator should not take actions that arbitrari-

---

6. *Behavioral (or conduct) regulation* is defined for the purposes of this handbook as close scrutiny of the actions and interactions of the company and its staff members, including the possibilities of governing behavior by a formal code of conduct. *Structural regulation* is defined for the purposes of this handbook as the management, business, corporate, or full legal separation of different business activities (for example, the separation of electricity generation from transmission or natural gas pipelines from wholesale and retail natural gas sales).

ly reduce asset values—such as holding regulated tariffs below economic cost—unless there is a specific justification to do so, such as arising from imprudent or unjustified expenditures.

The valuation of assets in regulation is an often subjective and controversial matter. Respect for property rights does *not* require that the regulator necessarily agree with an owner's valuation. It does, however, mean that the regulator must have a rational, coherent, and legally defensible basis for making a valuation.

A number of examples exist where regulators may, for good reasons, not value the property in the same way an owner might. One example, often encountered in cost-of-service regulation, is where owners have been found to have incurred expenses they need not have incurred, such as undocumented, or inadequately documented, expenditures or imprudent expenditures. In cost-of-service regulation, companies are not permitted to recover those costs from captive consumers.

The issue of imprudence in particular almost always raises difficult and contentious issues that regularly arise in cost-of-service regulation. Similar issues—for example, on future cost assumption—arise in price cap and revenue cap regulation.[7]

Similarly, constraints on the use of property, such as not allowing utility property to be used to cross-subsidize a regulated company's activities in other markets without appropriate compensation to the regulated activity, must have a basis in fact and policy to justify the imposition of the constraint.

Another frequent controversy in regulation results from a circumstance where a regulated entity believes that the price it is allowed to charge for its goods and services does not cover the costs it incurred in acquiring and operating the assets necessary for rendering services. The regulator needs to have a reasonable economic and factual basis for such decisions to defend against such criticism.

One important note in this context is that the tariffs set by the regulator need not *guarantee* the regulated entity the recovery of the full value of property. They should, however, provide the entity with a *reasonable opportunity* to recover the full value of the asset, including the cost of capital,[8] and must not erect unreasonable barriers to the owner doing so. Indeed, there is a *very compelling* argument that guarantees to regulated entities are counterproductive in that they remove incentives for increasing efficiency and productivities.

---

7. Issues such as imprudence, cost assumptions, and the like raise difficult issues concerning the boundary between regulation and company management. These issues are highly judgmental and deeply controversial in both theory and practice. Hence, it is very difficult to make valid generalizations. Each country and the cases that arise can be evaluated only on a case-by-case basis.

8. This may also be specified as the reasonable expectation of a normal, risk-adjusted rate of return on the business in question. A weaker—and less satisfactory—criterion is the obligation that regulated businesses have the financial resources at their disposal to finance their activities.

The critical element for regulatory respect for property rights is the duty of the regulator to act reasonably, respectfully, and transparently, and to have a factual and, of course, lawful basis for decisions that affect property rights.

3.2. Respect contractual obligations

Contracts between parties shall be afforded the full respect to which they are entitled under applicable law, and contract rights should not be unduly limited or abridged.

Lawful contracts should be accorded the same respect as that accorded to property rights. Indeed, for regulatory purposes, contract rights are substantially similar to property rights.

In consequence, much of the same discussion in the previous subsection, with respect to property rights, is applicable to contracts and contractual rights and need not be fully repeated here.

A couple of contract-related circumstances, however, should be noted as special cases for regulatory scrutiny. The first relates to *contracts between a regulated entity and an affiliated, unregulated company.* Examples are of a distribution company buying energy from an affiliated generating company, or billing services from an affiliated utility in another country, or a distributor buying information technology from its parent corporation. Because such contracts are self-dealing arrangements, it is only reasonable that they be subjected to greater regulatory scrutiny than freely negotiated contracts between willing, unrelated parties.

For example, the regulators may do one or more of the following:

- Limit the right of regulated entities to enter into such agreements.
- Subject them to some sort of market test to ensure that the terms, conditions, and prices in the contract are reasonable.
- Impose strict antidiscrimination clauses to prevent favoritism to affiliated companies or businesses, a procedure that is important in telecom regulation.
- Take other necessary steps to guarantee appropriate levels of scrutiny to ensure that captive consumers are not paying more than they should for any product or service and are not cross-subsidizing an unregulated affiliate of a regulated entity.

In general, the regulators who find particular self-dealing arrangements to be above market value can simply leave the contract alone, but refuse to allow recovery of above-market expenses. There, may, however, be circumstances where the regulator feels compelled to interfere with the fulfillment of the contract. Although this should be done only in particularly exploitative circumstances, it must be widely anticipated that self-dealing contracts are not entitled to the same respect and deference that should be accorded a transaction between unrelated parties.

The second case that merits special attention is that *contract disputes between regulated entities may be treated differently from other contracts when disputes arise.* Ordinary commercial contract disputes are generally resolved in the courts. However, for a variety of perfectly

A

valid public policy reasons, contract disputes between regulated entities are sometimes submitted to the regulatory agency for resolution.

3.3. Undertake transparent and public actions

No action that affects property or contract rights in any way shall be undertaken without first affording all affected parties proper notice of the action(s) being contemplated and affording such parties full, fair, and transparent opportunity to be heard on the matter before final decisions are taken.

Although property and contract rights are entitled to respect from regulators, it is unrealistic to expect that they will always remain unaffected by changed circumstances and regulatory responses to them. If such rights are to be affected in any significant way, however, those whose rights are potentially at risk should have sufficient advance notice of what is contemplated. This is so that they have full opportunity to address the regulators about those rights and how those rights might be affected.

The net effect of this consideration is that, assuming the regulator follows reasonably transparent and participatory decisionmaking processes (to be discussed in more detail below), the holders of affected property or contract rights to be affected by a proposed regulator decision will have sufficient opportunity to protect their interests.

It should be noted, however, that the regulator may well make decisions that have inadvertent or unintended consequences that the agency did not or could not anticipate. The likelihood of unintended consequences is, indeed, a major reason for regulators to have genuine, extensive, and meaningful public consultation processes.

It is not reasonable, however, to expect the regulators to be obliged to provide individual or specific notice of a proposed decision to each affected interest. Public notice of what is under consideration should be sufficient.

3.4. Clarify accountability

No regulated entities should be held to account for any activity, unless standards or expectations with which they are expected to comply are formally in place and publicly available.

No regulated entities can reasonably be held to account for failure to adhere to a policy or standard that was not fully articulated in advance of a finding of violation. It is, therefore, critical that the law—either primary or secondary—clearly set out the obligations and responsibilities of regulated entities, and the standards with which they must comply.

4. Clarity of Roles in Regulation and Policy

4.1. Set out clear responsibilities

The law should also provide for clear and comprehensive provisions concerning the allocation and demarcation of responsibilities, powers, and duties between the regulatory agency, governmental bodies, and all other agencies (for example, market administrators) that have authority over the sector.

One of the perils of the regulatory systems throughout the world is jurisdictional disputes between agencies over who has which responsibilities. These are often not simply bureaucratic turf fights, but are often the result of private interests, regulated or otherwise, that are shopping for a forum favorable to them for decisionmaking.

Regardless of their derivation, such battles and debates are at best diversionary and at worst destructive of the mission of providing effective and efficient regulation. They are costly both in terms of resources and in terms of depriving the regulatory system of the coherence and consistency desired.

Typical of these kinds of battles are disputes between sector regulators and competition regulators, or between sector regulators and securities regulators over who has authority concerning particular matters. Perhaps more common in developing countries are disputes between ministries and regulatory agencies with responsibilities within the same sector. These disputes are not particularly surprising, given that the regulatory agencies are often new entities created to carry out significant responsibilities that had previously been assigned to sector or line ministries.

Typical of such disputes is the often-heard question: Who sets policy? To the extent possible, the laws regarding the sector and its regulation should clearly delineate the respective responsibilities of all relevant agencies and carefully distinguish between them. Additionally, it is very desirable for the institutional arrangements in regulation to be as simple as possible. Stated more succinctly, the more agencies are asked to play a role or assigned responsibilities without clear, well-defined responsibilities, the more likely it is that there will be confusion and uncertainty of who is to do what. The result will almost certainly be incoherent and contradictory signals to market participants.

4.2. Set out formal policy

Basic policy for the regulated sector should be formally set out in law by legislative and/or executive branch action and made prospectively binding on the regulatory agency.

The basic policy to be applied for the regulated sector in question should be articulated in law. Regulators are obliged to follow those policies and to enforce them.

Ideally, the law articulates the basic framework, methods, and broad public policy for regulation and for the regulated sector. It is highly advisable for the policymakers to avoid getting into great detail, simply because it may be more prudent to delegate responsibility for that to technical experts.

It is very important to note that policymakers can act only on a prospective basis, in the sense that they can determine future policy, but they should not be able retroactively to change policies in order to undo a decision that has already been made by the regulators. Allowing retroactive policymaking would have the effect of politicizing regulation, undermining the integrity of the regulatory process, and rendering the entire system less stable and less predictable.

4.3. Enforce policy

The regulatory agency should implement and enforce all public policy as embodied in the law and relevant government pronouncements consistent with other legal obligations. To do so, it should be able to make subsidiary determinations on policy issues to fulfill its obligations.

Concerning the legal framework (section 1), it was noted that the regulator will need sufficient discretion to make subsidiary policy (what was earlier defined as "secondary policy") in order to fill out the details of what is set forth in law and other binding policy documents.

Unless the basic policy is set out in complete detail, something that is not only impossible to do but counterproductive even to attempt, regulators will have to make secondary policy in order to implement the law and to fulfill their responsibilities. Although it is often stated as a truism that regulators are not to make policy, as with many truisms, this is not true. Regulators cannot help but make policy. *What they cannot—and must not—do is to make policy contrary to the law or act beyond their legal authority.*

As long as they are making policy that is not inconsistent with the law, and they are acting within their legal powers, regulators can, and often must, make policy—at least in the sense of secondary policy.

4.4. Adhere to publicly articulated government policies

Regulatory agencies cannot be required to adhere to government policies that are not publicly articulated in advance of decisions.

In some instances, regulators have been criticized for not following an unarticulated policy.

It should be understood that regulators are only bound by policies that are formally set out in law or in other binding documents, such as a concession contract. It is contrary to principles of transparency and fairness to have an unwritten, perhaps not generally known, government policy that regulators are obliged to follow.

4.5. Influence decisions transparently

Ministers and government agencies seeking to influence regulatory decisions should be able to do so, but only in a fully transparent and open manner.

Once an independent regulatory agency is established, the role of the government and its ministries in regulatory decisionmaking is, in a procedural sense at least, no different from that of any other party. The regulators are obliged to listen to what the government has to say, but are not obliged to follow its direction.

In reality, it may well be that on some matters, the regulators will give some deference to what the government has to say. *What is critical is that if the government or any ministry has a position it wants to advance, it should do so, but it should do so on a completely transparent basis where all interested parties have the opportunity to know what the government is saying and to respond to it as they feel necessary.* If the government or finance ministry wishes, for example, to tell the regulator to consider the inflationary pressure a tariff increase would cause, it should do so, but only in public where adverse parties will have the opportunity to know what is being said and to respond.

One further note on the government's communications with the regulator is that if communication is not carried out in an open and transparent manner, some might see it as an opportunity to lobby the government to secretly try to persuade or pressure the regulators to decide a matter in their favor. In effect, such private lobbying can easily undermine an otherwise transparent regulatory decisionmaking process.

5. Clarity and Comprehensiveness of Regulatory Decisions

5.1. Set out clear methodologies in the law

The key principles and methodologies on which major regulatory decisions will be made (for example, tariff reviews, compliance with service quality requirements, market surveillance, and approvals for investment) should be set out clearly in advance in appropriate legal documents (for example, statutes, decrees, or guidelines).

All stakeholders in regulatory matters should be entitled to have a clear picture of the rules of the game in which they are going to be participants. Investors, for example, cannot make intelligent decisions about how much, if any, of their capital they are willing to put at risk, or what risk premiums they will require if they are deprived of the opportunity to know what the principles and methodologies in the regulatory regime will be. In consequence, it is also important that regulatory agencies consult on and discuss in advance the content and reasoning for key methodologies, codes, and so forth before they are put into effect.

The result of a lack of knowledge is likely to be little investment or, where any is forthcoming, it will be with a very high risk premium attached. Although, as noted above, the critical principles or basic policy articulated in law may not be thorough, it should clearly provide substantive guidance on key principles.

Hence, the primary law should be sufficiently complete and clear, in at least a conceptual sense, to provide potential participants, particularly investors, with a clear idea of the following:

- What obligations are being imposed.

- What incentives, positive and negative, will be in place.
- What the market structure and regulatory regime will be.
- What methodologies will be employed.

5.2. Lay out complete rules for all stakeholders

The rules should, to the extent possible, be thorough, complete, and clear as to the rights, responsibilities, expectations, and consequences that all stakeholders enjoy or face.

The rules should, to the extent possible, be laid out in advance in a reasonably thorough manner.

Although, as noted above, the details may be sketchy in the law, to the extent possible, the regulators should flesh them out in advance in the rules, codes, guidelines, and so forth that they adopt. Although it is certainly impossible to anticipate all potential issues that might be encountered before they arise, some matters concerning standards and methodologies can be fairly thoroughly laid out in advance. Additionally, as the regulatory system evolves over the course of more and more decisions, if those decisions are well articulated, the details of the regulatory regime will be more thoroughly set out. This helps significantly in providing a degree of continuity and predictability in decisionmaking.

Although regulatory agencies, such as governments, cannot bind their successors, the methods discussed above help ensure that regulatory policy evolves in a steady and predictable way.

One caveat to be noted is that, while the rules should be set out in advance in a reasonably thorough manner, they are always subject to change. To provide guidance about that, it also would be very useful to adopt rules that explain the process by which changes will be made in the policies, standards, practices, and methods of the regulators.

A

6. Predictability and Flexibility

6.1. Make decisions consistent with set precedents

Regulatory decisions should, to the extent reasonable and feasible, be consistent with previous decisions with previous determinations on similar matters.

The regulatory process is an iterative one. As has already been noted, predictability and consistency are generally desirable in regulation. Each major decision that is made should cast additional light on the nature of the policies and practices market participants can expect. Thus, although regulators are not necessarily bound to follow precedent in a legal sense, it is generally advisable for them to do so, unless there is good—and demonstrable—reason for them not to do so.

Stated another way, it should be reasonable to expect that regulators will treat each new matter as a case of first impression. One should be able to expect that, when faced with the same set of facts and circumstances a second time, the regulators will decide a matter the same way unless there are particular reasons for not doing so, in which case, the reasons should be publicly explained.

Similarly, once the regulators make subsidiary policy or interpret the law in a particular way, it would be prudent for them to adhere to that policy or interpretation in future cases. By doing so, they will provide assurance of the stability and solidity of the regulatory regime and provide some degree of assurance to those who might otherwise be risk averse.

6.2. Provide sufficient public notice of decisions that deviate from precedent

When deviation from previous practice is necessary, it should be undertaken by regulators only after first providing public notice of such a possibility and providing all interested parties with a meaningful opportunity to be heard on the matter.

Although predictability, consistency, and stability are generally desirable in a regulatory system, they should not be confused with rigidity in the face of changing circumstances. Inflexibility where adaptation is called for can be as destabilizing to a regulatory regime as inconsistency and unpredictability.

Some change is inevitable as the structure and ownership of the sector change. The successful management of change is a critical hallmark of a viable regulatory regime. One critical element of change is to provide all affected parties, to the extent possible, with sufficient notice of the types of change being contemplated and the rationale for these changes. The purpose of the notice is twofold. The first is to allow time to prepare for it, and the second is to afford affected parties a meaningful opportunity to provide input on the issue raised. That input might include an opportunity to argue against the change, to support it, or to modify or help shape it or whatever other position a party might choose to take.

The idea is to provide a cushion both in time and in the process to allow people to think about, seek to influence, and adjust to change. It is an inherent part of achieving a balance between providing the benefits of continuity and avoiding the pitfalls of rigidity.

6.3. Apply change gradually and prospectively

Any fundamental change in regulatory practice or policy should, to the extent feasible, be undertaken on a gradual basis and be applied prospectively.

In addition to providing notice concerning change, striking the appropriate balance between volatility and rigidity suggests that change, particularly of a fundamental type, be implemented on a gradual rather than sudden basis in order to afford affected parties time to adjust to change and to avoid unnecessary disruption. It might be noted in this regard that one of the principal benefits of regulators' being independent is that they have a greater ability to manage change over a longer period than do more overtly political agencies.

A

7. Consumer Rights and Obligations

7.1. Protect consumers

The central purpose of regulation is to protect consumers in the short and long term, including future consumers. To help achieve this, regulatory agencies should adopt a consumer statement of rights. This should, at a minimum, include the following:

7.1.1. Maintain standards of quality for consumers

Maintain quality-of-service standards consumers are entitled to expect.

One of the most fundamental functions of a regulatory agency is to protect consumers. A key element of that is to ensure that they have an acceptable level of quality in the services they receive.

To carry out this function, formal, published standards must be in place, which tell the consumers what they are entitled to expect and tell service providers precisely what is expected of them. Such standards should include

- Schedules for achieving service connections.
- Outage guidelines (for volume and duration).
- Response times to customer inquiries and complaints, bill formats, and information requests.
- Customer communications.
- Billing accuracy.
- Meter quality and reading frequencies.
- Voltage quality.
- Line maintenance.
- Service expansion.
- Customer privacy.
- Public safety.

The regulatory agency should require periodic, systematic reporting by regulated companies concerning the achieved performance relative to the stated standards. The reports should list the following:

- Every violation and how it was corrected.
- The location and duration of all service interruptions and the number of customers affected.
- Complaints received from customers and the status of each complaint.
- Statistics on the types of inquiries received from customers, injuries related to company equipment or personnel, and whatever other information the regulators believe to be important to their monitoring of the performance of regulated entities.

The reports should be provided to the regulatory agency and made public, although the identities of individual customers should be redacted to avoid violating customer privacy.

7.1.2. Establish remedies for breach of standards

Establish remedies to which customers are entitled in case of breach.

While the penalty for a company in breach of the standards should be proportionate to the violation, the code of standards should at least include the type of relief due a customer as the result of a breach of the standards by the regulated company.

Remedies might include refunds, rebates, compensatory damages, specific orders to perform, and escrow of bill payments to provide relief or compensation to individual customers. If the breach is particularly serious or if it caused harm to many customers, the penalty might include more severe sanctions, such as conditioning or suspension of the license or, where there is a consistent pattern of severe and repeated violations or fraud, even termination of the license.

7.1.3. Provide customers with easy access to resolve complaints

Ensure access to the regulatory agency to seek redress of grievances.

Regulated entities should seek to resolve consumer complaints and inquiries without regulatory intervention. Unfortunately, that may not always be possible. As a result, customers should be able to easily access the regulatory agency for redress of their complaint.

The agency should provide customers with easy access. Regulated entities should be required to provide the customer with the regulatory agency's contact information. The agency should, in turn, provide personnel to assist in the resolution of complaints and should have a published procedure for attempting to resolve complaints. The process may include any number of steps, including informal and formal mediation, but must also ultimately provide a forum for deciding the merits of a complaint in the event that a negotiated resolution proves to be impossible to achieve.

The regulatory agency should keep careful records of all complaints received from customers and periodically publish a report on the number of the complaints in the aggregate by type of complaint (for example, billing error, service outage, or personal injury) against each regulated entity and periodically match them against the company reports and publish the results in the aggregate.

7.1.4. Set out consumer obligations

Set out the obligations of consumer to the regulated utility.

Regulated companies are themselves entitled to certain expectations about their customers. Without certain expectations, they can hardly be expected to perform satisfactorily. Such expectations might include timely payment of bills, enforcement of laws concerning theft of service, reasonable access to customers' premises, and respect for the utility's property and equipment and for its prudent use. The utility ought to be entitled to regulatory or police protection, or both, concerning the enforcement of its rights and enforcement of consumer obligations.

8. Proportionality

8.1. Keep regulation to the minimum necessary for efficiency and fairness

Regulation should always be kept to the minimum necessary to ensure efficiency and fairness. Regulatory intervention should only be made in the following cases:

8.1.1. Where there is demonstrable market failure that cannot be removed by other means
Markets, in practice, almost always are imperfect in one way or another. This is why countries often adopt competition policy and create institutions to carry it out. There are, of course, circumstances where the market simply cannot support competition (see the discussion below).

Market imperfections arise for any number of reasons, such as inadequate or asymmetric flow of information, poor price signals, abusive or collusive behavior, essential facility or bottleneck constraints, or natural monopoly. Regulatory interventions also, of course, are imperfect as well. Hence, whether regulatory intervention is required depends on the following:

- The seriousness of the market imperfection(s).
- Whether or not they can be *permanently* removed or significantly reduced—for example, by a structural intervention—without major new problems.
- Whether the benefits of the specific, identified regulation are sufficient to justify the costs of bringing in the regulation.

The key point that results from this is that *appropriate judgment must be exercised as to when intervention is merited.* In addition, it is crucial that the nature and extent of the regulatory intervention should be calibrated to the degree of market imperfection.

As an example, there is no need to impose pervasive price regulation to cure price-fixing by supposed competitors. The proportionate response would be to penalize the wrongdoers and compensate the victims. Conversely, where there is a natural monopoly, there are no wrongdoers to penalize, but an inherent market failure that can only be remedied by the imposition of a pervasive regulatory structure.

These examples show the importance for regulators to be given an array of regulatory tools to enable them to appropriately calibrate their response to the actual degree of market

A

imperfection and resulting harm. Likewise, it is important to consumers and regulated companies for the regulators to respond in carefully calibrated ways.

8.1.2. Where the economic and social benefits of intervention can reasonably be expected to exceed the likely economic and social costs

The costs of regulation can, of course, be quite high. The rigors of regulatory decisionmaking processes carry with them high transaction costs.

First, the existence of the regulatory arena provides competitors with an opportunity to gain an advantage by using or, in some cases, abusing the regulatory process. Second, regulators can err in ways that cost enormous sums of money or that waste societal resources. Because of those risks, it is best to employ regulation only where the benefits of doing so can clearly be expected to exceed the costs. That principle, of course, is simple to state, but not so simple to ascertain readily.

It should, of course, be noted that the failure of regulators to act when they should can be enormously costly as well. Many see the failure of federal energy regulators to act in a timely manner as one of the principal causes of, or at least an exacerbating factor in, the California energy crisis.

Some have contended that the regulatory agency itself needs to be regulated by an entity that evaluates the costs and benefits of proposed regulatory actions, or that there should be some sort of regulatory impact assessment, similar in concept to environmental impact statements. That may be excessive. If regulation itself is expensive, it obviously becomes even costlier to superimpose an additional level of regulation to oversee the regulator.

A

However, it is also the case that the term *regulatory impact assessment* is used to describe a *process* by which the regulatory agencies themselves do the following:

- Define objectives.
- Specify targets.
- Identify targeted methods of achieving the objectives.

This is very different from the requirement that all regulatory agencies carry out a full ex ante cost–benefit analysis of regulatory interventions before proceeding. The latter is clearly a substantial and onerous burden, particularly for young regulatory agencies with limited staff resources in developing countries. However, the much more modest *process* version of an RIA does not carry a substantial resource requirement, and it represents sensible calibrated regulatory practice as described elsewhere in this handbook. A simple listing on these lines also provides a good foundation for ex post evaluations, for example, by identifying much of the information that would be needed to establish whether the intervention had achieved its objectives.

The key point is that regulators will have to exercise careful judgments about when and how to intervene. They need the discretion to be able to evaluate the benefits of various approaches to a problem against reasonably anticipated costs associated with each. It is for that reason that the laws governing regulation *not* lock the regulators into straitjackets. Discretion and the reasonable professional judgments that are exercised are required on a case-by-case basis.

8.1.3. *Where a natural monopoly is an important element of the industry*

Wherever major and fundamental economies of scale or scope are present and the service being rendered is essential, as in the case of electricity transmission and distribution networks, there may well be a natural monopoly.

Under such circumstances, a competitive market either cannot exist or is too costly to create, and it is far superior to impose a scheme of regulation under which prices, service offerings, contractual relations between customer and company, and service quality are regulated. It is in these circumstances that ex ante regulation fits most comfortably compared to ex post competition policy. However, an almost infinite variety of ways exist to carry out such regulation. Nonetheless, a natural monopoly in the provision of an essential service, almost by definition, must be regulated

In electricity, it is not at all unusual that the market is partially competitive and partially a natural monopoly. Wires services—such as transmission and distribution—and system operation are, for the most part, natural monopolies, whereas generation and perhaps retail supply are not. In telecoms, only the local loop approaches being a natural monopoly; whereas in water and sewerage, all the service elements in a locality may comprise a natural monopoly.

Some electricity companies will be vertically integrated and, therefore, engaged in both monopolistic and competitive aspects of the business. Regulators will have to pay close attention to make certain that no company uses its control of monopoly bottleneck facilities to leverage its position in the competitive sector of the business. This issue is also critical in telecoms and can be very important in railways, particularly in passenger rail services.

Vigilance is also required to make certain that costs incurred in the competitive market are not allocated to monopoly services in order to cross-subsidize a company's position in the competitive market. These are complex issues in which regulators will need many legal and accounting tools, as well as professional judgment and technical skills, to deal proportionately with the problems associated with vertical market power (as defined below).

8.1.4. Where significant market power exists (for example, because of market design problems or abusive behavior)

The possession of significant market power can be, and often is, destructive of competition. This can arise, for instance, when one market participant or set of market participants is in a position to dictate prices or when the supply of a particular product (or closely related set of products and services) is dominated by a single company or group of companies. The market power can be either *vertical* (for example, ownership or control of bottleneck facilities, *as well as* some competitive sector elements, such as transmission *and* a major share of generation) or horizontal (for example, concentrated ownership of generating capacity), or both. Similar issues arise in both telecoms and railways (for example, track and train services.)

Once it is determined that the use of market power has made it impossible to rely entirely on competitive market forces to yield efficient results, regulators will have to intervene. The scope of intervention can vary depending on whether the problem is systemic, isolated, or behavioral.

Depending on the nature of the problem, the remedy might include one of the following:

- The imposition of a full ex ante system of regulation (for example, fully regulated prices) in the case of systemic failure where it has become apparent that the market or industry design is seriously flawed. (Of course, this should only be a temporary fix until a better structure can be put in place, but it may take some time. In general, regulation is a poor and costly remedy for bad market or industry design.)
- Price caps on specific generators in problematic locations or circumstances (for example, load pockets).
- Divestiture orders where market power is concentrated (for example, where one company has 50 percent–plus market share).
- Codes of behavior in cases of abusive behavior (for example, price fixing or collusion).

As suggested in a different context above, when the regulators have responsibilities for promoting competition, they have a specific obligation to monitor the markets carefully and to intervene appropriately when market failure occurs.

8.1.5. Where fundamental consumer protection requires it

Protecting consumers against monopoly power is widely recognized as a critical element of consumer protection that regulators are expected to provide. Even when competitive choices exist, however, the mere right to choose service providers does not necessarily

A

mean that consumers are no longer in need of protection. Protection against fraudulent or misleading sales practices, slamming (switching customers from one supplier to another without their consent or knowledge), and licensing or bonding requirements on suppliers of essential services even in competitive markets, and assurance of number portability in cellular telephony are all examples of consumer protection that regulators should be able to provide.

The law should mandate those areas of consumer protection that lawmakers want to compel regulators to provide on an ongoing basis, and should provide the regulators some discretion to decide where else consumer protection should be provided. The regulators should also be provided with some degree of discretion to decide what specific measures are necessary and appropriate to ensure the requisite level of consumer protection.

8.1.6. Where government-mandated social policy requires action and where regulation is likely to be the most efficient means for implementing this policy

Regulatory intervention may well be required by law or policy to achieve a social objective that cannot readily be attained through the normal operation of the market.

Examples of such legally mandated interventions might include the following:

- Subsidies for low-income households.
- Promotion of economic development, as well as system expansion.
- National security considerations.
- Environmental concerns.
- Resource allocations, or for some other externality.

Regulatory intervention in such non-economic matters is almost always the subject of some controversy. Many will see it as inefficient, whereas others will see it as a form of indirect taxation. *Without making any judgment on such contentions, it is appropriate for the regulators to undertake such interventions only where they are required to do so by law or another binding declared policy.*

In some countries, regulators are able to act in such ways with discretionary powers, for instance, where they can demonstrate that such action is required for the good of society. However, it is also argued in many countries—particularly countries with very low tariffs—that such discretion can distort the prices and jeopardize the financial viability of the regulated entities.

It should also be emphasized that, if such subsidies are to be allowed, it is imperative that they are narrowly targeted both to be effective and to minimize distortions and potential adverse financial consequences.

8.2. Keep regulatory actions well focused and appropriate to the problem being addressed

Where regulatory actions are necessary, they should be well targeted, proportionate to the problem being addressed, and measured against the alternatives. A regulatory agency should possess the legal latitude to vary its regulatory methods and practices so that it can accomplish the objective at minimum cost.

Regulation, as practiced, can be either a blunt instrument or a finely tuned one. Given the goal of encouraging efficiency and the likelihood of unintended consequences, finely tuned regulation is the more sophisticated and preferred course. In deciding what course of action should be followed, regulators are well advised to define as precisely as possible the nature of the problem being encountered and the result desired. Once that task is completed, the regulators should lay out all reasonable alternatives for action, including inaction if reasonable, and determine which alternative or set of alternatives is the most likely to produce the desired outcome and the least likely to cause unintended harm.

Public, transparent consultations, with ample opportunity for public participation, can often be of great value in assessing such matters.

It is vital, as has been noted elsewhere in this handbook, that regulators be given a broad array of remedial tools and broad discretion in employing them. If regulators are more prescriptive and limited in fashioning remedies, it is more likely for regulation to be either a blunt instrument or woefully ineffective.

8.2.1. Act with proportionality

Act with proportionality. For example, do not revoke a license for a small offense or limit mandated refunds for an offense to affected customers.

The regulatory response to any situation should be proportionate to its gravity. It would be a gross overreaction, for example, to revoke a license for a minor billing error or single service outage of short duration by a regulated company.

At the other end of the spectrum, the mere issuance of a public reprimand by the regulator for continuing and sustained service outages over a broad geographic area seems wholly inadequate to remedy the problem and compensate consumers.

Any number of examples are available, but the principle is clear. Regulatory actions need to be proportionate to the problem being addressed.

8.2.2. Use remedies that are relevant to the regulated entity

Use remedies in ways that are relevant to the nature of the regulated entity (for example, state or privately owned, small or large).

An element of proportionality in regulatory actions is relevance to the entity being regulated. Thus, for example, financial penalties assessed a privately owned company that affect the enterprise's profitability can be quite effective. The effectiveness of penalties, of course, can be destroyed if the regulators allow the regulated entity to recover the costs of the penalty from captive customers.

Penalties assessed against state-owned companies, to whom the bottom line is less consequential than for a private entity, may be less effective. Public criticism of a state-owned and politically sensitive company, by contrast, particularly if they are well-documented and well-publicized criticisms, may be more effective than for a private company. Some commentators have suggested that for state-owned and regulated companies, in order to provide relevant and powerful incentive, regulators should have more input, or perhaps some control, over such internal matters as incentives and compensation for managers and corporate governance. Although that may or may not be worth considering in some circumstances, the important point is that the incentives for state-owned and investor-owned regulated companies may need to be varied if they are to be meaningful.

The key point is that the regulatory response to any situation must not only be proportionate in scale and scope to the problem being encountered, but it must be carefully tailored in light of the nature of the parties involved.

8.2.3. Delegate regulatory responsibilities

Delegate regulatory responsibilities to other agencies or entities (for example, from national to regional or local regulators, or NGOs), although the regulatory agency should remain responsible for the performance of these delegated bodies.

Proportionality in regulation can sometimes be enhanced by delegating certain regulatory responsibilities to agencies or entities that have a narrower focus or mandate than the overall sector regulator.

An example in electricity or natural gas would be if the responsibility to regulate the distribution company were assigned to local or provincial regulators, while the balance of the sector were regulated at the national level.

Similarly, in electricity, system planning and reliability regulation is sometimes assigned to a private, not-for-profit organization, which focuses its attention narrowly on its area of responsibility, although it is also held accountable to the sector regulator.

The advantage of delegating responsibility, from the perspective of proportionality, is that the narrow focus and powers of the entity to whom responsibility is delegated reduces the likelihood of disproportional regulatory response. The other side of the equation, as noted earlier, is that diffused regulatory powers can cause loss of clarity and confusion.

If delegation of power is made, care needs to be taken to carefully and clearly delineate the respective responsibilities of the agencies to whom authority is given.

Note on Decentralization

It is also worth recognizing here that some decentralization of regulatory authority has its benefits, particularly in regulating what are largely local businesses, such as those that provide electric and gas distribution, water and wastewater services, and urban transport.

Those benefits include better access for consumers, better understanding of and sensitivity to local circumstances and needs, and perhaps more diversity and experimentation in the country as a whole. The downside is the risk of policy confusion and, arguably perhaps, greater risk of politicization of regulation.

An evaluator of regulatory regimes should consider the country in which he or she is working over whether delegation and decentralization of the regulation of infrastructure services would be of value on a sector-by-sector basis.

8.3. Review activities and methods regularly

Regulatory agencies should periodically and regularly review their activities and methods to determine their relevance or need in changed circumstances. These periodic reviews should include public consultation as appropriate.

Regulatory agencies should periodically and publicly review their activities, methods, and legal power to make certain that they fully appreciate the impact of the actions they have taken and how they have gone about doing things. Similarly, the regulators should review the powers they have to make certain that they have all the requisite legal tools to respond proportionately to the circumstances with which they will have to contend.

A

9. Regulatory Independence

In some countries, *independence* and *autonomy* have different meanings. For purposes of this handbook, the terms are interchangeable.

Independence for a regulatory agency means that it should be free of any constraints from either the government or the private sector in exercising its authority, except for those constraints written in the constitution, law, or other document (for example, a concession contract) that set forth on a prospective basis the rules and policies the regulator is obliged to follow. If independence has been granted to the regulator, it is empowered to make all final decisions within its scope of authority without obtaining the approval of any other party or agency, subject only to a lawfully established process of appeals.

Independence does not mean that the agency is beyond the ordinary fiscal and administrative (that is, nonsubstantive) controls of the state, as long as those controls are exercised toward the regulatory body in the same fashion as they are applied to other branches of the state. Specific mechanisms for safeguarding independence are set forth below.

9.1. Create regulatory agencies through primary law

Regulatory agencies should be created by law (or constitution), rather than by decree or other subsidiary legislation.

Regulatory agencies should be created in primary law or in the constitution rather than by decree. Such a legal standing enhances the agency's independence by precluding any legal interference with its standing or power other than through a formal legislative and executive action.

When an agency is created by decree, the executive branch of the government has far more ability to tinker with the agency and its powers on an ad hoc, nontransparent basis that could well subject regulators to short-term political repercussions from which they should be insulated.

9.2. Establish legal powers and characteristics

Under the law, regulatory agencies should have the following powers and characteristics.

9.2.1. Delegate decisions to a board of commissioners

Regulatory decisions should, if possible, be made by a board of three, five, or seven commissioners. Regulatory agencies headed by a single person are, in general, not recommended except for an initial period either (a) during which the agency is being established or (b) in countries with major resource constraints, or both.

Multiple-member boards are preferable to single regulators for a variety of reasons. First, it allows for the appointment of people with the diverse professional skills required for the job (for example, law, economics, engineering, and accounting) and with diverse backgrounds and perspectives (for example, different parts of society and different parts of the country). Such diversity assists in providing credibility, both political and intellectual, for the agency.

Second and more important, such blending is an excellent backdrop for the deliberative decisionmaking that is so well suited for regulatory agencies where the issues are complicated, multifaceted, multidisciplinary, and demanding of careful analysis. Deliberative decisionmaking, by its very nature, serves to enhance transparency and to act as a barrier to both arbitrariness and corruption. If commissioners have to reason together with peers and to defend their position against those with different points of view, they have less room to be either arbitrary or unethical.

The mere existence of internal discussion and debate within the regulatory agency injects a level of transparency into the process that single-regulator subsystems cannot provide. However, it is also the case that it may not be possible to have a multimember board in some cases (for example, in some countries and/or during the initial stages of establishing a regulatory agency). This can create problems of transparency and affect the quality of decisionmaking.

In consequence, if the regulator is a single-person office head, measures to enhance the opportunities for meaningful public participation are likely to be needed, as well as very clear and reasoned justification for his or her decision.

9.2.2. Maintain a stable source of revenue for operations

Regulatory agencies should have a stable and reliable source of revenue for their operations.

Although this topic is explored in considerably more detail below, the agency's independence can be severely impinged if it is constantly forced to struggle for funding, and perhaps has to make compromises to obtain such funding.

A stable and well-founded formula and revenue source should be set out in law for the funding of regulatory activities.

9.2.3. Offer staff competitive compensation packages and appropriate training

Regulatory agencies should be able to offer staff competitive compensation packages and viable career opportunities, as well as appropriate training and education.

The ability to recruit and retain competent, skilled staff members for the regulatory agency is of intrinsic importance. This ability is also critical for the agency's independence.

The agency needs to be able to undertake very difficult and complex tasks, either on its own or under its supervision (for example, using consultants). It needs to have the internal capability to do that from its own resources rather than having to rely on other government agencies or any party that may have an interest in the outcomes of any decision. This does not mean that regulators cannot work in cooperation with such agencies where appropriate and helpful, but they should not be forced either to rely on these others or to work with them except on a fully transparent basis.

The agency further needs to make certain that neither staff nor commissioners are looking to the regulated sector for subsequent employment. The same applies to any other future benefit (for example, future consulting opportunities).

9.2.4. Establish the administrative structure of the agency and make personnel decisions

Regulatory agencies should have the power to establish the administrative structure of the agency and make all relevant personnel decisions, including the authority and ability to hire personnel on a full- or part-time basis, or a permanent or temporary basis, and to engage the services of consultants as needed.

Regulatory agencies should be free to structure and staff their organizations as they see fit. They should not have to be dependent on the government for making very basic personnel decisions.

A

If every personnel decision, or even the most consequential ones, had to be negotiated with the government, there would be almost limitless opportunity for the government, if it chose to do so, to extract compromises that could jeopardize regulatory independence.

9.2.5. Set the rules and policies that are needed to carry out responsibilities

Regulatory agencies should have the authority to set such rules and policies as may be needed to carry out their responsibilities.

Regulatory agencies require the discretion, within their legal authority, to establish the rules and policies by which they will conduct their business. Without that authority, the agencies could be subject to procedural and policy constraints that could easily interfere with the exercise of their independent authority and judgment.

If the government is of the view that important constraints need to be placed on an agency, for example, to protect procedural fairness, it should write those considerations into law. That way the agency would know that it always had to adhere to those provisions, but would not be subject to constantly having to renegotiate them or face interference in its internal affairs.

9.2.6. Proclaim and enforce a code of ethics

Regulatory agencies should have the authority to promulgate a code of ethics applicable to agency personnel and to those who conduct business at the agency, so as to ensure both the reality and the appearance of honest, fair, and impartial decision-making.

The code of ethics and its specifics are discussed in greater detail below. The document is important not only for its intrinsic value but also as a safeguard for independence.

It should include provisions that explicitly prohibit commissioners and staff from having any current or prospective financial or employment interests in enterprises that the agency regulates for a specified period. The same prohibition should be extended to engaging in any activity that could have or could be regarded as having the effect of compromising a person's ability to exercise fully independent judgment in carrying out his or her responsibilities.

9.2.7. Retain the services of independent experts as needed and justified

Regulatory agencies should have the authority to retain the services of such independent experts as may be required to carry out their obligations and, where justified by the circumstances, order any affected regulated entities to pay the consulting fees.

There are exceptions to the regulatory agency's self-sufficiency in internal resources to carry out its work. One is that regulators, from time to time, will need to be able to hire consultants to assist them. This would be true, for example, when something requires the services of a specialist in a particular matter, where the workload on the staff is unusually heavy, or where the agency simply wants an independent or fresh look at something. In those cases, a consultant who is completely free of any conflicts of interest might be retained.

In some cases, budget constraints are a problem when a consultant is needed and the agency should be able to hire the consultant and assess the costs to the regulated entity involved. If this is done, the regulator must retain all control over the consulting arrangement (such as hiring decisions and terms of reference) to avoid any conflict of interest.

9.2.8. Participate in relevant professional organizations

Regulatory agencies should be encouraged to join or participate in relevant professional, research, and educational groups, as well as in regional and international cooperative regulatory organizations.

Continuing education and sharing experiences with colleagues throughout the world is extremely valuable for regulators. Joining regulatory organizations, education groups, professional organizations, and the like enriches both the individuals involved and the entire regulatory environment.

Although belonging to a trade organization of participants in the regulated market might somewhat compromise independence or the appearance of it, participation in the educational sessions of such groups or belonging to regulatory organizations generally does not.

A

9.3. Determine conditions of service for agency management

Regulatory agency commissioners or directors should serve under the following conditions.

9.3.1. Commissioners and directors should be appointed to fixed terms of office

One of the central protections of regulatory independence is that they be appointed to fixed terms of office, thereby assuring that they will be in office at least for the duration of the terms to which they are appointed. Typically, although there are examples of both shorter and longer terms, the terms range anywhere from four to seven years. By having some degree of tenure, the commissioners are able to make decisions without fear of being fired.

9.3.2. Their terms of office should not be coincident with the terms of governments and legislatures

The fixed terms of commissioners not only provide security for commissioners, but if properly administered, they can protect against sudden swings in policy and practice. Thus terms of the commissioners should not be coincident with the terms of the government. Hence, the new government will only gradually be able to change the personnel in charge of the regulatory agency.[9]

9.3.3. Commissioners or directors should be appointed only if they are not legally precluded from serving their full terms (for example, because of mandatory retirement conditions in the law)

Because it takes a new commissioner considerable time to master the position, it is best that appointees be available to serve out the entirety of their terms.

In some instances, individuals have been appointed who are reasonably close to mandatory retirement. Hence, those people were unable to serve out their full terms. As a result, there has been more turnover than desirable and fewer experienced commissioners.

9.3.4. Appointments of single-person agency directors, commission chairs, and other commissioners or board members should be made by the head of government or head of state, with possible legislative approval

To enhance the standing of the regulatory agency and to emphasize such independence, commissioners should be appointed by the highest civil authorities in the country.

In some countries, the appointments are made by the sector minister, an unfortunate circumstance that suggests that the regulators are somehow subordinate to the minister for the sector. As a practical matter, the minister is almost certain to be consulted about regulatory appointments in his or her sector, although the appointments must still be blessed by the head of state or government.

It would also be beneficial for the appointments to be made subject to legislative approval. This would be advantageous because it would help make the appointment of a regulator a more diffuse process in which appointments will have many sponsors and the regulator may feel less obliged to any individual and more independent in carrying out his or her responsibilities.

9.3.5. In the case of collegial bodies, the terms of the directors or commissioners should be staggered to ensure continuity

Staggering the terms of commissioners provides a much greater possibility that regulatory practice and policy will be more predictable and less susceptible to sudden or drastic change than if all the seats on the board came open at the same time.

---

9. It is also important that the government be required to fill vacancies in a timely fashion, or at least to allow an incumbent to remain in office until his or her successor has been chosen. There have been examples of political manipulation on specific cases by not filling vacancies, and other related types of manipulation.

Staggering simply means that each seat on the board expires at a different time. An example would be that if there were five commissioners, each with a term of five years' duration, one seat would be vacated every year. In this example, it would take five years for a complete turnover of the board, except in the case of a resignation or death.

9.3.6. Directors or commissioners should be removed only for good cause as defined in the law (that is, proven, nontrivial, legal or ethical misbehavior, or nonperformance of their duties) as found by an independent investigation of a complaint

The fixed terms for commissioners would be meaningless if they could be fired for any reason. To make the term of office meaningful and to insulate commissioners from undue political interference or retaliation, it is important that commissioners can openly be removed from office *only* for proven, nontrivial legal or ethical misbehavior, or for failure to perform their duties.

To ensure that the allegations are not trumped up, the allegations must be proven to the satisfaction of an independent investigator or fact-finder.

9.3.7. The terms and conditions of employment of any regulatory commissioner or director should not be altered during the course of a term (except where there are predetermined automatic adjustments not subject to administrative discretion)

Just as the term of office would be meaningless if commissioners could be removed for any reason, it would also be of no value if the terms and conditions of a commissioner's employment (for example, salary or benefits) could be altered at will.

Accordingly, the terms and conditions of a commissioner's employment during his or her appointed term of office must be set at the time of the appointment and should not be altered until the term is over, unless the original appointment provided for automatic adjustment (for example, salary adjustments tied to inflation) that were not subject to discretionary change.

9.3.8. Directors or commissioners should come from diverse professional backgrounds and training (for example, economics, law, engineering, and accounting)

Given the multidisciplinary nature of regulation, it is highly advisable that the board be composed of commissioners from diverse professional backgrounds reflective of the skills required to fulfill the agency's responsibilities.

Some countries also have merit selection boards that screen candidates for appointments and provide a short list from which the appointing authority must choose to fill a vacancy on the board. There is some value to this method of selecting commissioners.

A

10. Financing of Regulatory Agencies

10.1. Maintain sufficient levels of funding for operations

By law, the level of funding of the agency should be adequate to allow it to meet all its responsibilities competently, professionally, and in a timely manner. A minimum level of funding, expressed as a percentage of regulated revenues, should be set out in law.

The sustainability and vitality of the regulatory system is inextricably linked to the financing available for the regulatory agency. Therefore, the law should set out specifically that the level of funding be sufficient to enable the agency to carry out its responsibilities competently, professionally, and in a timely manner. It is also important that the law should further set out a percentage of revenues in the regulated sector that is to be provided for purposes of regulation. Typically, that number in electricity might vary between 0.25 percent and 0.5 percent, but for small countries, the upper limit may need to be a little higher.

10.2. Obtain funding from special levies

The agency funding should be obtained from a levy assessed on regulated entities, and not from the general treasury except (a) where the government requires a specific project that is beyond the scope of normal regulatory functions or (b) possibly where the government needs to provide the agency's startup costs.

The funding source for the regulatory agency should, if at all possible, be independent from the national treasury. In fact, given that regulation is part of the overall cost of operating the power sector, the costs of regulation should be internalized into electric rates.

The only exceptions to that principle are where the startup costs of the agency require an infusion of money from the treasury, or where the government asks the regulator to undertake a particular activity or course of action that is external to the agency's central regulatory mission. In such a case, electricity consumers should not have to pay. The government—that is, the taxpayer—should pay.

Regulatory fees should be collected from the regulated companies. The levy on the companies should be viewed not as a tax but rather as a fee for regulatory services.

10.3. Allow for levied fees to be passed through to consumers

Regulated entities should be able to pass through funds collected for the levy to their customers in their tariffs.

Because the regulatory fees levied on regulated entities are an unavoidable cost of doing business for a regulated company, the costs should be passed through to the consumer. This practice, because it is mandated by law, rather than being voluntary, avoids even the appear-

A

ance of any impropriety resulting from the fact that the regulators' funds are obtained from regulated companies. The automatic pass-through ensures that it is consumers—not regulated companies—who pay for regulation.

10.4. Assess levies according to the revenues, not profits, of regulated entities

The levy should be assessed as a percentage of the revenues of a regulated entity, not tied in any way to the profits of regulated entities.

It is critical for the regulatory fee to be tied to revenues—not profits. The regulator should be indifferent to the profits of regulated entities. Tying regulatory fees to the profitability of regulated enterprises is a clear conflict of interest for regulators and should be avoided.

10.5. Hold levied funds in a special account

Funds collected from the levy should be held in a special account and earmarked for the exclusive use of the regulatory agency. Any other use should be expressly prohibited.

Because the regulatory levy is a fee for service fully internalized to the regulated sector, the funds are not ordinary tax revenues collected by the state, and they should not be treated as such. The levy is reflective of very specific costs and, consistent with economic theory on cost causation and efficiency, the revenues collected under it should be allocated solely to the specific use for which it is intended.

Apart from economic efficiency, the earmarking of the funds ensures the regulators of a secure, stable source of revenue to finance their activities, and frees them from budgetary retaliation or other compromises of the regulatory independence.

10.5.1. Return surplus funds to customers or use them for sectoral improvements

If there is a significant surplus of funds, the surplus should be returned to the customers of the regulated entities or to a public benefits fund for sector improvement (for example, to assist low-income customers). The surplus should not be available to the government to divert for other purposes.

Consistent with the principles set out above, any funds collected pursuant to the regulatory levy, but not spent for regulation, should not be diverted to any use other than either (a) to returns to the regulated entities for refunding to their customers who had paid the levy or (b) for use to finance a public benefit within the regulated sector (for example, subsidizing low-income customers or system expansion).

In addition to such a policy being consistent with good economic theory, it also removes the ability of the government to divert regulatory funds to other uses, something that has, unfortunately, occurred on too many occasions.

A

10.5.2. Allow government cuts in spending authority only if they apply consistently to all agencies

Any reduction in the spending authority of the regulatory agency in the middle of a normal budget cycle should occur only as part of an overall reduction in government spending—not as a mandated reduction applicable only to the regulatory agency.

Governments need to have discretion over their spending. Thus, if the government decides to cut back spending in the middle of a budget cycle and wishes to spread the reduction across all agencies, it is not inappropriate for regulatory agencies to share in the pain.

By contrast, when the government has unbridled discretion to single out regulatory agencies for budget cuts, the door is opened to the very types of retaliation and intimidation that can—and, in practice, does—severely compromise independence. Thus, although mid-cycle cutbacks in regulatory agency funding (for example, as part of an overall, across-the-board cutback in spending) are acceptable, discriminatory budget curtailment actions taken against regulatory agencies are highly problematic.

10.5.3. Follow the government's fiscal controls

The ordinary fiscal controls, auditing policies and practices, and budgetary controls of the government should apply to the regulatory agency. The overall spending authority of the agency should be subject to government approval. If government approval is not obtained in a timely fashion, the agency should be allowed a budget authorization (in real terms) equal to its budget in the previous fiscal period.

The government, of course, needs to have the power to determine its own budget. During the normal budget cycle, that should be applied to regulatory agencies, as well as every other part of the government. Thus, the overall level of regulatory agency spending, even if funded from levies collected from electricity consumers, should be subject to the same approval process as that required for any other government department or agency.

The same principle should apply to the government exercise of fiscal controls (for example, auditing and business practices, such as procurement and contracting). The only exception is where the government fails to approve the budget in time to authorize spending in a new fiscal period. If this should happen, regulatory agencies should be able to simply carry over budget authorization from the previous fiscal period until the new budget obtains final approval. That would allow for continuity and stability.

One other budgetary matter is that the regulatory levy—given that it is not a tax, but rather a fee for service—should be removed from the government's balance sheet. That would not only be good fiscal policy but would also insulate regulatory agencies from the effects of pressure from external lenders to the government to curtail spending.

A

10.5.4. Retain consultant services, as needed, for specified tasks

The regulatory agency should, where circumstances warrant, and without regard to agency spending authorization, be able to retain the services of a consultant to perform specified tasks and to require payment for the specific costs of that engagement from the regulated entities affected.

This concept has already been discussed above. In the context of the budget constraints, however, it must also be noted that this power provides the regulators with some degree of flexibility to reply to an emergency or other type of unique circumstance without having to undergo a full budget review.

11. Regulatory Accountability

Although it is vital for regulators to have the ability to make decisions independently, that autonomy must nonetheless be balanced against assuring accountability in the overall regulatory system.

Concerning management issues, the regulatory agencies ought not to be much different from any other agency of the state. As noted earlier, the ordinary fiscal and management oversight exercised by the government should apply to regulatory agencies.

Concerning substantive issues, however, balancing accountability and independence is a more complicated matter. About decisions that have already been made, the only effective means of assuring accountability on a retrospective basis without compromising independence is through the appeals process (which is fully discussed below). Other agencies of government (except for a designated court) should not have the authority to overturn the decision of a regulatory agency. On a prospective basis, however, including drawing lessons from experience to improve future regulation, accountability needs to be exercised on a fully transparent basis and, to be effective, must focus not only on how the regulators themselves have performed but also, as noted below, on how the overall system has functioned.

A

11.1. Conduct hearings to review the agencies' performance

Legislative committees and/or relevant ministries and executive task forces should periodically conduct hearings to review the performance of regulatory agencies.

The issues that should be covered include oversight of regulators, on a prospective basis, which should be exercised by policymakers who possess the authority to make meaningful and binding changes. That generally translates into the need for both legislative and executive officials to be involved in the process of oversight. Conducting the review at that level has the salutary effect of permitting effective review not only of the performance of the regulators themselves but, perhaps even more importantly, of the entire regulatory system, including laws, methods, processes, and other issues, both broad and narrow.

Such a process will produce two major benefits. The first is that it will encourage stakeholders to periodically focus inward on the regulatory process and evaluate their own performance and obtain the input of others on how things might be improved. The second is that the mere existence of a formal, periodic review process will help channel discontent with regulators into productive, less disruptive directions than might otherwise occur.

11.1.1. Define agency functions and the division of authority to prevent disputes

Define the functions of the agency and continued appropriateness of the division of authority between it and other relevant agencies.

Disputes often occur over the respective responsibilities and authority of regulatory agencies and other governmental entities. Typically, these are disagreements or, perhaps more often, confusion between ministries and regulators, or between regulatory agencies (for example, between competition regulators and sector regulators or between local and national regulators). These controversies have no single derivation. They are often related to overly aggressive regulators, or perhaps even to passive regulators or to litigants seeking to avail themselves of a forum more favorable to their interest. Regardless of the cause, the result of blurred lines of responsibility and bureaucratic turf battles can be quite negative. Incoherent or confused policy, inconsistent application of the law, diverse incentives at odds with each other, and diversion of resources and focus are not uncommon results. The lines of authority are an area worthy of continuing oversight.

11.1.2. Employ transparency, effectiveness, and timeliness in procedures

Employ transparency, effectiveness, and timeliness of regulatory procedures.

Regulatory processes should serve three fundamental purposes:

- The provision of adequate and fully tested information to decisionmakers.
- Efficient and coherent decisionmaking.
- Fairness and openness to all interested parties.

These objectives are not always consistent with one another. Efficient decisionmaking, for example, may well be inconsistent with having a fair and open process. Thus, balancing the varying interests can be a complex task that should be reexamined periodically.

One process question that is at the heart of the credibility of regulation is transparency. Any oversight proceedings should focus carefully on the transparency of regulation. This is discussed more fully below in the context of specific elements of transparency.

11.1.3. Make clear, coherent, consistent decisions in a timely manner

Ensure the clarity, coherence, consistency, and timeliness of agency decisions.

A regulatory agency has an obligation concerning decisionmaking that goes well beyond merely deciding the matters before it. An agency's decision should not only be clearly written in order to avoid any confusion or difficulty in compliance, but the decision should also be accompanied by a full and clear explanation of the rationale for the decision that was made. Doing so accomplishes three key objectives that should be examined in oversight hearings.

The first is to inject a level of intellectual discipline and reason into the process. It is very difficult to be arbitrary or dishonest, intellectually or otherwise, if one is required to publicly articulate a clear rationale for an action taken. The second is that in articulating the reasons for decision, those who must comply will be better positioned to do so. The third objective is that by explaining the reasoning, the agency over time will be better positioned to develop a consistent, predictable approach to regulatory policy and practice, and parties participating in agency proceedings will be better positioned to state their cases to the regulators.

Finally, agency decisions should be made in timely fashion. "Timely fashion," however, does not mean as soon as possible, or even as efficiently as possible. Rather, it means that all legal deadlines are met, that parties are not unduly inconvenienced, or that parties have not had their interests jeopardized by delays in rendering decisions. Expeditiousness, however, must be balanced against the need to provide all interested parties with a meaningful opportunity to participate in the process, although doing so may sometimes mean delay. It is the achievement of balance between the affording of meaningful opportunity for participation for all interested parties and the need for timely decisionmaking that is the objective that overseers of the regulatory process should be looking for. In this regard, those conducting oversight hearings should make certain not that the regulators are acting in timely and fair ways, but that they do not suffer under constraints that make attainment of the appropriate balance difficult (for example, unreasonable deadlines for making decisions).

11.1.4. Make decisions that are proportionate and targeted to the problem encountered
Ensure the proportionality and effectiveness of targeting in agency decisions.

As discussed above, regulators should be acting or intervening in markets in ways that are proportionate to the problems being encountered. Those conducting oversight proceedings should be looking not only to see if that is how regulators are behaving, but also whether the law has given the regulators the requisite legal tools and powers to enable them to respond proportionately.

11.1.5. Oversee the quality and sustainability of agency decisions
Oversee the quality of agency decisions and their sustainability on appeals and in practice.

Overseeing the quality of regulatory decisions is essentially a threefold process. The first is an examination of the agency's record on appeals. Does it have a history of staying within its lawful bounds? Do its processes meet the tests for fairness imposed by the law and by the courts? Are its decisions free from arbitrariness?

The second goes to the outcomes in the regulatory process. As is noted in chapter 5, the role of the regulator in outcomes in terms of investment, profitability, reasonableness of tariffs, and even quality of service is just one of many variables. Nonetheless, overseers of the regulatory process should be examining that role to ascertain the effect regulators and the regulatory system had in determining sector outcomes, positive or negative.

The third is to seek out the advice of neutral experts on the quality of regulatory decisions in intellectual depth and understanding, as well as quality of reasoning, and on how the decisions compare to those being made in other countries. The experts should also be called on to express their views on the regulatory environment as a whole, not just on the performance of current regulators. Doing so will provide overseers with a broader perspective on regulation.

11.1.6. *Manage the agency's resources efficiently*
Manage the efficiency of the agency's use of its resources.

The one area where oversight is largely identical to that exercised over any other government agency is in the area of management. Regulators, like any other officials of the state, should be held accountable for their use of resources and for their management of administrative tasks.

11.1.7. *Ensure independence, integrity, and credibility in agency processes and actions*
Ensure the degree of independence, integrity, and credibility in agency processes and actions.

Overseers should examine whether there have been any improprieties, either in law or in appearance, whether the agency has appropriate ethical standards and safeguards in place, and whether the regulatory agency is seen as honest, fair, and competent enough to ensure its credibility and integrity. Overseers should also examine the nature of the relationship between regulators and the government, as well as between regulators and market participants, to ensure that the agency is operating independently.

11.2. Hire outside experts to prepare reports on the agency's performance or other special topics

The government or legislative authorities should periodically engage the services of a panel of financially disinterested "outside" experts (which could include international experts and regulatory staff from neighboring or similar countries) to prepare a report on the overall performance of the agency, or on specific areas of interest.

As noted above, one very useful way of reviewing the regulatory regime, including but not limited to the performance of the regulators themselves, is to engage the services of financially disinterested, outside (international) experts to prepare periodic, public reports that analyze various aspects of the regulatory regime. Such outside perspectives allow for new ideas and ways of doing things to be brought into the system. They also allow regulators and policymakers to look at regulatory matters from different points of view, and provide useful guidelines for the future from international experience.

11.3. Conduct periodic audits

Regulatory agencies should be subject to periodic management audits and to other types of effectiveness review (for example, policy audits).

Regulatory agencies are no different from other types of organizations in the sense that they are well served by having their operations periodically evaluated by outside auditors (that is, consultants) who can evaluate the agency's organization, processes, and relations with the public and with other parts of government. Such consultants also have the advantage of being able to interact more freely with the participants in the regulatory process than the regulators themselves can ordinarily do. This allows them to look at the agency from both the inside and the outside.

Similarly, outside consultants can conduct policy audits as well. Policy audits can evaluate the consequences of pursuing a particular policy or course of action. These types of analyses are useful for both policymakers and regulators because they permit a disinterested analysis of issues in which partisans on various sides make contentions, often very loudly, that may or may not be true.

The use of management or policy auditors, or both, can also be quite useful in enriching the entire regulatory culture by adding new and differing perspectives and by performing professional, unbiased analysis of issues being debated within regulatory circles.

11.4. Submit an annual, public report on activities to the government

Regulatory agencies should be required, at least on an annual basis, to submit a report on their activities to legislative or executive authorities, or both. The report should be a public document.

The law should require the regulatory agency to submit, on at least an annual basis, a full report of its activities to legislative and/or executive authorities. The report should include, at a minimum, the following information:

- A full account of the budget and actual expenditures.

- Identification of the senior personnel at the agency and the positions they occupied in the reporting period.
- A list of the cases handled, other than consumer complaints, and a brief summary of the results and the time it took to process the cases from filing to disposition.
- The status of decisions that were appealed or pending on appeal in the reporting period, and the results of appeals decided in the reporting period.
- The number of consumer complaints handled in the reporting period (sorted by types of complaints, the companies against which they were made, and whether the complaints were resolved through negotiation, mediation, or full adjudication) and the number of public hearings held, along with the number of participants.

The report should be a public document.

12. Regulatory Processes and Transparency

The process of regulatory decisionmaking must be a credible one from at least two perspectives. The first is from the perspective of local customs and mores. To be acceptable, the process by which decisions are made must be consistent with local notions of fairness and justice. The other perspective that needs to be satisfied is that of the investors, many of whom are likely to be foreign, in the case of developing countries. Just as residents of the country need to be satisfied that the process is fair, so too do international investors who may have different views of fairness than local residents.

Satisfying both constituencies means that variations in the decisionmaking process from one country to another are likely. There should, however, be a baseline of principles, particularly in regard to transparency.

Some commentators have noted three essential principles for regulation: transparency, transparency, and transparency. It is essential that the process by which regulators decide matters be open in terms of the opportunity for input, the availability of information on which regulators rely, fully articulated decisions and the reasoning underlying them, and the absolute integrity and honesty of the entire process. Significantly, as is noted below, the intellectual discipline and rigor of the decisionmaking process is greatly enhanced by transparency.

12.1. Make decisions according to all applicable provisions

Except for defined emergency circumstances, no decision should be made by a regulatory agency until the following provisions have occurred.

The frequency of emergency actions should be relatively rare. Relatively commonplace emergency situations should be seen as a sign that something is amiss in the process. Thus, the following provisions should be the rule and deviation a rarity.

12.1.1. Give proper legal notice

Proper legal notice has been given, notifying all parties that a matter is under formal consideration.

The regulator should never take up matters without prior formal notice. Even in the rare circumstance where a matter is deemed confidential, the public should still be given the opportunity to at least know the subject that is under consideration. Although the legal requirements for defining what it means to provide adequate public notice may vary from country to country, the requirement to do so is essential for fairness and credibility. Optimally, regulatory proceedings will be advertised in formal legal notices. They will also be the subject of news stories, and otherwise be made known.

12.1.2. Provide appropriate, meaningful information in the public notice

The public notice has identified the matter being considered, the initiator of the action being contemplated, and a full schedule for the consideration of the matters.

The principle is quite simple. The public notice given must be meaningful in that it should advise interested parties what is under consideration, when and where the issue will be considered, and how interested parties can provide input on the matter. It should also provide all parties, including the regulated entities themselves, with an idea of how a particular case will be handled and what the schedule for the process will be.

12.1.3. Allow the opportunity for meaningful input

All parties who wish to do so have been afforded an opportunity to provide meaningful input to the agency.

This topic is more fully explored below in section 13. The principle, however, is quite simple. Meaningful public participation simply cannot occur without adequate public notice in advance that a matter is under consideration.

12.2. Allow for ex post review of emergency actions

In cases of emergencies, actions may be taken, but interested parties should be afforded a fair opportunity to participate ex post in any review of the matter. The criteria for defining an emergency should be stated in law.

As noted earlier, emergencies should be rare events, but when they do occur, it is important that actions taken on such a basis be reviewed after the fact in order to provide full opportunity to the public to be heard and, if necessary, to correct any defects in decisions taken on an emergency basis. Emergencies are perhaps the one case where it may be appropriate for regulators to act on a retroactive basis, because measures undertaken in haste are deserving of full review when there is more time to do so.

12.3. Issue publicly available, written decisions

No decision should be taken by a regulatory agency without its being set down in a publicly available, written document.

The fundamental principle is very clear. No regulatory decision can be valid if it is not in writing and on the public record.

12.3.1. Issue a clear statement of the decision

Issue a clear statement of the decision, comprehensible to affected parties.

Every regulatory decision must be clearly stated so that the meaning is easily comprehensible to all affected by it. It must be clear to those who must comply precisely what they must do.

12.3.2. Describe and analyze all evidence taken into consideration

Describe and analyze all evidence taken into consideration in arriving at the decision.

It is not sufficient for regulators to merely state the decision itself. Regulators should also describe the information and evidence on which they relied and how they used that information in arriving at their decision. All the information referenced should, with very limited exceptions, be available for public inspection.

Two basic reasons exist for setting out the evidence on which regulators relied. The first is that such action imposes a more disciplined decisionmaking model on the regulators and makes it difficult to be arbitrary, unreasonable, or even whimsical in decisionmaking. The second reason is that it is an essential element of transparency and procedural fairness that any evidence on which the regulators rely is readily available and known to others, and that the regulators' analysis and use of that information be clearly explained. It is also instructive for all participants in the regulatory process to see clearly how the regulators weigh and analyze information.

12.3.3. Provide a summary of the views

Provide a summary of the views offered by participants to the proceeding.

The purpose of summarizing the views of all parties in the case in the written decision is to again impose discipline on the regulators themselves. By at least repeating back to stakeholders what they told the agency and explaining how the regulators evaluated the information, the regulators demonstrate that they did consider all the input they were offered. This serves the dual purpose of assuring that all evidence offered is taken into consideration and provides some comfort to participants in the regulatory process that their positions are truly taken into consideration.

12.3.4. Provide a full discussion of the underlying rationale

Provide a full discussion of the underlying rationale for the decision.

Compelling the regulators to fully elaborate on their reasoning in arriving at a particular decision serves three key purposes. First, it provides all parties with an excellent opportunity to see how each of the regulators approaches matters. Second, it provides a fuller record to any court to which a decision is appealed. Finally, it imposes a disciplined reasoning process on the regulators.

12.4. Publish clearly defined procedures for decisions

All regulatory agencies should have clearly defined, published procedures under which they make, announce, and publish regulatory decisions and their justification.

No decisionmaking process can be regarded as fair or transparent unless the rules governing it are published in advance and adhered to in practice. All parties have a right to know precisely what process will be followed, what the schedule is for various milestones in the process (for example, filing deadlines or public hearings), what requirements they must meet in order to participate in an ongoing case or to initiate one, and such other matters as a participant in the process must know in order to be fully involved.

The procedure, to be meaningful, cannot be developed ad hoc or cavalierly disregarded. Any deviation from the procedural rules during the course of a specific case should be taken only with great reluctance, and only for one of two reasons. The first is a clear demonstration of good cause for doing so, in which case it should not be done until adequate notice is provided to all affected parties. The second circumstance is where all parties have consented to such a change, and the regulators decide to acquiesce to the consensus.

Procedural rules, of course, need not be rigid or unchanging. It is prudent for regulators to look at the rules from time to time and to solicit the opinions of interested parties on what changes, if any, should be undertaken. Such a process, however, should be undertaken independently of any specific case, and changes should be contemplated only on a prospective basis.

12.5. Establish methods for making decisions

Multimember regulatory agencies normally make their decisions either by (a) majority voting or (b) consensual, nonvoting methods.

Multimember regulatory boards make decisions in at least two ways. The first is by open vote at a public meeting, where each director (commissioner) casts his or her vote. The second is where the decision is made through some form of consensual nonvoting process. The first is more transparent and perhaps more accountable, but the second may seem to be more collegial and less divisive.

Given this split in viewpoints, it is useful to look at each process separately with the objective of assuring the optimal level of transparency attainable under each.

12.5.1. Procedures for announcing decisions made with the majority voting method

If a multimember regulatory agency decides to use a formal voting process for making decisions, the result of the vote should be made publicly available at or soon after the date of the decision.

When a formal voting process is used, the following procedures should be followed:

a. **All decisions should be made at a meeting at which or following which the votes of all members should be made public.**

   The decisions should be made in votes at a public meeting, for which the time, place, and agenda were announced and officially noticed in advance. Each director's vote, yea or nay, should be cast in the meeting and duly noted in the official meeting minutes. [10]

   If the agency's rules permit proxy voting, the rules governing that procedure should be published in advance.

b. **Board members voting "no" should have the option to file formal opinions expressing the rationale for their vote.**

   Each director who votes against a decision approved by the majority of his or her colleagues should publicly state his or her reasons for doing so, and should have the option of filing a formal dissenting opinion in the official record of the case. Dissenting opinions should be attached to and published with the majority decision.

c. **Board members who concur in the result, but do so for different reasons set forth in the decision, should have the option to file concurring opinions expressing the rationale for their opinions.**

   At times individual directors will agree with the agency's decision, but for reasons that are different from those written by the majority. A director in that circumstance should have the option of filing a formal concurring opinion. Concurring opinions, like dissenting opinions, should be attached to and published with the majority decision.

---

10. Directors also may wish, for any reason, to abstain from voting. If they choose to do so, they should publicly state the intention to do so. On occasion, directors, because of a case-specific conflict of interest or some other reason, might want to entirely recuse themselves from any participation in a case. If they do so, it should be specifically noted in the meeting where the voting takes place and should be written in the decision and recorded in the minutes. There is a difference between abstention and recusal. Abstention merely indicates that the director did not cast a vote on the final decision. He or she may or may not have otherwise participated in the case. One may abstain for any reason. Recusal, on the other hand, indicates that there is a case-specific conflict of interest or other impediment to a director's participating in the case. Unlike in an abstention, recusal means that the director not only does not cast a "yea" or "nay" vote, but also entirely removes himself or herself from participation of any kind in the case.

12.5.2. Procedures for announcing decisions made with the consensual approach

If the regulatory agency decides to use a consensual approach for decisionmaking, the following procedures should be followed:

a. **A record of the discussion should be made, reflecting the range of opinions expressed, both supporting and dissenting.**

    The agency should keep official, publicly available minutes of meetings at which the decision was discussed. The minutes should be sufficiently detailed to reflect the range of opinions expressed or questions posed on the critical issues in the case under consideration.

b. **A summary of the discussion should be made publicly available along with or soon after the publication of the regulatory decision and its justification.**

    The minutes, or an accurate summary of them, should be publicly made available or perhaps, preferably, attached to the decision itself. By doing so, the decision can be seen in context, and the flavor of the discussions among the decisionmakers can be made known.

c. **Board members should have the right to state their views concerning the decision publicly and on an attributable basis.**

    Just as in the case of public voting, any director who desires to do so should be afforded the full opportunity to file a dissenting or concurring opinion. Such opinions should be attached to and published with the majority decision.

    Whichever approach is adopted, the reasons for decisions should always be published by the agency together with the decision.

12.6. Make all supporting documents publicly available

All documents in the possession of a regulatory agency, particularly those being relied upon in making decisions, should be presumed to be available for public inspection, unless the regulator rules otherwise (for example, on the grounds of commercial confidentiality).

It is central to the principle of transparency in regulation that all documents in the possession of the agency—with only those few exceptions noted below, particularly those used in making decisions—be publicly available. The reasons for this are straightforward. It would do harm to the credibility of the agency's decisions if the documents and information on which they are based are hidden from public view. Not only should the information be available, but also parties who wish to examine and possibly challenge the accuracy or validity of the documents or the information contained in them in the case in which they are being used should be afforded full opportunity to do so. That is not only part of transparency, but it also has the practical value for the decisionmakers of not only having the information itself but also having the analysis or critique of that information by another, possibly adverse, party.

A

To put into context the importance of the principle of making documents public, it is useful to think in terms of what would happen if the reverse were true and documents on which the agency relied were kept confidential. The agency would have to proclaim that the information it relied upon for its decision in a case was confidential and not even subject to the scrutiny of other parties to the case. It is hard to see how the decisionmaking process would not be impoverished by such circumstances. More importantly, the credibility of the agency's decision would almost certainly suffer as a result.

12.6.1. The appropriate criteria for designating supporting documents as confidential should be applied

No document should be treated as confidential unless the regulator finds that the document (or some part of it) falls specifically into a category that the law or binding articulated policy deems legitimately confidential (for example, personnel matters, verifiable trade secrets, draft decisions not yet finalized, or documents related to pending litigation). Confidentiality issues, it must be noted, involve *only* the question of how the regulator treats the document. Claims of confidentiality *never* constitute grounds for a party to withhold a document from the regulator.

It is not at all unusual for a party to ask the regulators to keep a document or piece of information confidential. For reasons noted above, however, it should be unusual for a regulator to grant such a request. The only time a request for confidential treatment of a document should be granted is when the document falls into a category that has been determined to be confidential by preexisting law or rule.

Typically, the type of information that might be identified as confidential would include personnel matters, documents related to preparation for litigation that is ongoing or about to be commenced, verifiable trade secrets, or information whose premature release would unreasonably affect prices of a company's securities. The point is not to list all areas where confidentiality is justified, but rather to point out that no document should be deemed confidential unless it falls into a category that the law or rule has allowed the regulator the discretion to designate as confidential.

Even if a document falls into an area where the regulator has the discretion to grant confidential treatment, the regulator need not automatically agree to a confidentiality request. The burden of proving that a particular document or information falls into one of the approved categories and that it should be accorded confidential treatment falls entirely on the party who is asking for it.

Finally, allowing a document to be treated as confidential merely means that the regulators and all parties to the proceeding who have access to the document are explicitly prohibited from circulating the document to anyone other than those actively involved in the proceeding in question. In short, confidentiality is never grounds

A

for denying the regulators or other parties to a specific proceeding access to any document. Rather, it is simply a limit placed on everyone's ability to disclose the documents beyond the confines of the proceeding in question.

12.6.2. The primary law (or, failing that, the regulatory agency) should publish in advance its criteria for judging whether documents (or some parts) will be treated by them as confidential and should also establish systems for handling and storing confidential material

It is best if the law itself sets out those categories of information or documents that may be deemed confidential. The law should not mandate that regulators treat all documents or information in a particular category as confidential, but should merely enable the regulators to exercise discretion. If the document does not fall into one of the categories, the regulator lacks the discretion to even consider such a request. If it does fall into an eligible category, the regulator will have to be persuaded that acceding to a request for confidentiality is warranted in the case at hand.

If the law fails to designate categories of information eligible for confidential treatment, the regulators should themselves issue such a rule in order to avoid ad hoc determinations. It is best, however, for the law to set the categories, because that would limit regulatory discretion on a matter so central to transparency and fairness.

12.7. Announce publicly the rules the agency will follow in making decisions

The procedure the agency will follow in making decisions should be set out in clearly defined rules and should be made publicly available.

This has already been discussed in section 12.4 above. Suffice it to note here that if the process rules are not set out in advance and adhered to, all parties will be at a distinct disadvantage in meaningfully participating in agency proceedings, and the agency will be deprived of many of the benefits of effective input from all parties. Moreover, the process itself would become a confused bureaucratic maze, rather than the orderly and systematic collection of information and testing of that information that should characterize the regulatory decisionmaking process.

13. Public Participation

There must be ample opportunity for all affected parties who wish to participate meaningfully (that is, in a time and form that will reach the regulators in such a fashion that they could take it into account before rendering a decision) in regulatory proceedings to do so. Regulatory agencies should take all reasonable steps to facilitate and encourage public participation.

Public involvement in the regulatory process is an essential element of the credibility of regulation and of the regulatory agency. It can also provide the regulator with a broader perspective and additional insight on the question before him or her. In small countries in particular, but in large ones as well, public participation can serve as an effective antidote to regulatory capture by the regulated entities.[11] Meaningful opportunities for all parties, including regulated companies, need to be available to be heard by the regulators in specific matters that affect them.

There are essentially two forms of public participation in the process. The first is where small consumers and members of the public can formally and directly offer their point of view. The second form of participation is where a party wishes to invest more time and effort in the process by offering particular evidence (for example, expertise), or wishes to formally challenge information submitted to the regulatory agency by a regulated entity or other adverse party. In both cases, the involvement of the public is likely to enrich the process, stimulate productive public debate, and make regulation more credible as a result.

In order to facilitate public participation, regulatory agencies should undertake efforts to inform the public through legal notices, news stories, and advertising about where, when, and how members of the public can participate.

14. Appellate Review of Regulatory Decisions

14.1. Direct appeals to a single, independent appellate forum

All appeals from a regulatory agency decision should be directed to a single, independent appellate forum, the decision of which would be final, in the absence of a constitutional issue.

The appellate process should be simple and direct, and conducted by an independent, nonpolitical entity. It should also be designed to avoid the possibility of conflicting appellate decisions that contradict one another and lead to incoherence and confusion for investors and consumers.

Ideally, there should be only one appellate forum—an independent one—the decision of which is final. In many countries, however, the constitution, laws, or longstanding practice makes this difficult to achieve. There may be requirements of multiple levels of appeal or a permissive view of allowing appellants to go forum shopping for a court or tribunal sympathetic to their position. Some countries allow for appeals to the government, whereas others do not. Some countries have special administrative tribunals to hear appeals, whereas others have direct appeals to the courts. Almost all countries ultimately allow for access to the courts to pursue appeals at some point in the process. Bringing order, coherence, and simplicity to the appellate process may be a complex task.

---

11. *Capture* is the term used to describe the process by which the regulators come to view matters in the same frame of reference as the regulated entities—or, perhaps, occasionally as other types of parties. Capture usually does not denote or suggest corruption, but rather an intellectual process fed by an environment inhabited primarily by regulators and the regulated and where, in their isolation, they come to think alike.

Although the ideal may be a single, independent, and final forum, the political and institutional realities may impede it from coming into existence. Second best is to develop a mechanism for channeling appeals toward very specific, independent forums (for example, a specific court in the capital city), for promoting interaction between judges and regulators, and for taking other steps that increase the likelihood of the development of a coherent, consistent body of regulatory law.

14.2. Handle appeals in a specifically designated court or a specialized appellate tribunal

The appellate forum should be either a specifically designated court or a specialized appellate tribunal with the authority to review the decisions of one or more infrastructure regulatory agencies. In either case, the forum should possess relevant expertise in regulatory matters.

In addition to the appellate forum's being an independent and final forum, it is helpful if the body also possesses expertise in regulatory matters. Ideally, there might be an administrative tribunal or special court to hear all regulatory appeals. Such a tribunal or court would specialize in regulatory matters and would, therefore, possess the expertise that is highly desirable in an appellate forum. It would also increase the likelihood that legal interpretations would evolve coherently, and in ways that strengthen the regulatory regime.

14.3. Provide parties with an opportunity to seek an appeal

The regulatory agency must provide parties with an opportunity to seek rehearing or de novo review by the agency or by some other body designated in the law (for example, a competition agency). The time deadlines for filing an appeal should be suspended during the rehearing application and process.

The appellate process should be limited to the legal and process issues discussed below in section 14.6. On policy, factual, and substantive matters, however, the appellate process should be closed. To make sure, however, that parties have the right to ask for a "second look" (de novo review) at those matters that are not subject to appeal, a process should be in place to allow a party the right to seek review.

The right to such a review can be served by two possible mechanisms. The first, the easier of the two, is simply to allow a party to seek reconsideration by the regulators themselves. The second, in use in some countries, is to have a specialized tribunal that, upon petition by a party, may conduct a de novo review of the agency's decision. If there is such a tribunal, the cumulative processes followed by the regulatory agency and the special tribunal should be closely examined to make sure the process is not inordinately complicated or unnecessarily repetitive.

If either of these courses is followed, the appeals deadline discussed in section 14.4, below, should be suspended until a final decision on the de novo review is complete.

14.4. After a decision is made, provide a reasonable period in which an affected party can seek an appeal

Any party who believes that he or she is adversely affected by an agency decision should have the right to make an appeal on that decision within a reasonable period after the decision has been made (for example, 30 days). This right, however, should belong only to a party who formally participated in the agency proceedings on the matter in question and who raised that issue in the regulatory proceeding (including any rehearing process).

It is important that the original forum for all matters related to the economic regulation of the sector in question (for example, electricity, telecommunications, or water)—such as tariffs, service quality, or enforcement of market rules—be the regulatory agency. In some countries, the law or constitution may provide a mechanism, such as direct recourse to the courts or to the government, to bypass the regulator entirely. Unless the courts or government somehow involve the regulators and treat them deferentially, bypass of that nature could lead to a great deal of confusion in the evolution of precedent and practice in the regulation of the sector in question. Similarly, bypass of that nature could easily reduce transparency to unacceptably low levels.

In short, allowing bypass of the regulatory agency runs directly contrary to two of the fundamental reasons for creating regulatory agencies, namely, assuring that decisions for the sector are made by agencies with expertise and technical competence and that decisions for the sector are made to increase the probability that critical decisions for the regulated sector will be consistent, coherent, and predictable over the long term. The objective of having an appellate process is to constrain regulatory agencies and hold them accountable, not to allow them to be bypassed entirely.

Although the right to make an appeal should be guaranteed, the time for doing so cannot be forever. It is reasonable that some deadline be imposed on the exercise of that right, for example, within 30 days of the issuance of the agency's final decision.

14.5. Prohibit new issues and evidence from appeals

No interested party should be able to put forward new issues or new evidence on appeal that was not first raised in the proceedings at the regulatory agency (including any rehearing).

Two of the basic reasons that independent regulatory agencies are created are to ensure that critical decisions about the regulated sector are made by agencies with specific expertise and technical competence, and to make it more probable that decisions will be more predictable and consistent over the long term. Thus, the same rationale for avoiding agency bypass set forth above applies to issue bypass, where a party can raise issues on appeal that he or she never gave the regulatory agency the opportunity to decide. An appellate process is designed to review agency decisions, not to provide a means for bypassing them.

14.6. Use the appeals process primarily as a check on the agency's ability to act unlawfully or beyond its lawful authority

Regulatory agency decisions should be affirmed on appeal unless the agency acted unlawfully or exceeded its lawful authority, failed to follow the required processes in making its decision, or made decisions that were clearly flawed in the light of evidence presented at the appeal.

Appellate bodies, as a general principle, ought not to second-guess regulatory agency decisions simply because they disagree with them on policy grounds. The role of the appellate body is not to serve as a second regulatory forum, but rather to serve as an effective check on the regulators' ability to do the following:

- Exceed their legal authority.
- Fail to follow appropriate and fair processes.
- Act arbitrarily or unreasonably (for example, where they have no evidence to support their decision).

Thus, unless the appellant(s) can demonstrate to the satisfaction of the appellate body that the agency failed to meet one or more of those criteria, the decision of the regulatory agency should be affirmed.

14.7. Enforce decisions during appeal

The decision of the regulatory agency should remain in effect for the duration of the appeal, unless the agency or the appeals tribunal decides otherwise. Such a delay should not be granted without a demonstration of irreparable harm to the appellant and a likelihood that the appeal will succeed.

A

There should be a presumption of validity that attaches to agency decisions until such time as a legally constituted appellate body rules otherwise. Thus, the decision of the regulatory agency should, with very limited exceptions, remain in effect during the time that the appeal is pending. If the mere fact that a party's appeal from the regulatory agency decision has the effect of delaying the implementation of the decision, there would be a very powerful incentive for parties to make appeals on very weak grounds simply to delay implementation of decisions. Given the very slow processing of cases in many court systems around the world, the delay in implementation could have grave consequences.

The only exception to the rule that the regulatory decision stands until an appellate body rules otherwise is where an appellant persuades either the regulatory agency or the appellate body to issue an order delaying implementation of the agency decision pending the outcome of the appeal. To obtain such an order, an appellant would have to show two things: irreparable harm to himself or herself if the order is allowed to stand, and a high probability that the appeal will be successful. Failure to meet both of those standards should result in a denial of the plea for delaying implementation of the decision.

14.8. Send decisions that were overturned on appeal back to the agency for reconsideration

If the appellate forum reverses or changes the decision of the regulatory agency, the preferable course is for the matter to be sent back to the regulatory agency to conclude a remedy consistent with the decision of the appellate forum.

The best practice for an appellate body that reverses the decision of a regulatory agency is not to redecide the matter itself, but rather to return the case to the regulators with sufficient instruction to them to reconsider their decision in light of the appellate body's decision and instructions. The reason for such a course is that it allows the regulatory agency to follow the appellate body's instructions, but to do so in a way that is most consistent with general practice in the regulated sector. In this way, the outcome is more likely to be contributory to stability and predictability in the regulatory arena. If the regulatory agency fails to adhere to the decision and instructions of the appellate body, the body, of course, retains the authority to substitute its judgment for that of the regulators.

15. Ethics

To the extent not already covered by applicable law, regulatory agencies should promulgate a binding Code of Ethics applicable to all agency personnel, including directors and commissioners. Such a code should, at a minimum, include the standards set out in the sections below.

Regulatory agencies, along with their directors and staff, must be above reproach. All regulatory personnel should be held to the highest standards of conduct, not only so that they do not engage in any impropriety but to avoid even the appearance of any. The list of ethical restrictions below constitutes minimal standards that ought to apply. Other matters may well exist that could be included in a list of restrictions on regulatory personnel.

Although it is immaterial whether the ethical standards are set out in law for all government employees, or established in the agency rules, it is imperative that the ethical standards be binding and be vigorously enforced.

15.1. Prohibit favors and gifts from parties involved in agency business

Prohibit gratuities, favors, or other gifts from parties having any business involving the agency.

The acceptance of something of value or the extortion of something of value in exchange for favorable treatment by a government official, including regulators, is obviously unlawful. The mere acceptance of gratuities or favors (for example, tickets to sporting events, travel, or meals) without an explicit understanding of what is expected in exchange may or may not be unlawful. Nevertheless, it clearly carries the appearance of impropriety, and regulatory personnel ought to be strictly prohibited from accepting anything of value from any party having business before the agency.

15.2. Prohibit regulatory personnel from negotiating employment or business opportunities with parties having business before the agency

Limit subsequent employment on matters of parties doing business with the agency.

Regulatory personnel, while still employed as a regulator (staff or director), should be strictly prohibited from negotiating employment or business opportunities with commercial entities or persons having business before the agency. This constitutes an intolerable conflict of interest. The only exception to this is where the person involved discloses his or her actions to the relevant authority and then removes himself or herself from any activities involving the person or business with which the negotiations are being conducted.

In addition to the restrictions on negotiating employment, it is appropriate to put some distance between a person's service at the regulatory agency and his or her subsequent appearance at the agency on behalf of a participant in a regulatory proceeding, or perhaps even advising a person or business on agency-related matters. Certainly a former regulator should be precluded from using inside information gained from employment at the agency for personal gain of any type.

Because of the concerns noted, all regulatory personnel should be subject to a general quarantine for a period of at least one year, which would prevent them from appearing at the agency or providing consultation or advice on agency-related matters. In addition, there should be a lifetime prohibition on involvement with specific cases on which a person worked while employed as a regulator.

15.3. Prohibit conflicts of interests for all personnel and close family members

Prohibit actual or apparent financial or other conflicts of interest involving agency personnel or their immediate family.

It is simply intolerable for any regulator, or close family member of a regulator, to have any financial interest in the outcome of a case or in any business that has business pending before the agency. The term, "financial interest," for purposes of an ethical code, should be defined in a very broad fashion so as to include at least stock ownership, debtor or creditor relationship, and partnership.

15.4. Prohibit favoritism and ethical compromises

Prohibit conduct giving rise to an appearance of favoritism or ethical compromise.

Certain types of conduct, apart from those already discussed, either constitute or give the appearance of favoritism or another form of ethical compromise. Examples might include discriminating in the furnishing of access to information, providing access to the agency and its decisionmaking processes in ways that are denied to other parties, or making pronouncements that appear to prejudge pending matters at the agency.

Identifying all types of actions that might fall into this category of undesirable actions is difficult, so perhaps some broad prohibition should be adopted, which would preclude all actions or behavior that either are or appear to be unethical, improper, or unfair, or that otherwise compromise the integrity of the regulatory process or agency, or both.

15.5. Require regulatory personnel to disclose their financial interests

Require appropriate financial disclosure.

Requiring regulatory personnel to disclose all their financial interests above a minimal level will be useful in assuring the public that no financial conflicts of interest exist and in making it difficult for regulatory personnel to have any conflicts of interest without public knowledge of it. Financial interests that are required to be disclosed include stocks, debts, creditors, and partnerships.

15.6. Prohibit agency personnel or family members from deriving financial benefit in companies related to agency work

Prohibit employment or other work by agency personnel (or their close family) in companies or areas of work covered by the agency for a reasonable period after leaving the agency.

This is largely discussed in sections 15.2 and 15.3, above, but expands it to preclude close family members (for example, spouses, children, or parents) from deriving a financial benefit related to the relative serving at the regulatory agency.

A

Background Documents for Mid-Level and In-Depth Evaluations

1. *The World Factbook 2004.* Washington, DC. Brief on the country; available at http://www.cia.gov/cia/publications/factbook/.
2. Articles and papers that describe the structure and operation of the sector over the past 10 years.
3. All relevant laws, acts, and decrees that govern the operation of the electricity regulator and regulation of the electricity sector, and the dates when each of these became effective.
4. Any proposed bills, laws, and decrees.
5. Licenses or comparable documents for major operators in the sector.
6. All major regulations issued by the regulator or other government entities with regulatory authority in the past three years.
7. All draft regulations and policy statements issued for consultation.
8. Statements, press releases, and other documents that explain the current objectives and strategies of the regulatory entity.
9. Annual reports and annual management plans of the regulator for the past three years.
10. Annual reports of major participants in the sector for the past three years.
11. Organizational chart for the regulatory entity.
12. Budget requests and budget allowances obtained during the past five years, broken down if possible by source of funding (including license awards, license fees, government appropriation, regulatory fee, fines and penalties, grants from international organizations, payments from sector participants based on turnover, financial income, and other).
13. Recent assessments of the power sector or regulatory system sponsored by the government, sector organizations, or nongovernmental organizations.
14. Recent public statements or position papers on regulation and sector reform of major industry participants, associations, and the government.
15. Questionnaires on power sector reform and regulation completed by government or regulatory officials.

B

Questionnaires for Short Basic Evaluations of Infrastructure Regulatory Systems

Answer Yes, No, N/A (not applicable), or D/K (don't know), or note a checkmark and add explanation where appropriate.

A. General Regulatory Issues

1. Name of country, province, region, or other:

_____

2. What government body has the primary legal responsibility for economic regulation (e.g., tariff setting, quality of service, consumer protection, investment, promotion of competition) of the sector?

_____

Is the body:
  (a) An independent/autonomous regulatory agency?　　Yes ❏　No ❏　N/A ❏　D/K ❏ ___
  (b) A regulatory agency within ministry?　　　　　　Yes ❏　No ❏　N/A ❏　D/K ❏ ___
  (c) An independent advisory agency reporting to
      minister?　　　　　　　　　　　　　　　　　　Yes ❏　No ❏　N/A ❏　D/K ❏ ___
  (d) The minister/ministry?　　　　　　　　　　　　Yes ❏　No ❏　N/A ❏　D/K ❏ ___
  (e) Other?　　　　　　　　　　　　　　　　　　　Yes ❏　No ❏　N/A ❏　D/K ❏ ___
     If Yes, specify: _____
  In what year was the regulatory agency established?　　　　　Year: _____

  (f) If there is no independent regulatory agency or advisory
      agency (i.e., unless answer of Yes to *either* 2[a] *or* 2[b]
      above), is there an infrastructure concession or
      franchise contract for monitoring and enforcement
      or a similar "quasi-regulatory" body?　　　　　　　Yes ❏　No ❏　N/A ❏　D/K ❏ ___

If Yes, go to Question 18.

3. Does the agency/ministry derive its legal authority to
    carry out economic regulation from

        Constitution?   Yes ❑   No ❑   N/A ❑   D/K ❑ ___

        Law or statute?   Yes ❑   No ❑   N/A ❑   D/K ❑ ___

        Government decree?   Yes ❑   No ❑   N/A ❑   D/K ❑ ___

        Contract?   Yes ❑   No ❑   N/A ❑   D/K ❑ ___

        Combination of the above? (if Yes, explain)   Yes ❑   No ❑   N/A ❑   D/K ❑ ___

    _____

    _____

        None of the above? (if Yes, explain)   Yes ❑   No ❑   N/A ❑   D/K ❑ ___

    _____

    _____

        In what year was the law or decree, etc., enacted?   Year: _____

        In what year was the law or decree, etc., last amended?   Year: _____

        Is there a sector law (e.g., electricity, telecommunications)
    separate from any regulatory law?   Yes ❑   No ❑   N/A ❑   D/K ❑ ___

        If, so, in what year was the sector law enacted?   Yes ❑   No ❑   N/A ❑   D/K ❑ ___

4. Indicate what percentage of the regulatory agency's
    budget comes from the following sources:

        Government budget   _____ %

        Identified payment by regulated entities (e.g., license fees)   _____ %

        Identified payment by consumers (e.g., specific fees or taxes)   _____ %

        Other (explain) _____ _____ %

        For what year do these percentages apply?   Year: _____

        How are these percentages obtained? _____

    _____

        From a published source? (If Yes, name the source)   Yes ❑   No ❑   N/A ❑   D/K ❑ ___

    _____

        Estimated? (If Yes, indicate source of estimate)   Yes ❑   No ❑   N/A ❑   D/K ❑ ___

    _____

        Are regulatory funds legally earmarked for use only by
    the agency, or are they subject to government
    reallocation?   Yes ❑   No ❑   N/A ❑   D/K ❑ ___

5. Is the regulatory agency headed by

        A single person (e.g., director general/president)?   Yes ❑   No ❑   N/A ❑   D/K ❑ ___

        Multimember body (e.g., 3–5 regulatory
    commissioners)?   Yes ❑   No ❑   N/A ❑   D/K ❑ ___

        Other? (explain) _____ Yes ❑   No ❑   N/A ❑   D/K ❑ ___

    _____

    _____

C

6. Who is legally responsible for appointing the head(s) of
    the regulatory agency? (mark one or more in the case
    of shared legal responsibilities)

    President/head of state   Yes ❑   No ❑   N/A ❑   D/K ❑ ___
    Cabinet   Yes ❑   No ❑   N/A ❑   D/K ❑ ___
    Prime minister   Yes ❑   No ❑   N/A ❑   D/K ❑ ___
    Departmental minister   Yes ❑   No ❑   N/A ❑   D/K ❑ ___
    Legislature   Yes ❑   No ❑   N/A ❑   D/K ❑ ___

    Other (explain): _____

    _____

    Under the law, are these appointments subject to
    approval by

    Legislature?   Yes ❑   No ❑   N/A ❑   D/K ❑ ___

    Other body (explain): _____

    _____

7. Under the law, are regulatory agency head(s) appointed for

    Fixed terms? (if Yes, specify length of term) _____   Yes ❑   No ❑   N/A ❑   D/K ❑ ___

    Indefinite periods? (if Yes, specify at whose discretion   Yes ❑   No ❑   N/A ❑   D/K ❑ ___

    the appointment is ended) _____

    If terms are fixed, are they the same term as the period between elections   Same ❑
    or different from the period between elections?   Different ❑

    Are regulatory agency head(s) limited in the number of
    terms they are permitted to serve? If Yes, specify the
    maximum number of terms. _____   Yes ❑   No ❑   N/A ❑   D/K ❑ ___

    For regulatory agencies with 3, 5, or more commissioners,
    indicate whether their terms of office are

    Staggered and overlapping   Yes ❑   No ❑   N/A ❑   D/K ❑ ___
    Common, so that they all begin and end together   Yes ❑   No ❑   N/A ❑   D/K ❑ ___

8. Under the law, are regulatory agency head(s) subject to
    dismissal (within terms if terms are fixed)?   Yes ❑   No ❑   N/A ❑   D/K ❑ ___

    If Yes:
    For any reason?   Yes ❑   No ❑   N/A ❑   D/K ❑ ___
    For specific causes only?   Yes ❑   No ❑   N/A ❑   D/K ❑ ___
    If only for specific causes, list main types of specific
    cause: _____

    _____

    _____

    Under the law, indicate who has the power to remove regulatory agency

    head(s): _____

C

If removal can be made only for specific causes, under the law, do the causes have to be proved before the agency head(s) can be removed?　　　　　　　Yes ❑　No ❑　N/A ❑　D/K ❑ ＿＿

    If Yes, is an independent investigation required?　　Yes ❑　No ❑　N/A ❑　D/K ❑ ＿＿

    If Yes, identify who is identified in the law to carry out

    the investigation: ＿＿＿＿＿＿＿＿＿＿＿＿＿＿＿＿＿＿＿＿＿＿＿＿＿＿＿＿＿＿＿

＿＿＿

9. For fixed-term regulatory appointments, how many times in the past 5 years have agency head or regulatory commissioners served less than a complete term?　＿＿＿＿＿＿＿＿＿＿

For non–fixed-term appointments, how many times in the past 5 years have agency head or regulatory commissioners served less than 5 years?　＿＿＿＿＿＿＿＿＿＿

For fixed-term appointees who have served less than full terms, were removals voluntary or involuntary under the law? (include compulsory retirement as involuntary, but specify separately)　　　　　Voluntary ❑　Involuntary ❑　N/A ❑　D/K ❑ ＿＿

For fixed-term appointees, can terms and conditions of employment be changed midterm under the law?　　Yes ❑　No ❑　N/A ❑　D/K ❑ ＿＿

    (if Yes, explain): ＿＿＿＿＿＿＿＿＿＿＿＿＿＿＿＿＿＿＿＿＿＿＿＿＿＿＿＿＿＿＿

＿＿＿

10. Under the law, how are the pay scales of regulatory staff in the agency established (excluding directors/ commissioners, etc.)?

    According to civil service pay scales/rules　　　　Yes ❑　No ❑　N/A ❑　D/K ❑ ＿＿

    Regulatory agency discretion　　　　　　　　　Yes ❑　No ❑　N/A ❑　D/K ❑ ＿＿

    Other (explain): ＿＿＿＿＿＿＿＿＿＿＿＿＿＿＿＿＿＿＿＿＿＿＿＿＿＿＿＿＿＿＿

＿＿＿

Under the law, is the regulatory agency free to make its own personnel decisions (e.g., hire, fire, promote, discipline)?　　　　　　　　　　　　　　Yes ❑　No ❑　N/A ❑　D/K ❑ ＿＿

11. How many staff are employed in electricity regulation (independent agency/ministry)?　　　　　　　　　　　　　　　　　　＿＿＿＿＿＿

How many of the staff are professional (e.g., lawyers, economists, accountants, engineers)?　　　　　　　　　　　　　　　＿＿＿＿＿＿

How many of the staff are support staff (e.g., secretaries, administrative personnel, drivers)?　　　　　　　　　　　　　　　　＿＿＿＿＿＿

What percentage of the staff is

    Permanent?　　　　　　　　　　　　　　　　　　＿＿＿＿＿＿%

    Temporary?　　　　　　　　　　　　　　　　　　＿＿＿＿＿＿%

    On fixed contract?　　　　　　　　　　　　　　　＿＿＿＿＿＿%

    Seconded from ministry?　　　　　　　　　　　　＿＿＿＿＿＿%

    Seconded from regulated companies?　　　　　　＿＿＿＿＿＿%

Is there an organization chart for the agency?   Yes ❑ No ❑ N/A ❑ D/K ❑ ___
If Yes, attach a copy.
If No, list main departments/branches of agency with staff numbers in each, if available:

_____

_____

12. If there is an independent regulatory agency (i.e., Yes to
Question 2[a]), does it regulate only the power sector?   Yes ❑ No ❑ N/A ❑ D/K ❑ ___

If No, what other sectors does it regulate? (mark all
that apply)
Natural gas   Yes ❑ No ❑ N/A ❑ D/K ❑ ___
Telecommunications   Yes ❑ No ❑ N/A ❑ D/K ❑ ___
Transport (e.g., highway, rail, bus)   Yes ❑ No ❑ N/A ❑ D/K ❑ ___
Water   Yes ❑ No ❑ N/A ❑ D/K ❑ ___
Sewerage   Yes ❑ No ❑ N/A ❑ D/K ❑ ___
Petroleum products (e.g., gasoline/petrol, kerosene)   Yes ❑ No ❑ N/A ❑ D/K ❑ ___
District heating   Yes ❑ No ❑ N/A ❑ D/K ❑ ___

Other (identify): _____

_____

What percentage of staff effort is dedicated to the power sector?   _____ %

13. Who (subject to appeal) has the legal responsibility for making decisions on the following
issues?

Decision	Regulatory agency	Ministry	Company/enterprise (identify which company/enterprise)	Other (identify); (identify "no one identifiable" as N/A)
Tariff structure				
Tariff level				
Service quality				
Consumer complaints				
Sector expansion plans				
Investment plans/decisions (ex ante approval)				
Investment decisions (e.g., ex post prudence review)				
Wholesale market structure				
Anti-competitive behavior				
Merger/acquisition reviews				
Technical and safety standards				

C

14. Is there a legally defined process for appealing
regulatory decisions?   Yes ❑ No* ❑ N/A ❑ D/K ❑ ___
  *Includes reconsideration by agency without wider
  appeal route.*
  If Yes, indicate by whom appeals are considered:
    General law courts   Yes ❑ No ❑ N/A ❑ D/K ❑ ___
    Specifically designated court (identify)_____   Yes ❑ No ❑ N/A ❑ D/K ❑ ___
    Ministry/government   Yes ❑ No ❑ N/A ❑ D/K ❑ ___
    Minister (identify) _____ Yes ❑ No ❑ N/A ❑ D/K ❑ ___
    Special administrative tribunal   Yes ❑ No ❑ N/A ❑ D/K ❑ ___
    Combination of above (e.g., to courts and government)

    (explain):_____

    Other (explain): _____

Under the law, can parties appeal on all matters, including the substance of   Can appeal ❑
decisions, or are they limited (e.g., only to questions of law and regulatory   Limited ❑
process)?

  If appeals are limited, explain limitations on appeals: _____
  _____
  _____

Under the law, are there limits on who may seek appeals
(e.g., regulated companies, consumer agency)?   Yes ❑ No ❑ N/A ❑ D/K ❑ ___

  If Yes, identify or explain:_____
  _____
  _____

15. Does the regulatory agency publish an annual report on
its activities?   Yes ❑ No ❑ N/A ❑ D/K ❑ ___

  If Yes, how many annual reports have been published in the past 5 years?_____

Does the regulatory agency publish audited accounts?   Yes ❑ No ❑ N/A ❑ D/K ❑ ___

  If Yes, how many times have audited accounts been published in the past 5 years?_____

Who audits the accounts?
    International accounting firm   Yes ❑ No ❑ N/A ❑ D/K ❑ ___
    Local accounting firm   Yes ❑ No ❑ N/A ❑ D/K ❑ ___
    Internal audit facility   Yes ❑ No ❑ N/A ❑ D/K ❑ ___
    Government audit office   Yes ❑ No ❑ N/A ❑ D/K ❑ ___

    Other (explain):_____
    _____

Does the regulatory agency have a Web site?   Yes ❑ No ❑ N/A ❑ D/K ❑ ___

Does the regulatory agency publicly answer questions
from the legislature (e.g., from a parliamentary
committee)?   Yes ❑ No ❑ N/A ❑ D/K ❑ ___

C

16. Have there been any serious disputes or controversies
involving the electricity regulatory agency or the
regulatory system within the past 3 years?   Yes ❑ No* ❑ N/A ❑ D/K ❑ __
No disputes.

If Yes, have they involved disputes
(a) between the regulatory agency (including ministry
    regulator) and regulated companies?   Yes ❑ No ❑ N/A ❑ D/K ❑ __
(b) between the regulatory agency and the
    government/ministry?   Yes ❑ No ❑ N/A ❑ D/K ❑ __

(c) with others? (specify) _____

If Yes to (a), (b), or (c), give a brief description, and provide documentary references, if
available: _____

17. Have there been any major changes in the past 3–5 years
in the responsibilities of the regulatory agency?   Yes ❑ No ❑ N/A ❑ D/K ❑ __

If Yes, have they been
Increases in responsibilities?   Yes ❑ No ❑ N/A ❑ D/K ❑ __
Decreases in responsibilities?   Yes ❑ No ❑ N/A ❑ D/K ❑ __
Other (specify): _____

Give a brief description of changes, and list documentary sources for documentary

changes, if available: _____

C

**18. To be answered only for countries with an infrastructure concession/franchise contract for
monitoring and enforcement, or a similar "quasi-regulatory" body, but no regulatory
agency or advisory agency (i.e., Yes to Question 2[f]):**

When did the infrastructure concession/franchise contract monitoring
and enforcement or similar "quasi-regulatory" body start operating?   Year: _____

Does the infrastructure concession/franchise contract-
monitoring and enforcement, or similar "quasi-
regulatory"body operate under a specific law or decree?   Yes ❑ No ❑ N/A ❑ D/K ❑ __

If Yes, name law/decree: _____

In what year was law/decree first enacted?   Year: _____

In what year was law/decree last amended?   Year: _____

Is the infrastructure concession/franchise contract-
monitoring and enforcement or similar "quasi-
regulatory" body separate from the agency that
awards infrastructure concession/franchise contracts?   Yes ❑ No ❑ N/A ❑ D/K ❑ __

If Yes, name agency/ministry, etc., that awards infrastructure concession/franchise

contracts: _____

Does the infrastructure concession/franchise contract-monitoring and enforcement or similar "quasi-regulatory" body operate with clear and defined procedures?   Yes ❏ No ❏ N/A ❏ D/K ❏ ___

How much discretion does the infrastructure concession/franchise contract-monitoring and enforcement or similar "quasi-regulatory" body have in deciding whether the concession franchise holder has violated the terms of the contract?

A lot of discretion	Yes ❏ No ❏ N/A ❏ D/K ❏ ___
Some discretion	Yes ❏ No ❏ N/A ❏ D/K ❏ ___
A little discretion	Yes ❏ No ❏ N/A ❏ D/K ❏ ___
No discretion	Yes ❏ No ❏ N/A ❏ D/K ❏ ___

In finding remedies for contract problems and disputes?

A lot of discretion	Yes ❏ No ❏ N/A ❏ D/K ❏ ___
Some discretion	Yes ❏ No ❏ N/A ❏ D/K ❏ ___
A little discretion	Yes ❏ No ❏ N/A ❏ D/K ❏ ___
No discretion	Yes ❏ No ❏ N/A ❏ D/K ❏ ___

Can decisions of the infrastructure concession/franchise contract-monitoring and enforcement or similar "quasi-regulatory" body be appealed or reviewed in the courts or elsewhere?   Yes ❏ No ❏ N/A ❏ D/K ❏ ___

If Yes, where are they appealed or reviewed? _____

Have there been any serious disputes or controversies involving the infrastructure concession/franchise contract-monitoring and enforcement or similar "quasi-regulatory" body during the past 3 years?   Yes ❏ No ❏ N/A ❏ D/K ❏ ___

If Yes, have they involved disputes

(a) Between the agency and regulated companies?	Yes ❏ No ❏ N/A ❏ D/K ❏ ___
(b) Between the agency and government/ministry?	Yes ❏ No ❏ N/A ❏ D/K ❏ ___
(c) With others? (specify)	Yes ❏ No ❏ N/A ❏ D/K ❏ ___

If Yes to (a), (b), or (c), give a brief description, and provide documentary references, if available:_____

_____

Have there been any major changes in the past 3–5 years in the responsibilities of the infrastructure concession/franchise contract-monitoring and enforcement or similar "quasi-regulatory" body? (indicate the type of change)   Yes ❏ No ❏ N/A ❏ D/K ❏ ___

Increases in responsibilities	Yes ❏ No ❏ N/A ❏ D/K ❏ ___
Decreases in responsibilities	Yes ❏ No ❏ N/A ❏ D/K ❏ ___

Other (specify): _____

Give brief description of changes, and list documentary sources for changes, if available:

_____

_____

19. Provide answers for all countries.

What is the overall score for the country on the Kaufmann-Kraay Governance Indicators for the latest year available (currently 2004)?*_____

What was the score for 1996?* _____

What is the score for the Rule of Law measure on the Kaufmann-Kraay Governance Indicators for the latest year available (currently 2004)?*_____

What was the score for 1996?* _____

See http://www.worldbank.org/wbi/governance/data.html for the database with the scores for all countries.

B. Electricity Industry Issues

1. What is the size of the electricity industry in the country, province, region?

    Length of transmission lines (km)? _____ km

    Length of distribution lines (km)? _____ km

    Installed generation capacity (Megawatt [MW])? _____ MW

    International interconnection capacity (MW)? _____ MW

    Imports (MWh/year)? _____ (MWh/year)

    Exports (MWh/year)? _____ (MWh/year)

    Total number of customers? _____

    Percent residential? _____ %

    Percent of households connected to grid? _____ %

    Percent of households without any electricity (grid or off-grid)? _____ %

2. What is the fuel mix of installed generation capacity?

    Percent coal? _____ %

    Percent natural gas? _____ %

    Percent hydro? _____ %

    Percent nuclear? _____ %

    Percent renewable? _____ %

    Percent solar? _____ %

    Percent wind? _____ %

    Percent small hydro (less than 1 MW)? _____ %

    Percent geothermal? _____ %

    Percent other? (identify) _____ %

C

What are the estimated transmission and distribution losses? _____

    Percentage of technical losses? _____ %

    Percentage of nontechnical losses? _____ %

If data are separately available for transmission and distribution, what are the

    (a) Estimated transmission losses? _____

        Percentage of technical losses? _____ %

        Percentage of nontechnical losses? _____ %

    (b) Estimated distribution losses? _____

        Percentage of technical losses? _____ %

        Percentage of nontechnical losses? _____ %

To what year do the statistics above relate?   Year: _____

3. Assuming some electricity prices are regulated, under the law, does price regulation apply to

    Residential customers?   Yes ❏ No ❏ N/A ❏ D/K ❏ __

    Other small customers (e.g., small farmers)?   Yes ❏ No ❏ N/A ❏ D/K ❏ __

    Commercial customers? (identify exceptions, if any)   Yes ❏ No ❏ N/A ❏ D/K ❏ __

_____

    Industrial customers? (identify exceptions, if any)   Yes ❏ No ❏ N/A ❏ D/K ❏ __

_____

Are there any groups of customers who are supplied with electricity at a *zero price* (i.e., free of charge)?   Yes ❏ No ❏ N/A ❏ D/K ❏ __

    Identify any that apply:

    (*Possible examples are some groups of households, small farmers, street lighting, specific industries, some government departments, and the armed forces.*)

_____

_____

_____

_____

Are there any groups of customers who are supplied with electricity at a *very low price* (e.g., less than US$0.03/kWh)?   Yes ❏ No ❏ N/A ❏ D/K ❏ __

    Identify any that apply:

    (*Possible examples are some groups of households, small farmers, street lighting, specific industries, some government departments, and the armed forces.*)

_____

_____

_____

_____

C

4. Under the law, are electricity purchases by distribution/ retail sales entities for resale to customers subject to any form of review (e.g., for the reasonableness of the purchase price)?   Yes ❑ No ❑ N/A ❑ D/K ❑ ___

   If Yes, indicate type of review. _____

   _____

   _____

   Under the law, does the regulatory entity impose any other **mandatory requirements on electricity purchases** by distribution/retail sales entities (e.g., competitive procurement, procurement benchmarks)?   Yes ❑ No ❑ N/A ❑ D/K ❑ ___

   If Yes, indicate type of requirement. _____

   _____

   _____

5. Under the law, are there any **resource allocation or portfolio requirements** imposed on electricity purchases by distribution/retail sales entities (e.g., preferences for hydropower or CHP [combined heat and power] use, obligations on purchases of renewables, or obligatory purchases to ensure security of supply)?   Yes ❑ No ❑ N/A ❑ D/K ❑ ___

   If Yes, indicate type of requirement. _____

   _____

   _____

6. Indicate whether electricity tariffs are bundled or unbundled.

   (i) Bundled (i.e., with a single price covering [a] generation, [b] transmission, [c] distribution, and [d] retail sales)? Yes ❑ No ❑ N/A ❑ D/K ❑ ___
   or
   (ii) Unbundled (i.e., with separate cost/price elements for one or more of generation, transmission, distribution, and retail sales)?   Yes ❑ No ❑ N/A ❑ D/K ❑ ___

   If unbundled, identify which of the cost/price elements (a)–(d) are combined together and which are separated. _____

7. Under the law, how frequently are regulatory reviews of **either** Bundled tariffs **or** Separate retail sales tariffs, **or both**, conducted (e.g., every 12 months, every 5 years, upon application)?   _____

   Are they regulated by (mark one of the following)
   ❑ Price caps?
   ❑ Revenue caps?
   ❑ Rate of return?
   ❑ Mixed/other? (explain): _____

   _____

   _____

C

8. Industry structure/characteristics

   (i) Is there a single **national** electricity industry company/entity?   Yes ❑   No ❑   N/A ❑   D/K ❑ ___

     If Yes, is it fully vertically integrated (i.e., generation, transmission, distribution retail sales/supply all provided by a single company/entity)?   Yes ❑   No ❑   N/A ❑   D/K ❑ ___

     If Yes, what is its ownership structure?
- ❑ State-owned enterprise
- ❑ State owning at least 50 percent of shares
- ❑ Private sector owning at least 50 percent of shares

       ❑ Other (specify):_____

       _____

   (ii) Are there separate **provincial/regional** electricity companies/entities?   Yes ❑   No ❑   N/A ❑   D/K ❑ ___

     If Yes, are the provincial/regional companies fully vertically integrated (i.e., generation, transmission, distribution retail sales/supply all provided by a single company/entity)?   Yes ❑   No ❑   N/A ❑   D/K ❑ ___

     If Yes, what is their ownership structure?
- ❑ State/region/provincial government-owned enterprise
- ❑ State/region/provincial government owning at least 50 percent of shares
- ❑ Private sector owning at least 50 percent of shares

       ❑ Other (specify):_____

       _____

C

9. How many generation companies/entities are there?
- ❑ Only 1
- ❑ 2–3
- ❑ 4–5
- ❑ 6–10
- ❑ More than 10

What percentage of generation capacity is owned by the largest generation company/entity?   _____ %

Does this company/entity also own or manage transmission assets?   Yes ❑   No ❑   N/A ❑   D/K ❑ ___

Is this company/entity
- ❑ 100 percent owned by the state/province/region?
- ❑ At least 50 percent owned by the state/province/region?

What percentage of generation capacity is owned by the 3 largest company/entities?   _____ %

What percentage of generation capacity
   Is owned by independent power producers?   _____ %
   Is accounted for by self/auto-generation?   _____ %
   Is off-grid?   _____ %

Is *any* electricity generation sold under PPAs (power purchase agreements)?   Yes ❑ No ❑ N/A ❑ D/K ❑ ___

If Yes, what percentage of generation is sold under PPAs?   _____ %
And what percentage is sold under PPAs of more than 15 years' duration?   _____ %

Is generation subject to any form of price regulation?   Yes ❑ No ❑ N/A ❑ D/K ❑ ___

If Yes, is this (mark one of the following):
- ❑ Advance regulatory approval of prices in PPAs (power purchase agreements)?
- ❑ Annual or similar regulation of bulk supply tariff?
- ❑ Annual or similar regulation of prices charged by generators?

- ❑ Other (specify): _____

10. Who in the nation/province/region is allowed to buy and sell bulk power (including imports and exports)?
- ❑ (a) Main national/provincial/regional power company/entity only
- ❑ (b) Transmission company/entity only
- ❑ (c) Distribution/retail sales companies/entities only
- ❑ (d) Distribution/retail sales companies/entities and large industrial consumers only

- ❑ (e) Other (explain): _____

If bulk power can only be bought and sold *either* by groups (a) *or* (b) above, is there any separation of the activities of the bulk power purchase buyer from the other activities of the company/entity?   Yes ❑ No ❑ N/A ❑ D/K ❑ ___

If Yes, is this
- ❑ Separate accounts?
- ❑ Separate management?
- ❑ Separate businesses?
- ❑ Separate (legally defined) companies?

11. Is bulk electricity traded on a contract basis?   Yes ❑ No ❑ N/A ❑ D/K ❑ ___

If Yes, outline who can contract with whom, length of contracts, and percentage of electricity bought and sold on contract:

_____

_____

_____

Are there wholesale markets in which generators and others can buy or sell bulk electricity?   Yes ❑ No ❑ N/A ❑ D/K ❑ ___

If Yes, who is allowed to participate as buyers and sellers?

_____

_____

_____

C

Outline the nature of wholesale market(s) (e.g., imbalance market, bilateral trading market, power pool):

_____

_____

_____

_____

Are there any financial trading markets for bulk power
(e.g., futures markets)?   Yes ❑   No ❑   N/A ❑   D/K ❑ ___

If Yes, who is allowed to participate as buyers and sellers? _____

_____

Outline nature of financial trading market(s) for electricity (e.g., futures markets, hedging markets, etc.):

_____

_____

_____

_____

12. Is transmission fully separated from generation?   Yes ❑   No ❑   N/A ❑   D/K ❑ ___

If Yes, who owns the transmission entity? _____

_____

If No, is there any separation of transmission from
generation? (indicate any separation)   Yes ❑   No ❑   N/A ❑   D/K ❑ ___
    ❑   (a) No separation
    ❑   (b) Separate accounts
    ❑   (c) Separate management
    ❑   (d) Separate businesses
    ❑   (e) Separate (legally defined) companies

If transmission is classified as in categories (c), (d), or (e)
above, does the transmission entity also control system
operation?   Yes ❑   No ❑   N/A ❑   D/K ❑ ___

If the transmission entity does **not** control system
operation, is there a separate system operator?   Yes ❑   No ❑   N/A ❑   D/K ❑ ___

If Yes, is the system operator independent?   Yes ❑   No ❑   N/A ❑   D/K ❑ ___

Who owns the system operator? _____

Is there a defined generation market operator?   Yes ❑   No ❑   N/A ❑   D/K ❑ ___

If Yes, who owns the generation market operator? _____

Is there a wholesale generation settlement system?   Yes ❑   No ❑   N/A ❑   D/K ❑ ___

If Yes, who owns the generation settlement system? _____

C

13. How many distribution/retail sales companies or entities are there in the nation/province/region?
- ❏ Only 1
- ❏ 2–3
- ❏ 4–5
- ❏ 6–10
- ❏ More than 10

Are the distribution/retail sales companies/entities
- ❏ 100 percent owned by the state/province/region?
- ❏ At least 50 percent owned by the state/province/region?
- ❏ At least 50 percent owned by the private sector?
- ❏ Other (e.g., municipally owned)? (specify)

Is there any separation between (a) distribution
activities and (b) retail sales?   Yes ❏ No ❏ N/A ❏ D/K ❏ ___

    If Yes, is this:
- ❏ Separate accounts?
- ❏ Separate management?
- ❏ Separate businesses?
- ❏ Separate (legally defined) companies?

Do distribution/retail sales companies/entities have a
local monopoly on sales to *all* retail customers?   Yes ❏ No ❏ N/A ❏ D/K ❏ ___

Are some customers (e.g., large industrial customers) currently able to buy electricity from generators or suppliers
other than the local distribution/retail sales company?   Yes ❏ No ❏ N/A ❏ D/K ❏ ___

(a) If Yes, what percentage of retail sales are to non-monopoly customers? _____ %

    Is this planned to change over the next 3–5 years?   Yes ❏ No ❏ N/A ❏ D/K ❏ ___

      If Yes, outline the expected changes:

_____

_____

_____

_____

(b) If No, are there any plans to relax the monopoly over
the next 3–5 years?   Yes ❏ No ❏ N/A ❏ D/K ❏ ___

    If Yes, outline the expected changes:

_____

_____

_____

_____

C

C. Electricity Policy and Design Issues

1. Outline the government's policy toward private sector participation in the electricity supply industry. If appropriate, distinguish between (a) generation, (b) transmission, (c) distribution, and (d) retail sales:

_____

_____

_____

_____

2. List the most significant controversies in the country/region in electricity regulation in the past three years:

_____

_____

_____

_____

_____

3. How well does the current industry/market structure appear to function?
   - ❏ Very well
   - ❏ Well
   - ❏ Adequately/OK
   - ❏ Poorly
   - ❏ Very poorly

   Provide a brief explanation with references, if possible:

_____

_____

_____

_____

4. Have there been any serious problems (e.g., shortage of supply) in electricity supply over the past 3 years?   Yes ❏   No ❏   N/A ❏   D/K ❏ __

   If Yes, indicate nature and scale of problem(s):

_____

_____

_____

   Provide brief description and references, if possible:

_____

_____

_____

_____

C

D. More Detailed Electricity Structure and Regulatory Questions

1. If there are separate cost/price elements for *high-voltage transmission services,* under the law, how frequently are the regulatory reviews conducted (e.g., every year, every 5 years, upon application)?

    Are they regulated by
    - ❏ Price caps?
    - ❏ Revenue caps?
    - ❏ Rate of return?
    - ❏ Mixed/other? (explain):

    _____

    _____

    _____

    _____

2. If there are separate cost/price elements for *low-voltage distribution services* (i.e., network costs, *excluding* retail sales), under the law, how frequently are the regulatory reviews conducted (e.g., every year, every 5 years, upon application)?

    Are they regulated by
    - ❏ Price caps?
    - ❏ Revenue caps?
    - ❏ Rate of return?
    - ❏ Mixed/other? (explain):

    _____

    _____

    _____

    _____

3. If the regulatory agency has responsibility for more than one sector, do agency staff have multisector responsibilities?   Yes ❏   No ❏   N/A ❏   D/K ❏ ___

    If Yes, is this
    - ❏ For all staff?
    - ❏ For a few high-level professionals only (e.g., chief legal adviser, chief economist)?
    - ❏ Other (explain):

    _____

    _____

    _____

    _____

C

Questionnaires for Mid-Level and In-Depth Evaluations of Infrastructure Regulatory Systems

A mid-level evaluation is intended to provide a good understanding of important regulatory issues: what aspects work well, what arrangements work less well or badly, and what changes might be made. The analysis and conclusions of a mid-level evaluation should be written up in a substantive and public report by utility sector and/or regulatory specialists.

Mid-level evaluations should provide a full analysis and understanding of the sector and its regulatory arrangements, including both formal (legislative) and informal (in practice) elements of *regulatory governance* and *regulatory substance.* These two dimensions of regulation effectively define a country's regulatory system. Mid-level evaluations should also gather information on sector outcomes: the volume of investment in the industry, access growth, efficiency, quality, costs, and prices. A more complete listing of sector outcomes is set out in chapter 4.

The evaluation of industry outcomes should include, as far as possible, the contribution of regulatory arrangements and decisions to outcomes. This does not mean that the evaluator should spend a lot of time and effort trying to quantify the effect of regulation on the overall sector. Instead, our recommended approach, as discussed in chapter 5, is to look at specific elements of the regulatory system that relate to both regulatory governance and regulatory substance and to evaluate whether they help or hinder sectoral outcomes that the government has specified as goals in either legislation or policy statements. This means that the evaluation will be qualitative rather than quantitative.

Mid-level evaluations should be carried out using both a structured questionnaire and more open-ended interviews based on topic headings. Although governance issues tend to be similar across countries, this is not true for substantive regulatory issues. The important substantive issues will depend very much on market and industry structures, pricing regimes, the "starting points" for overall cost recovery and access, and legal and constitutional arrangements.

For example, a Central European regulator, whose country is seeking membership in the EU, is likely to focus primarily on issues of bulk power market design, the terms and conditions of transmission access, and the legal obligations of "a supplier of last resort." In contrast, a new

D

sub-Saharan African electricity regulator is much more likely to be interested in issues such as grid and off-grid electrification, methods of improving access rates, and the coordination of externally provided subsidies (including aid) with retail tariff setting. Appendix E provides guidelines and questions for regulatory decisions and actions in six major substantive areas. The relevance of these substantive areas will vary from country to country, so the evaluator will need to make an informed judgment on which lines of inquiry to pursue.

The starting point for mid-level evaluations will be structured questionnaires that focus on collecting preliminary information on the characteristics of the sector and disputed issues that have arisen in the sector. These disputed issues should then be pursued in more detail in open-ended interviews. In other words, the information collected through the questionnaires will provide initial indications as to the specific governance and substantive issues that merit a more detailed investigation. Naturally, the topics chosen will also provide indications of the individuals who should be interviewed for the more in-depth evaluation. The questionnaire responses and the background documents and information on the sector (appendix B) will provide the main body of information that will be used in preparing for the interviews.

As recommended in chapter 6, completing the short basic questionnaire (appendix C) is also likely to be a useful part of the preparatory scoping exercise for a mid-level evaluation.

1. Questionnaires for Mid-Level Evaluations

D

Mid-level evaluations will cover regulatory arrangements for electricity, telecommunications, and other infrastructure industries, such as natural gas, water, or transport.

1.1 Mid-Level Evaluations of Electricity Regulatory Arrangements

For mid-level evaluations of electricity sector and associated industries, the following "screening" questionnaires should be used:

- The short basic interview schedule in appendix C.
- The American Enterprise Institute (AEI)–Brookings Institution electricity regulation survey, which is provided in this appendix.

Completing these questionnaires (with possible additions, but preferably without deletions or amendments to the questions) would not only go a long way toward identifying the issues and topic headings relevant for the particular evaluation, but would also provide a common core data set for different evaluations. These data would help in comparisons between different evaluations and would provide useful information for policymakers within the country, as well as for officials at donor agencies and multinational banks. It would also, over time, help build up a larger sample of comparable data for developing countries on their electricity industries that will facilitate future cross-country quantitative analysis.

Because experienced consultants and researchers would carry out the mid-level evaluations, they should be aware of previous studies, questionnaires, and information tools. A number of examples from the literature of regulatory standards and evaluation are listed and described in the bibliography. Key findings and principal conclusions for actual evaluations of six electricity regulatory systems are presented in appendix G.

It appears that the 2003 Prayas Energy Group Report on electricity regulatory commissions in Indian states is the only major electricity regulatory evaluation of the type discussed in this handbook to have used a formal questionnaire. The questionnaire was used primarily as the starting point for subsequent discussions between Prayas researchers and the staff of the various commissions discussed in the report. Unfortunately, the published version of the report does not include the questionnaire. However, Prayas is now participating in a multicountry study of "electricity governance" being undertaken by several NGOs, and the regulatory component of the study includes a detailed questionnaire that also includes guidance to evaluators on the significance of each of the questionnaire items.[1]

The annotated bibliography to this handbook includes the Pierce Atwood (2004) survey of electricity regulation in southeastern Europe and the associated questionnaire. These documents have detailed—and useful—questions on the formal, legal aspects of regulation and includes questions on what happens in practice. The various evaluations summarized in appendix F discuss how electricity regulatory arrangements operate in practice, but do not cover issues of outcomes. The contracting-out survey by Trémolet, Shukla, and Venton (2004), cited in the appendix, discusses some issues of practice for all infrastructure regulators and has a self-completion questionnaire.

The questionnaire in Stern and Holder (1999) is more of a set of topic headings than a formal questionnaire. It includes some questions on regulatory practice, as well as formal arrangements. It covers all regulated infrastructure industries, not just electricity. It can still be useful as a starting point for specifying mid-level issues and topic headings.

1.2 Telecommunications

A number of questionnaires have been developed for substantive mid-level evaluations of regulatory arrangements for telecom industries in developing countries. Of all infrastructure industries, more academic and similar studies have been conducted on the impact of privatization and regulation on outcomes in the telecommunications industry than for any other industry. (See Stern and Cubbin [2005] and its bibliography for an introduction to this literature.)

Among the evaluations are major studies carried out by the International Telecommunication Union (ITU) in 2001 for five developing countries where telecom regulation had ap-

---

1. The Prayas questionnaire can be downloaded from this Web site: http://governanc e.wri.org/pubs_description.cf m?PubID=4040.

peared to work well (Botswana, Brazil, Morocco, Peru, and Singapore).[2] Like the electricity evaluations discussed earlier, they concentrated primarily on process issues, but included some limited discussion on outcomes of regulatory decisions and events. It appears that they did not use a structured questionnaire, but instead they relied on extensive background information collected in the regular ITU regulatory survey.[3]

Among the background questionnaires available for evaluators is the AEI–Brookings telecom questionnaire, which is a companion to the electricity questionnaire reproduced in appendix E. This, like the AEI–Brookings electricity questionnaire, provides an excellent screening tool.

At present, we are aware of only one questionnaire that deals systematically with outcomes, as well as the process of telecom regulation. This is the National Economic Research Associates (NERA) study for the World Bank on African telecoms and their regulation.[4] This questionnaire is also a useful starting point for constructing both formal questionnaires and general interview topic headings for electricity and other regulated infrastructure industries. Its questions are directly related to government goals and governance attributes. The full report and questionnaire were issued in 2005 by the World Bank.

1.3 Other Infrastructure Industries

For other infrastructure industries, such as natural gas, water, or transport, there has been less private investment or privatization—and fewer autonomous regulatory or quasi-regulatory agencies have been established.

A number of case studies have been done on private sector participation in these industries, but there is no obvious multicountry questionnaire tool like the AEI–Brookings questionnaire.[5]

2. Issues to Be Covered

For issues of regulatory governance and process, the items discussed and identified in chapter 3, and more fully developed in appendix A, should provide a good starting point, particularly on the formal, legal arrangements, as well as on how regulatory business is actually conducted. For issues relating to outcomes of the regulatory process and evaluations of substantive decisions

---

2. These evaluations are available at http://www.itu.int/ITU-D/treg/Case_Studies/index.html.
3. The survey can be found at http://www.itu.int/ITU-D/treg/Events/Survey/FormSurv_E_2004.rtf.
4. NERA, 2004, *Framework for Evaluating the Effectiveness of Telecommunications Regulators in Sub-Saharan Africa,* a final report for the Global Information and Communication Technologies Department of the World Bank (London: NERA); available at http://www.nera.com.
5. For water and sewerage, see Mary M. Shirley, ed., 2002, "Thirsting for Efficiency: The Economics and Politics of Water Reform" World Bank. It contains substantial discussion of both transport and water concession contracts in Latin America and the Caribbean, including the role of regulatory and quasi-regulatory bodies.

and actions of the regulator, the items discussed and identified in chapter 5 and the topics and interview guidelines in appendix E should provide a good starting point, as well as the topic and query lists for in-depth interviews found in appendix E. Additional insights can be gained from some of the evaluations summarized in appendix G.

Substantive policy and regulatory decisions will be driven by the specific reforms that the government wishes to pursue. In the electricity sector, the evaluator will need to look at some or all of the following:

- Policies and regulatory arrangements for rural electrification, including grid expansion and off-grid solutions and service provision.
- Policies and regulatory arrangements for the creation of open access regimes.
- Policies and regulatory arrangements for the establishment of bulk power markets.
- Policies and regulatory arrangements for the promotion of renewable energy.
- Policies and regulatory arrangements for rationalizing pricing, subsidies, and cross-subsidies.
- Policies and regulatory arrangements for countries introducing private sector involvement in distribution through divestiture and/or long-term leases and concessions.
- Policies and regulatory arrangements for reducing theft or other nontechnical losses.
- Policies and regulatory arrangements for meeting specific poverty relief targets.

Specific questions for each of these areas are presented in appendix E.

3. Coverage

D

The focus of a mid-level evaluation is on key issues arising from regulatory and sector developments. Hence, we would suggest that it include the following:

- A thorough overview, with a list and appraisal of key issues—both formal and informal (in practice) elements of regulation and also of sector outcomes.
- Detailed investigation of two to three governance or process issues.
- Detailed investigation of two to three outcome or key decision issues.[6]

The recommended framework is primarily intended for the evaluation of regulatory frameworks with autonomous regulatory agencies that are either fully independent or merely advisory. But it should also be applicable to countries with ministry regulators, if the ministry regulator and its staff are clearly identifiable and operate under a legal mandate that defines the ministry regulator's powers and duties.

This evaluation framework is unlikely to be well suited for a ministry regulator operating without a set of defined legal obligations. The suggested screening questionnaires (including

---

6. The in-depth evaluation would examine all major regulatory governance and substantive issues.

the short basic questionnaire in appendix C) may be useful, but a mid-level evaluation is unlikely to provide much additional useful information.

As discussed in chapter 4, we also observe a number of intermediate or quasi-regulatory agencies for electricity and other infrastructure industries. The framework set out in this appendix was not designed specifically for use with such agencies. Further work will be needed to develop mid-level and detailed evaluation tools to address these types of regulatory systems. The framework set out earlier will be useful in a country that has an autonomous concession contract-monitoring and enforcement agency with defined legal obligations and processes.

For other countries with less developed regulatory or quasi-regulatory frameworks (including "failed states"), we suggest that, to devise appropriate evaluation tools, evaluators use this handbook along with other sources, including the studies cited in chapter 5. This handbook should provide some useful criteria for evaluating such arrangements and guidance on the general approach. However, establishing the objectives of such agencies and devising appropriate evaluation frameworks and tools is clearly a task for experienced infrastructure industry and regulatory specialists. The same applies to carrying out such evaluations. Indeed, it would be desirable to commission one or two pilot evaluations in countries with differing infrastructure industry regulatory or quasi-regulatory arrangements.

D

Electricity Regulation Survey

Competition Policy and Regulation

Development Research Group (DECRG)

The World Bank

The World Bank
1818 H Street NW
Washington, DC 20433
USA

D

The electricity survey used to collect data was presented in the following publication and is presented here with permission: Scott Wallsten, George Clarke, Luke Haggarty, Rosario Kaneshiro, Roger G. Noll, Mary Shirley, and Lixin Colin Xu, 2004, "New Tools for Studying Network Industry Reforms in Developing Countries: The Telecommunications and Electricity Regulation Database." *Review of Network Economics* 3 (3): 248–82. Please cite appropriately. *Note:* These codes may not correspond to the data. Please refer to the online database and paper for the data and correct codes: http://www.AEIENNNbrookings.org/publications/abstract.php?pid=724.

Questionnaire for Electricity Regulators

Please circle or place a cross in front of the relevant answer(s) when there are multiple choices.

Section 1. Electricity Law

Has the parliament passed any framework laws aiming at reforming the electricity sector?

............................Q11   Yes   **Go to 1.2**
           Q11y (year)   No   ***Go to Section 2***

1.1 Please list names, years of publication, and numbers for relevant laws, including laws related to privatization or investment that affect the electricity sector.

1. _____ Q12a _____ Q12ay _____

2. _____ Q12b _____

3. _____ Q12c _____

4. _____ Q12d _____

5. _____ Q12e _____

D

When did the electricity sector reform actually start? (please enter year) _____ Q13

Does the law explicitly forbid operators from joint ownership of electricity
services (such as generation, transmission, distribution, and retail/supply)?   **Yes/No**   Q14

Does the law allow the entry of new private power companies?   **Yes/No**   Q15

Does the law allow the electricity sector to be privatized in part or in whole?   **2 = In Whole**   Q16
                                                                                                1 = In Part
                                                                                                0 = Not at All

Section 2. Restructuring

Which of the following market models describes the power sector in your country?

Q21a	**Vertically integrated monopoly**	**0/1**
Q21b	**Single buyer market**	**0/1**
Q21c	**Wholesale competition**	**0/1**
Q21d	**Supply/Retail competition**	**0/1**
Q21e	**= Note**	

2.1   Please indicate the years the following reform measures were **first initiated** in your country:

Reform measures	Year
Regulator established	Q22a _____
Privatization	Q22b _____
Vertical separation	Q22c _____
Entry of new private power producers	Q22d _____
Wholesale power market (pool, contract, spot, etc.)	Q22e _____

2.2   Degree of vertical integration from generation to supply

Q23

2 = **Unbundled**
0 = **Integrated**
1= Mixed

2.3   Has transmission been separated from generation?

Q24

2 = **Separate companies**
1 = **Accounting separation**
0 = **Integrated**

Are there vertical restrictions on joint ownership of generation and transmission facilities?

Q25

1 = Yes
2 = No

2.4   Are there *horizontal* restrictions on the maximum market share of generation and retail supply companies?

Q26

1 = **Yes**
0 = **No**

D

273

2.5 Are there any constraints in the number of operators in Generation?   **Yes**
Q27   **No**

2.6 Please fill in the following sector information:

Q28		t0 **At the Time of Reform** Year: *Q28t0y* (In case of no reform, please enter information 5 years ago)								**Post-Reform** Year: *Q28y* (In case of no reform, please enter most recent information)							
		N Number of Companies				S Percent of Total MW				N Number of Companies				S Percent of Total MW			
		a	b	c	d	a	b	c	d	a	b	c	d	a	b	c	d
		Public	Minority Private	Majority Private	Private	Public	Minority Private	Majority Private	Private	Public	Minority Private	Majority Private	Private	Public	Minority Private	Majority Private	Private
G	Generation	Q28t0Nag	Q28t0Nbg	Q28t0Ncg	Q28t0Ndg	Q28t0Sag	Q28t0Sbg	Q28t0Scg	Q28t0Sdg	Q28Nag	Q28Nbg	Q28Ncg	Q28Ndg	Q28Sag	Q28Sbg	Q28Scg	Q28Sdg
T	Transmission	Q28t0Nat	Q28t0Nbt	Q28t0Nct	Q28t0Ndt	Q28t0Sat	Q28t0Sbt	Q28t0Sct	Q28t0Sdt	Q28Nat	Q28Nbt	Q28Nct	Q28Ndt	Q28Sat	Q28Sbt	Q28Sct	Q28Sdt
D	Distribution	Q28t0Nad	Q28t0Nbd	Q28t0Ncd	Q28t0Ndd	Q28t0Sad	Q28t0Sbd	Q28t0Scd	Q28t0Sdd	Q28Nad	Q28Nbd	Q28Ncd	Q28Ndd	Q28Sad	Q28Sbd	Q28Scd	Q28Sdd
S	Supply	Q28t0Nas	Q28t0Nbs	Q28t0Ncs	Q28t0Nds	Q28t0Sas	Q28t0Sbs	Q28t0Scs	Q28t0Sds	Q28Nas	Q28Nbs	Q28Ncs	Q28Nds	Q28Sas	Q28Sbs	Q28Scs	Q28Sds
	Total	Q28t0Na	Q28t0Nb	Q28t0Nc	Q28t0Nd	Q28t0Sa	Q28t0Sb	Q28t0Sc	Q28t0Sd	Q28Na	Q28Nb	Q28Nc	Q28Nd	Q28Sa	Q28Sb	Q28Sc	Q28Sd

Q28t0NG = total number of generators at time of reform

Q28t0NT = total number of transmission companies at time of reform

Q28t0ND = total number of distribution companies' generators at time of reform

Q28t0NS = total number of supply companies at time of reform

2.7 Have the public (e.g., central government, state-owned, municipal, etc.) company(ies) been corporatized?   **Yes**
Q29   **No**

2.8 Are consumers allowed to choose among electricity suppliers?   **Yes**
Q210   **No**

2.9 Is there a customer size threshold (e.g., KW/KWh) for free consumer choice? **Yes**

Q211 **No**

2.10 Please provide the customer threshold(s) (in kW/kWh) for which consumers are free to choose among electricity producers/suppliers and the date this regulation(s) took (will take) effect:

Q212

Customer Type	Customer Size (kW/kWh) (a)	Percent of Total Consumption (b)	Date (c)
Industrial	Q212aI	Q212bI	Q212cI
Commercial	Q212aC	Q212bC	Q212cC
Residential	Q212aR	Q212bR	Q212cR

Section 3. Regulatory Bodies

3.1 Has a regulatory body that is separate from the utilities and from the Ministry started to work?

Q31 **Yes/No**

Please list all regulatory bodies involved in regulating/overseeing the electricity sector (including the ministry and/or incumbent if they are responsible for some areas of regulation) and the areas of regulation that they are responsible for.

D

Name (a)	Responsibilities (b)	Date of Creation (c)
1. Main Regulator Q31a1	Q31b1	Q31c1
2. Q31a2	Q31b2	Q31c2
3. Q31a3	Q31b3	Q31c3
4. Q31a4	Q31b4	Q31c4

3.2 Does your agency oversee multiple sectors? **Yes** Q32

No

3.2.1 If yes, which sectors? Q321

3.3 How is the regulatory body financed? (percent of regulator's budget)

Government budget   Q33a

Levies on companies/license fees   Q33b

Customer levies   Q33c

Other (Please describe): _____   Q33e

Note: Dummy if any from each source

3.4 Is the regulatory body headed by a single person or by a group of people (e.g., a regulatory board)?   **Single person**

     Multiple people   Q34

3.5 How many employees does your agency employ?   Q35
     Of these:

     3.5.1 How many technicians?   Q351

     3.5.2 How many engineers?   Q352

     3.5.3 How many accountants?   Q353

     3.5.4 How many economists?   Q354

     3.5.5 How many lawyers?   Q355

3.6 Who appoints the head and/or the commissioners of the regulatory body?

     President   Q36

     Ministry

     Parliament

     Other (specify) _____

D

3.7 If the president or Ministry appoints the head and/or the commissioners of the regulator body, is Parliamentary approval required?   **Yes**   1

     No   0   Q37

3.8 Is head appointed for a fixed term?   **Yes**

     No   Q38

     3.8.1 For how long?   Q381

     3.8.2 Can head be re-appointed?   **Yes**   Q382

     No

     3.8.3 Who has the authority to fire head/commissioners? (please mark all that apply)   Q383

       (a) President   Q383a

       (b) Minister   Q383b

       (c) Parliament   Q383c

       (d) Others (please list): _____   Q383d

3.8.4 For what reasons (e.g., incompetence, corruption, conflict of interest)?
Please list:

Q384a   Conflict of Interest _____

Q384b   Incompetence _____

Q384c   Corruption _____

3.8.5 How many heads have been removed since your agency's creation?   Q385

3.9   Who can veto the regulator's decisions?

Q39a	**President**
Q39b	**Minister**
Q39c	**Court**
Q39d	**Other**

3.10   Who can issue policy guidelines for the regulator?

Q310a	=	**President**
Q310b	=	**Minister**
Q310c	=	**Parliament**
Q310d	=	**Regulator**
Q310e	=	**Other**

3.11   Are the policy guidelines publicly available?

Q311   **Yes**
        No

3.12   Can the Minister/President give verbal instructions to the regulator?

        Yes
Q312   **No**

3.13   Have regional regulatory bodies been created?

        Yes
Q313   **No**

D

Section 4: Regulatory Process/Decisions

4.1   Can your agency compel financial and performance information from utilities?   Q41   **Yes**
        No

4.1.1 Is there a standardized reporting format for financial/performance
information?   Q411   **Yes**
                                                                           No

4.1.2 Is the financial/performance information audited by:

Q412a   (a) Regulator   Q412b   (b) Independent auditors

Q412c   (c) Others (please list): _____

4.2 Does the regulator make financial and performance information publicly available?

Q42	**Yes**
	No

4.3 Is there a consultation process prior to regulatory decisions?

Q43	**Yes**
	No

4.3.1 If so, what type? (a) Consultation papers   Q431a
                          (b) Hearings   Q431b
                          (c) Meetings   Q431c
                          (d) Other (please list):_____ (No other)

4.4 Please circle all groups who have the right to participate in regulatory proceedings:
Q44 (Study)

(a) Consumer groups   Q44a   (b) Utilities   Q44b
(c) Industry associations   Q44c   (d) Others (please list): _____ Q44d

4.5 Can the utilities appeal if they disagree with the regulator's decisions?

	Yes
Q45	**No**

4.6 Who can the utilities appeal to in each instance? (i.e., Ministry, Executive, Other executive body, Judiciary, Formal domestic arbitrator, Formal international arbitrator, no appeal)

4.6.1 First instance   Q461a: At what stage appeal to regulator

4.6.2 Second instance   Q462b: At what stage appeal to ministry

4.6.3 Third instance   Q463c: At what stage appeal to court

4.7 Can other parties appeal?

Q47	**Yes**
	No

4.8 Circle all other parties that can appeal:

Q48a   (a) Consumer groups   Q48b   (b) Utilities
Q48c   (c) Industry associations   Q48d   (d) Others _____

4.9 Are regulatory meetings open to the public in practice?

2 = In Whole	Q49	**2 / 1 / 0**
1 = In Part		
0 = Not at All		

4.10 Are regulatory meetings required to be open to the public by law?   Q410   **Yes/No**

4.11 Are regulatory decisions publicly available?   Q411   **Yes/No**

4.12 Does the law REQUIRE the regulator to publish decisions   Q412   **Yes/No**

4.13 If so, where?   Q413

4.14 Does the regulator publish decisions in practice?　　　　Q414　**Yes/No**

　　4.14.1 If so, where?　　　　　　　　　　Q4141

4.15 Does the law REQUIRE the regulator to publish explanations of decisions　**Yes/No**　Q415

　　4.15.1 If so, where?　　　　　Q4151

4.16 Does the regulator publish explanations of decisions in practice?　**Yes/No**　Q416

　　4.16.1 If so, where?　　　　　Q4161

Section 5. Price Regulation

5.1 Are the following end-user prices regulated?

　　5.1.1 Electricity prices for industry?　　**Yes/No**　Q511

　　5.1.2 Commercial electricity prices?　　**Yes/No**　Q512

　　5.1.3 Electricity prices for households?　　**Yes/No**　Q513

5.2 Please provide the following information about end-user price regulation (Please mark all that apply).　　　　Q52

Prices	R Regulatory			M Ministry			P Parliament			C Competitively decided
	M Monitors	A Advisers	D Deciders	M Monitors	A Advisers	D Deciders	M Monitors	A Advisers	D Deciders	
Industrial I	Q52R MI	Q52R AI	Q52R DI	Q52 MMI	Q52 MAI	Q52 MDI	Q52P MI	Q52P AI	Q52P DI	Q52CI
Residential R	Q52R MR	Q52R AR	Q52R DR	Q52 MMR	Q52 MAR	Q52 MDR	Q52P MR	Q52P AR	Q52P DR	Q52CR

5.3 Type of existing power market (Please mark all that apply):

Q53a　(a) Bilateral contracts　　Q53b　(b) Spot market

Q53c　(c) Pool　　　　　　　　Q53d　(d) Forward market

Q53e　(e) Balancing market　　Other: _____

　　5.3.1 Is participation in the wholesale markets mandatory?　**Yes/No**　Q531

　　5.3.2 If so, in what type of market?　Q532　_____

5.4 What is the price control method for:

5.4.1 Transmission?

	RC	**Revenue Cap**
Q541	PC	**Price Cap**
	RR	**Rate of Return**
	None	**None**
	Other	**Other:** _____

5.4.2 Distribution?

	RC	**Revenue Cap**
Q542	PC	**Price Cap**
	RR	**Rate of Return**
	None	**None**
	Other	**Other:** _____

5.5 How long (in terms of years) is the period between price reviews? Q55

5.6 Does the government subsidize the use of specific generation fuels? **Yes/No** Q56

   5.6.1 If so, which? Q561

   (a) Natural Gas   (b) Coal

   (c) Oil   (d) Renewables: _____

   (e) Other:_____

5.7 Are prices for any consumer groups subsidized? Q57 **Yes/No**

   5.7.1 If so, which prices?

   Q571a (a) Residential   Q571b (b) Commercial

   Q571c (c) Industrial   Q571d (d) Other: _____

   5.7.2 What percentage of subsidies comes from the following sources? Q572
   (String)

   5.7.2.1 Government Budget   _____%

   5.7.2.2 Industry Levies   _____%

   5.7.2.3 Other (specify): _____   _____%

   5.7.2.4 Internal X Subs

   100%

D

5.8 Please fill in the following information:

Average End-User Electricity Prices (in Local Currency Unit)				
	At the Time of Reform Year: *Q58t0y* (In case of no reform, please enter information 5 years ago)		Post-Reform Year: *Q58y* (In case of no reform, please enter most recent information)	
	R Residential	**I Industrial**	**R Residential**	**I Industrial**
Generation	Q58t0RG	Q58t0IG	Q58RG	Q58IG
Transmission	Q58t0RT	Q58t0IT	Q58RT	Q58IT
Distribution	Q58t0RD	Q58t0ID	Q58RD	Q58ID
Supply	Q58t0RS	Q58t0IS	Q58RS	Q58IS
Total	Q58t0R	Q58t0I	Q58R	Q58I

Section 6. Access/Interconnection Policies

6.1 Does the law require non-discriminatory access to transmission and distribution networks (Third Party Access TPA)?   Q61   **Yes/No**

D

6.2 Does the law require that all entrants receive the same technical terms and conditions for access?   Q62   **Yes/No**

6.3 Does the law require that all entrants receive the same prices for access?   Q63   **Yes/No**

6.4 How are access fees/interconnection rates set between the generation and transmission/distribution operators?   Q64

                             Negotiated TPA
                             Regulated TPA
                             Other (specify): _____

6.5 If operators cannot agree on access/interconnection terms/fees, who can intervene to resolve conflicts?   Q65   _____

6.6 Is transmission access controlled by an independent system operator (ISO)?   Q66   **Yes/No**

6.7 Is the transmission network operator required to extend the network to meet demand?   Q67   **Yes/No**

Section 7: Licenses

7.1   Is there a formal procedure for granting/renewing licenses for the following areas?

7.1.1 Generation?	Q711	**Yes/No**
7.1.2 Transmission?	Q712	**Yes/No**
7.1.3 Distribution?	Q713	**Yes/No**
7.1.4 Retail Supply?	Q714	**Yes/No**
7.1.5 Imports?	Q715	**Yes/No**
7.1.6 Exports?	Q716	**Yes/No**

7.2   Who approves licenses?

	Regulator	*President*	*Ministry*	*Parliament*	*Other (please specify)*
Q72G Generation					
Q72T Transmission					
Q72D Distribution					
Q72S Retail Supply					
Q72M Imports					
Q72X Exports					

D

7.3   Is there a mandatory bidding for granting licenses?

7.3.1 Generation?	Q731	**Yes/No/No Experience**
7.3.2 Transmission?	Q732	**Yes/No/No Experience**
7.3.3 Distribution?	Q733	**Yes/No/No Experience**
7.3.4 Retail Supply?	Q734	**Yes/No/No Experience**
7.3.5 Imports?	Q735	**Yes/No/No Experience**
7.3.6 Exports?	Q736	**Yes/No/No Experience**

7.4   Can a license be revoked?   Q74   **Yes/No**

7.4.1 If yes for what reason?   Q741   _____

Section 8: Universal Service Obligations/Quality of Supply

8.1 Are utilities allowed to cut off service for non-payment?　　　　　　Q81 **Yes/No**

8.2 Is there a clearly stated policy addressing issues such as:

Q82a　(a) Non-Payment/Credit problems　　　Q82b　(b) Cost of new connections

Q82c　(c) Support of low-income groups　　　Q82d　(d) Supply of rural customers

Q82e　(e) Non-discrimination among consumers　　Other: _____

8.2.1 What are the bodies involved in protecting consumer interests? (please mark all that apply)

Q821a　(a) Independent interest/consumer groups　　Q821b　(b) Regulator

Q821c　(c) Other government agencies　　Others: _____

8.3 Are there well-defined targets or minimum standards for quality of service (e.g., number of interruptions, minutes lost per customer, SAIFI, SAIDI, etc)?　　Q83 **Yes/No**

8.3.1 If so, are there well-defined penalty schemes for noncompliance?　　**Yes/No** Q831

8.3.2 Have there been any quality-of-service improvements after reform?　　**Yes/No** Q832

8.3.2.1 If yes, please describe improvements: Q8321

_____

_____

8.4 Number of connections/customers: _____ Q86

8.5 Please enter the following information:

Degree of Electrification (e.g., Percentage of Population, Percentage of Households)			
At the Time of Reform (In case of no reform, please enter information 5 years ago)		**Post-Reform** (In case of no reform, please enter most recent information)	
Percentage (specify indicator)	*Year*	*Percentage (specify indicator)*	*Year*
Q86t0	Q86t0y	Q86	Q86y

D

283

Section 9: Sector Characteristics

9.1 Please fill in the following sector information:

Resource Base (Generation)		
Q91	At the Time of Reform Year: *Q91t0y* (In case of no reform, please enter information 5 years ago)	Post-Reform Year: *Q91y* (In case of no reform, please enter most recent information)
Generation Type	*Installed Capacity in MW*	*Installed Capacity in MW*
O Oil	Q91t0O	Q91O
C Coal	Q91t0C	Q91C
G Natural Gas	Q91t0G	Q91G
H Hydro	Q91t0H	Q91H
N Nuclear	Q91t0N	Q91N
OTH Other	Q91t0OTH	Q91OTH

9.2 System Losses:

Transmission/Distribution Losses			
At the Time of Reform (In case of no reform, please enter information 5 years ago)		Post-Reform (In case of no reform, please enter most recent information)	
MWh	*Year*	*MWh*	*Year*
Q92t0	Q92t0y	Q92	Q92y

+ Shr   =   Percentage
Q92t0t   =   trans losses   Q92t0Tshr   =   pct losses trans
Q92t0d   =   dist. losses   Q92t0dshr   =   pct losses dist

9.3 Please fill in the following tables:

	Q93	E Number of Full-Time Sector Employees		MW / MWh (Generated, transmitted, distributed, sold)	
		At the Time of Reform Year: *Q93Et0y* (In case of no reform, please enter information 5 years ago)	Post-Reform Year: *Q93Ety* (In case of no reform, please enter most recent information)	At the Time of Reform Year: *Q93Mt0y* (In case of no reform, please enter information 5 years ago)	Post-Reform Year: *Q93My* (In case of no reform, please enter most recent information)
G	Generation	Q93Et0G	Q93EG	Q93Mt0yG	Q93MG
T	Transmission	Q93Et0T	Q93ET	Q93Mt0yT	Q93MT
D	Distribution	Q93Et0D	Q93ED	Q93Mt0yD	Q93MD
S	Supply	Q93Et0S	Q93ES	Q93Mt0yS	Q93MS
	Total	Q93Et0	Q93E	Q93Mt0	Q93M

	Companies	G Corporation		R Retail Supply	
		M Market Share (Percent)	O Ownership Status State-owned, minority private, majority private, private)	M Market Share (Percent)	O Ownership Status State-owned, minority private, majority private, private)
1	Largest	Q931GM1	Q931GO1	Q931RM1	Q931RO1
2	Second Largest	Q931GM2	Q931GO2	Q931RM2	Q931RO2
3	Third Largest	Q931GM3	Q931GO3	Q931RM3	Q931RO3

D

Comments

_____

_____

_____

_____

D

Guidelines and Questions for Mid-Level and In-Depth Evaluations of Infrastructure Regulatory Systems

It is better to know some of the questions than all the answers.

— James Thurber

Interviews with key players in the regulated sector are absolutely essential for in-depth evaluations of a regulatory system. Unlike a questionnaire, interviews give the evaluator the opportunity to interact with subjects and to probe deeper on critical questions. Given the relative spontaneity and dynamic nature of an interview, the responses obtained are often more candid and less calculated than are responses to written queries. Thus, for the evaluator, they present an excellent opportunity to obtain insights and perspective that might otherwise not be available.

The selection of those who will be interviewed should be heavily influenced by their involvement in, and knowledge of, the topics that are of interest to the evaluators. The interviews should also be reflective of diverse interests and perspectives on the topics being queried. Typically, interviews regarding power sector regulation should be conducted with the regulators themselves, policymakers in both the executive and the legislative branches of government, judges who hear regulatory appeals, generators, distributors, transmission owners and operators, representatives of large and small consumers, environmental groups, academics in relevant disciplines, investors and financiers, market administrators and monitors, and perhaps even journalists who cover energy-related issues. Although some of those interviewed may have little to say about an issue with which they are not involved, and, therefore, they need not be asked about these topics, it is important that for each question, answers be sought from a cross sample of interviewees who do have experience on the issue. The reason, of course, is to make sure that each question is approached from a variety of perspectives. This reduces the probability that an issue of consequence will "get swept under the carpet."

Unlike a questionnaire, where the questions are narrowly framed to elicit concise answers, the interview questions should be clear but somewhat open ended. An evaluator gains insight not only by a direct response but also by the fact that respondents may well, in the course of answering an

E

open-ended question, open up new areas for inquiry that, although not anticipated in advance, may prove quite fruitful for the exercise as a whole. Thus, the interviewer needs to maintain some degree of flexibility in order to adequately follow up on unanticipated insights and perspective.

The primary purpose of the exercise is to identify problem areas and to recommend changes that will improve the regulatory system in those areas. Thus, the interviews will focus primarily on substantive policies, regulations, and practices that can be improved. Although the evaluators will need to have a firm base of knowledge about the regulated sector of the country in which the work is being done, the main focus of the interviews is on the more subjective areas, where diverse opinions are likely to be encountered. The evaluator will need to understand and weigh those opinions, decide how they bear on policy and regulation, and then determine whether recommendations should be made and, if so, what they should be. The evaluator's principal judgment should be whether continuation of the status quo is likely to result in "bad" outcomes, such as those discussed in chapter 5.

In an interview, the evaluators are urged to ask the questions in the way best calculated to elicit meaningful, substantive responses. How the questions are asked may well be as important as what questions are asked. Thus, the interviewer might want to use phrases such as the following:

- "Let me see if I understand what you just said. . . ."
- "Did you mean [this] or did you mean [that]?"
- "I want to make sure that I fully understood your point"
- "Here is what I heard you say: . . . Is that correct or did I misunderstand?"
- "Is this written down anywhere?"
- "Some people claim that. . . . Is there any validity to that concern?"
- "Which issues have been the most controversial? Why is that the case?"
- "Is the problem you discussed a policy problem or one of implementation?"
- "Did anything happen that was not anticipated?"
- "A problem that emerged in regulation in [another country] was . . . Is that also a problem here?"
- "Is there a way to improve regulation in this area? Does the change you suggest involve changes in the law or in the constitution? Do you think the regulator or the government would go along with that?"
- "What are your biggest concerns with regulation as it is practiced?"

It is impossible to identify all of the questions that might be appropriate for power sector regulation in every country where regulatory evaluation would be valuable. As a result, no effort to compile such an exhaustive list of queries for interviews has been made. It is, however, important to illustrate the type of questions that would be of value in regard to both regulatory governance and regulatory substance. The list of questions below is focused exclusively on six substantive areas of power sector reform as examples of how implementation and regulation of

E

these industries might be approached in interviews. Model questions are not provided in this appendix for regulatory governance because this aspect of regulation is discussed in considerable detail in both chapter 2 and appendix A.

Electrification

Asia, Latin America, and Sub-Saharan Africa

- **Forms of Electrification.** What are the major forms of electrification (for example, grid extension, solar home systems, and minigrids)? Does the regulatory entity have legal jurisdiction over all or some forms of electrification?
- **Types of Programs.** Are these "top down" (government mandated or supported) or "bottom up" (not government mandated) programs?
- **Obligation to Serve.** What is the obligation of distribution companies to connect new customers? Where there is an obligation, is the technology that will be used for electrification specified?
- **Subsidies.** Has the government agreed to provide any capital or operating cost subsidies to promote electrification?
  a. Who decides on the level of these subsidies? What are the magnitudes of the subsidies? Are any of the awarded subsidies the outcome of a formal bidding process? Do they differ by the type of electrification?
  b. Are the subsidies channeled through a separate electrification fund?
  c. Who administers the fund?
  d. Are there clearly specified criteria for deciding which communities will receive the electrification subsidies?
  e. Are the subsidies targeted to suppliers or consumers, or to both?
  f. Have there been any problems or complaints about the operation of the funds? Is there any evidence that the subsidy mechanism is badly targeted (that is, does not reach the intended audience) or is overly complex?
  g. Does the regulator have any authority to adjust tariffs if the government does not provide the subsidies that were promised?
- **Tariffs.** Who decides on allowed tariffs for the different forms of electrification? The regulator or some other entity?
  a. If there are caps on the maximum prices that can be charged, how are these price caps determined? Are the caps based on benchmarks or the supplier's own costs?
  b. What is the structure of the tariffs? Flat monthly fee, by time-differentiated tariff, or by non–time-differentiated tariff? Has the tariff level or structure created any problems for operators or customers?

E

   c. If a concession is awarded on the basis of a bid tariff, is the regulator obligated to accept this tariff?
- **Quality-of-Service Standards.** Who decides on the commercial and technical quality-of-service standards? Are the standards the same for all entities (for example, grid and off-grid providers)?
   a. Who monitors and enforces these standards?
   b. Has monitoring been effective?
   c. Are there penalties for noncompliance? What are the levels of the penalties?
- **Contracting Out.** Has the regulator contracted out, either formally or informally, some regulatory functions relating to electrification to other entities (for example, other ministries, local or regional government entities, community organizations)?
- **Regulatory Forbearance.** Does the regulator have the legal authority to "forbear" (that is, refrain) from regulating? Does the regulator have the authority to vary the scope and intensity of its regulation depending on the type of entity (private, large grid company versus community-based, off-grid enterprise) that is being regulated?

Grid-Based Renewable Energy[1]

All countries

1. **Government Policy.** Has the government publicly stated its intent to support renewable generation because of concerns regarding:
   a. Security of supply (reducing dependence on fossil fuels)?
   b. Fuel diversification (protection from macroeconomic shocks caused by fluctuations in internationally traded fuels)?
   c. Environmental impact (effect of fossil fuels on climate change)?
   d. Foreign exchange savings (reduction in foreign exchange demand)?
   e. Other?
2. **Subsidies.** What subsidies are available to renewable generators?
   a. Investment subsidies (input subsidy)
      i. Direct capital cost subsidies
      ii. Soft loans
      iii. Tax exemptions or holidays

---

1. The analytical framework for these questions draws heavily from Wolfgang Mostaert, 2004, *Policies for Wind Integration into the Nicaragua National Grid System: Review of International Experiences and Scheme Proposal for Nicaragua,* a report prepared for the National Energy Commission and the Energy Sector Management Assistance Program. The report is available at www.esmap.org.

E

   iv. Import duty exemption
   v. Accelerated depreciation
   vi. Part or all of grid connection costs paid for by utilities or consumers
   b. KWh subsidies (output subsidy)
   i. Topping up premiums in organized bulk power markets
   ii. Mandated above-market "feed-in tariffs" (FITs)
   iii. Green electricity purchases by public institutions
   iv. Renewable portfolio standards with or without tradable renewable energy certificates
   v. CO_2 certificates
   c. Grid and electricity market subsidies (input delivery subsidy)
   i. Wheeling tariffs below the true opportunity cost of the transmitting utility
   ii. Undercharging for balancing and/or reserve costs
   iii. Use of system charges below cost
3. **Provider of Subsidies.** Who initially and finally pays for these subsidies—taxpayers, domestic consumers, or outside providers of CO_2 credits?
4. **Subsidy Delivery Mechanisms.** How are the subsidies delivered?
   a. **Feed-In Tariffs (FITs).** An FIT that involves an above-market price for the electricity produced by one or more types of renewable generators. Is the FIT reduced after a certain number of years, or for an assumed level of productivity improvement? Is it limited to a predetermined level of renewable energy generation?
   b. **Renewable Portfolio Standards.** Renewable energy portfolio standards that require consumers, retail suppliers, and electricity generators to obtain a minimum percentage of their supplies from eligible renewable generators. Is this system also combined with a system of tradable certificates? Has the government specified that electricity suppliers must obtain an increasing portion of their supply sources from renewable generation?
   c. **Tender Systems.** An MW-Tender System through which annual tenders are organized for 10- to 20-year PPA contracts for specified volumes of renewable energy generation. Who conducts the tender? What is the price-setting method in the tender? Are price caps specified? How are the above-market prices recovered? Are bidders required to have permits in place before they are allowed to bid?
   d. **Negotiated PPA Schemes.** Under a negotiated PPA scheme, the government fixes a certain target for renewable energy production and invites developers to present their proposals to the government. Is this approach limited to a one-time transaction or does it seem to be conducted on an ongoing basis?
5. **Pass-through Mechanisms.** If renewable generators are receiving above-market prices from retail suppliers, has the regulator established a mechanism for the pass-through of

E

these above-market prices? Is the cost spread across all electricity consumers or targeted for certain categories of electricity consumers?

6. **Connection Agreements.** Is there any standardization of the process and requirements for connecting renewable and other forms of distributed generation to the main grid?

7. **Capital Costs for Connection to the Grid.** Is the renewable generator charged "deep connection charges" (all capital costs, including grid reinforcement to absorb the electrical output of the generator) or "shallow connection charges" (only the capital costs of connecting the generator to the nearest substation)? Do renewable generators receive more favorable connection charges than nonrenewable generators?

8. **Use of System Charges.** These are the costs incurred by a market or system operator to integrate the supply of the renewable generator onto the grid. These would include administrative costs, market transaction costs, additional balancing costs, and the costs of additional reserve capacity. What are they, and how are they calculated?

9. **Wheeling Charges.** Do renewable generators pay the same wheeling charges as nonrenewable generators?

10. **Net Metering.** Are there any provisions for small generators to sell electricity back to the grid? What is the cap on the size of such generators? How is the buy-back price determined? Is there a simple, standardized interconnection agreement?

E | Distributor and Retail Supplier Regulation

All countries

1. **Capital Structure.** Does the regulator have standards for a debt-to-equity ratio? If so, what is the standard, and how is it monitored? Concerning both equity and debt, does the regulator monitor the source of the capital (for example, government or private sources, domestic or foreign sources)?

2. **Supply Obligation.** Does the distributor have a monopoly for supply, as well as delivery of energy? If there is retail competition, is the distributor the supplier of last resort, or does that responsibility lie elsewhere (for example, generators or customers themselves)? Who is the default provider in the event that the consumer does not make a choice of supplier? How is the default product designed? Even in the absence of retail competition, does the ultimate supply obligation fall on the distributor, or does it fall elsewhere (for example, generators or transmission system)? If it falls on the distributor, what are the penalties for failure to supply? Who bears the risks for oversupply?

3. **Energy Costs.** Is the cost of fuel and/or purchased energy passed through to consumers through a specific mechanism apart from base rates, or is it internalized into base rates? If so, how often are adjustments made to the monitored mechanism? How is the prudence of

purchases monitored and assured? Are energy and fuel costs merely passed through to consumers, or is the distributor permitted to "mark up" the price for a profit? If the latter, what is deemed to be a reasonable level of profit? How are costs for hedging energy or fuel purchases treated?

4. **Currency Risks.** Does the distributor or retail supplier bear the risk for currency fluctuations, or are those risks passed on to consumers? How are the costs of hedging currency risks treated?

5. **Country Risks.** Are tariffs adjusted to reflect country risks, such as political or regulatory volatility? If so, how are those adjustments calculated and made? How are the costs of political risk insurance treated?

6. **Capital Costs.** How is the total rate base (that is, total capital investment) determined? Is it the replacement cost? Is it the actual investment made less depreciation, and if so, how is depreciation determined? Is it based on some benchmark, and if so, how is that benchmark determined and applied? Are new investments approved on a "before-the-fact" or "after-the-fact" basis? Are the investments approved on an aggregate basis or by individual investments above the threshold?

7. **Operations and Maintenance (O&M) Costs.** How are O&M costs determined? Are they based on actual expenditures? If so, what is the period for which the costs are tested (for example, future or historic test years or some combination of the two)? If actual costs are used, how is the prudence of the expenditures determined? Are the rules clear concerning which costs are recoverable in rates and which are not? If some O&M basis other than actual expenditures is used, what is that basis, and how is it derived (for example, benchmarks)?

8. **Pricing Methodology.** However the costs plugged into rate making are derived, what is the methodology used for setting tariffs (for example, rate of return regulation, price caps, revenue caps, or just and reasonable rate)? How often is the regulator required to conduct a full review of tariffs? Are there other triggers to tariff reviews besides mandated time intervals? If so, what are they, and how often have they been utilized? Are the tariffs composed of separate components for fixed and variable costs, or are they one-part tariffs? If two-part, what costs do the regulators consider to be fixed and which variable? Does the regulator use any forms of benchmarking of costs or operations?

9. **Service Quality.** Are the rules governing quality of service clearly articulated? If so, who establishes them, and how often are they reviewed? Are the rules reasonable in terms of the expectations of both distributors and consumers? How are they enforced (for example, regular reporting requirements, systematic or random audits, consumer complaints, or some combination)? What are the penalties for failure to comply with the standards? Does the regulator have a variety of enforcement mechanisms to use in the case of violations, so that the penalty is proportionate to the infraction?

E

10. **Consumer Complaints.** How are consumer complaints handled? How do consumers interface with the regulator on complaints? Are distributors or retail suppliers given an opportunity to resolve complaints before the regulator intervenes? Does the regulator systematically keep track of the volume and characteristics of complaints (for example, billing errors, service outages, or property damage)?

11. **Affiliate Transactions.** How are purchases of goods and/or services from—or other transactions with—affiliates treated (for example, prohibited, market tested, or administratively reviewed)?

12. **Vertical Integration.** Are distribution companies permitted to be in the generation, energy trading, or transmission businesses? If so, what kinds of separations, if any, are required (for example, accounting, corporate, or other structural, behavioral)?

13. **Cross-Subsidies.** What cross-subsidies, if any, are embedded into distribution/retail tariffs (for example, urban to rural, industrial to residential or vice versa, or affluent to poor)? Are the cross-subsidies made transparent?

14. **Nontechnical Losses.** What regulatory policies are in place to monitor and/or deal with nontechnical losses (for example, nonbilled, nonpayment, or theft)? What risks do distributors/retail suppliers bear? Does sufficient political, management, and regulatory will exist to reduce nontechnical losses?

15. **Energy Efficiency.** What incentives, if any, are in place to encourage distribution companies to use effective demand-side management and discourage wasteful use of energy, and to manage load efficiently (for example, time-of-use tariffs, demand-side bidding, decoupling profits and sales, or compensation for lost sales)?

16. **Licenses.** Who issues licenses to distributors and retail suppliers? What is the duration of these licenses? What are the criteria for obtaining one? How is it decided what distribution company rights and obligations are articulated into law or a license, or left to the discretion of the regulators? What are the grounds for suspension or revocation of a license? How can the terms and conditions of a license be altered and by whom? What is the role of the regulator in writing, issuing, enforcing, administering, and suspending or revoking a license?

Effect on the Poor as Consumers

All countries

1. **Low-Income Tariffs.** Are there tariffs specifically designed to assist low-income households (for example, lifeline rates, low-use rates, percent of income payment plans, or other cross subsidies)? Are there tariffs that focus more on variable rather than fixed

costs in serving the poor, thus reducing or eliminating barriers to service, such as high connection or line extension charges, and putting the size of the bill for poor household more within their control by emphasizing charges for actual use rather than fixed, unavoidable costs? Are connection charges subsidized? Have any studies been conducted to determine whether subsides are actually approaching their targets?

2. **Externalities.** How, if at all, does the regulatory system account for the external costs of failure to provide electric service to the poor (for example, health and safety effects, effects on literacy, environmental impact, and increased productivity)?

3. **Service Options.** Does the regulatory system authorize service offerings of particular value to the poor (for example, use limitations, prepayment cards, or subsidized provision of high-efficiency instruments to reduce consumption of electricity, such as high-efficiency light bulbs)?

4. **Distribution Company Obligation.** Are there conditions attached to tariffs or licenses imposing obligations on distribution companies in dealing with low-income households (for example, more tolerance for nonpayment or partial payment, assistance in gaining access to public subsidies to which they might be entitled, or shared meters)? If so, what are they? Is the obligation to serve defined in ways that obligate distributors to connect and maintain service to low-income households?

5. **Public and Cross-Subsidies.** What public subsidies are available to support service to the poor, and how does the regulatory system make certain that they are deployed efficiently? Are there cross-subsidies embedded in electric rates to provide financial means for serving low-income households? If so, how are they designed, are they effective, and do they efficiently target the intended beneficiaries?

6. **Public Participation and Outreach.** How easy or difficult is it for low-income consumers to access regulatory agencies to let their needs be known and their service-related complaints heard? Does the regulatory system provide a mechanism for sustained advocacy on behalf of low-income people?

E

Open Access and Customer Choice Regimes

East and South Asia, Eastern Europe, and Latin America

1. **Transmission Access Regime.** Is the transmission system open to all generators? If not, to whom is it closed (for example, small-scale distribution generators, or nonutility generators)? On the purchaser side, do all distributors have access? If any do not, who is precluded from access? Which end users, if any, are entitled—or even required—to buy energy directly off the transmission grid (that is, bypass distributors)? How does the regulator enforce the access rules, and what role does the regulator have in formulating those rules?

2. **Transmission Market Structure.** Is there a single transmission company or multiple transmission owners? If so, is it (are they) permitted to have any business affiliation with other industry sectors (for example, trading, generating, or distributing)? If permitted, do those linkages exist? If they do, what, if any, regulatory protections are in place to protect against the exercise of monopoly power at the transmission bottleneck?

3. **Transmission Expansion.** Who, if anyone, has the obligation to build new transmission facilities or to build new lines to interconnect new generators? Who determines the need for new transmission facilities? Who determines how that need will be met (for example, construction of new lines, expanding capacity of existing facilities, modernizing technology on existing facilities, or better load management)? Are system enhancements or expansions put out for competitive procurement, or are they assigned to a specific entity (for example, transmission company, or incumbent utility in location where the need exists)? What, if any, is the role of the regulator in system planning and expansion?

4. **Transmission Operations.** Who dispatches the system? Is there an independent system operator or transmission owners who do so? If there is an independent operator, how is it governed? Is it for profit or not for profit? How is it governed? Whether independent or not, what incentives and disincentives are in place to guide the operator in carrying out its responsibilities? How do system users interface with the system operator? What is the scope of the operator's responsibilities (for example, dispatch, redispatch, system planning, acquisition of reserves, and provider of last resort)? How is regulatory oversight exercised? Does the system operator also operate some power markets?

5. **Transmission Service Options.** How is transmission service provided? Is it on a systemwide (that is, network) basis, on a point-to-point basis, on a flow-gate model, on a zone-by-zone basis, on a nodal basis, or on some other basis? Is the dispatch subject to security constraints? If so, how are those constraints dealt with (for example, redispatch)?

6. **Congestion Management.** How is congestion dealt with? Is an administrative (that is, nonmarket) process in place for assigning dispatch priorities at times of constraint, or are there nodal (or perhaps zonal) prices that allow for pricing dispatch priorities? If there is an administrative process, how does it work, who makes what decisions, and how does the regulator exercise oversight? If locational prices are being used, is there a hedge market for firm transmission rights to allow for managing the risks associated with congestion? If there is nodal pricing, is it a sufficient incentive for attracting investment in necessary new capacity? Whatever the management (or pricing) system, how well does it function, and how does the regulator exercise oversight?

7. **Ancillary Services.** How are ancillary services (for example, voltage support, spinning reserves, cold reserves, or reactive power) provided? Are there competitive offerings or are they assigned to the transmission owner(s), generators, purchasers, or the system operator?

E

8. **Transmission Pricing.** Setting aside nodal prices and ancillary services, how are transmission investors compensated? Is it through rolled-in average prices, long-term or short-term marginal cost pricing (which, in the short term might be at least partially reflected in nodal pricing, although the revenues from nodal prices may not go to investors in transmission), or some other methodology? Are price caps, revenue caps, rate of return, or some other methodology used for determining base rates? Are transmission use of system tariffs one part or two parts (that is, fixed and variable)? What is the underlying cost basis used for determining costs—historical, future, or a benchmark—and how is it determined?

9. **Transmission Planning.** Who has responsibility for transmission planning? How is it carried out? (That is, through public participation? How transparent is the process?) What is the role of the regulator?

10. **Transmission Licensing and Siting.** What types of transmission facilities or upgrades require licenses? Who issues the required licenses? What are the criteria for issuing one? Are economic and reliability criteria looked at in assessing need? What role does the regulator play?

11. **Reliability.** Who is responsible for maintaining reliability in the short term and who is responsible in the long term? Who decides on transfer capability specifications and the related calculations? Is there a grid code or some other documentation of these determinations? What are the reliability standards? Who decides them, how are they publicized, and how are they administered?

E

Competitive Bulk Power Markets

Eastern Europe and South America

1. **Generation Pricing.** Are generating prices set by the market or by regulation? How is it determined which method will apply? Are "must-run" units treated differently from other generators? If so, how are they treated differently, and what are the criteria for including them in the "must-run" category? What about generators located in load pockets?

2. **Market Monitoring.** How do regulators monitor the market to assure themselves and market participants that competition is effective? Is there a designated market monitor, or is it done by the regulatory agency itself? If there is a separate market monitor, is it independent? To whom does it report and how? Are its findings public? What powers does it possess?

3. **Market Power.** Are there standards for determining market power in generation? If so, what are they? What constitutes an inordinate market share? Are there limitations to how much generation a single corporate entity can control? (That is, what level of market share is impermissible?)

4. **Competition Enforcement.** How does the electricity regulator interact with the competition regulator (assuming one exists) on competition issues in the power sector? What powers do regulators have to enforce competition policy and to remedy undue concentration of market power (for example, to mandate divestiture of assets or to impose behavioral controls)?

5. **Market Structure and Design.** Are generating units dispatched by virtue of bilateral transactions in existence, or are they dispatched in pool arrangements with known protocols on dispatch order? If pool arrangements are used, to what extent do buyers and sellers enter into bilateral arrangements to hedge their risks? If pool arrangements are used, how are bids made? Are they cost based or price based? Are there real-time bids and day-ahead or other forward markets? Are bids hourly or at some other time interval? Are successful bidders paid the bid price, the market-clearing price, or some other price? How, and to what extent, do the regulators oversee the market operations and hedging arrangements?

6. **Market Administrator.** Is there a separate market administrator? Is the administrator separate from the transmission operator? What are the market administrator's functions (for example, serving as a forum for all energy purchases and sales, billing, collecting and disbursing all the funds from sales and purchases, and adopting and enforcing market rules)? What is the governance system for the market administrator? What kind of oversight does the regulator exercise over the market administrator? How is that oversight conducted? What incentives does the market administrator have? How is the administrator held accountable? Is the administrator a for-profit or not-for-profit organization?

7. **Capacity Market.** Is the bulk power market just for energy, or is there a capacity or long-term contract market as well? If there is a capacity market, how does that market function? How does the regulator exercise oversight? Is it competitive? How is capacity obtained (for example, self built, transparent auctions, or bilateral negotiations)?

8. **Resource Adequacy.** Are there resource adequacy requirements imposed by law or regulation, or is it assumed that the market will produce sufficient power to meet demand? If there are adequacy requirements, how are they determined (for example, a stated percentage of energy purchased or sold)? Who has the obligation to make sure that there are adequate resources to meet demand? Is there a generation planning function? If so, who carries out the planning, and what powers does that entity possess? What is the role of the regulator concerning resource adequacy, and how is that responsibility carried out?

9. **Resource Mix.** Is it left to the market to decide the energy resource mix in a country's generation sector, or is there a public policy mandate for the resource mix? If there is a preference, what is it (for example, renewables, coal, hydro, gas, or nuclear), and who decides on it (for example, regulatory agency, government, legislature, or energy ministry)? If there are resource preferences, how are they exercised (for example, separate

procurement processes for each resource, or mandated portfolio standards)? Are the preferred resources subsidized or cross-subsidized in order to attain the quantity sought?

10. **Energy Trading.** Is there energy trading? How, if at all, are traders licensed? What role do they play (for example, merely as brokers who purchase for and sell from their own portfolio)? Do they enhance liquidity in the market? Are traders allowed to be affiliated with generators, transmission companies, or distributors? Can traders sell to retail, as well as to wholesale customers?

11. **Multinational Markets.** Is the energy market multinational? If so, are there common market rules? How does the national market interface with the multinational markets? How do the regulators interact? Who exercises regulatory oversight over the multinational market?

12. **Licensing and Siting.** Who issues licenses for new plants? Do all plants require licenses? If not, which ones do not? What criteria must new licensees meet (for example, on the basis of need or economic, environmental, or safety criteria)? Are licensing and siting coordinated with planning? If so, how is that coordination carried out?

13. **Billing and Metering.** Is the metering adequate to provide the requisite information for operating the system, allocating costs, assigning liabilities, and averting use that exceeds system limitations? Is it sufficient for identifying costs associated with real-time load balancing and producing accurate customer profiles? Does the billing system accurately rack the costs and direct bills to the appropriate parties?

E

Sample Terms of Reference for Mid-Level and In-Depth Evaluations of Regulatory Systems

The purpose of this appendix is to provide sample terms of reference (TOR) to guide those who actually organize and carry out the evaluations envisioned in this handbook, as well as to guide those who seek to provide training to either avoid or correct the problems that are often encountered in infrastructure regulation.

Background

The TOR below are generic in nature and, therefore, will require some modification or tweaking to reflect more specifically the realities encountered in the country chosen for study. The TOR are designed solely for in-depth evaluations. The TOR for the short and mid-level evaluations are effectively embodied and are self-explanatory in the questionnaire tools and general discussion found in appendixes C (short basic evaluation of national, regional, and provincial utility regulation) and D (questionnaires for mid-level evaluation). Hence, no further discussion of the TOR for these is necessary here. For the in-depth evaluation, as discussed in chapter 6, there may be considerable value to having completed the short- and possibly also the medium-term questionnaires prior to undertaking the in-depth evaluation and a requirement to do so may be included in the TOR.[1]

---

1. The information gleaned from the use of those instruments well may turn up background information or highlight some specific issues that need to be addressed, both of which situations could prove to be useful precursors to the consultants doing the deeper evaluation. On a case-by-case basis, the drafters of TOR for in-depth evaluations may want to consider making one or both of those tools part of the scoping effort, or they might want to make certain that the work is done before undertaking the scoping activity discussed below. These are case-by-case determinations based on such matters as the urgency of completing the in-depth analysis, the familiarity of the consultants (especially the international consultant) with the country and the sector in which the evaluation is to be conducted, the audience for whom the work is intended, and other such matters.

The TOR also assume that no preliminary work has been done at the time that the TOR are actually produced (for example, scoping out critical topics to be explored).[2] Many of the evaluations are likely to be triggered by certain events, whereas others may simply be the result of a general sense within a government that the regulatory system and agency have been operating for a while. As with any other activity and institution, it makes sense to periodically reevaluate what is being done and how it is being carried out.

The TOR also assume that the project is a stand-alone effort rather than simply one aspect of a larger project, such as looking at the restructuring of the entire power sector of a country. There, is, of course, some likelihood that the regulatory evaluation will be part of a larger project, in which case the sponsors of the project can simply incorporate the TOR into that larger document. For that reason, as well as because the immediate precipitating factors that motivate any single evaluation are not knowable as this document is being written, the background section of the TOR cannot be fully articulated in this appendix.

Finally, of course, as the name Republic of Hypothetica (RH) indicates, the TOR are intended to be generic in nature and not drawn uniquely from any single country's experience. For that reason, as noted above, the TOR will have to be modified, particularly in regard to narrowing its substantive focus on a country-by-country basis.

Terms of Reference for In-Depth Evaluation of the Republic of Hypothetica Power Sector Regulatory System

F

This section, of course, will provide a brief context of the work to be performed. The context will essentially consist of two elements. The first element is a brief historical description of the creation and evolution of both the power sector and its regulation. It will provide a quick look at characteristics of the power sector that are of particular relevance to the evaluators. Although the description need not be exhaustive, because the evaluators will have to thoroughly familiarize themselves with the sector, it might typically include a brief overview of the following:

- Ownership status and history (that is, state whether local, regional, national, or private, or some mixture thereof).
- Energy resource mix (for example, hydro, gas, and coal).
- Basic sector statistics (for example, installed capacity, consumption, and miles of transmission).

---

2. Although it is assumed that the preliminary scoping will not have been done before the consultant is retained, the draft TOR do assume that the client has already been identified. This is important to note, not as part of the TOR but as an essential element of the evaluation process. There must be a clearly identified in-country client who takes on sponsorship of the effort. There are any number of potential client sponsors, such as the government itself, a ministry, the regulatory agency, a neutral NGO, or some other entity with credibility and stature, but with no partisan axe to grind or financial interest to serve.

- Social characteristics (for example, market penetration, cross-subsidies, and environmental issues).
- Market design (for example, competition or monopoly, or transmission or distribution access regimes).
- Degree of vertical integration.
- Load and consumption patterns (for example, percentage industrial, household, or commercial, and peak load).
- Allocation of planning and supplier of last-resort obligations.
- Prices and pricing methodologies.

In addition to sector characteristics, a brief overview of the regulatory structure should also be included. The overview might typically address the following in brief:

- Description of the powers of the regulatory agency.
- Description of the structure of the agency.
- Discussion of the governance of the agency.
- Description of the resources, financial and human, of the agency.
- Discussion of the methodologies used by the agency (for example, pricing).
- Discussion of market governance and institutions that interact with the regulator in the marketplace (for example, system operator or market administrator).
- Relationship of the sector regulator with other parts of the government (for example, competition regulators, ministries, or state and local governments).
- Discussion of the regulatory decisionmaking process and the interaction of the regulators with stakeholders.
- Description of all significant recent controversies concerning regulation and how it is carried out.

F

The second element that is critical to the statement of background is the immediate precipitator of the evaluations. In Brazil, for example, the precipitating circumstance that led to the evaluation was the supply crisis and subsequent rationing of electricity in the country. There was a feeling among many that the crisis had harmed the regulatory process, thereby necessitating a reevaluation. Others, coming from a different perspective in the public debate about the crisis, fairly or not, had attributed at least some of the responsibility for the shortage to faulty regulation. In Russia, the precipitator of the evaluation was concern that the regulatory institutions would be unable to handle their new responsibilities under a proposed sector restructuring. Another Latin American country contemplated such an evaluation because of a fierce controversy over the respective roles of the regulatory agency and the energy ministry.

An African nation was open to the suggestion of an evaluation because it was concerned that liberalization and some privatization in infrastructure had resulted in disappointingly little international private investment being attracted to its infrastructure. It also wanted to determine whether its regulatory system was partly responsible for that result. One can envision any number of reasons why such an evaluation should be conducted, including simple ones like the evaluation being a condition of a loan from a multilateral lender or bilateral donor or, even more simply, because the system has been in place for several years, and it is useful to take a fresh look at what the system has been doing and how. In writing the background section for a regulatory evaluation TOR, setting out the key factors motivating and precipitating the evaluation is essential. Doing so will put all potential consultants on more precise, although not necessarily detailed, notice of the issues with which they will be expected to grapple. It will also serve as a useful tool for those who will select the consultants based on who has the most relevant experience, and which might have disqualifying conflicts of interest.

Goal and Purpose of the Evaluation

The purpose of the evaluation is to examine those aspects of a regulatory system where careful, expert analysis, critique, and recommendations for going forward would add the greatest value for all concerned. The term "regulatory system" is meant in the broadest sense. It encompasses governance, process, substance, institutions, and behavior (that is, all of which are covered in chapters 3, 4, and 5, and in appendix A).

In addition to providing expert, disinterested analysis and recommendations, charging the consultants to carry out their work on a highly interactive and consultative basis will serve an important second purpose. The interactive process, including the use of seminars, will provide a useful forum for airing the most critical aspects of the regulatory system.

Consultant Characteristics

There should be a team of consultants, all of whom must possess relevant training and experience, and none of whom have any conflicts of interest that might either bias or appear to bias their recommendations. The lead consultant should be an international expert. The international expert should be teamed with an in-country expert who is deeply familiar with the sector. It is also very valuable to retain the services of an in-country attorney to help frame the recommendations most readily in the country's legal system. The consultant qualifications should be as follows:

- **International Expert.** The international expert should be experienced in both regulatory and sectoral matters in both his or her own country, as well as in other countries and cultures. Ideally, he or she will have advanced academic credentials in relevant disciplines (for example, law, economics, engineering, and/or accounting). He or she should be capable of, and comfortable in, working in cross-cultural settings and diverse legal systems. Experience as a regulator, knowledge of relevant languages, and/or expertise in the country whose regulatory system is being evaluated are desirable, but not necessarily a prerequisite. Experience in conducting similar evaluations in other countries would also be a major plus.

- **In-Country Expert.** The in-country expert must possess many of the same credentials as the international expert. In addition, he or she must be very familiar with and experienced in both the regulatory system and the infrastructural sector in the country. He or she should possess excellent contacts in the sector and should be seen as a respected, unbiased observer within the industry. Multilingual skills are a must (for example, native languages in the country, the native language of the international expert, and/or English).
- **In-Country Attorney.** The credentials of the attorney are identical to those of the in-country expert, except, of course, that the attorney must be trained and licensed as a lawyer in the country.

Work Plan

The work should take place in four phases, and a possible fifth. They are as follows:

1. **Scoping and Definition.** The first task for the consultants will be to collect information on recent developments in the regulated sector, particularly concerning the most significant controversies in the sector in recent years. They will also compile background materials related to relevant laws and rules, sector information, and detailed information about the regulatory agency, its rules, resources, processes, and policies. As recommended in chapter 6, completing the short basic and/or mid-level questionnaires could be helpful in this context.[3]

   The consultants will then work closely with the sponsor to finalize a list of topics that are to be pursued in greater detail. These will be drawn from the background materials, from the client's priorities, from conversations with others, and from professional judgments as to what is most important. The issues could be of a variety of types, including process, governance, substance, or any other related matters (see, for example, chapters 3, 4, and 5 for the range of possibilities).[4] *The test for prioritizing subjects for analysis*

---

3. Using the questionnaires might provide an additional benefit useful for developing comparative material.
4. It is impossible to define generically what the priorities are for in-depth evaluation. Every country will have different priorities, and every moment in time is likely to have different priorities. They will simply have to be worked out on a case-by-case basis, although any events that served as precursors or motivations for the evaluations are likely to be at least partially definitive of the most pressing needs. In any event, two examples might be useful. In Brazil the evaluation focused primarily on process and governance. Among the key issues addressed in

should be relevance, overall significance to the regulatory system and regulated sector, the likelihood of having a real impact, and practicability.

The list of priorities concerning the subjects to be addressed should be used as a guide for preparation, but not a final determination. Almost certainly, as the consultants go about their work, they will uncover other issues that merit scrutiny, so some flexibility needs to be retained for the consultants to look at unforeseen issues that arise.

There should also be an agreement between the clients and consultants on the schedule and process to be used. All these agreements should be set out in an inception report that is written and submitted by the consultants before the interview and in-depth research effort goes further. *Time is important because issues change over time, so timeliness and relevance are closely interrelated. Ideally, assuming no unforeseen complexities, the process should be completed in 90 to 120 days.*

Finally, the client and consultant will need to agree on two matters that need not be included in the inception report. The first is a minimal list of who needs to be consulted in the evaluation. The agreed-upon list of contacts (for example, specified persons, interest groups, organizations, or agencies) is minimal solely because it is the client's "must call upon" list. It is not meant to be a limit on the consultant's discretion to add additional persons or entities. The second agreement is on feedback and communications between the client and consultants as the process unfolds. The client and consultant should communicate at regular, periodic intervals and should agree on how and when these communications should occur.

2. **Research and Consultative Process.** The consultants will conduct whatever research and collect whatever documents they need. They will also prepare an outline of questions on appropriate topics for the people with whom they intend to meet.

It is critical that the evaluation process be interactive and participatory. Care must be taken to ensure that all sides of critical issues are listened to and factored into the final analysis. Thus, the consultants will set up meetings (preferably in person, but telephonically if necessary) with the relevant people on the chosen topics. The consultants will not necessarily be limited to interviewing those they meet with based on prepared

---

that evaluation were financial and human resources available to regulators, clarification of the respective roles of government and regulators, regulatory independence, the relationship between regional (state) and national regulators, transparency in decisionmaking, appellate processes, consumer representation, ethics, and regulatory oversight of market institutions. It also might have included issues related to the setting of distribution tariffs, but there was a concurrent parallel effort sponsored by the World Bank to assist the power sector regulators on tariff-related matters. In Russia the evaluation was driven by analysis of what the regulatory agency would be required to do under a proposed new model for the power sector. Thus, such issues as tariff methodology, regulatory independence, and market oversight capabilities took on a greater importance.

questionnaires. The process is meant to be fully interactive. The meetings, unless agreed to otherwise by the interviewee, are to be on a "not for attribution" basis. Thus, although knowledge of the existence of meetings between consultants and interviewees will not necessarily be confidential (although some interviewees may ask for such confidentiality), no one will be quoted by name, either in the report or in conversations with anyone other than the consultants themselves.

The interview process is absolutely critical for two reasons. The first is that it may be the most effective way for the consultants to gain a full understanding of the various perspectives on a given topic. It also provides key players with a sense of involvement and input into the report. That sense of being involved can play a role in obtaining support for the recommendations that are ultimately produced.

3. **Drafting and Obtaining Feedback.** On completion of all of the research, including the interviews, the consultants will write a draft report. The report will be composed of three parts. The first will cover the background of the process followed and the work undertaken. The second part of the report will be a topic-by-topic discussion of the issues being evaluated, with a brief description of the issue, a summary of all of the critical information obtained, the consultant's own analysis, and recommendation(s). The third part of the report will simply be a recapitulation of the recommendations on a stand-alone basis. The recommendations will also include an explanation of what will legally be required to implement them, with particular focus on whether implementation can be done by regulatory action, by ministerial or other form of government decree, by legislative action, or by altering the constitution.

The consultants will provide the client with a first draft of the report for review and feedback. The client should have ample opportunity to provide meaningful feedback, but the ultimate content of the report should be left to the consultants.

Once the client's feedback is obtained and considered, the revised draft will be circulated to all those interviewed in order to seek their feedback. A few weeks after this draft is circulated, the client and consultants, perhaps with the assistance of a funding entity (such as the World Bank), will set up a workshop for an informal presentation of the draft and a full discussion of its contents. The consultants will take note of all of the feedback obtained.

4. **Delivery of the Final Product.** The consultants will analyze all the feedback and prepare a final report. Before that document is made public, however, the client will be given one more opportunity to provide feedback to the consultants. After that feedback is obtained, the report will be made public. Part of the process of making it public will be a forum, open to all interested parties, where the consultants will formally present their evaluation, recommendations, and reasons for them.

F

5. **Post-Report Effort.** The consultants should be willing to undertake any work that they may be called upon to provide to implement the recommendations of their report.[5] Although they should be entitled to additional compensation for such additional work (given the need for continuity and expertise that only the report's authors are in a position to offer), it is important that they be contractually bound to provide that work for additional pay at the same rate at which they were paid in the first four phases of the project.

Deliverables

The deliverables are, as noted in the inception report, a draft report followed by a final report. The consultants will also be required to provide two formal presentations—at both the workshop at the conclusion of the draft and at the forum where the final report is delivered. The draft report shall be submitted no later than 60 to 75 days after the work is undertaken, and the final report should follow 30 to 45 days thereafter.

Level of Effort

The precise level of effort required is difficult to state on a generic basis because the amount of work is likely to vary depending on the issues, the number of interviews required, and other matters that can be highly variable. The bulk of the writing is likely to be done by the international consultant, whereas the burden of coordination and logistics is likely to fall disproportionately on the in-country consultant. The in-country lawyer will probably be called upon for considerably less effort than the other two consultants, but the precise level of legal effort is also likely to vary greatly, depending on the circumstances. Given the time frames called for in completing the work, it is roughly estimated that both the international and the in-country consultants would be called upon for 6–7 person-weeks each, whereas the lawyer would probably be called upon for 10 person-days of effort. Those numbers, however, reflect an educated guess, because circumstances could dictate that either more or less effort would actually be required.

---

5. The types of post-report effort that might be required would include, although not necessarily be limited to, drafting rules, decrees, or laws; providing training; and testifying before legislative bodies, or meeting with government officials or others as the client deems necessary.

Summaries of Some Mid-Level and In-Depth Country-Specific Regulatory Evaluations

This appendix contains summaries of mid-level and in-depth evaluations of regulatory systems for the electricity sectors in Brazil, Chile, India, Russia, South Africa, and Ukraine. In general, the evaluations examine both regulatory governance and regulatory substance. The summaries present principal findings and principal recommendations of each evaluation. Not surprisingly, the focus of the evaluations is on recommended changes that would improve the operation of the existing regulatory systems.

Brazil

Title: Strengthening of the Institutional and Regulatory Structure of the Brazilian Power Sector
Author: Ashley C. Brown and Ericson de Paula
Context: Prepared in 2004 for the World Bank as an evaluation of the Brazilian electricity sector regulatory framework.
Level of Assessment: In-depth
Availability: http://wbln0018.worldbank.org/ppiaf/activity.nsf/files/brazilP091503.pdf/$FILE/brazilP091503.pdf

Background

The National Electricity Regulatory Agency (ANEEL)was established as the Brazilian national electricity regulatory agency in 1996. This report, which is a follow-up to a 2002 report, assesses the operation of the Brazilian electricity regulatory system with particular emphasis on governance issues.

Principal Findings

The report identifies various areas where the Brazilian electricity sector regulatory framework can be further improved.

Governance

ANEEL's human and financial resources, as well as the operation of the market and the functions of its various participants, are the major issues that emerge from an examination of regulatory governance issues.

ANEEL's Human and Financial Resources

- Although recently passed legislation has removed barriers and addressed some problems, the report finds that the law is still not adequate for enhancing the institutional and regulatory structure of ANEEL.
- ANEEL's ability to hire experienced or inexperienced but well-trained professionals is severely impaired by the requirement that it can only provide entry-level compensation for new hires. ANEEL cannot offer its employees compensation packages that differ from those offered to the civil service as a whole, which creates an incentive for agency personnel to leave ANEEL and work for the regulated entities. This constraint leads to a waste of public resources, given the amount of funds dedicated to their training, as well as a reduction in the quality of regulatory service and a serious ethical dilemma.
- The government collects 0.5 percent of regulated company revenues, which are intended to support ANEEL activities, and allows ANEEL to spend only 40 percent of the collected funds in an apparent attempt to reallocate those funds to contribute to the government's targeted budget surplus as part of its overall fiscal austerity program.

Market Operations and Functions

- There are several concerns over the specifics of the operation of the Wholesale Electricity Market, including how ANEEL will exercise regulatory oversight over the new market administrator, the Chamber of Electric Energy Commercialization (CCEE). Moreover, the closeness of the board of the National System Operator (ONS) to market participants leads to concerns and creates more frequent interventions by ANEEL than necessary. A clarification of ANEEL's regulatory role and its responsibilities relative to the system operator (ONS) and market administrator (CCEE) is necessary.
- ANEEL does not appear to have taken advantage of its budgetary review powers over ONS and CCEE budgets to create incentives for more efficient and effective performance by these entities. The incentives at present are not symmetrical and balanced, and they focus primarily on negative incentives.
- A need exists for an independent "market monitor" with well-defined monitoring authority, as well as the ability to report its findings publicly.

G

Principal Recommendations

The report makes a set of recommendations that would enhance the regulatory governance and substance in the Brazilian electricity sector.

Governance

With respect to regulatory governance, the recommendations address a range of issues that include ANEEL's human and financial resources, accountability and transparency, decentralization of certain regulatory powers, mechanisms for tackling disputes and appeals, and details of the operation and functioning of the market.

ANEEL's Human and Financial Resources

- ANEEL should be provided with authority under the law to establish its own hiring practices, or at least be allowed to deviate from generally applicable practices.
- ANEEL should be allowed to establish civil service employee compensation packages that are benchmarked to the levels of compensation paid by regulated companies, or ANEEL salaries should at least be comparable to other government agencies that compensate their staff above generally applicable government pay scales. In return, ANEEL staff and directors should be made subject to the more stringent ethical restrictions, including those relating to holding financial interests in the industry, employment by sector participants after the termination of their ANEEL tenure, and prohibitions on accepting gifts and gratuities from sector participants.
- The law should specifically preclude the funds collected from consumers for purposes of regulation from being diverted to other uses by the government. The law should prevent the government from reducing the budgetary funds allocated to ANEEL for a specific fiscal year, unless the reduction is part of a broad cutback applicable across the public sector and does not disproportionately affect ANEEL.

Accountability, Transparency, and Participation

- The law should be amended—or policies put into place—to provide for periodic, public, transparent review of the activities of ANEEL by designated legislative or executive authorities, or both.
- All communications between ANEEL and any party, including a government agency, on a matter pending before the agency should be made in a publicly accessible, completely transparent way.
- When appropriate, ANEEL should conduct public hearings, with the participation of its own staff, as well as representatives of various stakeholders, and allow for presentations, debate, and cross-examinations during the hearings.

G

- ANEEL should establish a seven-member Consumer Advocate Board (CAB) of Directors, which would be selected through consultation with local governments, labor unions, consumer organizations, and the Ministry of Mines and Energy. ANEEL should require each distribution company to contribute a specified percentage of their revenues for an NGO designated by CAB to serve as the consumer advocate.

Decentralization

ANEEL should promote greater interaction with state regulatory agencies by conducting joint public hearings and allowing the state agencies to have an advisory or formal role during the review of the distribution tariffs in their region; establishing staff exchange programs, joint training, and other cooperative efforts; and experimenting with delegating some authority to the state agencies in setting distribution tariffs.

Disputes and Appeals

- If legally possible, all appeals of regulatory agency decisions should be directed to a single expert forum whose decision would be subject to a single level of judicial review, unless there are constitutional issues.
- The possibility of creating a specialized court (Vara) should be explored to hear appeals from ANEEL and the Petroleum National Agency, as well as all matters related to energy regulation, whether these are appeals of regulatory decisions or cases initiated in the courts without first being considered by the regulators. If such a court is created, ANEEL should be consulted in electricity sector–related cases where it was not involved before or when new information presented during a hearing had not been brought to ANEEL's attention earlier.

Allocation of Policy and Regulatory Functions

- The government should give serious consideration to the merger and full consolidation of all national regulatory responsibilities for both the electric and the natural gas industries into a single agency.
- The respective powers of various government entities involved in energy sector policy and regulation should be clarified. Although the congress and the executive power should make primary policy, subsidiary policymaking should be left to regulators.
- The adoption and publication of the rules and protocols, as well as the implementation of the auctions in the wholesale market and the granting of concessions, should be carried out transparently. ANEEL can delegate the responsibility for conducting auctions to CCEE in accordance with guidelines that ANEEL would issue on implementation of the auctions.

- ANEEL should make its exercise of regulatory oversight of both the ONS and the CCEE more transparent and more open to public participation.
- ANEEL should perform one role in the planning process: the determination of whether certain costs or risks should be socialized by passing them through to consumers.

Substance

With respect to regulatory substance, the recommendations of the report cover such areas as the creation of incentives for sector participants and the need to focus on transmission congestion and demand-side measures, as well as planning, monitoring, and consumer protection.

- ANEEL should develop proposals on how it will use its power to approve the CCEE and ONS budgets more effectively to provide incentives for improved overall performance. ANEEL should also explore, through a public consultation process, how to make the overall incentives for the CCEE and the ONS more symmetrical, balanced, and effective.
- The Ministry of Mines and Energy, ANEEL, ONS, and CCEE should collaborate in formal studies on managing transmission congestion and incorporating demand-side management options into the capacity and energy markets.
- The Monitoring Committee for the Electricity Sector, through engaging independent consultants and/or advisory committees, should focus on transmission issues, the use of demand-side resources, the interplay between the free and regulated markets, and the effects of segregated auctions on supply security and efficient sector outcomes.

G

Chile

Title: Electricity Reform in Chile: Lessons for Developing Countries
Author : Michael G. Pollitt
Context: Revised version of a report prepared for the World Bank.
Level of Assessment: In-depth
Availability: http://www.econ.cam.ac.uk/electricity/publications/wp/ep51.pdf

Background

This report describes reform in the Chilean electricity sector and the lessons to be learned from this experience. Although it is not specifically intended as a regulatory evaluation, it contains a detailed discussion of regulatory substance and regulatory governance issues.

Principal Findings

The report identifies various areas where the Chilean electricity sector regulatory framework can be further improved, in terms of both regulatory governance and regulatory substance.

Governance

In terms of regulatory governance, the report finds that improvements can be made in the allocation of regulatory responsibilities, institutional capacity, transparency, and participation, among others.

Allocation of Regulatory Responsibilities

- The allocation of regulatory responsibilities is unclear and confusing. The division of roles between the National Energy Commission (CNE) and the Superintendency for Electricity and Fuels (SEC) creates the impression that there are two regulatory bodies. The CNE has responsibility for advising the Minister of Economy on electricity policy and for setting regulated distribution charges, which would then be formally imposed by the ministry. The SEC has responsibility for collecting data on regulation and enforcement and for handling consumer complaints and the enforcement of fines for service quality issues and customer compensations.
- The advisory role of the CNE fails to create incentives for it to behave in the public interest. Rather, the agency tends to lobby with the government to have its advice accepted.

Regulatory Discretion

Regulatory discretion has been limited by legislation, and no major changes in the system have been made since 1982. Although this arrangement has contributed to the success of investment in the sector, it has also prevented the appropriate updating of the regulatory regime in light of new information and developments. Any change to market design and rules has to be carried out through a change in legislation.

Disputes and Appeals

The ultimate responsibility for resolving disputes, hearing appeals, deciding on the need for rationing, and determining the reserve capacity levels assumed in the calculation of peak capacity payments currently rests with the Ministry of Economy.

Public Participation, Transparency, and Accountability

- Small consumers are not adequately represented in the regulatory process and the governance of the market. Intervention by the Ministry of Economy to represent the interests of those consumers in the process is not effective.
- There is a striking lack of published information about regulatory actions. The CNE does not publish reports on how it assesses the distribution charges, and the SEC does not produce an annual report at all.

Substance

The report discusses regulatory substance issues, such as the scope of the regulatory framework, competition, governance of the load dispatch centers, network access, tariffs, and rural electrification.

Applicable Regulatory Framework

- The law governing the electricity sector provides detailed specifications for regulation of the sector, especially on issues concerning market design, threshold levels of competition (0.5 MW), maximum number of CNE staff (45), weights assigned to reports prepared by consultants of the distribution companies (1/3) and regulatory agency (2/3) for determining the distribution charges, the share of transmission costs to be paid by the generators, and the way ancillary services will be remunerated. The extensive details provided on sector regulation have made the electricity law inflexible and unable both to keep up with the evolution of the market and to adapt to changes in the sector and unforeseen technical progress.
- The rules governing the sector are based on the requirements of the Central Interconnected System (SIC)—and not the Northern Interconnected System.
- The Chilean regulatory system relies more heavily on engineering models with less input from economic analysis. This creates a bias toward an ideal model-based solution for determinations such as nodal prices and the setting of distribution tariffs, instead of one that is based on economic analysis. This bias toward engineering analysis is likely

G

to be a reflection of the restrictions on the mix of professional skills in the CNE and the SEC. These restrictions limit the effectiveness of their regulatory activities.

Governance of the System Operator

The disputes that arise within the governing board of the system operator, namely the Economic Load Dispatch Center (CDEC) have been problematic, because of the divergence of interests of the parties that are represented on the board, coupled with the fact that the law requires unanimity in voting for any rule change. The CDEC governing board is not representative of the entire market. It is composed only of incumbent supply-side entities, that is, generators and transmission companies.

Network Access and Associated Charges

- The ability of generators to integrate with distributors has an adverse effect on the ability of "nonintegrated" generators to compete for customers of the distribution business. Relatively little competition exists between generators for customers embedded in the distribution network because the access charges and terms to the distribution network are not properly regulated to prevent discriminatory access charges.
- Allowing negotiated transmission access to new generators means that new entrants can impose congestion costs on existing users of the network. This also puts the transmission company in a weak negotiating position with the generators, because even in the absence of an agreement from the transmission company, generators can go ahead with connections and settle access prices through arbitration.
- The rates charged by the central system (SIC) transmission monopoly Transelec were unregulated until the passage of the "short law" (*Ley Corta*) in 2004, which introduced minor changes to the regulatory framework. Transelec's charges will now be regulated, based on a 10 percent real rate of return on assets and competitive bidding for operation and maintenance, capital upgrades, and system extensions. This is not efficient, because the company does not exploit economies of scale, scope, or learning in transmission operation and building. Moreover, the transaction costs of such a system are significant. In the short term, bidders may be willing to absorb losses to gain a place in the market, but in the long term, as the number of bidders is likely to fall, the bidding costs will be fully reflected in their prices.

Rural Electrification

Significant progress has been made in rural electrification, but the regulatory framework does not create incentives for least-cost connections to increase access. Generous connection subsidies have been granted, and most grid extensions are made by local distribution companies based on incurred costs, instead of through bids that are the outcome of a competitive process.

G

Principal Recommendations

The report makes a number of recommendations that would enhance the regulatory governance and substance in the Chilean electricity sector.

Governance

With respect to regulatory governance, the recommendations of the report focus on the consolidation of regulatory roles, strengthening of the regulatory institutions, the clarification of dispute resolution, and review mechanisms, among others.

- The roles of CNE and SEC should be merged so that there is one energy regulatory agency.
- The CNE should be freed from the operational control of the Ministry of Economy. It should be set up as an independent regulatory agency instead of being an advisory body.
- The head of the independent regulatory agency should be appointed for a fixed term by the relevant minister and should be removed only in exceptional circumstances.
- The dispute resolution and review mechanisms should be made clearer and should be expedited, especially for disputes involving agencies with regulatory functions and the regulated companies. Given the technical nature of the subject, the dispute resolution process should involve specialist arbitration panels.
- Regulatory discretion should be increased.
- Legislation should be amended to reflect the differing circumstances of the central and northern systems.
- A formal role should be given to small consumers to ensure their participation in the governance of the industry. This could be accomplished, for example, by establishing a formal consumer association to represent consumers and handle complaints. The activities of such a body could be funded by a levy imposed on sector participation.
- The transparency of industry regulation and oversight needs to be improved.
- Representation on the CDEC governing board should be expanded to include demand-side participants, as well as potential entrants on the supply side. Increased participation in the CDEC governing board should be accompanied by reforms of the unanimous voting and dispute resolution procedures within the board.

Substance

The report's recommendations address such issues as the unbundling, as well as integration of market activities, the creation of an ancillary services market, the composition of load dispatch center boards, the regulation of transmission charges, and rural electrification.

- Generators should be allowed to merge with retailers, but not with both retailers and wire businesses.

G

- A market for ancillary services should be introduced, with a price-based bidding system for the provision of the services by generators, transmission companies, and large customers.
- Regulated transmission charges should be combined with a system of congestion cost recovery aimed at covering the cost of the whole network, instead of just paying for the cost imposed on the system in the "influence area," where power is deemed to flow from generators to their customers. The arrangement ignores the effect of a generator on the rest of the system and the fact that other transmission lines outside this influence area provide backup capability to the whole system.
- Both generators and customers should pay for transmission.
- Transelec, the transmission monopoly, should be regulated in a way consistent with the regulation of distribution companies: price controls set for a four-year period based on a model company's costs.
- A regulated third-party access charge is needed in order to correctly regulate access to the monopoly distribution network by third-party suppliers.
- Grid extensions for rural electrification should be based on a competitive and open bidding process.

G

India

Title: A Good Beginning but Challenges Galore: A Survey Based Study of Resources, Transparency and Public Participation in Electricity Regulatory Commissions in India
Author: Prayas Energy Group
Context: Based on a 2002 survey of several regulatory commissions in India.
Level of Assessment: In-depth
Availability: http://www.prayaspune.org/energy/36_Prayas_ERC_Survey.pdf

Background

The Prayas Energy Group is an Indian NGO that emphasizes health, energy, learning, parenthood, resources, and livelihood issues. It focuses on issues relating to power sector reforms and regulation. It conducted a survey of electricity regulatory commissions in India to assess the adequacy of their resources and to analyze the degree of transparency and public participation in regulatory processes. A Panel of Eminent Persons, comprising three experts, commented on the survey questionnaire and the final report presenting survey results. The report has heavy emphasis on governance issues.

Principal Findings

The report finds that regulatory governance can be improved in various areas.

Governance

The report finds that the autonomy and independence of the regulatory agencies need to be improved considerably and that the regulatory processes are deficient in the areas of accountability, transparency, and public participation.

Autonomy and Independence

- Most electricity regulatory commissions (ERCs) are dependent on the government for financial resources. With two exceptions, any fees or charges received from the market participants must be deposited with the government, and the commissions cannot use these funds for their own expenditures. More than half the ERCs covered in the survey received less than 70 percent of the budget they requested in at least one of the past two years.
- Most of the ERCs have no permanent staff for performing crucial technical, financial, economic, and legal functions. This is caused, in part, by the widespread practice of appointing staff on deputation or contract.

G

Accountability, Transparency, and Public Participation

- The orders issued by the ERCs are not sufficiently comprehensive and self-contained. This makes it difficult to understand the rationales for the decisions and consequently dilutes the accountability of the ERCs.
- Many ERCs have either submitted annual reports with significant detail or have not submitted them at all. Where they exist, annual reports of the ERCs have tended to be cryptic and superficial.
- Although all the ERCs surveyed reported that all proceedings were open to the public and that they have ensured full transparency in their processes, in practice, few commissions seem to have taken adequate steps to operationalize transparency. As a result, public participation in the regulatory process is restricted only to the public hearings conducted during the tariff revision process.
- Governments and utilities appear not to be sufficiently committed to their new roles in the new sector structure. Governments are lax in appointing new commissioners, they provide inadequate financial support, and they do not make significant attempts to ensure public participation. Some governments go one step beyond noncooperation and actively try to restrict the autonomy and powers of the ERCs. Utilities fail to submit data required by the ERCs, they refuse to undertake studies necessary for the regulation of investments by the ERCs, and they delay implementation of key performance and evaluation systems that would facilitate public scrutiny of their performance. Utilities also resort to litigation as a means to oppose or at least delay crucial regulatory actions.
- There have also been instances where the positions of powerful vested interests in the government and private or public utilities have led to blatant violations of law.

Principal Recommendations

The report proposes a range of solutions to address the issues identified during the analysis.

Governance

The regulatory governance issues addressed by the recommendations focus on two main areas: the autonomy and independence of the regulatory agencies, and accountability, transparency, and public participation in regulatory processes.

Autonomy and Independence

- The effectiveness of the ERCs should be enhanced by making commissioner appointment and removal procedures more objective and free from political interference, through the creation of a standing statutory committee in charge of the selection of

G

the members of state ERCs, by not allowing persons known to represent certain political interests as commissioners, and through various other measures.

- There should be no statutory provision for the government to issue directives to the ERCs.
- Commissioners, upon the end of their term, should not be allowed to accept any form of employment with any utility or on any power project in the state they serve.
- To ensure that the ERCs perform their functions effectively, all the regulatory, licensing, and other related powers of the ERCs assigned to them in the ERC Act of 1998 should be incorporated as inherent powers of the ERCs.
- The primary accountability of the ERCs should be to the parliament or the concerned state legislature.
- To prevent governments from using the ERCs' financial dependence to their benefit, the financial autonomy of the commissions needs to be ensured by allowing them to impose a small surcharge on electricity consumption in their states and making sure that the collected funds are fully at the disposal of the commissions.
- Each ERC should have at least a few permanent staff members in order to develop an institutional memory and to ensure consistency in decisions and regulatory approach. The ERCs should have reasonable pay scales to be able to attract and retain capable staff.
- The procedures for selection and appointment of commissioners needs to be improved to ensure timely appointments, sufficiently long tenures, and enhanced transparency through the incorporation of some new provisions in the governing laws of the ERCs.
- After consultation with different stakeholders, a voluntary Code of Conduct should be developed for regulators and the regulatory process.
- Active public participation, especially from civil society institutions, is necessary to support effective regulatory processes and to prevent vested interests from sabotaging the newly created ERCs.

Accountability, Transparency, and Public Participation

- The ERCs should submit their annual reports to the parliament or the concerned legislature within the prescribed time limit, and the legislatures should be notified of any breach of this legal requirement.
- The ERCs' annual reports should contain explicit disclosures on the public hearings held and the orders issued, and on whether they were implemented by the concerned government or utility. The annual reports should also indicate any directives, as well as any administrative and financial constraints, imposed on them by the government.
- Remedies to enhance public participation and transparency include setting up a system for informing the public about the content of the hearings, organizing workshops and training courses, providing information on regulations and orders in all local languages, and enhancing consumer participation.

G

- The relevant laws should provide for the creation of new institutional structures, similar to the "Office of Public Advocate," which would be in charge of public information efforts, actively participating in all cases before the commission, and acting as a party in all of them by representing and protecting consumer interests and creating consumer awareness.
- Governments, through their relevant agencies, should be required to develop specific programs for supporting consumer groups, awareness creation, capacity building, and training, along with funding support.
- A "nodal agency" should be created to develop coordination and networking between civil society institutions by acting as the central information clearinghouse and as a forum for regular interaction.
- Academic institutions should be encouraged to help interested civil society groups and to contribute to the regulatory process.
- Academic courses, ranging from two-year postgraduate degrees to short-term diploma and certificate courses, can be created.
- Regulatory commissions should make efforts to produce as many documents in local languages as possible.
- The civil society groups that are already active in the regulatory process should form a "Citizens' Coalition on Electricity Regulation" that could host joint efforts by its members to create public awareness and build capacity.

G

Russia

Title: Policy Perspective and Analysis of the Regulatory Regime in the Restructured Russian Power Sector
Author: Ashley C. Brown
Context: Prepared in 2004 for the World Bank as part of an overall assessment of the state of Russian power sector reform.
Level of Assessment: Mid-level
Availability: http://www.worldbank.org.ru/

Background

This report analyzes the proposed regulatory regime for the Russian power sector from practical and policy perspectives. It was prepared as part of an ongoing dialogue between the World Bank and the Russian government.

Principal Findings

The report finds that the proposed regulatory structure is complicated. It then identifies specific areas where it can be enhanced.

Governance

The report identifies several areas where regulatory governance can be improved, ranging from the allocation of regulatory tasks to regulatory independence and transparency, and the human and financial resources required for the performance of regulatory functions, as well as specific issues, such as tariff-setting, accounting, and market monitoring.

Overall Regulatory Framework

The proposed regulatory structure is complicated. It consists of a web of state regulatory agencies and ministries at national and regional levels, each responsible for separate regulatory tasks, such as market monitoring, market power mitigation, implementing and enforcing of market rules, service quality regulation, tariff-setting, tariff supervision, and establishing of rules and methodologies for formulating tariffs. This division of responsibility is further complicated by the fact that these agencies report to different parts of the government.

Allocation of Regulatory Tasks

Within this complex regulatory framework, it is unclear which entity is in charge of critical responsibilities. The problem of fractured regulatory jurisdiction is compounded by the fact that authority is divided among agencies with uncertain levels of discretion and varying degrees of independence and autonomy.

G

Regulatory Independence and Transparency

The overall independence of the regulatory regime from both government and vested private interests appears seriously compromised. The regulatory agencies derive their authority from a variety of laws. The statutes adopted from those laws generally delegate power to the government, not directly to the regulator. Hence, the regulators derive their power from a subdelegation of authority from the government, which suggests that the government has considerable discretion to remove the authority it has delegated. The ability of private companies to require confidential treatment of any information they provide to the regulatory agencies hampers regulatory transparency.

Regulatory Decisions

The decisionmaking process under the new model is, at present, highly uncertain. Not all the regulatory agencies have clearly defined decisionmaking processes.

Market Monitoring

The regulatory responsibilities for promoting, maintaining, and monitoring competition in generation markets are highly diffused among different agencies and may prove to be ineffective.

Tariffs

At present, distribution tariffs are set through a complicated, three-step process involving the regional electricity commissions, the Federal Tariffs Service, and the Ministry of Economic Development and Trade. The tariffs rarely include incentives to reduce costs, improve productivity, or cut losses. The regulators will face the difficult tasks of deciding what energy and supply contract costs to pass through to consumers. It is also unclear what approach will be used to reduce and eventually eliminate cross-subsidies embedded in existing tariffs.

Cross-Subsidies

The elimination, or even substantial reduction, of cross-subsidies will be a difficult and contentious process, because it runs counter to the traditional ways tariffs were negotiated and will lead to rate shocks and worse for many customers.

Accounting Practices

The regulators appear to lack authority to impose specific accounting requirements for purposes of regulation. The deficiency in legal accounting powers is compounded by a shortage of personnel in regulatory agencies that could perform audits of the information submitted.

Flow of Information

The lack of information flow needed for both regulation and effective market monitoring is caused by inadequate metering.

Ethics

The only ethical standards applicable to the personnel of the regulatory agencies are general provisions of law that are applicable to the Russian civil service as a whole. The general ethical rules are inadequate for regulatory agency staff, given the nature and sensitivity of electricity regulation.

Human Resources

The human resources required for the multiple regulatory functions required to implement the new sector model are insufficient at present. The compensation packages for regulatory personnel are inadequate for the recruitment and retention of a fully trained, technically competent, professional staff.

Financial Resources

The current practice of funding regulatory activities out of general treasury funds leaves the door wide open to political retaliation against regulators through budgetary actions, to cross-subsidies to rate payers from taxpayers, and to destabilization of regulatory activities.

Principal Recommendations

The report provides a comprehensive set of recommendations to address specific issues related to regulatory governance and substance.

Governance

With respect to regulatory governance, the recommendations of the report include a focus on the overall regulatory framework, as well as specific issues of market monitoring, tariff-setting, appeals, human resources of the regulatory agencies, and ethics.

Overall Framework

The regulatory framework should be reviewed to ensure harmonious, consistent, coherent and comprehensive interaction between the relevant agencies. If that is not legally possible, its complexity should be reduced through merging of functions or institutions, or both, and establishing clear division of responsibilities.

G

The decisionmaking processes of all regulatory agencies should be more transparent, more user friendly, and more informative. All decisions should be written in a consistent and systematic format. Submissions and other material, such as consultant reports or research commissioned by the stakeholders or the regulator, should be in the public record. All communications between regulators and the government and/or commercial entities on pending regulatory matters should be made part of the public record.

Market Monitoring

Policies and procedures for promoting, maintaining, and monitoring competition in generation markets should be carefully coordinated. The responsibilities of relevant agencies should be clearly defined, and the necessary information collection systems should be in place before the market becomes operational. Required information should be shared among agencies.

Tariff-Setting

A clear understanding of the allocation of regulatory responsibilities needs to be in place, and all relevant institutions involved in the tariff-setting process should work in order to build human and technical capacity swiftly, so that they can perform the necessary regulatory tasks.

Appellate Bodies

It would be desirable to establish a single, specialized appellate tribunal to hear regulatory appeals. In case of an appeal, the decision of the regulatory agency should be presumed to be valid until adjudged otherwise by the appellate forum. The only circumstance where the implementation of a decision should be delayed is upon successful application by an appealing party to either the regulatory agency or the appellate forum for an order to delay implementation.

Human Resources

The regulatory agencies should assess their human resources requirements and inform the government. The issue of compensation of regulatory staff should be considered together with stricter ethics rules, so that higher salaries are linked to restrictions on the job mobility and investment opportunities for regulatory personnel.

Ethics

An ethics code applicable to all regulatory officials should be written and adopted. This code should cover subjects such as prohibitions on conflicts of interest, acceptance of gratuities, accepting employment in regulated companies, financial disclosure of holdings by regulatory officials, and rules concerning communications with regulated companies or traders in the securities of such firms.

Substance

The report makes specific recommendations on tariffs and subsidies.

Tariffs

To the extent that price caps for particular customer classes or limitations on pricing methodologies are necessary, they should be specified, as far as possible, at the outset in the framework within which the regulator operates rather than imposed on an ad hoc basis by the government. There needs to be an open and public debate on what methodology should be used to establish tariffs for monopoly services and the providers of last resort obligation. Clear rules need to be developed for the pass-through of energy costs. Before the market becomes operational, the Federal Anti-Monopoly Service should publish the criteria that might cause a plant to be subjected to tariff regulation, how often its status will be reviewed, and under what circumstances its tariff status will be changed.

Subsidies

The government should publish a plan for the gradual phasing out of subsidies and solicit public comment to stimulate a national debate. A public education campaign should be implemented to acquaint all consumers with the plans and to help them cope with the consequences. The necessity to alleviate the effect of the removal of cross-subsidies through such measures as subsidies to low-income households should be made an explicit part of the public debate.

G

South Africa

Title: Review of the Effectiveness of Utility Regulation in South Africa
Author: Grove Steyn
Context: Prepared for the Office of the Presidency of South Africa as part of a broader 10-year review of the effect of regulators.
Level of Assessment: Mid-level
Availability: Contact the Office of the Presidency.

Background

This report provides an overview of regulatory governance and substance issues facing the power sector in South Africa. It reviews the institutional structure of the National Electricity Regulator (NER), its mandate, resources, and organization, as well as its activities.

Principal Findings

The report identifies areas where the South African electricity sector regulatory framework can be further improved.

Governance

The report identifies a set of issues concerning regulatory governance.

- Much work remains to be done in building necessary institutional capacity.
- The NER has experienced long delays while the Department of Minerals and Energy and the Department of Finance processed its budget requests. As a consequence, the NER has been forced to make unauthorized expenditures during the early months of some fiscal years.
- The NER is substantially under-resourced in skilled personnel, which has hindered its performance. The problem will get worse as the reform process evolves.
- Although the NER states that it encourages participation, most regulatory procedures and decisions are not open to the public in practice.

Substance

The report discusses the NER's regulatory performance and focuses on specific regulatory substance issues.

- The NER has made significant progress in improving Eskom's governance, limiting price increases, rationalizing municipal tariff structures, reducing disparities in price levels, and facilitating progress in sector reform.
- The delays and uncertainties in the restructuring of the electricity distribution subsector have had a significant effect on the ability of the NER to regulate the sector.

G

- The government envisages a "managed" liberalization, whereby the vertically integrated utility Eskom will be unbundled and two state-owned companies will be created—one for transmission and one for generation. Thirty percent of the generation assets of this company would be divested and the remaining power plants would be organized into clusters that would compete with each other in the open market while still under public ownership. The state-owned generation company will not be allowed to construct new generation capacity.
- The government's current power sector liberalization policy leaves the NER with a dilemma with respect to new generation capacity. It is projected that new capacity will be needed by 2007 to meet growing demand. Calling upon Eskom to provide the new capacity would strengthen its dominance and hamper the development of competition.
- The NER does not have the ability to do a full cost review to implement its rate of return tariff-setting methodology.
- The NER has made significant gains with respect to price regulation, but it has not been able to create managerial incentives for efficient behavior by Eskom and the municipal distributors.
- Issues that need to be addressed include the methodology for price regulation, the allocation of Eskom's financial resources, regulation of local authority distributors, policy development, regulatory independence, and securing of new generation investments.

Principal Recommendations

The report makes a set of recommendations to address the issues identified during the analysis.

Governance

With respect to regulatory governance, recommendations focus on capacity building, transparency, participation and accountability in regulatory processes, and appeals mechanisms.

Improvements are needed in governance and accountability, in the NER's resources, and in transparency of processes.

Capacity Building

Institutional capacity should be enhanced by development of internal technical competencies in the NER, the regulated firms, potential entrants, the government, the press, and consumers.

Transparency and Public Participation

As sector reform progresses, it will be imperative that the NER's decisionmaking processes become more transparent and enable public participation. Greater transparency, public awareness, and access to the regulatory process should be encouraged.

G

Accountability

Given the limited resources of the Department of Minerals and Energy to monitor NER activities, it is important that the NER should regularly appear before the Parliament to report on its activities.

Appeals

Potential conflicts of jurisdiction that may exist between the NER and the Minister of Minerals and Energy should be resolved, for instance, through making matters of substance appealable to the Competition Tribunal.

Substance

Recommendations specific to regulatory substance cover issues such as price regulation, clarity of policy, and the construction of new generation capacity, among others.

- In order to implement the rate of return methodology, the NER should use independent auditors for future Eskom price reviews.
- The NER should consider other forms of price regulation, such as incentive-based systems, profit-sharing arrangements, or a combination of the two, because they could provide more certainty of regulatory outcomes and create efficiency incentives that do not currently exist.
- The government will have to resolve the uncertainties caused by policy contradictions and expedite the electricity supply industry reform process.
- In relation to the construction of new generation capacity, interim procedures to facilitate investment in the generation subsector should be developed to avoid obstructing the movement to a more fully competitive market at a later stage. An interim arrangement for generation investment is likely to rely substantially on the NER as the only technically competent body independent of Eskom. This role, in turn, will necessitate new capabilities for the NER.

G

Ukraine

Title: Strengthening the Administrative and Financial Independence of the Sector's Regulator
Author: Rafael Moscote
Context: One section of a World Bank–financed report on the power sector of the Ukraine.
Level of Assessment: Mid-level
Availability: Contact the National Electricity Regulatory Commission.

Background

This report outlines the current legal framework applicable to the electricity sector in Ukraine, discusses the status of the National Energy Regulatory Commission (NERC), describes novel features of proposed legislation, identifies the shortcomings of the proposed legislation, and makes recommendations to improve the regulatory framework.

Principal Findings

The report reviews the regulatory governance and substance issues and identifies problem areas.

Governance

The report finds that further improvements are needed for NERC's regulatory independence, its authority over tariff-setting, market monitoring, investment review, and quality of service, and that in most cases the proposed law falls short of adequately addressing main issues.

Independence

The NERC falls short of being a wholly independent regulatory agency, because it lacks financial, administrative, and organizational independence from the executive branch of the government and from the industry's interests in a sector with significant state ownership of assets. A recently approved law imposes further restrictions on its independence by making the commission's decisions subject to the Cabinet of Ministers and a specially authorized central body. A new proposed law on the organizational and legal bases of state regulation of natural monopolies and markets in Ukraine's energy sector includes provisions that may address some of the concerns relating to the NERC's lack of independence. However, the draft law does not adequately address the issue of administrative, organizational, or financial independence.

Tariff-Setting Authority

The NERC does not currently regulate residential prices. This regulatory task is carried out by the Cabinet of Ministers even though the law laying out the NERC's functions and its relations with other government entities assigns this task to the regulatory agency.

G

331

Investment Review Authority

The NERC reviews investments of the privately owned entities in the sector, whereas the Ministry of Fuel and Energy performs this task for state-owned enterprises in its capacity as a representative of the shareholders.

Authority over the Wholesale Market

The NERC does not have sufficient authority over the wholesale electricity market or its participants. Neither is it able to monitor the operation of the market, as well as the pricing of the energy bought and sold in the market, or to promote competition and penalize non-competitive practices in the market.

Quality of Service

The NERC has not set any service quality standards. The only standards that exist are a set of basic technical parameters, and no government body monitors compliance with these standards, except in the case of specific complaints by customers.

Principal Recommendations

In order to address the issues identified, the report makes a set of recommendations.

Governance

The report recommends that the draft law should do the following:

- Enable the NERC to operate without interference from other governmental bodies by establishing that its decisions will not be subject to state registration procedures that allow the Ministry of Justice to refuse registration of NERC decisions if the ministry concludes that the decision is in conflict with Ukrainian or EC legislation, and by exempting the NERC from the provisions of the recent law that requires its decisions to be reviewed by a special state committee.
- Allow the NERC to set its own staffing and salary policies.
- Establish a source of funding for the NERC that is separate from budget allocations, as well as set an overall limit for its expenditures.
- Incorporate specific provisions with respect to the NERC's functions, rights, and limitations, including its rights to access information necessary to perform its regulatory functions, to determine standard accounting methods, to impose prespecified penalties in case of regulated parties' noncompliance with the regulatory framework, to require access to networks and interconnections, to approve or object to mergers and acquisitions

in the sector, and to establish an obligation to respect the confidentiality of commercially sensitive information.

- Include measures to ensure the NERC's accountability by providing for annual or biannual public review of its activities by legislative and executive authorities designated by law.
- Ensure that the NERC's activities, proceedings, communications, and findings are subject to an appropriate level of transparency.
- Concentrate all tariff-setting responsibilities exclusively in the NERC and provide for clear policy guidelines on social goals to be achieved through tariffs or subsidies, or both.
- Authorize the NERC to use benchmarking as an instrument for tariff regulation.
- Specify the NERC's responsibility with respect to customer protection measures, especially quality-of-service standards.

Substance

The report recommends the following:

- With respect to the wholesale market, the NERC should consider allowing regulated plants to quote prices in response to the requests for proposals to be issued by distribution companies, or alternatively, it should regulate the prices so that they reflect all relevant economic costs, including capital costs at replacement value instead of just short-term operating and maintenance costs.
- The NERC should ensure that transmission tariffs include all capital costs and that the tariffs reflect congestion or the relative scarcity of transmission capacity at different points on the network.
- The NERC should begin to set targets for quality of electricity supply both for distribution and transmission service providers.

G

Alternative Regulatory Governance Models

Although the independent regulator model is the governance model underlying the handbook's questionnaires and interview guidelines, we must point out that it is only one of several possible regulatory governance models. The purpose of this appendix is to give an overview of other types of regulatory systems. This is done by comparing and contrasting two major regulatory governance models: (a) the independent regulator model as it has evolved in the United States and other English-speaking countries; and (b) the public service concession model as it has evolved in the French water industry and elsewhere. This is then followed by a description of some hybrid models that have emerged in a number of developing countries.

Regulatory systems are largely defined by four design decisions:

- Whether there is a separate, designated regulator.
- Whether the regulator has final or advisory decisionmaking authority.
- The substantive areas that have been assigned to the regulator (for example, tariff levels and structure, technical and commercial quality-of-service standards, and access condition).
- The degree of prespecificity and detail in the regulatory rules.

Inevitably, our descriptions of different regulatory systems are stylized descriptions of general characteristics. Like all generalizations, they will not be totally accurate representations of all observed variations. Instead, they describe principal characteristics and central tendencies.

H

The Anglo-American Independent Regulator Model

The Anglo-American model of regulatory governance is one variant of the independent regulator model. It has been adopted in recent years, at least on paper, in a number of developed and developing countries, including both common and civil law countries. Therefore, the "Anglo-American" designation refers more to its origin than its current locations. The U.S. version of the independent regulator model has three distinguishing features. First, U.S. regulators have significant financial, administrative, and decisionmaking independence. Second, U.S. regulators place a heavy emphasis on "due process," so that tariff proceedings often resemble court cases. And third, U.S. regulators operate under general tariff-setting principles specified in their regulatory statutes.[1]

Not all independent regulators look like the U.S. model. For example, Australia has adopted independent regulators for its state-level regulation of electricity, but the Australian and U.S. systems differ in a number of important respects.[2] For instance, in deciding tariff changes, the Australian state electricity regulators use informal consultations (such as workshops, roundtables, and forums) rather than the formal "rate cases" that are the norm in the United States. Under the Australian approach, lawyers are usually not allowed to participate in the discussions before the regulators. Even where a proceeding is labeled as a "hearing," the Australians, unlike their U.S. counterparts, do not use legal affidavits or sworn testimony. The U.K. regulatory system is closer to the Australian model in terms of process, with formal legal processes being reserved for appeals from the regulator.

Another difference is the degree of specificity in licenses. U.S. licenses tend to be very general. Most of the detailed regulatory obligations and decisions are made in a series of orders that are issued by the regulator over time. In contrast, Australian state regulators, like U.K. regulators and most new independent regulators outside the United States, employ very detailed licenses. Another difference is that Australian state regulators tend to focus on average prices or total revenues rather than individual prices and tariff structures. In contrast, U.S. regulators usually examine total revenues, as well as the prices charged to individual customer groups. Australia also uses a different governance approach for its national electricity regulator. Unlike in the United States, there is no separate federal electricity regulatory agency in Australia. Instead, all federal and interprovincial issues are handled by the Australian Competition and Consumer Commission, the national competition and consumer protection agency.[3]

Perhaps the biggest difference between U.S. independent regulators and their counterparts in other countries is the degree of prespecificity in tariff-setting systems. Most independent regulators outside the United States operate under much more detailed and prespecified tariff-setting systems than is the case in the United States, especially (a) for the first five years or so after a privatization and (b) in cases where customers are not given the legal right to choose alternative suppliers.

---

1. For a discussion of the origins of the U.S. variant of the independent regulator model and how it has spread over the past decade to developing and transition-economy countries, see Isabel Bjork and Catherine R. Connors, 2005, "Free Markets and Their Umpires: The Appeal of the U.S. Regulatory Model," *World Policy Journal* 22 (2): 51–58.
2. Eric Groom, 2005, "Perspectives on the Development of Regulation in Australia," draft, World Bank, Washington, DC, photocopy.
3. See www.acc.gov.au for more details. In 2005, the national government started a process to establish a new national energy regulator that would be called the Australian Energy Regulator. Although it would remain as a division within the Australian Competition and Consumer Commission, it would be granted administrative and decisionmaking independence by statute.

Initial post-privatization tariff-setting systems are usually established by ministers or legislatures in the context of trying to encourage private investment into power sectors that were largely publicly owned. In contrast, the typical U.S. regulatory statute usually contains very broad language that states that tariffs should be "just and reasonable" and "not unduly discriminatory." This general language means that the statute is "enabling" rather than "prescriptive." Such broad statutory language, however, does *not* mean that U.S. regulatory commissions have total discretion when setting tariffs. During the past 70 years, U.S. courts have issued many decisions that define the meaning of "just and reasonable" and "not unduly discriminatory." Taken together, these judicial decisions place significant limits on the decisionmaking discretion of U.S. regulators.

Because this body of prior judicial decisions will not exist in other countries that chose to establish a new independent regulator, most of these countries have opted to create other mechanisms to limit the discretion of their regulators, especially in their early years of operation. The most commonly used mechanism, as noted above, is a commitment to a prespecified regulatory system (for example, tariffs, quality of service, and connection obligations), which contains many of the elements of the French concession or contract model described in the next section. The tariff-setting system will often build on vesting contracts between existing generators and new distribution companies.[4]

A common confusion is to assume that "independence" is synonymous with "broad discretion." A regulator may be independent, in the sense of having final decisionmaking authority, except for court review, but this in itself does not necessarily imply that the independent regulator's decisionmaking authority will be extensive. A government may choose to assign decisionmaking authority over only a relatively small set of decisions to a new regulator. This may be done because the government perceives that investors will be reluctant to invest if they perceive that a new, untested regulator has too much discretion. Therefore, the new regulator, while having independent, final decisionmaking authority, may have this authority only for a limited set of decisions and may be tightly constrained by a prespecified tariff-setting formula for an initial tariff-setting period. Over time, the independent regulator's decisionmaking authority may be expanded.[5] Consequently, when someone says that a country has an independ-

---

4. Vesting contracts usually are assigned to distribution companies as part of a reform or privatization package. They typically are accompanied by a requirement that the regulator automatically pass through the costs of power purchases incurred by the distribution company. This requirement can have a major effect on retail tariffs because power purchase costs often constitute more than 50 percent of the final tariffs paid by the distribution company's retail customers. Such vesting contracts have been used in Argentina, El Salvador, Panama, Romania, and Uganda. See Beatriz Arizu, Luiz Maurer, and Bernard Tenenbaum, 2004, "Pass Though of Power Purchase Costs: Regulatory Challenges and International Practices," Energy and Mining Sector Board Discussion Paper 10, World Bank, Washington, DC; available at www.worldbank.org/energy.

5. Expansion of the regulator's decisionmaking authority is not inevitable. For example, Littlechild argues that the authority of the electricity regulator in England and Wales has diminished over time. See Stephen Littlechild, 2005, "Beyond Regulation," IEA/LBS Beesley Lectures on Regulation Series XV, Institute of Economic Affairs, London; pp. 3–4; available at www.iea.org.uk.

ent regulator, this characterization by itself does not reveal very much. One must ask two additional questions: Is it an independent regulator with extensive or limited regulatory responsibilities? How much discretion does it have in making decisions over the tasks it has been assigned?

The reality, then, is that discretion is limited even for independent regulatory systems. All successful independent regulatory frameworks operate with **bounded and accountable** discretion. The U.S., U.K., Australian, and similar independent regulatory models may differ to some degree in how they operate, but in all instances they operate with limits on their discretion—limits that are set by law and by evolving regulatory practice.

The Public Service Concession Model: French Water and Sanitation

In the French water and sanitation system, the dominant regulatory system is usually described as the "public service concession model."[6] It is designed to accommodate different types of long-term leasing arrangements rather than a full transfer of asset ownership to a private entity. However, for practical regulatory purposes, there is very little difference between a privatization and a long-term lease (for example, 50 years or more), and none at all if the concession holder is given a long rolling franchise period.

In the French water industry, leasing is required because French municipalities are legally prohibited from selling their water and sanitation assets to private companies.[7] Given this legal limitation on outright asset sales, public authorities in France "delegate" their public service obligation to private operators. For example, at present about 85 percent of water and sanitation services in France are provided by private operators under various types of leasing agreements.

The French regulatory model that accompanies these leasing arrangements has three distinguishing characteristics. **First, it relies on a detailed concession contract.** As a consequence, the French system is sometimes referred to as "regulation by contract." This characterization is not totally accurate, however. In particular, it does *not* mean that there is contract between a separate regulator and a regulated entity. Instead, the contract is between a municipality (which buys the services for its own facilities and acts as an agent for the citizens and commercial enterprises with-

---

6. The traditional concession model does not appear to be used in the French electricity sector. Instead, the new regulatory system for France's electricity sector combines an independent regulator to adjudicate grid access issues and bulk power market disputes (as required by the EU electricity directive) with a performance contract for EDF, the state-owned utility

7. Two African countries, Lesotho and Uganda, recently have chosen the concession model in seeking private participation in electricity distribution, even though their legal systems, unlike the French system, would permit full asset sales. It appears that the decision of both countries to pursue concessions rather than full privatization was based on political determinations that long-term concessions, in which the government retains ownership of existing assets, would be less politically controversial than full asset sales. Both countries operate under common law systems. This contradicts the conventional wisdom that concessions can be established only in civil code legal systems.

in its jurisdiction) and the private operator. The contract can take different forms: a concession contract under which the private operator has both operational and investment responsibilities and an *affermage* contract under which the private operator has operational but no investment responsibilities. For ease of exposition, we will refer to both arrangements as "concession contracts."

Second, concession contracts perform two functions in a single document. A typical concession document will transfer *operating rights* to the private operator, while at the same time also imposing *regulatory obligations* on the operator. Under the first function, the contract will transfer many of the property rights that would normally be associated with full ownership of the assets. For example, most concession contracts provide private operators with full management discretion in deciding how to operate existing assets and what new investments should be made. Under the second function, the concession contract imposes regulatory standards, targets, and obligations on the operator with respect to maximum tariff levels, required quality-of-service standards, obligations to serve new and existing customers, and procedures for the transfer and disposal of assets.[8] Consequently, the municipality is, in effect, wearing two hats. It is granting operating rights to assets it owns, and it is acting as a de facto first-level regulator.[9]

A third distinguishing characteristic of the French model is that there is no separate, designated regulator. Instead, the contract is legally enforceable by France's highest administrative court, the Conseil d'Etat. Because there is no formally designated regulator, the French model is sometimes also described as "regulation without a regulator." Although there is no formally designated water regulator, this does not mean that the two parties to the contract—the municipality and the private operator—have total freedom in designing the contract. Just as U.S. regulators are constrained by a body of law that interprets the meaning of "just and reasonable" and "not unduly discriminatory," French municipalities and water companies are constrained by several general legal doctrines that have been developed or accepted by the Conseil d'Etat. These include an operator's right to receive tariff adjustments for adverse government action (*fait du prince*), hardship (*imprévison*), and unexpected constraints (*sujétions imprévues*). Even though the French legal system is a civil law system, in this instance the regulatory system has made liberal use of "legal precedents," which are usually presumed to exist only in common law legal systems. Therefore, this is another instance where "labels" may overstate differences in actual regulatory practices.

H

---

8. These two functions do not always need be combined in a concession document. In Turkey, the government may issue two documents in conjunction with private participation in electricity distribution: a concession to transfer long-term operating and investment rights to the private operator and a license to impose regulatory obligations on the operator. Lesotho and Uganda also are using separate concession and license documents.

9. The specific terms and conditions of the concession contract usually are not developed de novo by each municipality. Most French municipalities rely on "model" concession contracts developed by a central government ministry or an association of French municipalities. Similar model documents exist for the rural and peri-urban private water operators in Paraguay and have been proposed for the several hundred private operators of electricity minigrids in Cambodia. A minigrid is an autonomously run distribution system that may or may not be physically connected to the main high-voltage grid.

Some have asserted that, even though the Conseil d'Etat is not designated as a sector regulator, it effectively functions as a "quasi-regulator" or "super-regulator" because it performs at least one of the traditional functions of a regulator: it resolves disputes between customers (the municipalities) and suppliers (the private operators).[10] Moreover, through a series of decisions, the Conseil d'Etat has effectively modified the acceptable tariff-setting system from a fixed price cap with no adjustments allowed for the contract period to a cost-of-service tariff regime with indexed adjustments for input cost changes. Arguably, these actions of the Conseil d'Etat, although embedded in a different institutional and philosophical framework, have led to regulatory processes and day-to-day regulatory actions that are not very different from those in the England and Wales water industry, which combines privatization with long rolling franchises and an independent regulator (Ofwat).

Hybrid Models

The U.S. regulatory model is not the only possible version of the independent regulator model, nor is the French regulatory model the only possible version of the "regulation by contract" model. *A country need not be limited to choosing either the French or the Anglo-American model of regulation.* Moreover, the French and Anglo-American systems are not mutually exclusive. Some common law (United Kingdom and Uganda) and civil law (Brazil and Romania) countries have combined independent regulators (the U.S. or other variants) with a detailed and prespecified tariff-setting system (the French model). Such hybrid regulatory arrangements have been used for both long-term leasing of government-owned assets and full asset transfers.

In the United Kingdom, most utility sector regulation relies on an independent regulator to interpret and modify fairly detailed licenses. Even within the United Kingdom, however, other regulatory governance models exist. For example, U.K. railway regulation has substantial contract elements, and the London Underground has a 30-year, private-public partnership concessions overseen by a private-public partnership arbiter, the PPP Arbiter—an entity that is somewhere between a regulator and an arbitrator.[11]

Among these hybrid regulatory systems exist many variations. In many developing countries, the tariff-setting system may be established by a ministry as part of the bidding or negotiation process with private operators, and then administered by a regulator *either* (a) on an advisory basis *or* (b) on a full decisionmaking basis. In either case, the regulator, although independent, will have limited discretion with respect to setting tariffs for distribution entities,

---

10. **Frilet** (2004) and **Pezon** (2003). The Pezon article provides a comprehensive historical review of disputes before the Conseil d'Etat. It can be downloaded at www.isnie.org.
11. For more details on the role, powers, and duties of the PPP Arbiter, see http://www.ppparbiter.org.uk.

at least for an initial post-privatization period. For the initial period, the regulator essentially monitors a tariff-setting system that has been negotiated by a minister.[12]

This does not mean that the regulator's discretion is constrained in all areas, however. A regulator that finds itself limited to supervising a prespecified tariff system for distribution entities may have at the same time considerably more discretion over market monitoring and the terms and conditions for granting access to the transmission and distribution grids.

What Are the Differences between the Anglo-American and French Regulatory Models?

Several fundamental differences in philosophy exist between the Anglo-American and French approaches to regulation, although, as we have suggested, the practical differences are more often less pronounced than the labels would seem to imply, especially in infrastructure industries involving private finance for investment.

The Anglo-American approach, as embodied in the independent regulator model, tries to "depoliticize" economic regulation. In other words, it tries to remove politics and government (at least in the form of ministries) from the business of regulation once a separate or independent regulator has been established. In contrast, the French concession approach seems to start with the presumption that the concept of an independent regulator is naïve and unworkable— government cannot and should not be removed from the business of specifying public service obligations. Instead, the traditional French solution is to specify the obligations and responsibilities of the two parties with more precision and with a well-functioning backup dispute resolution system, so that each party will have confidence in the commitments of the other.

The philosophical underpinnings of the French and the Anglo-American regulatory systems also appear to differ in another important way. The French tradition is that the provision of a "public service" is a government responsibility. Although a government may choose to delegate the "management" of this public service to a private entity, the ultimate responsibility for providing this service still remains with the government. In the Anglo-American tradition, there is no inherent presumption that utility services are necessarily government responsibilities.

Nevertheless, all countries accept, in practice, that services, such as the provision of electricity and water, are affected by "public interest" considerations, so that a government may want to achieve certain social outcomes that a private company would not pursue on its own volition. In addition, governments typically include strong safeguards in the regulatory framework, such as maintenance of service (for example, the U.K. legal provisions for electricity "suppliers of last resort"). In consequence, in all countries using the Anglo-American model, governments accept

H

---

12. This is sometimes described as "hardwiring" of the tariff-setting system.

that they have a strong political responsibility to ensure supplies of electricity, water, and similar, and to restore them as quickly as possible after any crisis-induced breakdown.[13]

Therefore, in the Anglo-American system, the normal freedom of private enterprises to run their businesses as they see fit is considerably restricted to satisfy these public interest considerations. In addition, the design of the regulatory system imposes considerable limits on the freedom of the regulated enterprise in electricity and some other infrastructure industries. So, again, it could be argued that the practical differences between the Anglo-American and French regulatory systems over the role of government in maintaining supply in important infrastructure industries are, in practice, more ones of emphasis than anything fundamental.

Most developing countries have decided that some government entity, usually other than the regulator, must develop the initial "regulatory deal" in a contract or concession. This is clearly in the French tradition. However, once the agreement is in place, most developing countries have chosen to establish a separate or independent regulator to monitor and enforce compliance with the terms of the contract or concession. This is clearly in the Anglo-American tradition.

It appears that many developing countries have chosen this hybrid approach for two reasons. First, most developing countries simply do not have a credible administrative court such as the French Conseil d'Etat to perform the dispute resolution and regulatory functions. Second, if the reform involves new entities and a variety of transactions, it will be difficult, if not impossible, to prespecify all the necessary commercial and technical relationships in one or more contracts.[14] Alternatively, if such contracts exist, they will need some entity to facilitate changes over time. The presumption is that a technically competent regulator will be better able to do this than a court.

What Are the Elements of a Hybrid Regulatory Approach?

This hybrid approach can be thought of as a "third way" because it combines the independent regulator from the Anglo-American regulatory system with the detailed, prespecified tariff-setting system of the French regulatory system.[15] Depending on a country's legal system, this

---

13. The United Kingdom's and other countries' regulatory laws include force majeure clauses that allow for the temporary suspension of markets and regulators where there are states of emergency creating major supply disruptions.

14. Prosser expresses skepticism about the durability of regulatory contracts for other reasons. While accepting that regulatory contracts may be workable for some limited elements of regulation (for example, an initial multiyear tariff-setting system), he argues that they cannot be the dominant or durable regulatory model because "regulators have to have regard to a wide range of interests in reaching decisions, not just the well being of the regulated firm . . . " (p. 45), and that "[regulatory] relationships are both too complex and too unpredictable" (p. 53) to be specified in a contract. See Tony Prosser, 2005, "Regulatory Contracts and Stakeholder Regulation," *Annals of Public and Cooperative Economics* 76: 35–57.

15. This hybrid approach is not limited to power sector regulation. A very similar hybrid arrangement has emerged

commitment to a prespecified tariff system, which could be described as a prespecified regulatory contract, might exist in one of the following forms:

- A license.
- A concession agreement.[16]
- A privatization support agreement.
- A tariff order of the regulatory entity.
- Some combination of legal documents.

The specific substantive elements of a regulatory contract may vary significantly depending on who established the agreement within the government (for example, a ministry, the parliament, or the regulator). However, if the contract is to be of any practical use, it needs to include elements such as the following:

- Its duration.
- Its level of specificity with respect to important tariff elements.
- How risks are shared.
- The level of legal commitment on the government's side.
- The extent to which it is legally enforceable.[17]
- How tariffs are reset at the end of the first tariff-setting period.[18]
- The extent to which other government entities, such as ministries and municipalities, will administer elements of the contract.[19]

H

---

in Latin American regulation of water and sanitation. See Vivien Foster, 2005, "Ten Years of Water Service Reform in Latin America: Toward an Anglo-French Model," Water Supply and Sanitation Discussion Paper Series 3, World Bank, Washington, DC, p. 5; available at www.worldbank.org/watsan.

16. A concession will transfer operating rights of government-owned facilities to a private operator while imposing regulatory rules and obligations on the operator. A license is a more limited document. It does not transfer operating rights to the licensee. Instead, it just specifies regulatory rules and obligations. The advantage of concessions and licenses is that they allow a government to specify regulations on an individualized basis.

17. Strictly speaking, in most legal systems a "promise" is not a contract unless it is legally enforceable.

18. Drawing on their water sector experience, Shugart and Ballance argue that regulatory contracts are most likely to fail at the end of the first tariff-setting period. As an alternative to independent regulators with considerable discretionary power, they argue that tariff levels should be reset using expert panels given detailed guidelines. See **Shugart and Ballance** (2005).

19. For example, when there are many small entities providing service, such as the 1,700 water and sanitation providers in Colombia and the several hundred minigrid operators in Cambodia, it will be neither possible nor desirable for a national regulator to try to actively regulate these entities. Therefore, Section 79 of the Colombian national water law explicitly allows provinces and municipalities to act on behalf of the national water regulator. Any agreements that these subnational entities reach with private operators, whether through a concession or lease, are required to be consistent with general principles enunciated by the national water regulator. In practice, it is unclear if the national regulator does much actual monitoring. Similar arrangements exist in rural electrification. For example, in Cambodia the national electricity regulator has approved a license that uses a

Therefore, the concept of a "regulatory contract" is very broad and can mean very different things depending on the specifics of the arrangement. We observe various combinations of regulation and contracts in different countries.[20] However, this hybrid approach—the combination of a prespecified tariff-setting system with a separate regulatory entity that has either advisory or final decisionmaking authority over implementation of the tariff-setting system—has, in fact, become the most common regulatory governance model in most developing and transition economies that have created new regulatory systems.

H

village electrification committee to particularize general regulatory principles for a particular minigrid serving about 500 families. See Ky Chanthan and Jean-Pierre Mahe, 2005, "Rehabilitation of a Rural Electricity System: Smau Khney Village, Trapeang Sab Commune, Bati District, Takeo Province, Cambodia," General Report GRET and Kosan Engineering, Phnom Penh; available at www.gret.org.

20. The different variations of prespecified regulatory agreements are discussed more fully in chapter 4.

Infrastructure Regulation in Failed States and Post-Conflict Countries

The World Bank has recently published some major research on the provision of infrastructural services and the role of private finance in infrastructure in post-conflict societies (that is, countries emerging from war or prolonged periods of civil conflict), including Somalia, which, post-1991, was a clear example of a failed state. Post-conflict countries (and even more failed states) are classic instances of countries with few effectively functioning governmental institutions.[1]

In both cases, privately owned and operated infrastructure companies have been important and have provided significant amounts of reasonable quality service—both in absolute terms and relative to neighboring stable countries. However, the limits on the development of the utility industries from the absence of any regulatory oversight—or, in Somalia's case, any stable, formal mechanisms for institutional contract enforcement—provide clear boundaries on how far the industries can expand their services. The extremely limited contractual and regulatory framework also creates major network coordination and rollout problems once initial, more easily satisfied demands have been met.

Options for Failed States:
Infrastructure Development in Somalia

Somalia has had no recognized government since 1991, and a recent World Bank paper describes the country as "the quintessential failed state." There are several local currencies, and the legal system for commercial matters "is either fully dysfunctional or riddled by delays and corruption."[2] Nevertheless, telecom services are functioning to a remarkably widespread de-

---

1. Most of these countries are in the bottom third of the Kaufmann rule of law index.
2. See Tatiana Nenova, 2004, "Private Sector Response to the Absence of Government Institutions in Somalia," World Bank, Washington, DC, photocopy, p. 9; available at http://rru.worldbank.org/Documents/PapersLinks/Nenova-Somalia-PrivateSector.pdf. See also Tatiana Nenova and Tim Harford, 2004, "Anarchy and Invention: How Does Somalia's Private Sector Cope without Government?" Public Policy for the Private Sector Note 280, World Bank, Washington, DC.

gree, considering the circumstances. Urban electricity is available to a lesser extent, including to areas that were unserved before 1991—and at reasonable prices relative to those in neighboring countries. The quality of service is markedly less adequate for water, roads, and airports.

Telecommunications

Mobile telecom services have flourished with call rates for local service of US$0.10 per minute and 15 telephones per 1,000 people as of 2002—a coverage rate that is 50 percent higher than in neighboring countries or West Africa in general. Overall, there are 112,000 fixed lines and 50,000 mobile subscribers relative to 17,000 fixed lines in 1991. The absence of any regulatory agency also means, however, that first, there is no standardization of numbers or frequencies, and second, interconnection between operators has been limited. However, interconnection in Mogadishu has been achieved by negotiations within the Somali Telecom Association, and set up with the help of the ITU. The issue of settling interpayments remains to be resolved.

Electricity

A number of cities have supplies of electricity where local monopoly suppliers combine generation from secondhand generators imported from Dubai and supply electricity over local distribution networks.[3] Customers are offered three choices of service—evenings only, daytime only, or 24 hours—and households are charged according to the number of lightbulbs in the dwelling (that is, a daily tariff rate of US$0.35 per light bulb). The private contracts that are observed in Somalia represent a form of "quasi-regulation." This arrangement may or may not lead to a more formal regulatory system.

There are limits to the type of investments and industry structures that can be supported by these quasi-regulatory arrangements. As in the United Kingdom before 1914, the Somalian system of local "island" monopolies is likely to run into difficulties in creating citywide or regional power companies that could benefit from economies of scale and more efficient generation usage. In addition, these private contractual arrangements cannot support regional or national electricity systems. For example, in Somalia there have been no major new investments in new generation, or in transmission or distribution networks. This suggests that the expansion of

---

3. Similar informal and non-interconnected minigrid systems exist in Bolivia, Cambodia, Ethiopia, and Indonesia. As Reiche, Tenenbaum, and Torres point out, these are spontaneous, "bottom-up" investments that are not the result of any "top-down" government program. Kilian Reiche, Bernard Tenenbaum, and Clemencia Torres, forthcoming, "Promoting Electrification: Regulatory Principles and a Model Law," Energy and Mining Sector Board Discussion Paper, World Bank, Washington, DC.

electricity service in Somalia may be reaching its limits in the absence of a more formal system of regulation.[4]

What actions would be required to support a better-functioning and more efficient electricity sector in other failed states or post-conflict countries? Initially, the following steps would seem to be priorities:

1. Developing a greater ability to write, monitor, and enforce commercial contracts.
2. Establishing dispute resolution procedures that can go beyond the current informal, clan, or religious grouping arrangements.
3. Improved coordination between supplying companies to help develop and extend the market served.

Note that none of these actions require the existence of a formal regulator, either inside or outside a ministry.

A second level of formalization would require several additional actions. These include the following, most of which might well require assistance from the World Bank and the donor community:

- To provide assistance in arbitration/dispute resolution (as the ITU has done in Somalia over telecom interconnection).
- To help develop more formal contracts, for example, by developing model contracts.
- To help develop contract and enforcement procedures that go beyond the current informal methods.
- To provide technical support, for example, by ensuring panels of advisers and experts who can develop a knowledge and understanding of local circumstances and be brought in at short notice.
- To provide support in establishing an understanding of infrastructure industry costs and in creating much more reliable accounting frameworks.

Some of these actions could be accomplished through conditionality clauses in regular International Development Agency or grant aid programs. These actions could be complemented through guarantee programs for initial new investments—particularly where they involve foreign investors who would otherwise not invest or would require very high-risk premiums. As is discussed in more detail below, support from the Multilateral Investment Guarantee Agency (MIGA) has been used substantially to support private finance in infrastructure in post-conflict countries.

---

4. See Nenova (2004) for a full discussion.

Options for Post-Conflict Countries

Somalia is an extreme example of a conflict country, but World Bank research by Paul Collier and associates identifies 31 conflict or post-conflict countries in 2001.[5] Schwartz, Hahn, and Bannon (2004) divide these into 25 countries with weak or nonfunctioning states (including Cambodia, the Democratic Republic of Congo [DRC], El Salvador, and Somalia,) and 5 with functioning states, but serious regional conflicts (including Colombia and the Philippines). The majority of the former group (19 of the 25 countries) are classified as low-income countries.[6]

A recent paper by Schwartz, Hahn, and Bannon (2004) provides a good survey of infrastructure—and the private finance of infrastructure—in conflict and post-conflict countries, including information on helpful transitional and intermediate regulatory and other steps.[7] The discussion that follows draws on this paper extensively.

Conflict countries have very low infrastructure service rates and, not surprisingly, they find it very hard to attract private investment into these industries. However, some positive level of service exists, as well as some positive level of investment, particularly from local entrepreneurs—even though the absence of effective regulatory arrangements (and, in some cases, of contract law and its enforcement) means that such investment is very limited in scale other than for mobile telephony.

In consequence, average electricity consumption was 96 kWh per capita in 2003 in conflict-affected sub-Saharan African countries as against 384 kWh per head in non–conflict-affected countries of sub-Saharan Africa. For telecoms, conflict-affected sub-Saharan African countries had 19 fixed and mobile lines per 1,000 population in 2003, compared with 67 in non–conflict-affected countries of sub-Saharan Africa.[8]

The key features of private investment flows and regulatory support by MIGA and the World Bank for the main infrastructure industries are as follows.[9]

Telecommunications

Private investment in telecoms, particularly mobile telecoms, begins to develop immediately after—or in some cases even before—the end of conflict. Mobile telecom investment does not

---

5. See Paul Collier and Anke Hoeffler, 2001, "Greed and Grievance in Civil War," World Bank, Washington, DC.
6. See Jordan Schwartz, Shelly Hahn, and Ian Bannon, 2004, "The Private Sector's Role in the Provision of Infrastructure in Post-Conflict Countries: Patterns and Policy Options," Social Development Group, Conflict Prevention and Reconstruction Working Paper 16, World Bank, Washington, DC.
7. Ibid. This paper has an extensive list of references for those who wish to follow up on this topic.
8. See Schwartz, Hahn, and Bannon (2004), table 1, p. 4.
9. The source for the private investment data is the detailed analysis by Schwartz, Hahn, and Bannon (2004) of data from the World Bank Private Participation in Infrastructure database.

appear to need specific regulatory support for relatively widespread service to appear (as was the case in Afghanistan, the DRC, El Salvador, and Iraq.

Mobile telephony is in a favorable position because the cost recovery period required for greenfield mobile investments is much shorter than for any other infrastructure industry. The absence of regulation, however, does lead to problems in mobile provision with interconnection, interference, and technical incompatibility, and the substitution of mobile for fixed telephony can lead to delays in Internet and broadband rollout.

Schwartz, Hahn, and Bannon (2004) report MIGA guarantees since 1995 for mobile telecom investments in two conflict countries with weak or nonfunctioning governmental institutions: Azerbaijan and Burundi, as well as Colombia, Indonesia, and Nigeria.

Electricity

Private investments in electricity generation and distribution only begin to develop in conflict countries after about three years post-conflict. However, they are small-scale, and it takes five or more years before large-scale construction or rehabilitation investment in generation and transmission or distribution is undertaken. This indicates the need for greater stability. Particularly in the initial years, private investment is more likely when generation and distribution or retail sales can be combined.

New-entry, small-scale electricity providers are generally important in post-conflict countries. In 2004, 9 out of 16 countries with small-scale electricity companies were post-conflict countries. In addition, some local small-scale electricity providers also start operation before the end of conflict, as was the case in Cambodia and Somalia. Unlike larger and foreign operators, they can operate on existing equipment with little or no regulatory support (this has some similarities with the late-19th-century U.K. position).

Of course, small-scale companies provide only local and sometimes interrupted service, and many do not provide power at a regulated frequency. Nevertheless, a major risk is that regulatory entities for electricity impose tough conditions on these new entrants. This has the effect of restricting their activities or forcing them out of business. Schwartz, Hahn, and Bannon (2004) call for "minimal levels of oversight to alleviate extreme cases of rent-seeking and quality of service deficiencies."[10] This judgment is one that would be well-taken by many, including the authors.

MIGA has provided risk guarantees for power sector investments in a number of developing countries but, among conflict countries, only for a few distribution companies in the Philippines. However, the World Bank's guarantee facility has been used for power sector investments in Colombia and Lebanon, as well as the Sasol natural gas project in Mozambique. Mozambique

10. Ibid., p. 8.

is the only low-income conflict-affected country where MIGA or World Bank guarantees appear to date (mid-2005) to have been used for energy-related projects.

Other infrastructure industries

The volume of private investment in conflict-affected countries in water, railways, and roads is very low and greatly delayed relative to conflict end. This reflects trends in all developing countries, particularly low-income countries.

For these industries, even more than electricity or natural gas, stability and effective regulation are crucial for investment, and conflict-affected countries are even more likely to have associated high-risk premiums. In consequence, it is harder to devise even initial contractual and regulatory arrangements for these industries that are sound enough for IFI or donor guarantee support.

Some conflict countries have legal and legislative systems that allow the writing and implementation of franchise or concession contracts or licenses (for example, Algeria, El Salvador, and the Philippines). That allows the development of *regulation by contract.* This is the first step in developing effective regulation, as occurred in the 19th century for electricity and other infrastructure industries in the United Kingdom and elsewhere, and has happened more recently in many developing countries. Regulation by contract is typically a *transitional stage* for regulation by an independent regulatory agency, but it allows us to consider these countries as having functioning governmental authority, at least for utility regulation.

Other conflict countries (for example, Rwanda, Tajikistan, and Yemen) are not yet in a position where the legal arrangements allow regulation by contract administered by the courts or a contract-monitoring body. For countries in this position, the available regulatory options are more limited and more constrained. One possibility is to provide contract enforcement by an agency outside the country, for example, an international arbitration body or an international group of experts, but this leaves major problems of enforcement within the country, which can be highly contentious politically. Otherwise, the options are likely to be very similar to those identified for Somalia, namely, technical assistance in arbitration and dispute resolution, devising of model contracts, contract monitoring and enforcement methods, establishing of costs, and accounting frameworks.

Schwartz, Hahn, and Bannon (2004) point to the potential for gradually introducing private participation in infrastructure, for example, with service or management contracts initially before progressing to leases with investment or long-term concessions. For incumbent companies, these contracts might usefully be combined with some of the basic regulatory developments suggested above. However, the clear risk is that concentrating on—and, even more, protecting—incumbents may hinder new entry, which, as in 19th-century electricity and other utilities in the United Kingdom and United States, can be very important for the long-term development of the industry. Management contracts may be more useful where privatization is less likely, at least in the near future. Hence, it has been explored more in the water and sewerage industry (for example, in South Africa).

Schwartz, Hahn, and Bannon (2004) also demonstrate how electricity investment can be supported by contracts with large new industrial consumers. This can provide the starting point for a rollout of distribution to neighboring areas, including small consumers. Policies on these lines have been tried apparently with some success in Mozambique (electricity supplies to a large aluminum plant) and, on a smaller scale, in Uganda.

These options provide both suggestions for policies to help start utility regulation in difficult circumstances and the basis for designing evaluations of existing regulatory arrangements that are in place. The latter includes potential issues and topic headings for questions in mid-level and in-depth assessments. (See appendixes C and D.)

Selected Annotated Bibliography: Evaluating the Effectiveness of Regulatory Systems for Infrastructure Industries

Note: Many documents cited in this handbook are described more fully in this annotated bibliography. To help users identify these documents, they are cited throughout the handbook in footnotes in author-date format and in boldface type. All other documents cited in footnotes are set in nonbold type; at first mention, the full bibliographic reference is given, after which the author-date format is used.

1. General Articles on the Design and Assessment of Regulatory Systems for Infrastructure Industries

Berg, Sanford V. 2000. "Sustainable Regulatory Systems: Laws, Resources, and Values." *Utilities Policy* 9: 159–70.

The article identifies organizational resources, the legal mandate, and core agency values as the three main factors that will affect regulatory performance. It describes each of these factors and explains how they affect the functioning of a regulatory agency. According to Berg, for the work of a regulatory agency to move forward, the agency must have adequate resources to perform its functions, a legal mandate that legitimizes its activities, and values or operational principles that uphold those activities. He notes that each of these factors is, in turn, shaped by the political and institutional forces that influence the associated reform process. Defining the overlap of all three factors as the "ideal state" for the realization of a regulatory agency's objectives, Berg proceeds to describe different situations that involve various permutations of the three factors and their impact on regulatory performance. The article also discusses how the three factors come into play during the life cycle of a regulatory agency, which Berg characterizes as beginning with youthful energy, protecting consumers and promoting objectives set in the legislation, but which could end up as a calcified agency that protects producers.

Available at www.sciencedirect.com/.

Castalia Strategic Advisors. 2005. "Explanatory Notes on Key Topics in the Regulation of Water and Sanitation Services." World Bank, Washington, DC.

In a series of four notes prepared for the World Bank, David Ehrhardt of Castalia Strategic Advisors asks basic questions about the design (that is, functions, organizations, and legal instruments) of regulatory systems for water and sanitation services. Ehrhardt's fundamental conclusion is that too much emphasis has been placed on creating independent regulators. He contends that regulation can be performed by a variety of institutional arrangements, not just by independent regulators. The notes describe alternative models that might be appropriate for water and sanitation services. Ehrhardt argues that the right regulatory approach will depend on the kind of problems that need to be addressed, the existing legal framework, and the levels of organizational capacity in the country. The last note contains a discussion of different approaches to regulating private participation in the water sector, focusing on the French contract-based approach and the Anglo-American independent regulator model. Ehrhardt emphasizes the need for caution in creating regulatory systems that combine these two approaches. He contends that the combination of these approaches easily could lead to "overregulation" and confusion about regulatory roles.

Available at www.castalia.fr.

Estache, Antonio. 2004a. "Emerging Infrastructure Policy Issues in Developing Countries: A Survey of the Recent Economic Literature." Policy Research Working Paper 3442, World Bank, Washington, DC.

This paper presents a succinct overview of major policy issues affecting the provision of infrastructure and infrastructure investment in developing countries in the 21st century. It covers the underlying economic problems and the contributions that academic economists have made, and it summarizes the results of applied research and relates them to policy choices. The focus is on what needs to be done to expand infrastructure services to the poor and on the role of infrastructure in delivering the Millennium Development Goals. Within this context, financing issues and regulatory challenges are discussed and related to these broader concerns.

Available at www.worldbank.org.

Gómez-Ibáñez, José. 2003. *Regulating Infrastructure: Monopoly, Contracts and Discretion.* Cambridge: Harvard University Press.

This book explores the advantages of different regulatory systems in solving the fundamental problem of "establishing a commitment to a fair and stable set of rules governing the relationship between the government and private infrastructure providers" (p. 2). Gómez-Ibáñez argues that there are three principal regulatory options: private contracts, concession contracts, and discretionary regulation. He contends that the success or failure of a regulatory system must be judged against whether the system produces outcomes that are "politically acceptable" and "economically sensible." Using these criteria and a "transaction cost" framework, he presents case studies of regulatory systems for Sri Lanka's buses, Argentina's railroads and electricity, the United States' telephones and electricity, and the United Kingdom's water and railroads. He contends that the future of private provision of infrastructure, especially in developing countries, will depend critically on the ability of governments to create regulatory systems that treat both investors and consumers fairly.

Available at www.hup.harvard.edu.

Guasch, J. Luis. 2004. *Granting and Renegotiating Infrastructure Concessions: Doing It Right.* Washington, DC: World Bank Institute.

In a very detailed empirical study, Guasch tries to determine the factors that lead to renegotiation of infrastructure concession contracts. His analysis is based on a review of the incidence of renegotiation using a large data set of more than 1,000 concession contracts in Latin America between 1985 and 2000 in the water and sanitation, roads, telecommunication, and energy sectors. He finds that more than 60 percent of infrastructure concessions are renegotiated within three years after the concession is awarded. However, the observed incidence of renegotiation is much lower in electricity, and lower still in telecommunications. For electricity, the renegotiation rate was 9 percent, and most of that was accounted for by two countries: the Dominican Republic and Honduras. Guasch's analysis shows that a concession contract is less likely to be renegotiated if a regulatory entity existed at the time the concession was awarded, the regulatory framework was embedded in a law (as opposed to a decree or just within the concession contract), tariffs were set using a cost-of-service rather than price-cap methodology, regulation was by objectives (for example, performance indexes) rather than by means (for example, level of investment), and the concession was awarded through noncompetitive bilateral negotiations rather than through competitive bidding.

Available at www-wds.worldbank.org.

Harris, Clive, and Ian Alexander. 2005. *The Regulation of Investment in Utilities: Concepts and Applications.* Washington, DC: World Bank.

This book provides an overview of different approaches for review of investments by regulated utilities. The issue of how to deal with the costs of new investments is especially important in developing countries because oftentimes the principal motivation for the sector reform is to obtain funding for new investment. Harris and Alexander's analysis focuses on issues relating to the inclusion and valuation of investment in the regulatory asset base and the recovery of the allowed investment costs through allocations between different users and between connection and usage charges. The book reviews the experience in regulating investments in various infrastructure sectors in several countries. It focuses on the regulatory approaches actually adopted and the practical implementation issues that were encountered. It concludes that the best approach will depend on the circumstances of each specific case, particularly the volume and predictability of investments. It stresses the importance of keeping the regulatory approach as simple as possible to limit compliance costs and minimize distortions to investment incentives.

Available at www.worldbank.org.

Kessides, Ioannis. 2004. *Reforming Infrastructure: Privatization, Regulation and Competition.* Washington, DC: World Bank.

The book presents a wide-ranging survey of recent infrastructure reforms in electricity, transportation, and water supply. Drawing on a number of empirical studies, it describes real-world pricing and governance issues encountered by new regulators in these three sectors in a number of developing and transition economies. Chapter 2 may be of most interest to users of this handbook. It presents a multisectoral analysis of the elements of effective regulation, the structure of regulatory institutions, methods for ensuring commitment, and pricing issues for access and poverty alleviation.

Available at wdsbeta.worldbank.org.

Laffont, Jean-Jacques. 2005. *Regulation and Development (Federico Caffe Lectures).* Cambridge, UK: Cambridge University Press.

This book represents the first serious effort to deal with issues of regulatory governance and substance for infrastructure regulatory institutions in developing countries. Written by a world-renowned economic theorist who traveled extensively throughout Africa, it pays special attention to utility pricing. Much of the book is highly mathematical, although the key results in each chapter are set out and discussed in nontechnical language. The most relevant chapters for readers of this handbook are likely to be the overview (chapter 1) and the chapter on the development of regulatory institutions (chapter 7). A central thesis of the book is that regulatory institutions and policies cannot be blindly transferred from developed countries. A similar conclusion was reached in Levy and Spiller (1994) and is expanded on in the discussion of possible transitional regulatory systems in chapter 4 of this handbook. Laffont's book does not give or support easy policy conclusions, but with respect to regulatory institutional design, it describes factors that should determine institutional design choices (for example, the choices between decentralized or centralized regulation and between single sector and multisector regulation).

Available at www.cambridge.org/uk/.

Levy, Brian, and Pablo Spiller. 1994. "The Institutional Foundations of Regulatory Commitment: A Comparative Analysis of Telecommunications Regulation." *Journal of Law, Economics and Organisation* 10 (2): 201–46.

This seminal article provides an excellent introduction to issues of regulatory governance. Its particular strength is its discussion of how the choice of effective regulatory arrangements is affected by a country's constitutional and political condition, as well as available resources. The article was written at a time of considerable optimism about the prospects for private investment in infrastructure and the prospects for the establishment of effective regulatory agencies for utilities. The article argues strongly for tightly defined regulatory arrangements with little or no regulatory discretion in most developing countries. Whether or not the readers agree with these views, this article is an essential starting point for considering the design of effective regulatory agencies in developing countries.

Available at intl-jleo.oxfordjournals.org.

Pardina, Martin Rodriguez, Richard Schlirf Rapti, and Eric Groom. Forthcoming. *Regulatory Accounting: An Introduction.* Washington, DC: World Bank.

This book is a good primer on regulatory accounting. The book first sets the stage for regulatory accounting by describing its objectives and the associated information requirements. It introduces basic concepts and principles of general accounting, such as corporate information systems, statutory financial statements, and management and cost accounting. It then presents an overview of the main elements of regulatory accounting and presents a detailed discussion of the separation of activities, the determination of the regulatory asset base, depreciation, and the treatment of transactions with related parties and transfer pricing. This is followed by a chapter on how to establish a regulatory accounting system. The chapter also presents a regulatory accounting guideline document, procedures for information exchanges between the regulator and other parties, and the competencies, tools, timing, rules, principles, and processes that are necessary for the regulatory agency to fulfill its duties. The book contains three case studies to illustrate some of the main issues relating to regulatory information and accounting systems. The case studies cover the privatization of a water and electricity utility in an African country, the separation of a Latin American electricity utility's activities into regulated and unregulated components, and the creation of a model efficient company to establish retail tariffs in another Latin American utility.

Ros, Agustin. 2003. "The Impact of the Regulatory Process and Price Cap Regulation in Latin American Telecommunications Market." *Review of Network Economics* 2 (3): 270–86.

The article presents a useful listing and statistical compilation of variables affecting performance by regulated entities. It is short, however, on the discussion and analysis of why the correlations are as described. It begins with a brief but valuable review of the relevant literature on the performance of telecom companies in a variety of regulatory environments. It also provides a brief overview of the telecom sector in 20 Latin American countries, with a discussion of the impact of various endogenous and exogenous factors on performance by regulated telecom companies. Its findings also may be of value to other regulated infrastructure sectors.

Available at rnejournal.com.

Srivastava, Leena. 2000. *Issues in Institutional Design of Regulatory Agencies.* New Delhi: Tata Energy Research Institute.

The publication provides a thoughtful discussion of the establishment of the new regulatory frameworks in South Asia, primarily India and Nepal. The description of the basic institutional arrangements of regulatory agencies in the power and telecommunications sectors of those two countries is concise and informative. It is relevant both as a survey of institutions and as a reminder of the political realities faced by embryonic regulatory institutions. Its methodology is largely that of statutory survey and analytical thinking by an astute observer of the regulatory process.

Available at www.teriin.org.

Stern, Jon. 2003. "Regulation and Contracts for Utility Services: Substitutes or Complements? Lessons from UK Railway and Electricity History." *Journal of Policy Reform* 6 (4): 193–216.

This article describes how regulatory systems evolved in the United Kingdom by providing different ways of monitoring, enforcing, and eventually revising concession contracts for the railway and electricity industries. The absence of effective review and revision procedures in both industries led to prices becoming significantly out of line with costs as technical progress took place. The development of regulation in these industries started with dispute resolution and the monitoring of concession contracts, and then evolved to regulatory institutions that were established with some powers to review and revise contract terms (including prices). However, these pre-1939 U.K. institutions for infrastructure industry regulation were not well designed and did not provide a stable solution to reconciling the needs of consumers with a reasonable rate of return to investors. The discussion in the article is related to the economic theory of incomplete contracts. It also provides support for the proposition that, in developing countries today, effective infrastructure regulatory agencies can promote better and simpler infrastructure concession contracts. In addition, the article offers useful insights on stages of regulatory development.

Available at www.tandf.co.uk/journals.

Stern, Jon, and John Cubbin. 2005. "Regulatory Effectiveness: The Impact of Regulation and Regulatory Governance Arrangements on Electricity Industry Outcomes: A Review Paper." Policy Research Working Paper 3536, World Bank, Washington, DC.

For utility service industries this paper provides surveys of (a) regulatory governance criteria, (b) regulatory performance, (c) outcomes of regulation, and (d) econometric studies of the impact of regulation on investment and efficiency in telecoms and electricity. The paper concentrates on developing countries, and identifies good regulatory practice and better study approaches, as well as information gaps and limits on current knowledge. The paper also discusses what has been learned for regulatory design and policy from various surveys and academic studies.

Available at www-wds.worldbank.org.

2. Ex post Evaluations of Regulatory Systems for Infrastructure Industries

Agarwal, Manish, Ian Alexander, and Bernard Tenenbaum. 2003. "The Delhi Electricity Discom Privatizations: Some Observations and Recommendations for Future Privatizations in India and Elsewhere." Energy and Mining Sector Board Discussion Paper 8, World Bank, Washington, DC.

This is an ex post assessment of the privatization of three state-owned distribution companies in Delhi. In addition to the components of the privatization process, such as bidding, measurement of losses, asset valuation, and subsidies, the paper provides an in-depth analysis of the regulatory governance and substance features of the multiyear tariff system that were applied following privatization. It analyzes and makes recommendations on the roles of the government and the regulator, the government's policy directive to the regulator, and the specifics of the regulatory framework that were applied after the transaction. The principal conclusion of this paper is that privatization of the Delhi distribution is a major improvement over the one in Orissa, which was the very first privatization of distribution in India. The authors stress that a series of technical and regulatory improvements is not likely to produce sustainable privatizations, unless there is serious political support for the privatization, and unless the distribution companies can become economically viable after an initial transition period. They argue that further improvements on the Delhi experience are possible over issues such as the treatment of new investments under the multiyear tariff system, the specification of technical and commercial quality-of-service standards, the mechanisms for the delivery of subsidies, and the provision of regulatory certainty to the investors concerning the tariff-setting system after the end of the multiyear tariff period.

Available at www.worldbank.org.

Brown, Ashley C., and Ericson De Paula. 2002 and 2004. *Strengthening of the Institutional and Regulatory Structure of the Brazilian Power Sector.* Washington, DC: Public-Private Infrastructure Advisory Facility (PPIAF) and World Bank

This study is a recent example of a major external review of the regulatory practices and procedures of the Brazilian electricity regulatory system. It demonstrates how an in-depth case study review can and should be conducted. The study illustrates the range of people who should be consulted, the information that needs to be collected, and the breadth of issues that should be addressed. Many of the issues discussed in the review of Brazilian electricity regulation also arise in other Latin American countries and elsewhere. An updated version of this study became available on the PPIAF Web site in September 2004.

The 2002 edition is available at www.ppiaf.org; the 2004 edition is available at www.world bank.org.

CEER (Council of European Energy Regulators). 2004. *Regulatory Benchmarking Report for the Athens MoU Signatory Parties and Observers.* Brussels: CEER.

This benchmarking report contains detailed information on regulatory development in 15 Southeast European countries. It was produced by Pierce Atwood and USAID, with the cooperation of a group of energy regulators from Southeast Europe whose countries were signatories or observers to the "Athens Memorandum." That memorandum proposes a series of actions to integrate the energy markets of these countries into the EU's internal energy market.

The report focuses on seven characteristics of regulation: independence, competencies, internal organization, procedures for core regulatory activities, international activities, enforcement, and accountability. The report finds differences in the competencies of the energy regulators in the region. It concludes that more attention needs to be devoted to developing secondary legislation, unbundling, and institutional strengthening of the regulatory authorities of the region.

Available at www.seerecon.org.

Commission of the European Communities. 2005. *Annual Report on the Implementation of the Gas and Electricity Internal Market.* Report from the Commission, COM (2004) 863 final and SEC (2004) 1720, Brussels.

This report, also known as the "Benchmarking Report," is the fourth annual report of the European Commission, the body responsible for monitoring the progress of implementing the electricity and gas directives. It is a multicountry review of the EU electricity and natural gas industry restructuring and reform programs for current members of the EU, candidate countries, and other neighboring countries. The technical annexes to the report provide more detailed information on the implementation of the EU directives concerning market opening, retail and wholesale competition, unbundling and network access, security of supply, public service obligation, consumer protection, and environmental issues. The report provides information on the formal, legal elements of the regulatory frameworks, but there is no description or analysis of how the regulatory frameworks operate in practice, nor is there an assessment of the quality of the regulatory decisions.

The main report is available at europa.eu.int; the technical annexes are available at europa.eu.int.

Correa, Paulo, Carlos Pereira, Bernardo Mueller, and Marcus Melo. Forthcoming. "Assessing Regulatory Governance of Infrastructure Industries: Lessons from the Brazilian Experience," World Bank and PPIAF, Washington, DC. Processed.

Using an 18-page questionnaire, the authors measured four dimensions of regulatory governance at 21 new federal and state infrastructure regulators in Brazil. The measured dimensions of governance were autonomy, decisionmaking, regulatory tools, and accountability. These are important governance elements of the independent regulator model. The authors estimate that 30 percent of the responses required factual or objective determinations and that 70 percent were judgmental or subjective. The study has several features that improve on earlier benchmarking studies. First, it goes beyond simply describing the formal characteristics as specified in laws and decrees to producing an evaluation of how they actually have been implemented. Second, it produces a single overall governance number, called the index of regulatory governance, for each regulatory entity. These governance numbers are used to produce an overall governance ranking of each of the regulatory entities from best to worst. Third, the researchers visited each of the 21 regulatory entities to provide guidance in filling out the questionnaires. This ensured a high response rate and consistency in answering the questions.

For further information, contact Paulo Guilherme Correa at the World Bank (pcorrea@ worldbank.org).

Cubbin, John, and Jon Stern. 2005. "Regulatory Effectiveness and the Empirical Impact of Variations in Regulatory Governance: Electricity Industry Capacity and Efficiency in Developing Countries." Policy Research Working Paper 3535, World Bank, Washington, DC.

This paper reports the results of an econometric assessment of the impact of regulatory governance on per capita generation capacity for 28 developing countries over the period 1980–2001. The authors use a four-element governance index. The results show that higher levels of governance quality are associated with up to approximately 35 percent higher generation capacity per capita in the long term, after having taken account of the level of gross domestic product and other effects, including country-specific fixed effects. They also show that it takes time for the effects of better regulation on capacity to build up. The impact is significantly higher after 3 years and seems to continue growing during the first 10 years and possibly longer. Among the regulatory governance variables, the largest impact is associated with having in place a primary law establishing the regulatory framework.

Available at www.worldbank.org.

EBRD (European Bank for Reconstruction and Development). 2004. *Transition Report 2004: Infrastructure.* London.

The EBRD *Transition Report* provides an overview of market reform and macroeconomic performance in countries in Central and Eastern Europe and in the CIS. It also covers one thematic issue each year, and in 2004 the theme was infrastructure. Chapter 3 of this report focuses on the regulation of infrastructure services. The chapter begins with an overview of the status of the infrastructure sectors of transition countries. It discusses the concept of regulatory effectiveness and identifies important key characteristics of an effective regulatory system: coherence, predictability, capacity, independence, transparency, and accountability. It points out a gap between the regulatory arrangements on paper and their application in practice. The report reviews the results of a 2004 EBRD survey of regulators of infrastructure industries in transition economies and provides an index of overall regulatory effectiveness based on independence, transparency, and accountability. The report concludes that results of efforts to establish modern regulatory regimes for network utilities have been mixed.

Many of the advanced countries in the region succeeded in establishing independent and accountable authorities, whereas others struggled to put credible arrangements in place. It finds that the effectiveness of the regulatory system is correlated with measures of "constitutional liberalism." It discusses challenges that regulators face; and it highlights areas for improvement, particularly in strengthening regulatory independence, accountability, and transparency.

Available at www.ebrd.com.

ERRA (Energy Regulators Regional Association). 2005. "Country Profiles." Budapest.

ERRA is an association of regulatory agencies in Central and Eastern Europe and the CIS. It has been providing technical forums, meetings, and study tours for the energy regulators of the region since 1999. It has produced a number of publications on energy regulation. The ERRA Web site contains country profiles for all its members, with key market statistics, information on regulatory frameworks, market structures, and latest developments. A database on the electricity and natural gas prices in 20 countries is also available.

Available at www.erranet.org.

Estache, Antonio. 2004b. "1990s' Utilities, Argentina Privatization: Cure or Disease?" In Christian von Hirschhausen, Thorsten Beckers, and Kay Mitusch, eds., *Trends in Infrastructure Regulation and Financing: International Experience and Case Studies from Germany,* pp. 199–224. Cheltenham, UK: Edward Elgar.

This article examines the history and performance of the 1990s privatizations of electricity, natural gas, telecoms, and water in Argentina. The author discusses why the privatizations became so unpopular in spite of the major societal benefits of higher efficiency, lower costs, and increased access. He examines the trade-off between allocative efficiency and fairness and, in particular, the consequences of tariff restructuring that led to higher prices for small and low-income users. A major issue discussed is the weaknesses of regulatory institutions—such as their delays to pass on cost savings to consumers. The role of the government is illustrated, including the government's financial benefit from higher corporate taxes levied on utility industry profits. The author also analyzes the problem of achieving effective regulation in circumstances of generally weak institutions and strong ideological divisions.

An earlier version of the working paper is available at www.ssrn.com; information on the book is available at http://wip.tu-berlin.de/en/index.htm.

Foster, Vivien, and Tito Yepes. Forthcoming. "Is Cost Recovery a Feasible Objective for Water and Electricity?" In World Bank, Latin America Regional Study on Infrastructure, Washington, DC.

This article evaluates the progress made in the Latin American water and electricity sectors in ensuring cost recovery. Because the authors do not have access to their ideal cost recovery measure (a comparison of average tariffs with full average cost of production), they use estimates of cost to assess the likelihood that a particular utility is recovering various levels of cost—O&M costs alone or O&M and capital costs. They find that the electricity sector is much closer to cost recovery than the water sector. They conclude that genuine problems with the affordability of water and electricity in Latin America appear to be limited to the lowest-income quintile of the population. They argue that targeted safety nets for utility services should be able to resolve the issue of reconciling cost recovery and social policy objectives. The report presents a detailed evaluation of the design and performance of social tariff schemes in the water and electricity sectors, using specific examples of tariff structure and subsidy arrangements in various Latin American countries. It concludes that, in general, inverted block tariff structures for electricity are much better designed than those for water. It finds a higher correlation between consumption and household income in electricity than in water. The article concludes that, if properly designed, the inverted block tariff structure in electricity has greater potential to redistribute income than that in water.

Frilet, Marc. 2004. "Building or Improving Public Infrastructure Services with the Private Sector: The French Experience." Presentation at the World Bank, Washington, DC.

This presentation, delivered at a meeting at the World Bank in Washington, DC, in November 2004, presents a detailed discussion of the public service concession model, which has been the dominant form of infrastructure regulation in France for the water and sanitation sector. In the presentation, Frilet provides an overview of the concept of public service concession, which has a heavy emphasis on "regulation by contract." He identifies several advantages of the French water concession model, including its applicability in other countries, low transaction costs over the long term, and the fact that very few disputes materialize during operation. The Conseil d'Etat, the French supreme administrative court, plays the role of a de facto or "super" regulator of these concession contracts, and its decisions are applicable to other cases. In effect, the Conseil d'Etat creates administrative laws, and Frilet defines concession as a practical example of convergence between case law and civil law. Frilet concludes that the French experience with concessions shows that, if well designed and well defined in an appropriate regulatory and partnering framework, concessions are in practice far less complex than many other public-private partnership schemes.

Global Competition Review. 2005. "Electricity Regulation in 2004." Produced in association with Freshfields Bruckhaus Deringer.

This report provides information on government electricity policy and regulation in the power sectors of 28 countries or political jurisdictions. It begins with a global overview and then proceeds with a detail analysis of regulation in individual countries: Austria, Belgium, Brazil, Canada, China, Croatia, the Czech Republic, the EU, Finland, France, Germany, Hungary, Ireland, Italy, Mexico, the Netherlands, Norway, Poland, Portugal, Russia, Singapore, the Slovak Republic, Spain, Sweden, Switzerland, United Kingdom, United States, and República Bolivariana de Venezuela. Because the report was prepared by lawyers who practice in each country, it is not surprising that the focus of the report is on formal legal elements. It also includes a discussion of the implementation of retail competition in several countries.

The survey covers government policy for the sector; alternative energy sources; market organization; cross-border electricity supply; public service obligations; the regulation of the generation, the transmission, the distribution, and the sale of electricity—including the authorizations required for each activity—and tariff regulation; transactions between utilities and their affiliates; and the enforcement of affiliate restrictions. Information is also presented on regulatory policy; the allocation of responsibilities between various government bodies in the sector; the establishment of a regulator; the authority of the regulator; the appeal of the regulator's decisions; the bodies that have authority over mergers, acquisitions, and transfers of control; the prevention and prosecution of anticompetitive practices; criteria for anticompetitive conduct; the remedy of anticompetitive practices; and special requirements for foreign companies.

A second Web site presents the information from the report and allows users to make cross-country comparisons by selecting from a list of questions and viewing responses for individual countries.

Available at www.globalcompetitionreview.com/.

Gutierrez, Luis H. 2003. "Regulatory Governance in the Latin American Telecommunications Sector." *Utilities Policy* 11 (4): 185–244.

This article constructs an index of governance indicators for telecommunications regulatory agencies in 25 Latin American and Caribbean countries for the period 1980–2001. It confines itself to formal legal features and does not cover regulatory practices or decisions. It describes how the quality of formal governance has changed for these countries. The methodology of the report could be used in other countries or groups of countries and in other infrastructure industries.

A companion paper (Luis H. Gutierrez, 2003, "The Effect of Endogenous Regulation on Telecommunications Expansion and Efficiency in Latin America," *Journal of Regulatory Economics* 23 [3]: 257–86) uses an earlier version of the index in an econometric study that demonstrates, using panel data estimation methods, that better regulatory governance is significantly associated with higher investment and efficiency in Latin American and Caribbean telecommunications industries.

Available at the publisher's Web site: www.sciencedirect.com. An earlier version of the second paper is available from the Public Utility Research Center Web site (http://bear.cba.ufl.edu/centers/purc/).

ITU (International Telecommunication Union). 2001. *Case Studies—Effective Regulation: 2001.* ITU, Geneva.

A series of five case studies were prepared in 2001 with a focus on regulatory independence and other dimensions of governance. Case studies were undertaken for Botswana, Brazil, Morocco, Peru, and Singapore. Although consultants were hired by the ITU, the views expressed do not represent official views of the ITU. With varying degrees of detail, each of these reports provides an overview of the structure of the telecommunications sector in the country, and discusses regulatory governance and, to a lesser extent, regulatory substance. The case studies discuss the organizational structure of the government bodies charged with regulating the telecommunications sector, and their relationships with other government entities, as well as their resources, independence, and accountability. The studies also analyze regulatory powers for specific issues, such as licensing, interconnection, universal service, quality of service, tariffs, and spectrum management. Each report concludes with an evaluation of regulatory governance in the country in question and makes recommendations for improvements.

Available at www.itu.int.

ITU. 2005. Databases as of this date: "Country Profile," "Regulators Profile," and "Universal Service Profile." ITU, Geneva.

This online database provides useful information on regulatory governance and substance in specific countries. It is an interactive Web site where the visitor can select a country and view information on the regulatory aspects of the telecommunications sector, such as existing legislation, specific institutional details relating to the structure, financing, and functions of the regulatory entity. The database also includes details on the status of universal service coverage, existing programs and financing for universal coverage, the level of competition, and the status of the primary fixed-line operators. The Web site also allows users to make regional comparisons on a number of dimensions.

Available at www.itu.int.

In addition to the "Country Regulatory Profiles" database, several other databases available through the ITU Web site contain such information as spectrum fees, tariffs policies, and financing institutions, as well as a directory of telecommunications operators worldwide and "Telecommunication Indicator Reports," which analyze trends and developments in the global telecommunications sector.

Available at www.itu.int.

Kelley, Elizabeth, and Bernard Tenenbaum. 2004. "Funding of Energy Regulatory Commissions." Energy and Mining Sector Board Working Notes 30525, World Bank, Washington, DC.

These working notes provide detailed descriptions of the funding systems for eight energy regulatory commissions in developed and developing countries. For each case, the notes describe the formal elements of the funding system, and discuss how these formal elements actually have been implemented. The information on implementation is based on lengthy telephone interviews with energy regulators and other government officials. The notes present 15 recommendations to achieve secure and adequate funding. Using these recommendations as a benchmark, the notes present a numerical ranking of the funding practices of the California and Bulgarian energy regulatory commissions.

Available at www.worldbank.org.

Moscote, Rafael. 2004. "Strengthening the Administrative and Financial Independence of the Sector's Regulator." World Bank, Washington, DC.

This is one chapter of a larger report on the Ukrainian electricity sector. The chapter provides a concise and clear assessment of the regulatory system from the perspectives of both regulatory governance and regulatory substance. It also compares actual implementation with what formally exists in the law. It outlines the current legal framework applicable to the electricity sector in Ukraine, discusses the status of the National Energy Regulatory Commission in the current framework, outlines changes proposed in draft legislation, identifies the shortcomings of draft legislation, and then makes recommendations. In evaluating each aspect of the regulatory system, the report compares Ukrainian practices to regulatory practices in other countries. The analysis and recommendations focus on governance issues, such as the financial, organizational, and administrative independence of the regulatory agency; its relationships with other government bodies; and the specific responsibilities that should be assigned to the regulator, as well as its accountability, the transparency of its procedures, and the appeals of its decisions. Many of these elements relate to the principles and standards in chapter 2 of this handbook. However, the report also provides an analysis and recommendations on regulatory substance: the details of the rate-setting process in the wholesale electricity market; the regulation of distribution, transmission, and retail tariffs; the regulatory treatment of losses; and quality-of-service standards.

National Audit Office. 2002. *Pipes and Wires.* Report by the Comptroller and Auditor General, National Audit Office, HC 723 Session 2001–2002. London: Stationery Office.

This report is an example of an ex post review of regulatory practice and its application to a range of utilities in an established OECD regulatory framework. It was prepared for the U.K. legislature. The report concentrates on the impact of price cap regulation on consumer welfare, investment, and regulatory risk. It contains useful technical annexes on incentives and regulatory risk. It provides a good example of a policy audit based on key regulatory concepts.

Available at www.nao.org.uk.

Ocaña, Carlos. 2002. "Trends in the Management of Regulation: A Comparison of Energy Regulators in Member Countries of the Organisation for Economic Development and Co-operation." *International Journal of Regulation and Governance* 3 (1): 13–32.

The article provides a useful comparative description of regulatory institutions and, to a lesser extent, processes in the OECD countries. The article is limited to a discussion of the formal structure of agencies and does not address actual practice or behavior in the countries covered. It is relevant for those who are seeking an overview of the basic institutional characteristics of the regulatory regimes discussed. It is founded on a review of the basic statutes governing regulatory institutions in each country, and it identifies four different institutional approaches to utility regulation: regulation by an independent regulatory agency and a ministry; by a ministerial agency that reports to and is located within a ministry; by a ministry and an independent advisory agency outside of the ministry; and by a ministry without a separate regulatory entity.

Available at www.teriin.org.

Pezon, Christelle. 2003. "Water Supply Regulation in France from 1848 to 2001: A Jurisprudence Based Analysis." Presentation at the Annual Conference of the International Society for New Institutional Economics, Budapest, Hungary, September 11–13.

An updated version of this report has been published with a number of other papers on the water industry in France, Spain, and other countries in the February 2005 special issue of Sciences de la Société *Civil Society and Water Commercialization,* edited by Catherine Baron.

This report presents a highly informative history of the French concession model for water and sewerage services and, in particular, of the evolution of the concession contracts. The author shows that the commercial arrangements began as classic concession contracts but, after 1900, municipalities increasingly became responsible for both investment and supplies. Since 1950, municipalities more frequently have been franchising out their responsibilities to private companies under *affermage* contracts which, particularly since 1993, have looked increasingly like U.K.–style regulatory licenses. These developments have been mirrored in changes of responsibility and decisionmaking by the relevant court of the Conseil d'Etat. Pezon concludes that the Conseil d'Etat has evolved from being primarily a dispute resolution body to something much closer to a standard regulatory agency.

Available at www.isnie.org.

Prayas Energy Group. 2003. *A Good Beginning but Challenges Galore: A Survey Based Study of Resources, Transparency, and Public Participation in Electricity Regulatory Commissions in India.* Pune, India.

This report provides an excellent study of regulatory practice in India because it describes the achievements and difficulties of new electricity regulatory agencies in a developing country. In particular, the report provides an insightful discussion on problems encountered in trying to implement what has been legally mandated. The focus of the report is on how electricity regulation actually has operated in the various Indian states relative to their official legal mandates. The report also describes how the state governments, legislatures, and electricity enterprises have responded to the new regulatory agencies. The methodology of the report is descriptive. A follow-

up study on "electricity governance" indicators will expand and formalize the evaluation methodology developed by Prayas. (See WRI [2004] in section 5.)
Available at www.prayaspune.org.

Rao, S. L. 2004. *Governing Power: A New Institution of Governance—The Experience with Independent Regulation of Electricity.* New Delhi: TERI Press.

The book begins with an overview of the evolution of policy and regulation and a discussion of the concept of independent regulation. It examines international experience in electricity sector regulation and then turns to the case of India in an attempt to identify common principles and frameworks that enhance the functioning of the new independent regulatory commissions. It focuses on the effectiveness of regulatory governance in India, including the legitimacy and independence of the regulatory commissions, their responsibilities and authority, decisionmaking processes, accountability, and the participation of stakeholders in the relevant processes. The book also examines regulatory substance through an analysis of the decisions of several state electricity regulatory commissions. It finds that in the first five states that established commissions, there have been distinct and contradictory approaches on some issues, but in the case of tariffs, the approaches have been consistent but not very successful.

Available at www.teriin.org.

Stern, Jon, and Stuart Holder. 1999. "Regulatory Governance: Criteria for Assessing the Performance of Regulatory Systems. An Application to Infrastructure Industries in the Developing Countries of Asia." *Utilities Policy* 8 (1): 33–50.

This article provides a good example of a systematic, comparative evaluation of regulatory practices for infrastructure utilities in seven Asian developing countries. The findings are now somewhat dated, but the conceptual approach and its survey application are still useful. It is strongest on the formal, legal properties of regulation and has some, albeit limited, information on how regulation actually operated in the countries considered. The approach, if adopted in future studies, should be extended to include more information on regulatory practice and outcomes of the regulatory process.

Available at www.nera.com.

Steyn, Grove. 2003. "Review of the Effectiveness of Utility Regulation in South Africa." Working Paper.

This paper, commissioned by the Office of the Presidency of South Africa as part of a broader 10-year review of the impact of regulators, provides an overview of regulatory governance and substance issues facing the power sector in the country. After an introduction to the organization of the power sector and the policy context, the paper describes institutional arrangements, such as the structure of the NER, its mandate, resources, and organization. It reviews the NER's activities; and describes price regulation, licensing, information gathering, rule making, and the NER's role in the policy process and electrification, as well as its dispute resolution function. Although the NER has made significant progress in terms of improving Eskom's governance, limiting price increases, rationalizing municipal tariffs, facilitating progress in sector reform, and developing its own capacity, important challenges remain that need to be addressed. The evaluation concludes that improvements are needed in governance and accountability, the NER's resources, the transparency of its processes, its methodology for price regulation, its regulation of local authority distributors, and its policies for securing of new generation investments.

Grove Steyn is on the faculty of the Infrastructure Industries Reform and Regulation Management Programme, Graduate School of Business, University of Cape Town, South Africa: http://www.gsb.uct.ac.za/iirr/home.asp.

World Bank. 2004. "Policy Perspective and Analysis of the Regulatory Regime in the Restructured Russian Power Sector." Europe and Central Asia Region Infrastructure and Energy Services Department Policy Note, World Bank, Washington, DC.

This note, largely based on the report prepared by Ashley C. Brown, analyzes the proposed regulatory regime for the Russian power sector from practical and policy perspectives. After providing an overview of the proposed regulatory regime, the paper discusses the issue of regulatory independence, starting with the theoretical background and then evaluating the current proposals based on the theoretical framework and international experience. It concludes that regulatory authority has been divided and diffused to a greater extent than is commonly found in other reforming countries. It also presents a discussion of the role of regulators in market development and in promotion and maintenance of competition. The paper identifies various shortcomings in the government's current proposals for tariff setting, accounting and information systems, appellate processes, the ethical standards applicable to regulatory personnel, and the human and financial resources available to regulatory entities.

Available at www.worldbank.org.

3. Ex ante Regulatory Impact Assessments

Alexander, Ian, Aftab Raza, and Joseph Daniel Wright. 2003. "KESC's 2002 Multi-Year Tariff Determination: Lessons for Pakistan and South Asia." *International Journal of Regulation and Governance* 3 (2): 161–94.

This article provides a good assessment of a proposed tariff-setting system. It presents a detailed analysis of the proposed regulatory framework to support privatization of the state-owned utility in Karachi. The article describes elements of a multiyear tariff scheme and evaluates the strengths and weaknesses in several dimensions: the certainty and predictability of the tariff for investors and customers, the form of control to be exercised by the regulator and the associated risks, the allowed rate of return, loss reduction and efficiency targets, the pass-through of uncontrollable costs, and the associated tariff review processes. It highlights the question of how to ensure a regulatory agency's commitment to the regulatory framework. Although the article concludes that there are many positive features in the proposed framework, it recommends that more attention should be paid to the treatment of investments, the adequacy of the projected real rate of return, and the amount of time that the regulatory agency will have to review the company's multiyear tariff proposal.

Available at www.teriin.org.

Kirkpatrick, Colin, David Parker, and Yin-Fang Zhang. 2004. "Regulatory Impact Assessment in Developing and Transition Economies: A Survey of Current Practice." Working Paper 83, Centre on Regulation and Competition, University of Manchester, United Kingdom.

This paper discusses the role of regulation in promoting economic and social welfare and the importance of a systematic appraisal of the impacts of any proposed and actual regulation. It provides some general principles for regulatory impact assessments (RIAs). The paper presents an overview of RIA practices in 40 developing and transition economies, based on the results of a questionnaire survey, which is available in the appendix to the paper. The questionnaire focuses on three main areas: RIA as an assessment method, RIA as a process, and RIA as part of a wider strategy for regulatory reform. The paper finds that a growing number of low- and middle-income countries are beginning to apply some form of regulatory assessment, but that the methods adopted are limited in their application and are not systematically applied across government. It finds that, where implemented, the RIA process usually includes consultation, but consultations tend to be limited to government and business, leaving consumers and other civil society groups underrepresented. The activities covered by the survey included economic, social, and environmental regulation. The authors report a growing use of RIAs in economic regulation.

Available at www.competition-regulation.org.uk.

OECD (Organisation for Economic Co-operation and Development). 2005. "Regulatory Impact Analysis in OECD Countries."

This Web site was established by the OECD as part of its Regulatory Reform Program. The site provides useful information on regulatory impact analysis and its current status in OECD countries, as well as recommendations on how it should be carried out.

Available at www.oecd.org.

U.K. Cabinet Office. 2003. *Better Policy Making: A Guide to Regulatory Impact Assessment.* London: Crown.

This guide was issued by the U.K. Cabinet Office, a central government body responsible for coordinating government policy and strategy. The guide covers the U.K. regulatory impact assessment process in detail. It begins by defining RIA, discusses when an RIA should be undertaken, and outlines the steps involved in performing an RIA. The guide describes a continuous process consisting of three phases: an initial RIA, a partial

RIA, and a full or final RIA. It discusses how to perform RIAs for legislative proposals introduced at the EU level for eventual implementation in the United Kingdom. Information is presented on competition and cost–benefit analyses. The guide also provides RIA templates and a useful bibliography.

Available at www.cabinetoffice.gov.uk/regulation/ria/.

4. Questionnaires Used for Evaluating Regulatory Systems

Global Competition Review. 2005. "Electricity Regulation in 2004." Produced in association with Freshfields Bruckhaus Deringer.

The report referred to in section 2 is based on a questionnaire. The questions are included in the report, and they are available on the related Web page. The report is organized around the responses to 33 questions.

Available at www.globalcompetitionreview.com.

Pierce Atwood. 2004. "Regulatory Benchmarking Questionnaire: SEE/REM States." Produced in cooperation with CEER Working Group and with USAID support.

This questionnaire forms the basis of the USAID Regulatory Benchmarking Report on South East Europe, which focuses on regulatory development in 15 countries that are members of the Energy Community of Southeast Europe. The questionnaire seeks to collect information from the respondents in several dimensions: the legal status of the energy sector regulatory authorities; the degree of legal, financial, and functional independence; their mandates; their powers with respect to various aspects of the sectors that they cover; their internal organization, resources, and capacities; their procedures for core regulatory activities; their involvement in international activities; their enforcement powers; and the accountability of the regulatory authorities.

Available at www.seerecon.org.

Trémolet, Sophie, Padmesh Shukla, and Courtenay Venton. 2004. *Contracting Out Utility Regulatory Functions.* Washington, DC: World Bank.

The objective of the survey was to gather information on the contracting-out practices of utility regulators around the world. The results of the survey were received from 51 agencies throughout the world, representing a 38 percent response rate. The survey showed that most regulators (75 percent of the survey sample) engage external parties in the administration of regulatory tasks and plan to continue to do so in the future. Appendix B of the report (listed in section 5) contains the questions used in the survey of regulatory agencies and a summary of the answers provided.

Available at rru.worldbank.org.

Wallsten, Scott, George Clarke, Luke Haggarty, Rosario Kaneshiro, Roger Noll, Mary Shirley, and Lixin Colin Xu. 2004. "New Tools for Studying Network Industry Reforms in Developing Countries: The Telecommunications and Electricity Regulation Database," Related Publication 04-05, AEI-Brookings Joint Center for Regulatory Studies, Washington, DC.

This working paper attempts to develop a comprehensive and consistent data set on regulatory characteristics and practices of telecommunications and electricity regulators in developing countries. It is based on the responses to a detailed questionnaire that focuses on both regulatory governance and regulatory substance. The database of telecommunications regulation provides information on 178 variables in 45 countries. The database of electricity regulations contains information on 374 variables in 20 countries. The information provided in the database was current as of the end of 2001 for telecommunications and April 2002 for electricity.

Available at www.aei-brookings.org.

5. Proposed Regulatory Principles and Standards

AFUR (African Forum for Utility Regulation). 2003. "A Framework for Utility Regulation in Africa." Position paper adopted at First Annual General Assembly, Yaounde, Cameroon, November 11–13.

This AFUR position paper proposes a framework for the principles and core issues relating to regulatory governance, nondiscrimination, investment protection, and the promotion of competition in Africa. The regulatory governance recommendations focus on principles, such as minimum regulation, proportionality, due process, transparency, independence, and accountability of the regulatory agencies. Although it recommends these general principles, the paper states that further work must be performed to adapt the principles to the cultural, political and legal differences between Anglophone, Francophone and Lusophone countries in Africa.

Information on the AFUR is available at www1.worldbank.org/afur/.

CEER (Council of European Energy Regulators). 2003. "Regulatory Benchmarking Standards for South East Europe Regional Electricity Market." WG SEEER Discussion Paper, Brussels.

This discussion paper focuses on basic principles, as well as specific standards derived from those principles. These principles and standards are intended to serve as guidelines to the regulatory authorities of the region, and to provide a basis for measuring the regulatory status and progress of reforms in countries of Southeastern Europe. Implementation of these principles and standards was assessed in the regulatory benchmarking report described in CEER (2004) in section 2.

The standards cover the independence of the regulatory authority; its competencies with respect to information access, security of supply, market operation, and monitoring; the regulator's internal organization, resources, and capacity; standards for core regulatory activities; and international activities and enforcement powers.

Two tiers of standards are presented. The first tier comprises "required minimums," which are universally required and which must be adopted promptly. These "minimums" reflect existing political and legal commitments—such as EU Directive 2003/54/EC on the Internal Electricity Market, the EU Regulation No. 1228/2003 on cross-border exchanges in electricity, and the Athens Memorandum of Understanding—that the parties will be expected to adhere to in the medium term.

An additional set of "preferred practices" is presented. It covers standards deemed desirable that should be adopted over the longer term, with the understanding that not every standard level ultimately may be deemed appropriate by every state. The discussion paper is provided in appendix 4 of CEER (2004) (see section 2 of this bibliography).

A presentation on the benchmarking standards is available at www.seerecon.org.

EU (European Union). 2003 "Directive 2003/54/EC of the European Parliament and of the Council of 26 June 2003 Concerning Common Rules for the Internal Market in Electricity and Repealing Directive 96/92/EC." *Official Journal of the European Union* L 176/37, July 15.

In 1996 the European Commission issued its first Electricity Directive. The directive was vague about regulation. It contained a general statement about the need to designate "a competent authority." In contrast, the second electricity directive issued in 2003 is much more explicit about the need for a separate regulatory authority in charge of the electricity sector, as well as the responsibilities that must be assigned to it. The 2003 directive requires all EU member-states to establish regulatory authorities wholly independent from the interests of the electricity industry, although not necessarily with decisionmaking authority independent from ministries or other government entities. Although member-states are allowed to specify the functions, competencies, and administrative powers of the regulatory authorities, the directive clearly states that the regulatory authorities in all member-states must share the same minimum set of competencies. For example, Article 23 of the directive states that regulatory authorities must at least be responsible for ensuring nondiscrimination, effective competition, and the efficient functioning of the market. In addition, the directive assigns regulatory authorities the responsibility for fixing or approving the tariffs, or at least the regulatory authority must provide the methodologies used to calculate or establish the terms and conditions for connection and access to national transmission and distribution networks and the provision of balancing services. This reflects the European Commission's overriding goal of creating a Europe-wide internal electricity market.

Available at europa.eu.int.

Office of Water Regulation. 1999. "Best Practice Utility Regulation." Utility Regulators Forum Discussion Paper, Office of Water Regulation, Perth, Western Australia.

This is a think-piece meant to stimulate discussion. It is almost exclusively theoretical with little mention of actual practice. It is essentially an outline of what the author sees as the critical principles of regulation. The discussion is divided into three categories: best-practice principles, best-practice processes, and best-practice organization. The paper provides a useful basic guide for those who are about to create a new regulatory regime or for those who need to be reminded of some of the key principles to be applied. The paper is largely limited to a statement of critical principles, an analysis of their meaning and significance, and of the dilemmas inherent in achieving them.

Available at http://www.era.wa.gov.au/.

WRI (World Resources Institute), National Institute of Public Finance and Policy, and Prayas Energy Group. 2004. *Electricity Governance Toolkit.* Washington, DC: WRI.

This report is written from the perspective of civil society organizations in several countries as part of the Electricity Governance Initiative, a joint effort by the World Resources Institute, the National Institute of Public Finance and Policy in India, and the Prayas Energy Group. This toolkit is intended to be used to make pilot assessments of governance of the electricity sector in several countries. It appears to have been motivated by a general dissatisfaction with power sector reform as implemented in several developing countries, especially with respect to transparency and public participation in decisionmaking processes and implementation. It provides an overview of good governance in the electricity sector and proposes qualitative performance indicators for evaluating processes in three areas: policy processes, regulation, and environmental and social actions. The authors identify a set of "priority indicators" that teams performing evaluations will apply to establish an overview of sector governance. Many of the document's suggestions on regulatory governance are similar to the recommendations in chapter 2 of this handbook.

The report is available at www.wri.org. More information on the WRI's electricity governance initiative is available at http://electricitygovernance.wri.org/.

6. Transitional and Alternative Regulatory Arrangements

Bakovic, Tonci, Bernard Tenenbaum, and Fiona Woolf. 2003. "Regulation by Contract: A New Way to Privatize Electricity Distribution?" Energy and Mining Sector Board Discussion Paper 7, World Bank, Washington, DC.

This paper argues that regulatory independence to promote successful privatization of electricity distribution should be combined with a regulatory contract. The regulatory contract must generally be negotiated by political authorities and should specify a performance-based, multiyear tariff-setting system. To demonstrate how regulatory contracts can be combined with independent regulatory commissions, the paper describes the real-world regulatory experiences of Argentina, Brazil, and India. The paper discusses the allocation of risks among different parties (consumers, investors, and government), and describes how dispute resolution mechanisms can be used with regulatory contracts. In effect, the paper attempts to explain how the "tightly defined regulatory arrangements" recommended by Levy and Spiller (1994) could be implemented to promote electricity privatization.

Available at www.worldbank.org/energy.

Castalia Strategic Advisors. 2004. "Final Provisions for Long Term PPP in the Water and Sanitation Sector, Volume I—Main Report." Draft Report to the World Bank and Water Operator Roundtable, Washington, DC.

This report analyzes different approaches for enhancing private sector participation in water and sanitation. One approach is the "Improved Concession Model." Drawing on six actual privatization or leasing examples and two model contracts from France and the United Kingdom, it provides specific examples and recommendations for improving concession provisions dealing with service standards, tariff indexation, exchange rate risk, transparency, termination, and dispute resolution. In addition to a proposal for a detailed multiyear tariff-setting system, the report recommends that such concession provisions be combined with four other institutional and financing arrangements: output-based subsidy mechanisms, PRGs for regulatory and subsidy agreements, the use of independent expert panels to perform some of the regulatory functions on either an advisory or a binding basis, and an outside monitoring entity for quality-of-service standards. Unlike Bakovic, Tenenbaum, and Woolf (2003), who argue that in the case of privatization of electricity distribution, "regulatory contracts" should be administered by independent regulatory entities, this report argues that the combination of these other elements can eliminate the need for a separate regulatory entity, at least in the case of water and sanitation. The report concludes that this approach—regulation without a separate government regulator—could be used to promote private sector involvement in water and sanitation projects in many developing countries.

This report and related reports prepared for the Water Operator Roundtable can be obtained by contacting the World Bank's Water Help Desk at whelpdesk@worlbank.org.

Gupta, Pankaj, Ranjit Lamech, Farida Mazhar, and Joseph Wright. 2002. "Mitigating Regulatory Risk for Distribution Privatization—The World Bank Partial Risk Guarantee." Energy and Mining Sector Board Discussion Paper 5, World Bank, Washington, DC.

This discussion paper focuses on how a World Bank PRG may be used to promote private sector investment in electricity distribution utilities as a means to address increased investor sensitivity to regulatory risk when contemplating investing in a developing country. The authors recommend that the World Bank's PRG be used as an instrument to mitigate regulatory risk by serving as a backstop for a government's commitment to a defined regulatory framework and a dispute resolution mechanism.

The paper starts with reviewing the regulatory risk facing investors in electricity distribution and discusses how a regulatory framework and a dispute resolution process can mitigate that risk. It outlines two possible financial structures for implementing a PRG—the Limited Recourse Structure and the Letter of Credit Structure—and provides details on the application of a PRG during privatization. The first real-world example of a regulatory PRG was used in the privatization of two Romanian electricity distribution companies (see chapter 4 of this handbook for a full discussion of the PRG).

Available at www.worldbank.org.

Kaufmann, Daniel, Aart Kraay, and Massimo Mastruzzi. 2003. *Governance Matters III: Governance Indicators for 1996–2002.* Washington, DC: World Bank.

The publication broadly defines governance as "the traditions and institutions by which authority in a country is exercised" (p. 2). It identifies six dimensions of governance: voice and accountability, political stability and the absence of violence, government effectiveness, regulatory quality, the rule of law, and control of corruption. Indicators for these dimensions are used to calculate overall governance performance scores for almost 200 countries. The publication also includes a discussion of methodological issues in constructing indicators.

Closely related to this paper is the "2002 Worldwide Governance Research Indicators Dataset." It is an interactive Web site that enables users to create a "snapshot" of governance in individual countries or groups of countries. This versatile tool can be used to develop an overview of one country based on six governance indicators and a comparison across several countries based on one indicator. Users also have the option of comparing results with previous years, with regional averages, or by countries in different income categories.

Available at www.worldbank.org.

Shugart, Chris, and Tony Ballance. 2005. *Expert Panels: Regulating Water Companies in Developing Countries.* Washington, DC: World Bank.

Like Castalia (2005), this report focuses on issues of regulatory governance in water and wastewater services. The authors argue that the independent regulator model has not worked well in many developing countries because of continuing political influence and arbitrary decisionmaking. As an alternative, they propose the use of an independent, three-person, nongovernmental expert panel for conducting periodic price reviews. The expert panels, with strong technical capacity and true independence, would be empowered to make binding decisions, which could be subject to a limited scope of review. The report emphasizes the importance of carefully designing the process, and discusses how such panels differ from arbitration panels, how they relate to other dispute-handling mechanisms, and how a panel would carry out extraordinary tariff adjustments. The report then focuses on how the panel would work, and looks at issues such as the rules governing the panel's decisions, and whether those rules should be set in a contract or governing legislation, how the panel members should be selected, what the price review process would cover, how the decisions would be enforced and appealed, and how the costs associated with the panel would be covered. The report describes how expert panels have been used in several countries, and concludes with a discussion of possible objections and drawbacks to expert panels.

Available at rru.worldbank.org.

Trémolet, Sophie, Padmesh Shukla, and Courtenay Venton. 2004. *Contracting Out Utility Regulatory Functions.* Washington, DC: World Bank.

This report provides a review of international experience in contracting out regulatory functions, as well as five detailed case studies. It is based on a worldwide survey of regulators. The report begins by laying out an overall analytical framework for utility regulation that includes the objectives of regulation, a description of regulatory functions and tasks, and the requirements for regulatory effectiveness. It then discusses the rationale for contracting out regulatory functions, focusing on the choice between "making" and "buying" a certain service or product. The report describes various contracting arrangements and analyzes current practices in a sample of countries and sectors: a water divestiture in Chile, a water and electricity concession in Gabon, a water management contract in Gaza, a water and sanitation concession in Bucharest, and a regional regulator for the telecommunications sector in the Caribbean. The report concludes by outlining the implications of this analysis for regulators and recommends potential roles for donors and lending agencies.

Available at rru.worldbank.org.

Index

Boxes, figures, notes, and tables are indicated by b, f, n, and t, respectively.